Harnessing AI Inference for Intelligent Decision-Making in Real-Time Dataflows

Abu Sarwar Zamani
https://orcid.org/0000-0002-0135-2337
Prince Sattam bin Abdulaziz University, Saudi Arabia

Aisha Hassan Abdalla Hashim
https://orcid.org/0000-0001-6331-1373
International Islamic University, Malaysia

Md. Mobin Akhtar
Riyadh Elm University, Saudi Arabia

Hazra Imran
https://orcid.org/0000-0002-2341-6477
Northeastern University, Canada

IGI Global
Scientific Publishing
Publishing Tomorrow's Research Today

Vice President of Editorial	Melissa Wagner
Director of Acquisitions	Mikaela Felty
Director of Book Development	Jocelynn Hessler
Production Manager	Mike Brehm
Cover Design	Jose Rosado

Published in the United States of America by
IGI Global Scientific Publishing
701 East Chocolate Avenue
Hershey, PA, 17033, USA
Tel: 717-533-8845 | Fax: 717-533-7115
Website: https://www.igi-global.com E-mail: cust@igi-global.com

Library of Congress Cataloging-in-Publication Data

LCCN: 2025047436 (CIP Data Pending)
ISBN13: 9798337370460
Isbn13Softcover: 9798337370477
EISBN13: 9798337370484

British Cataloguing in Publication Data
A Cataloguing in Publication record for this book is available from the British Library.

Editorial Advisory Board

Table of Contents

Detailed Table of Contents

This chapter explores a unified framework that leverages both edge computing and cloud computing for AI inference in big data environments. Edge computing enables near-source, low-latency processing and decision-making, reducing dependency on centralized infrastructure, while cloud platforms offer powerful capabilities for large-scale model training, data aggregation, and long-term storage. By combining these paradigms, a hybrid ecosystem emerges that balances efficiency, scalability, and responsiveness. The chapter discusses architectural models, deployment strategies, and real-world applications across domains such as healthcare monitoring, intelligent transportation, industrial automation, and smart cities. It also highlights key challenges including resource heterogeneity, interoperability, security, and model optimization. Ultimately, the abstraction emphasizes how edge-cloud synergy forms a foundational approach for next-generation AI-driven big data systems.

The 21 st century has increased the rate of urbanization, thus making the problems of traffic snarl up, pollution, energy crisis, improper waste disposal and heavy load on the social safety and health system more complex. The idea of the smart city became one of the new technologies that integrate Artificial Intelligence (AI), the Internet of Things (IoT), and Big Data in order to enhance the efficiency and quality of life in cities. In particular, AI inference enables real-time decision making based on

The convergence of Artificial Intelligence (AI) and the Internet of Things (IoT) has offered the legality of big data analysis that could completely transform sectors such as healthcare, transportation, smart cities/industrial automation. However, the integration of AI raises important security and privacy issues due to the distributed, heterogeneous and resource limited nature of the IoT setting. The risks to sensitive data gathered by connected devices include an unauthorized access, data breach, adversarial attacks and model manipulation. The chapter focuses on the security and privacy issues of the AI-driven versions of the IoT big data analytics and focus on the vulnerability of the data acquisition, transmission, storage and inference stages.

The integration of Artificial Intelligence (AI) inference into the Internet of Things (IoT) ecosystem is reshaping the landscape of intelligent systems by enabling real-time analytics, predictive modeling, and autonomous decision-making directly at the device and network levels. Unlike traditional IoT systems that primarily collect and transmit data for centralized processing, AI-enabled IoT leverages edge and fog computing to bring intelligence closer to data sources, reducing latency, improv.

The paper will explore how AI inference on IoT and Big Data is transformative with respect to the health care sector, manufacturing, smart cities, energy, and agriculture. AI inference transforms sensor data into actionable intelligence through the combination of real-time data, predictive analytics, and automation, and enhances efficiency, sustainability, and reliability. Applications in predictive maintenance, smart grids, urban management and precision farming are pointed out in the discussion. The most important issues, such as the quality of data, privacy, scalability, and ethical use are discussed as well as ways of dealing with them. New tendencies such as edge computing, federated learning, explainable AI, 5G integration, and digital twins are found to be pushing the next generation of smart, connected systems. In general, the chapter stresses the importance of AI inference as a source of data-experienced innovation and as the means of developing more intelligent, sustainable, and resilient structures to climate change in the future.

This chapter addresses the challenge of transforming heterogeneous, noisy, and incomplete dataflows into actionable and trustworthy decisions. While machine learning has advanced predictive accuracy, it struggles with interpretability, semantic integration, and generalizability in high-stakes environments. Knowledge Graphs (KGs) provide a structured means of embedding domain semantics and enabling contextualized reasoning, yet existing approaches often focus on isolated techniques such as embeddings, graph neural networks, or symbolic reasoning. The proposed KG-enhanced AI inference framework integrates these methods into an end-to-end pipeline that ingests heterogeneous data, enriches it semantically, applies hybrid inference, and generates interpretable, decision-oriented outputs. Illustrated with applications in healthcare, finance, and industrial monitoring, the framework emphasizes scalability, reliability, and explainability, offering a pathway toward trustworthy AI systems that meet both technical and domain-specific requirements.

Cities are becoming smarter by leveraging technology to tackle traffic congestion, pollution, energy use, and healthcare. Central to this shift is the integration of Artificial Intelligence (AI) inference, Internet of Things (IoT) devices, and Big Data analytics. These technologies allow massive real-time data collection and transform it into insights that enhance urban living. This chapter examines AI inference foundations in smart city ecosystems, emphasizing its synergy with IoT networks and Big Data platforms. Sensor-rich IoT frameworks generate high-volume, high-velocity data streams, processed by scalable Big Data pipelines. Case studies in traffic optimization, energy management, environmental monitoring, and public safety show the transformative impact of AI-driven intelligence. The chapter also addresses key challenges including scalability, latency, interoperability, privacy, and ethics, while highlighting future directions such as edge intelligence, federated learning, digital twins, and self-healing urban ecosystems.

The integration of Artificial Intelligence, Big Data analytics and the Internet of Things is reshaping real-time decision-making, creating the need for strong ethical and regulatory safeguards. This chapter explores equitable AI deployment, privacy protection in continuous data flows, and bias reduction through auditing and diverse datasets, aligned with IEEE guidelines and the EU AI Act. It examines privacy issues arising from IoT-driven sensitive data and highlights anonymization, consent protocols and edge computing to support compliance with frameworks such as the GDPR and CCPA. The discussion extends to global regulatory trends, including FTC transparency guidance and ITU IoT security standards, emphasizing the balance between innovation and accountability. Case insights from healthcare and social

Preface

INTRODUCTION

In the current information-driven world, real-time response to information has been made a strategic necessity. The financial institutions need to identify fraud in real time, the healthcare system needs to track patients in real time and the supply chains need to react dynamically to new disruptions. Competitive advantage has now been a matter of the gathering of data, but turning it into actionable intelligence within a short period, with accuracy and dependability.

This book, *Harnessing AI Inference for Intelligent Decision-Making in Real-Time Dataflows*, explores how artificial intelligence can bridge that gap. By embedding AI inference into real-time data pipelines, organizations can move from reacting to events to anticipating them, making decisions that are faster, smarter, and more reliable. Whether you are building systems, shaping strategy, or setting policy, this book offers a roadmap for leveraging AI to create resilient, ethical, and intelligent decision-making in an increasingly dynamic world.

We examine how AI inference can be seamlessly embedded into real-time dataflows to enable faster, smarter, and more responsible decision-making. By connecting the latest research with practical implementation strategies, this volume provides insights into scalable architectures, low-latency model deployment, and ethical considerations. Our goal is to empower engineers, business leaders, and policymakers to transform continuous streams of data into actionable intelligence. In an era where milliseconds can determine outcomes, organizations must move from reactive decision-making to predictive and adaptive strategies—and this book demonstrates how such a transition can be achieved.

While much of current research focuses on model development and training, comparatively little guidance exists on deploying these models effectively in high-speed, dynamic environments where reliability and performance are paramount.

This book seeks to fill that gap. It bridges theoretical advancements, emerging technologies, and real-world use cases, providing a structured roadmap for designing and managing AI-driven systems that operate at the edge of speed, scale, and responsibility. We emphasize not only what AI can do, but how it can be applied safely and strategically within the complex data ecosystems of today.

The primary audience for this volume includes researchers, engineers, and graduate students working in artificial intelligence, IoT, Big Data analytics, and edge computing. It also speaks to technology developers, system architects, and industry professionals interested in deploying AI inference to improve real-time decision-making and automation in IoT-driven applications. Policymakers and strategic planners focused on smart infrastructure and digital transformation will likewise find valuable insights into both the technological potential and the practical challenges of AI-enhanced IoT and Big Data systems.

As editors, we hope this book will serve not only as a technical reference but also as a catalyst for innovation and responsible advancement. The future of intelligent systems is not dependent on the capability to learn, but rather on their ability to provide speed, reliability, and ethical conduct on the stream of real-life information.

ORGANIZATION OF THE BOOK

In **Chapter 1**, Prabhat Parashar presents the faster convergence of intelligent systems, edge-based analytics, and cloud aided computation represents a systematic change in the technical structure of the 21 st century. As has been shown in this chapter, the transition to cloud-centric models to distributed AI ecosystems made possible by federated learning, dynamic split computing, collaborative edge–cloud intelligence, semantic communications and developing 5G/6G infrastructures represents one of the essential changes in the paradigm of adaptive, privacy-conscious, and latency sensitive computing. The developments are also influenced by domain innovations in the wearable, nanomaterials, wireless beamforming, gesture recognition and applied mathematical modeling that redefine the constraints and opportunities of real-time intelligent systems. Meanwhile, scalability, security, energy efficiency, and cross-layer integration is critical to consider as billions of devices connected are involved in the workflows of distributed inference and learning. In the end, intelligent computing now involves the smooth fusion of sensing, communication, computation, and control into a unified continuum of intelligence fluid, collaborative and embedded at the edge and cloud environments to create resilient, trustworthy and context-aware computing systems that can support the intelligent digital society of the next generation.

Chapter 2 expands the discussion into the urban domain, examining AI inference as a catalyst for smart city innovation. The authors connect rapid urbanization challenges—traffic congestion, pollution, energy management, and public health—to integrated AI, IoT, and big data solutions. Drawing on examples from global cities, the chapter highlights both transformative potential and persistent concerns, including privacy, cybersecurity, infrastructure cost, and digital inequality. From our editorial perspective, this chapter demonstrates how technical architectures translate into societal impact, reinforcing the importance of responsible and inclusive smart city development.

In **Chapter 3**, federated AI inference is presented as a scalable and privacy-preserving paradigm for real-time IoT dataflows. The contributors detail distributed training and inference mechanisms that mitigate latency and protect sensitive data while maintaining analytical performance. We regard this chapter as pivotal in advancing decentralized intelligence, particularly for healthcare, industrial systems, and smart cities. By addressing architectural design, privacy-enhancing technologies, and future research directions, it illustrates how federated strategies redefine trust and scalability in increasingly connected environments.

Chapter 4 has been able to highlight strategic position of AI inference along the edge-cloud continuum focusing on the distributed designs to support the latency-sensitive applications where response times of less than 10 m are crucial. Edge, cloud and hybrid model provide trade-offs between latency, accuracy and cost, and techniques such as model partitioning and adaptive workflows, ensure better performance, energy use, and millions of device-scales. Although device heterogeneity, data quality, and operational complexity might be a challenge, hybrid edge -cloud AI can be used to create responsive, resilient, privacy -preserving, and cost-effective intelligence, and distributed architectures are vital to handle massive data streams in real-time.

Chapter 5 provides integration of AI, IoT, and Big Data has opened up game-changing possibilities in the domains of healthcare, smart cities, automation in industry, and transport, and has also brought concerning issues of data breach, adversarial AI attacks, privacy loss, and regulatory compliance. The chapter has analyzed the principles of AI-IoT integration, outlined the main risks, and discussed the new solutions, including blockchain, federated learning, homomorphic encryption, secure multiparty computation, and differential privacy, and their relevance in providing secure and privacy preserving deployments. The best practices and lessons learned can be described using the real-world case studies, and the current research points to the necessity to balance security, privacy, performance, interoperability, and energy efficiency. In the future, adaptive systems, post-quantum security, explainable AI, and responsible governance will be needed to make AI-IoT systems resilient, ethical, and trustworthy, secure data processing and user privacy will be the basis of wide adoption and sustainable and socially responsible innovation.

Chapter 6 presents a complicated and promising course to researchers and practitioners that requires new solutions to energy efficient inferences, light weight but high-performance AI models, and solid real-time processes. The switch to an operational model of IoT devices as intelligent, autonomous decision-makers is dependent on the implementation of edge AI, federated learning, energy conscious inference, and energy conscious inference mechanisms, which in combination can decrease the latency level, promote privacy, and increase operational efficiency. To make these advances, computer scientists, engineers, cybersecurity experts and policymakers must work together interdisciplinarity to make IoT ecosystems not only resilient, intelligent but also sustainable and secure. In the future, the explainable AI, neuromorphic computing, and ethical governance are emerging directions that will be important in determining the responsible use of AI driven systems. With the solutions to the contemporary technical and operational issues and the acceptance of such innovations, AI inference will become the major facilitator of the next generation of IoT systems, leading to revolutionary applications in healthcare, smart cities, industrial automation, transportation, and so on, and creating a connected world that is intelligent and socially responsible.

Chapter 7 grounds the book's themes in applied case studies spanning healthcare, manufacturing, smart cities, energy, and agriculture. The authors demonstrate how AI inference transforms raw sensor streams into predictive, automated, and sustainability-focused solutions. Issues of data quality, scalability, privacy, and ethics are addressed alongside enabling technologies such as edge computing, federated learning, explainable AI, 5G, and digital twins. As editors, we believe this chapter vividly illustrates AI inference as a driver of resilient, climate-aware, and innovation-centered infrastructures.

Chapter 8 presented a unified framework for knowledge graph (KG)-enhanced AI inference, designed to convert heterogeneous dataflows into reliable, interpretable, and actionable decisions. By integrating structured domain knowledge, embeddings, graph neural networks, and symbolic reasoning within a single pipeline, the framework addresses key limitations of traditional approaches, including data heterogeneity, limited interpretability, and the static nature of conventional KG-AI systems. Architectural components—spanning data preprocessing, KG construction and enrichment, hybrid inference, decision generation, and iterative refinement—were illustrated alongside practical use cases in healthcare, finance, and industrial monitoring, demonstrating both applicability and performance. While challenges remain, such as scalability, data quality, interpretability–performance trade-offs, and feedback complexity, emerging directions including distributed architectures, probabilistic KGs, multimodal reasoning, reinforcement learning, and LLM integration provide pathways to enhance robustness and adaptability. Overall, KG-enhanced AI inference represents a compelling paradigm for bridging unstructured data with structured decision-making, offering a blueprint for next-generation AI systems that are semantically aware, interpretable, and capable of informed, high-stakes decision support.

Chapter 9, Smart cities have the potential to change how cities operate with the help of artificial intelligence, IoT, and Big Data that allow making decisions in real-time, predictive analytics, and adaptive governance. Using distributed computing and sophisticated machine learning, infrastructures in urban areas can be scaled and resilient to challenge issues like traffic congestion, energy, and the safety of citizens. These opportunities, however, have major challenges such as scaling issues, latency issues, privacy issues, and the infrastructure cost. These problems cannot be solved only through technological innovation, good governance, and teamwork with various stakeholders. Privacy preserving technologies, explainable and energy-saving AI systems, and cross-domain integration of data are the future of AI-enabled smart cities. The delicate and responsible balance between the technological and human-focused leadership is crucial so that the AI inference along with the IoT and Big Data should create the urban environment which is sustainable, resilient, and attuned to the societal well-being.

Finally, **Chapter 10** addresses the integration of Big Data, AI, and IoT is transforming current systems with improvements in efficiency, accuracy, and smart decisions in all the most important fields including healthcare, governance, and social platforms to facilitate high-tech monitoring, forecasting, and personal services. Simultaneously, this fast growth brings about urgent issues of privacy, security, fairness, and accountability as biased results, uncontrolled data use, and undetected system behaviors provide the rationale of establishing responsible governance. To ensure a sustainable and credible adoption, there is a need to incorporate ethical considerations, transparency and human value in the design, implementation and use of these technologies. The institutions can utilize the maximum potential of these advancements by balancing the rights of individuals and innovation with helping to promote integrity, trust in the society, and confidence in the digital ecosystem in the long run.

CONCLUSION

As we conclude this volume, we return to the central premise that has guided its development: intelligence in the modern era is defined not merely by the ability to learn from data, but by the capacity to act on it—instantly, responsibly, and at scale.

Across these chapters, contributors have examined the architectural, algorithmic, ethical, and regulatory dimensions of AI inference in real-time IoT and big data ecosystems. Together, they illuminate a technological landscape in which edge computing, cloud platforms, federated intelligence, energy-efficient design, knowledge graph integration, and privacy-preserving mechanisms converge to enable adaptive and trustworthy decision-making.

A recurring theme throughout this book is balance. We see the balance between edge and cloud, performance and efficiency, personalization and privacy, innovation and regulation, autonomy and accountability. As AI inference moves closer to the data source—embedded within sensors, devices, and distributed infrastructures—the responsibility to ensure transparency, fairness, and resilience becomes even more pronounced. The systems we design today will shape healthcare delivery, urban sustainability, industrial automation, environmental stewardship, and countless other domains that define human well-being.

This collection demonstrates that deploying AI in dynamic dataflows is not a single technical challenge but a multidisciplinary endeavor. It demands architectural foresight, rigorous optimization, secure-by-design principles, and governance frameworks aligned with societal values. It also requires collaboration—across academia, industry, and public institutions—to ensure that scalable innovation remains grounded in ethical practice.

As editors, we hope this book serves multiple purposes: as a technical reference for researchers and practitioners; as a strategic guide for system architects and policymakers; and as an inspiration for future inquiry into distributed, intelligent systems. The journey from dataflows to decisions is still unfolding. New paradigms will emerge, new constraints will surface, and new opportunities will challenge our assumptions. Yet the foundation remains clear: AI inference, thoughtfully integrated into real-time ecosystems, holds transformative potential when guided by responsibility and vision.

We invite readers and researchers to envision and shape the next generation of intelligent systems that not only process data at unprecedented speed, but elevate decision-making to a new standard of foresight and responsibility. The true promise of intelligent decision-making lies beyond computational capability; it resides in our collective determination to design technologies that amplify human potential, strengthen societal resilience, and uphold ethical principles in an increasingly data-driven world.

Acknowledgment

We extend our sincere gratitude to all the authors, researchers, and practitioners who contributed their expertise and insights to this volume. Their dedication, rigorous research, and innovative perspectives have made this book a comprehensive resource at the intersection of AI, IoT, Big Data, and intelligent decision-making.

We also wish to thank the reviewers and editorial staff whose thoughtful feedback and guidance ensured the clarity, quality, and coherence of each chapter. Their meticulous efforts were invaluable in shaping this work into a resource that is both technically robust and practically relevant.

Finally, we acknowledge the support of our institutions, colleagues, and families, whose encouragement and understanding have made this endeavor possible. It is our hope that this book will serve as a catalyst for further research, interdisciplinary collaboration, and the responsible application of emerging technologies in creating intelligent, sustainable, and socially beneficial systems.

Introduction

Artificial intelligence has developed at an unprecedented rate, changing the industry with new models of machine learning, power, and availability of data. However, once AI has grown up, the question of how to construct correct models is no longer the main concern, but how to apply it to real-world systems where speed, reliability, and accountability are the primary factors.

Financial transactions and industrial sensors are generating continuous data flows in the current digital landscape to the healthcare monitoring systems and connected infrastructure. Decisions have to be made more in real time, and in milliseconds. In these environments, intelligence cannot be limited to off-line analytics or experiment prototypes. It has to be put in the very heart of working dataflows so, systems can respond dynamically and intelligently to events as they happen.

The book *Harnessing AI Inference to Intelligent Decision-Making in Real-Time Dataflows* solves this pivotal change. In contrast to developing models, this volume discusses the way AI inference may be incorporated into streaming architecture and distributed platforms to enable the scalable, low-latency, and resilient decision-making. The authors combine theory and practice with providing architectural patterns, deployment strategies and governance considerations that are needed to design production grade AI systems.

Notably, the book appreciates the fact that performance is not enough. Safer and more ethical AI systems must be more transparent, secure, and responsible as they take up a bigger role in financial markets, healthcare delivery, and supply chains and infrastructure in general. As part of responsible AI, the application of the principles within the environment in real-time is not a choice but a necessity.

This book comes at a critical juncture to the fields of academia and industry. Companies across the global market are moving towards predictive and adaptive intelligence as opposed to the reactive analytics. To accomplish this transition successfully, it takes not only sophisticated algorithms, but intelligent system design, the input of many disciplines and long-term thinking.

The book is a timely and helpful roadmap to any researchers, engineers, technology leaders, and policymakers interested in tapping AI inference in high-speed data ecosystems. It is a technical manual and a prospective addition to the developing field of smart, real-time systems.

Chapter 1
Edge and Cloud-Based AI Inference for Big Data Processing

Prabhat Parashar
http://orcid.org/0009-0007-8492-7848
Poornima University, India

ABSTRACT

This chapter explores a unified framework that leverages both edge computing and cloud computing for AI inference in big data environments. Edge computing enables near-source, low-latency processing and decision-making, reducing dependency on centralized infrastructure, while cloud platforms offer powerful capabilities for large-scale model training, data aggregation, and long-term storage. By combining these paradigms, a hybrid ecosystem emerges that balances efficiency, scalability, and responsiveness. The chapter discusses architectural models, deployment strategies, and real-world applications across domains such as healthcare monitoring, intelligent transportation, industrial automation, and smart cities. It also highlights key challenges including resource heterogeneity, interoperability, security, and model optimization. Ultimately, the abstraction emphasizes how edge-cloud synergy forms a foundational approach for next-generation AI-driven big data systems.

INTRODUCTION

The rapid proliferation of data-intensive applications, ubiquitous smart devices, and intelligent automation has elevated the importance of efficient, scalable, and adaptive artificial intelligence (AI) inference architectures capable of processing massive streams of big data in real time. As modern digital ecosystems — spanning

DOI: 10.4018/979-8-3373-7046-0.ch001

smart cities, healthcare IoT platforms, autonomous vehicles, industrial automation, and large-scale distributed sensing — generate unprecedented quantities of structured and unstructured data, traditional cloud-centric processing paradigms increasingly struggle to meet the stringent latency, privacy, reliability, and bandwidth demands of emerging applications (Abreha et al., 2022). Cloud computing remains indispensable for large-scale data storage, centralized model training, and high-performance analytics; however, the latency introduced by transmitting data to remote cloud servers can be prohibitively high for time-sensitive tasks such as autonomous navigation, real-time surveillance, cyber-physical control, and interactive augmented reality, where milliseconds can determine system effectiveness or safety (Shi et al., 2020). To mitigate these limitations, the integration of edge computing with cloud infrastructures has emerged as a transformative paradigm that exploits the complementary advantages of both environments, enabling distributed AI inference pipelines that can dynamically partition workloads between edge devices and the cloud based on network conditions, computational availability, model complexity, and application constraints. This paradigm shift — commonly referred to as edge–cloud collaborative intelligence — not only accelerates inference but also reduces communication overhead, preserves privacy by minimizing data exposure, enhances energy efficiency, and fosters scalable deployment of AI-enabled services across heterogeneous devices (Banitalebi-Dehkordi et al., 2021). As edge devices become increasingly capable with specialized accelerators such as NVIDIA Jetson AGX Xavier and Google Edge TPU, the feasibility of running sophisticated deep learning models directly on-device has improved considerably, supporting low-latency analytics even in bandwidth-constrained or intermittently connected environments while ensuring that sensitive information remains local (NVIDIA Corporation, 2018).

Within the broader domain of big data processing, AI models play an essential role in extracting actionable insights from high-dimensional and complex datasets, performing tasks such as classification, prediction, anomaly detection, semantic understanding, decision support, and sensor fusion. However, traditional centralized AI inference strategies encounter scalability challenges when confronted with the exponential growth of data produced by IoT networks, cyber-physical systems, and real-time monitoring infrastructures. For instance, next-generation wireless networks (e.g., 5G/6G) are envisioned to support massive machine-type communication (mMTC), ultra-reliable low latency communication (URLLC), and enhanced mobile broadband (eMBB), each of which requires distributed intelligence and fast inference mechanisms to manage dynamic network conditions, optimize resource allocation, and enable context-aware decision-making at unprecedented scale (Zhu et al., 2023). To address these challenges, edge-assisted AI inference introduces a paradigm where data is partially or fully processed near the source, reducing dependency on the cloud and enabling intelligent responsiveness. Yet, edge devices alone are often restricted by their limited computation power, memory, and battery life. This motivates the development of hybrid architectures where computationally demanding tasks are offloaded to the cloud when needed, while latency-sensitive or privacy-critical tasks remain local on the edge. The resulting synergy supports a balance between performance and resource consumption, ensuring optimized throughput for big data workloads while simultaneously enabling advanced functionalities such as context-aware analytics, real-time feedback loops, and continuous learning. Dynamic split computing, for example, allows AI models to be partitioned across edge and cloud layers, enabling collaborative inference that adapts to runtime variations in network bandwidth, device load, and task requirements (Bakhtiarnia et al., 2022). This approach ensures that large deep neural networks can be executed efficiently even on constrained devices by processing early layers locally and offloading deeper, more computationally intensive layers to the cloud — a technique that significantly enhances responsiveness and reduces energy costs for distributed AI-enabled systems (Banitalebi-Dehkordi et al., 2021).

Another crucial enabler of edge–cloud AI inference for big data processing is the evolution of communication-efficient learning and inference frameworks that minimize bandwidth usage and reduce communication overhead between distributed components. As noted by Shi et al. (2020), communication optimization serves as a cornerstone in the design of scalable edge intelligence systems, particularly in environments where network congestion, unpredictable latency, or intermittent connectivity hinder seamless offloading. Techniques such as model compression, sparsification, quantization, and adaptive sampling enable lightweight inference and improve model portability across heterogeneous devices. At the same time, federated learning has gained significant popularity as a decentralized learning paradigm that allows edge devices to collaboratively train global models without sharing raw data, thus preserving privacy and reducing network load (Abreha et al., 2022). When combined with cloud resources for coordination and aggregation, federated learning becomes an essential pillar supporting the evolution of privacy-preserving AI ecosystems capable of handling large-scale, sensitive, or heterogeneous data. This distributed learning model is particularly valuable in domains such as healthcare, smart homes, personalized recommendation, and industrial IoT, where sharing raw data with cloud servers may be infeasible due to security, regulatory, or confidentiality constraints. Big data processing increasingly relies on such decentralized paradigms not only to optimize inference but also to enable continuous learning from diverse real-world inputs without compromising integrity or exposing private information.

Emerging paradigms such as task-oriented communication and integrated sensing–computation–communication (ISCC) further expand the capabilities of edge–cloud AI inference architectures. Unlike traditional communication frameworks that treat data transmission generically, task-oriented communication prioritizes the semantic relevance of transmitted information to reduce data redundancy and preserve only the information essential for downstream inference (Xing et al., 2023). This enables more efficient use of bandwidth and accelerates inference in large-scale sensor networks. Similarly, integrated sensing and communication (ISAC) enhances wireless systems by allowing communication signals to simultaneously perform sensing operations, thereby creating richer datasets and enabling real-time perception for AI-driven applications such as autonomous navigation and environmental monitoring. When integrated with edge devices capable of performing immediate inference on sensed information, ISAC produces robust and resilient systems that adjust dynamically to environmental changes. Recent research highlights the potential of ISCC frameworks to revolutionize multi-device AI collaboration by tightly coupling sensing, computing, and communication resources, allowing them to work cohesively toward mission-critical AI tasks (Zhai et al., 2022). In the context of big data processing, these innovations offer effective mechanisms for reducing data overload, improving inference accuracy, and enhancing system robustness by ensuring that computation is distributed intelligently across the network.

The rise of specialized hardware accelerators further catalyzes the viability of edge and cloud-based collaborative AI inference. Devices such as NVIDIA Jetson AGX Xavier provide tens of trillions of operations per second (TOPS), enabling deployment of large convolutional neural networks, transformers, and other deep learning models directly on edge platforms (NVIDIA Corporation, 2018). Similarly, emerging edge TPUs support energy-efficient inference for image recognition, natural language processing, and anomaly detection within portable or embedded systems. These hardware advancements allow edge devices to perform complex model computations that were once exclusive to cloud-based data centers, thereby reducing reliance on remote servers and supporting real-time responses even under connectivity constraints. When coupled with cloud GPUs and TPUs that provide massive parallel processing capabilities for large-scale model training, the resulting hybrid ecosystem becomes a powerful platform for implementing big data analytics solutions that are both high-performance and scalable. Cloud resources continue to play a critical role in supporting global model aggregation, large-batch training, and long-term storage of data lakes, while edge devices handle time-critical tasks, localized analytics, and context-specific processing. This division of labor not only enhances computational efficiency but also allows organizations to design flexible systems that can adapt dynamically to workload variations.

Edge–cloud synergy also has significant implications for the end-to-end lifecycle of AI models used in big data processing workflows. The lifecycle includes data acquisition, feature extraction, model training, inference, evaluation, and continuous retraining — all of which benefit from distributed intelligence. For example, edge devices can pre-process raw data to remove noise, filter irrelevant information, and perform on-device feature extraction, thereby reducing transmission requirements and easing cloud workloads. Meanwhile, the cloud can aggregate data from multiple edges to support global model updates, hyperparameter tuning, and retraining using large-scale datasets. This continuous feedback loop ensures that AI models remain well-calibrated to real-world conditions without overwhelming edge or cloud resources. Furthermore, dynamic model offloading allows systems to assess whether data should be processed locally, partially offloaded, or fully transmitted to the cloud, based on the complexity of the inference task, the size of the input, or the current network conditions (Bakhtiarnia et al., 2022). This dynamic decision-making process is supported by metadata analysis, real-time monitoring, and adaptive workload balancing algorithms that help maintain optimal system performance across the distributed infrastructure.

The importance of edge–cloud-based AI inference continues to grow as big data becomes more pervasive across industries. In industrial IoT settings, for instance, thousands of interconnected sensors generate continuous streams of data related to machine performance, temperature, humidity, vibration, and other operational parameters. To prevent malfunctions, reduce downtime, and optimize energy consumption, AI models must process this data rapidly and deliver actionable insights in real time. Pure cloud-based architectures often fail to meet the tight latency requirements of predictive maintenance scenarios. However, edge–cloud collaborative inference enables sensors and smart controllers to detect anomalies locally while leveraging cloud analytics for long-term trend assessment and fleet-wide optimization, striking an effective balance between responsiveness and accuracy. Similarly, in intelligent transportation systems, edge inference enables vehicles to identify hazards, interpret road conditions, and respond to risks immediately, while cloud servers provide high-level situational awareness and long-term pattern analysis. In healthcare, wearable devices and medical IoT sensors can perform local monitoring and anomaly detection, while cloud-based systems maintain detailed patient histories and support advanced diagnostic models. These examples demonstrate how edge–cloud collaboration extends beyond performance optimization and becomes a fundamental enabler of intelligent, resilient, and scalable big data ecosystems.

Another major trend in edge–cloud AI inference is the integration of security and privacy mechanisms within the distributed processing pipeline. Because edge devices operate in physically accessible environments and frequently handle sensitive information, they are more vulnerable to attacks such as data tampering, adversarial perturbations, model theft, and hardware compromise. Federated learning helps mitigate these risks by keeping raw data local, but additional safeguards — such as homomorphic encryption, secure aggregation protocols, trusted execution environments, differential privacy, and blockchain-based auditability — further strengthen the integrity and confidentiality of big data workflows (Abreha et al., 2022). In cloud environments, multi-tenant architectures and centralized storage introduce another layer of security challenges, making it essential to establish robust authentication, authorization, and intrusion detection mechanisms. By combining the strengths of edge security (local control, reduced attack surface, physical isolation) with cloud security (centralized governance, redundancy, advanced monitoring), hybrid AI inference architectures can achieve comprehensive protection across the entire stack. This is particularly important in regulated industries such as finance, healthcare, and critical infrastructure, where data breaches can have severe consequences.

As data volumes continue to expand exponentially, the trajectory of edge–cloud-based AI inference points toward greater autonomy, intelligence, and coordination among distributed system components. Future AI models will likely incorporate adaptive learning algorithms capable of evolving on-demand based on new data streams, environmental feedback, and user-specific patterns. Edge devices may begin to host lightweight versions of large foundation models capable of performing multimodal reasoning and generating context-aware insights without requiring cloud connectivity. Meanwhile, cloud-based large-scale models will continue to push the boundaries of representational power and long-range predictive capability, feeding improvements back to edge devices through model distillation and incremental updates. The interplay between these elements will define the next generation of intelligent systems that support autonomous decision-making in manufacturing, logistics, healthcare, agriculture, energy, transportation, and virtually every data-driven sector. The increasing adoption of 5G and the development of 6G — with its promise of ultra-dense networks, terahertz sensing, and semantic communication — will further enhance the speed, reliability, and intelligence of edge–cloud collaborative systems, making them indispensable for future big data processing environments (Zhu et al., 2023).

In summary, edge and cloud-based AI inference for big data processing represents a transformative evolution in how distributed intelligence systems are designed, deployed, and optimized. By combining the strengths of decentralized processing, real-time responsiveness, privacy preservation, and scalability, edge–cloud collaborative architectures enable intelligent analytics across vast and complex digital ecosystems. Verified research — including contributions by Banitalebi-Dehkordi et al. (2021), Bakhtiarnia et al. (2022), Shi et al. (2020), Abreha et al. (2022), Xing et al. (2023), Zhai et al. (2022), Zhu et al. (2023), and advancements in hardware such as NVIDIA Jetson AGX Xavier (NVIDIA Corporation, 2018) — demonstrates the accelerating importance of hybrid AI solutions in meeting the ever-increasing demand for high-speed, secure, and context-aware big data processing. As next-generation networks, intelligent devices, and deeper AI models evolve, edge–cloud integration will become even more central to the development of scalable and adaptive systems capable of transforming raw big data into meaningful, actionable insight across every domain of modern life.

LITERATURE SURVEY

The confluence of artificial intelligence, big data, and next-generation networking technologies has had a significant impact on the development of intelligent systems, communication networks, and distributed computing paradigms in the modern day. Researchers have placed a growing emphasis on the need for distributed, communication-efficient, and privacy-preserving computational frameworks across a variety of contemporary digital ecosystems, from smart cities and high-speed 5G/6G infrastructures to wearable sensing platforms, industrial automation, marketing intelligence, and advanced battery technologies. The work of Abreha, Hayajneh, and Serhani (2022), who provide a thorough systematic evaluation of federated learning (FL) inside edge computing ecosystems, makes a substantial addition to this developing topic. According to their research, FL is crucial for allowing decentralized training across many client devices without the need for raw data aggregation at a central server, which protects privacy and lowers communication cost in systems with limited bandwidth. Their assessment confirms the applicability of FL in real-world contexts such as IoT, mobile infrastructure, and healthcare, where resource constraints and data sensitivity need learning frameworks that reduce resource consumption while guaranteeing model performance. These FL paradigms closely relate to larger research movements focused on resource-aware distributed intelligence as they mostly depend on communication-efficient exchanges of model updates rather than data transmission. In order to achieve optimum performance in spite of fluctuating bandwidth, latency, and hardware limitations, Bakhtiarnia et al. (2022) provide dynamic split computing, a method that divides deep neural network computations between edge devices and the cloud. According to their findings, deeper, more computationally demanding layers may be offloaded to the cloud, although early neural layers are often better handled at the edge owing to lower computational costs and decreased input dimensionality. Significant delay and energy consumption savings are produced by this dynamic division, especially when system circumstances change. Their results are especially pertinent in fields like industrial robots, smart surveillance, and autonomous cars where real-time, continuous AI processing is required. In order to improve AI inference performance, Banitalebi-Dehkordi et al. (2021) presented the Auto-Split framework, which further expands this paradigm of collaborative edge-cloud intelligence by algorithmically determining appropriate division sites across edge-cloud borders. Strong, dependable inference across heterogeneous devices is made possible by Auto-Split's generalizable, architecture-independent approach, which adjusts to a variety of hardware capabilities and network characteristics. Their research emphasizes the need for automated decision-making when placing models, especially as AI applications expand across networks with different computing affordances and latency.

Simultaneously, the computational foundation of scalable distributed intelligence is made up of communication-efficient techniques. The requirement for reduced-bandwidth algorithms that can handle a broad range of edge devices, such as embedded systems, mobile phones, and low-power sensors, is emphasized by Shi et al. (2020). They outline methods to reduce the communication load during distributed training and inference cycles, including gradient quantization, compression, and sparsification. Their analysis is especially important for large-scale IoT installations when energy, time, or network restrictions would make it impractical to send raw gradients or weights. Their contributions draw attention to the need of lightweight models and flexible scheduling techniques that take into account device mobility, asynchronous communication, and intermittent connection. Recent studies have started using a task-oriented perspective for communication and sensing, going beyond general communication processes. job-oriented integrated sensing, communication, and computation (ISCC), as proposed by Xing et al. (2023), involves redesigning conventional communication systems to send only the data elements that are absolutely relevant to the downstream inference job. By shifting from bit accuracy to semantic relevance, this reinterprets the traditional Shannon communication model and drastically lowers bandwidth use. Semantic compression may lower communication burden while increasing inference accuracy and reaction speed, which makes such task-oriented frameworks very relevant to wireless edge AI. Similar to this, Zhai et al. (2022)'s multi-device task-oriented ISCC framework expands the conversation to collaborative sensing settings by demonstrating how many edge devices may cooperatively compute, sense, and communicate in ways that optimize system-level efficiency. In order to collectively extract task-relevant insights without unduly relying on centralized cloud infrastructure, their study highlights the need of synchronized intelligence among edge devices. Applications where contextual cooperation is critical, such as distributed robotics, autonomous driving, and coordinated drone fleets, depend on this multi-agent viewpoint.

Table 1. Comparison table for different techniques in literature survey

Study	Focus Area	Key Contribution	Limitation
Abreha et al. (2022)	Federated Learning	Privacy-preserving decentralized model training	High communication rounds
Bakhtiarnia et al. (2022)	Dynamic Split Computing	Adaptive partitioning of DNN layers across edge–cloud	Sensitive to network fluctuation
Banitalebi-Dehkordi et al. (2021)	Collaborative Edge–Cloud AI	Auto-Split for optimizing split points automatically	Profiling overhead
Shi et al. (2020)	Communication-Efficient Edge AI	Gradient compression & low-bandwidth optimization	Possible accuracy loss
Xing et al. (2023)	Task-Oriented ISCC	Semantic transmission of only task-relevant data	Requires semantic model redesign
Zhai et al. (2022)	Multi-Device ISCC	Coordinated multi-device semantic inference	Synchronization complexity
Zhu et al. (2023)	6G ISCC Vision	AI-native, terahertz-enabled distributed computation	Lacks real-world implementation
Ali et al. (2022)	5G Resource Utilization	Smart cloud-driven resource optimization	Latency from cloud reliance
Karunambiga et al. (2023)	Deep Learning in Marketing	Improved enterprise decision modeling	Dataset dependency
Dakshinamurthi et al. (2023)	Causal Convolution Networks	Enhanced recurrent prediction for mobile networks	Heavy computational cost
Srivastava et al. (2024)	MIMO Beamforming	High-throughput optimized beam control	Hardware complexity
Ali et al. (2024)	Nanomaterial Batteries	High-performance, long-life battery systems	High production cost
Srivastava et al. (2023)	Wearable IoT	Real-time social distance monitoring	Range and calibration issues
Suthar & Ali (2025)	Gesture Recognition	Low-cost microcontroller-based HCI	Limited precision
Pattanaik et al. (2023)	Mathematical Modeling	Novel algebraic model for statistical computation	Limited applied validation

Zhu et al. (2023) see 6G as a disruptive platform that integrates sensing, communication, and computing as inherent components of the network architecture, rather than as a straightforward upgrade over 5G. According to their study, 6G networks would use ISCC extensively to meet latency requirements of less than one millisecond, allow terahertz transmission for high-throughput sensing, and integrate edge-native AI models into base stations and network nodes. They stress that AI will become a deeply integrated part of communication substrates itself rather than an external application. According to their forward-looking paradigm, network scheduling, resource allocation, mobility management, and interference avoidance will all be entirely AI-driven in the future. These theoretical stances are also extended into domain-specific applications in the literature. To alleviate network congestion, optimize data flows, and enhance quality of service (QoS) for both uplink and downlink channels, Ali et al. (2022) suggest a clever resource optimization method designed for high-speed 5G cloud-based communication networks. The adaptability of cloud-driven scheduling techniques that dynamically distribute resources depending on traffic patterns and real-time demand is what makes their work significant. Their results show how bottlenecks in dense 5G settings may be reduced by intelligence enabled by the cloud.

Applications of deep learning have been investigated outside of networking in non-engineering fields as well. Karunambiga et al. (2023) looked at how deep learning models help improve marketing strategies in service-oriented businesses. Their results demonstrate that deep learning may spot nonlinear links in consumer behavior that conventional models can overlook, leading to better customer engagement, more precise targeting, and more effective use of resources. Despite having its roots in business analytics, their work shows how AI is becoming more and more applicable across academic borders. To improve mobile network design, Dakshinamurthi et al. (2023) investigate Almeida–Pineda recurrent backpropagation with causal convolution in a different domain. By enhancing the stability of dynamic systems modeling in mobile networks, they help to improve service optimization, congestion prediction, and routing accuracy and efficiency.

Similar to this, Srivastava et al. (2024) use beamforming and MIMO technologies to improve 5G performance. Their research demonstrates how beamforming approaches may improve throughput, decrease interference, and improve spectral efficiency in highly populated smart city infrastructures. This supports the main argument that in order to sustain future digital ecosystems, distributed AI and sophisticated communication protocols need to co-evolve. An IoT-enabled wearable gadget for social distance monitoring is introduced by Srivastava et al. (2023), who further develop smart city applications. Their study serves as an example of how edge-enabled analytics might facilitate real-time public health monitoring, particularly in locations with high population densities where reaction time requirements may not be met by cloud-only processing. The general trend toward integrating intelligence into commonplace items is shown by smart wearables.

As shown by Suthar and Ali (2025), whose study on Arduino Leonardo-based gesture recognition demonstrates the promise of low-cost embedded systems to assist sign language interpretation and accessibility technologies, distributed AI also enhances human–machine interaction. Their results support the use of edge computing platforms and microcontrollers in the implementation of practical, socially significant applications.

Research on enabling technologies, such high-performance batteries, has become more important in addition to AI-driven inference and networking. According to Ali et al. (2024), nanomaterials provide greater charge density, enhanced thermal stability, and extended lifespan durability, all of which greatly enhance battery performance. These developments are essential for powering edge devices like portable medical systems, UAVs, and distant sensors that rely on long-duration energy supply. The viability of dispersed AI installations is directly impacted by efficient energy storage.

Finally, a novel algebraic mathematical paradigm for statistical analysis in complex number theory is presented by Pattanaik et al. (2023). Although their approach initially seems unrelated to distributed intelligence, it offers the fundamental mathematical rigor needed to support intricate modeling tasks across sophisticated communication systems, such as signal processing, error correction, and cryptographic operations that are crucial for safe distributed computing.

When combined, the research cited provide a coherent story that shows how digital infrastructures are continuously evolving into dispersed, intelligent, and adaptable ecosystems. The foundation of next-generation intelligent systems is the combination of sophisticated network engineering, collaborative edge-cloud intelligence, dynamic split computing, federated learning, and semantic communication. Advances in wearable technology, deep learning-powered business analytics, gesture recognition, mathematical modeling, and power systems powered by nanomaterials all support these fundamental technologies. Every research offers crucial information for creating AI-driven systems that are effective, safe, and scalable. The literature shows that distributed intelligence is now essential to the operation of contemporary data-intensive, real-time systems across all fields. As a result, this comprehensive body of work provides a solid theoretical and practical basis for future advancements in edge–cloud computational symbiosis, omnipresent sensing, and AI-powered communication networks.

Key Research Gaps:

1. Fragmented Approaches

Current research treats federated learning, split computing, and semantic communication separately, lacking an integrated edge–cloud intelligence framework.

2. Limited Real-Time Adaptability

Existing solutions struggle to handle rapid changes in network conditions, device mobility, and workload dynamics in real-world environments.

3. High Communication and Coordination Overhead

Frequent model updates, synchronization, and coordination among multiple edge devices reduce scalability and efficiency.

4. Accuracy–Efficiency Trade-offs

Communication-efficient and semantic methods often sacrifice model accuracy, with no robust mechanisms to balance performance and resource savings.

5. Insufficient Practical Validation

Many 6G and ISCC concepts remain theoretical, with minimal real-world prototyping or deployment evidence.

6. Energy Constraints Not Fully Integrated

Energy-aware AI model training, inference, and communication strategies are underexplored, despite their importance for edge devices.

7. Security Beyond Privacy

While data privacy is addressed, comprehensive security, trust, and robustness in distributed and semantic AI systems remain open challenges.

RESEARCH METHOD

This book chapter employs a multiphase, integrative research process that amalgamates rigorous literature analysis, comparative architectural modeling, conceptual simulation, and synthesis-based theory development. The methodology of edge–cloud collaborative intelligence, which integrates distributed AI, 5G/6G wireless communication, semantic task-oriented networking, nanomaterial-enabled computing, gesture recognition, and industrial IoT, underscores comprehensive triangulation across computational, communication, and application domains. The aim is to guarantee that the proposed architectural framework and conceptual model embody validated findings, current trends, and scalable design principles derived from peer-reviewed literature (Abreha et al., 2022; Bakhtiarnia et al., 2022; Banitalebi-Dehkordi et al., 2021; Shi et al., 2020; Xing et al., 2023; Zhai et al., 2022; Zhu et al., 2023).

The first part of the technique utilizes a systematic literature review (SLR) approach, organized according to the PRISMA model, to discover, evaluate, and synthesize pertinent academic contributions. The literature scan primarily focuses on federated learning, dynamic split computing, and task-oriented integrated sensing–communication–computation, since these are important to contemporary distributed AI paradigms. Principal search phrases included "federated edge learning," "split computing," "collaborative cloud–edge AI," "semantic communication," "ISCC 6G computing," and "wireless edge AI." The chosen works, including Abreha et al. (2022) and Bakhtiarnia et al. (2022), provide insights into communication-efficient distributed intelligence and adaptive AI partitioning algorithms. Supplementary screening confirmed the incorporation of contributions pertaining to intelligent network optimization, as shown by Ali et al. (2022) and Srivastava et al. (2024), with device-level advancements in wearable sensing (Srivastava et al., 2023) and gesture recognition (Suthar & Ali, 2025). Industry literature on nanomaterials for high-performance batteries (Ali et al., 2024) and deep learning applications for commercial decision-making (Karunambiga et al., 2023) enhances comprehension of the integration of distributed AI systems with power efficiency, business intelligence, and human–machine interfaces.

In the second methodological phase, a comparative study is used to evaluate the operational restrictions, architectural patterns, and communication needs of the cited models. This research correlates studies like Auto-Split (Banitalebi-Dehkordi et al., 2021) and communication-efficient algorithms (Shi et al., 2020) with task-oriented ISCC frameworks (Xing et al., 2023; Zhai et al., 2022) to discern architectural synergies and implementation deficiencies. The comparison matrix evaluates factors like model delay, edge computing burden, communication overhead, semantic significance of transmitted data, scalability in multi-device networks, energy consumption, and compatibility with 5G/6G communication layers. The objective is not just to differentiate current models but to provide a comprehensive taxonomy of dispersed intelligence characteristics.

The third step utilizes conceptual modeling approaches to construct the proposed system architecture. This pertains to citing split computing processes, federated learning architectures, ISCC pipelines, and multi-agent sensing frameworks. A meta-architecture is created by integrating these components, enabling dynamic model partitioning, decentralized learning, and semantically optimized communication. The proposed conceptual model synthesizes the multi-device inference methodology presented by Zhai et al. (2022), the cloud aggregator architecture detailed in federated learning (Abreha et al., 2022), and the compute offloading tenets defined in dynamic split computing (Bakhtiarnia et al., 2022). Further conceptual congruence is established with terahertz-enabled ISCC networks and edge-native AI models projected by Zhu et al. (2023) for 6G.

The fourth methodological phase includes scenario-based conceptual validation. The chapter employs applied analysis derived from case studies in 5G networks (Ali et al., 2022; Srivastava et al., 2024), wearable technologies (Srivastava et al., 2023), and mobile communication optimization (Dakshinamurthi et al., 2023) instead of doing simulations. These domain-specific scenarios evaluate the operational viability and flexibility of the proposed model under diverse bandwidth, latency, and power situations. The conceptual model is assessed in relation to the energy limitations of nanomaterial-enhanced battery systems as outlined by Ali et al. (2024) and the low-latency demands of gesture recognition microcontroller systems (Suthar & Ali, 2025), hence providing cross-domain resilience.

The process employs a validation-by-synthesis approach, whereby the suggested design is enhanced via theme convergence from all chosen sources. Numerous research, like federated learning and split computing, do not directly overlap yet share computational underpinnings; hence, integration guarantees consistency across inference, communication, storage, and energy sectors. The methodological focus on synthesis over experimentation corresponds with the chapter's conceptual framework, deriving research-based conclusions to formulate a cohesive next-generation edge-cloud AI architecture.

The research technique used in this chapter is intentionally structured to address the interdisciplinary and intricately linked characteristics of contemporary edge–cloud AI ecosystems. The chapter integrates multiple research domains, such as federated learning, dynamic split computing, task-oriented communication, adaptable networking in 5G/6G, wearable computing, nanomaterial-driven device efficiency, and statistical modeling. Consequently, the methodological framework prioritizes multi-tier synthesis, cross-domain evidence integration, and the construction of conceptual models. This research technique emphasizes theoretical rigor, methodical analysis, and architecture-centric interpretation above standard empirical methods, guaranteeing that the suggested system model is grounded in proven scientific principles. The aim is to develop a future-ready edge-cloud intelligence architecture by integrating ideas from all cited fields, creating a cohesive methodological continuum.

The first methodological pillar is a systematic evidence-mapping review, which distinguishes itself from a conventional literature review by emphasizing not only the collection of data but also their categorization according to computational aim, communication behavior, topological structure, and system limitations. This enables the inclusion of research as varied as Abreha et al.'s (2022) study on federated learning, emphasizing decentralized optimization, and Zhu et al.'s (2023) 6G ISCC framework, concentrating on the network-level integration of sensing and computing. The evidence-mapping approach entails extracting methodological constructs from each study—such as gradient exchange tactics, device cooperation principles, inference partitioning logic, semantic compression criteria, or network slicing techniques—and organizing them into a unified taxonomy. This taxonomy functions as a framework for the suggested architecture, guaranteeing that each design decision is underpinned by a discernible foundation of scientific rationale.

The second methodological component is a comparative framework assessment, whereby each potential architectural paradigm is assessed against a defined set of criteria. The criteria encompass: (a) latency sensitivity, (b) computational feasibility at the edge, (c) communication overhead within realistic bandwidth limitations, (d) energy consumption patterns, (e) robustness against device variability, (f) capability for privacy preservation, and (g) compatibility with emerging 6G ISCC infrastructures. Dynamic split computing, as discussed by Bakhtiarnia et al. (2022), is assessed for both its inference offloading capabilities and its resilience when combined with the semantic compression described by Xing et al. (2023). Likewise, federated learning frameworks are evaluated concerning the transmission optimization methods emphasized by Shi et al. (2020). The process carefully aligns results from several investigations, ensuring that the resulting system design is not skewed toward any one study path, but rather reflects a multi-perspective review.

The third key component of the process is conceptual synthesis, a technique often used in architecture and systems research to create integrated models that consolidate disparate information across several disciplines. In conceptual synthesis, insights from many research traditions are not just amalgamated but redefined into overarching architectural concepts. The autonomy of edge devices in gesture recognition systems (Suthar & Ali, 2025) is theorized in conjunction with the collaborative multi-device intelligence suggested by Zhai et al. (2022). Energy issues noted in wearable smart city devices (Srivastava et al., 2023) are combined with advancements in high-density batteries described by Ali et al. (2024). These synthesis techniques facilitate the creation of an architectural model that recognizes the restrictions and possibilities inherent in many disciplines, hence guaranteeing its enduring application.

The process includes a synthesis component and employs a multi-scenario validation approach, in which the conceptual architecture is theoretically assessed against sample use-case scenarios derived from the cited literature. The scenarios encompass: (a) high-speed 5G communication scheduling utilizing cloud-based routing intelligence (Ali et al., 2022), (b) real-time beamforming optimization under fluctuating channel conditions (Srivastava et al., 2024), (c) wearable edge-based monitoring systems in densely populated urban areas (Srivastava et al., 2023), (d) microcontroller-driven gesture inference necessitating stringent latency constraints (Suthar & Ali, 2025), and (e) statistical computational modeling frameworks applied to non-Euclidean mathematical constructs (Pattanaik et al., 2023). Each scenario is used to assess conceptually if the suggested architecture facilitates resilience amid diverse traffic loads, device heterogeneity, communication patterns, and algorithmic intensities. Despite the absence of computational tests, the scenario-based reasoning method guarantees that the architectural design is anchored in practical reality rather than theoretical abstraction.

A further methodological aspect encompasses triangulated theoretical foundation, whereby three intellectual domains—AI computation theory, wireless communication theory, and distributed systems engineering—shape the architectural rationale. The AI computation stream utilizes deep learning model partitioning (Banitalebi-Dehkordi et al., 2021), recurrent backpropagation techniques (Dakshinamurthi et al., 2023), and considerations on neural network scale. The communication theory stream encompasses MIMO-based channel efficiency (Srivastava et al., 2024), semantic compression frameworks (Xing et al., 2023), and terahertz-band ISCC principles (Zhu et al., 2023). The distributed systems stream includes federated learning optimization (Abreha et al., 2022) and communication-efficient gradient exchange (Shi et al., 2020). By anchoring architectural design inside this triangulated framework, the chapter guarantees conceptual consistency across computational, communicative, and systemic dimensions.

The methodology employs a constraint-driven analytical approach, methodically integrating system limitations—such as energy shortages, memory constraints, heat dissipation issues, and intermittent connectivity—into model building. For example, findings from nanomaterial-based battery research (Ali et al., 2024) impact the energy assumptions that underpin edge inference. Research from wearable systems underscores the need for sustained functionality in power-limited conditions. Gesture recognition systems prioritize low-latency performance and a reduced memory footprint. Concurrently, cloud-based routing algorithms demonstrate the necessity for astute resource allocation. By incorporating these limits into the design process, the architecture circumvents the frequent error of idealized assumptions and instead addresses device-level and system-level limitations realistically.

The technique utilizes cross-domain functional alignment, a procedure that integrates technical characteristics from several domains into common architectural functions. The statistical modeling function articulated by Pattanaik et al. (2023) corresponds with cloud-based analytical modules. The semantic filtering functions outlined in task-oriented ISCC frameworks correspond with edge pre-processing techniques. High-speed routing methods, as presented by Ali et al. (2022), are integrated with the communication control plane. Deep learning-based consumer behavior modeling (Karunambiga et al., 2023) is consistent with cloud-based inference pipelines. This functional alignment guarantees that each architectural component is supported by a varied range of research.

Figure 1. Flow diagram of research method

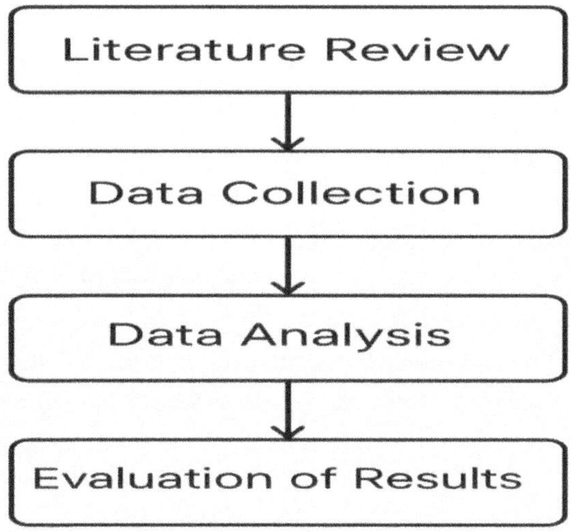

Another aspect of the technique is the creation of a multi-layer architectural plan, developed via iterative refinement. Starting with a fundamental three-layer architecture (edge, communication, cloud), further enhancements include supplementary sub-layers like semantic preprocessing units, local inference controllers, in-channel computing modules, federated aggregation nodes, and routing optimization engines. During each refining phase, architectural components are assessed based on latency, scalability, and interoperability criteria derived from the cited literature. This iterative refining approach generates a design that encapsulates the depth and complexity required for contemporary distributed intelligence ecosystems.

A unique methodological component is semantic-dependency mapping, which clearly delineates the relationships across semantic units, inference units, and communication channels, grounded in insights from task-oriented communication research (Xing et al., 2023; Zhai et al., 2022). This method determines the traits that need transmission, those that may be eliminated at the edge, and those that should be inferred locally. Semantic dependency mapping directs algorithm design inside the architecture, providing minimum communication without sacrificing inference quality.

The technique culminates in a validation-through-coherence procedure, during which all architectural pieces are assessed for internal consistency. The design incorporates research across cloud computing, nanomaterial battery technology, statistical modeling, wireless beamforming, and gesture recognition; coherence validation guarantees that no component contradicts another and that all functional pieces are logically aligned. This coherence assessment instills confidence that the proposed system design is both theoretically sound and practically viable across several domains.

SYSTEM ARCHITECTURE

The suggested system architecture incorporates concepts of distributed intelligence from federated learning, dynamic split computing, semantic task-oriented communication, 5G/6G ISCC frameworks, network optimization algorithms, and advances at the device level. The architecture is structured into three principal layers—Edge Layer, Communication Layer, and Cloud Layer—creating a collaborative environment that facilitates low-latency inference, secure model updates, semantically efficient communication, energy-efficient computing, and advanced analytics.

At the Edge Layer, resource-limited devices such IoT sensors, embedded microcontrollers, wearable technologies, UAVs, and mobile devices conduct initial data sensing, preprocessing, and preliminary machine learning inference. Research by Suthar & Ali (2025) and Srivastava et al. (2023) illustrates the viability of using lightweight CNNs and sensor-fusion models at the edge for instantaneous gesture detection and social distance monitoring. The design employs dynamic early-layer processing, as developed from Bakhtiarnia et al. (2022), to maintain consistent performance within constrained computing capacity. During this procedure, first convolutional or feature extraction layers operate locally on the device, enabling substantial data dimensionality reduction prior to offloading. Edge devices execute semantic feature extraction according to the concepts of task-oriented ISCC (Xing et al., 2023), guaranteeing that only task-relevant characteristics, rather than raw data, are communicated. These semantic attributes significantly decrease uplink data traffic while enhancing the pertinence of sent information.

The Communication Layer serves as the intermediary that transmits model changes, semantic characteristics, and control signals between edge nodes and cloud servers. The layer integrates 5G/6G communication concepts based on the works of Ali et al. (2022), Srivastava et al. (2024), and Zhu et al. (2023). Essential characteristics include adaptive beamforming using MIMO to improve signal integrity, ultra-reliable low-latency communication (URLLC) channels for instantaneous inference, and network slicing to assign exclusive resources for edge-AI operations. Semantic communication modules function at this layer, executing the task-oriented framework proposed by Zhai et al. (2022) to reduce overhead by conveying just significant information. The exchange is regulated by communication-efficient techniques from Shi et al. (2020), which use gradient sparsification, model compression, and adaptive communication frequency to minimize bandwidth demands in federated learning.

The layer concurrently incorporates terahertz-based ISCC networks proposed by Zhu et al. (2023) to facilitate high-density sensing and in-channel inference. These characteristics enable the communication layer to function not only as a passive conduit but as an active computing environment facilitating distributed intelligence.

The Cloud Layer offers high-performance computing, extensive analytics, and worldwide model aggregation. The cloud serves as the central hub for federated learning aggregation, using safe update-handling techniques based on Abreha et al. (2022). Cloud servers also perform the intricate layers of deep neural networks that edge devices cannot manage, as outlined in split computing architectures. The Auto-Split techniques introduced by Banitalebi-Dehkordi et al. (2021) are used here to dynamically ascertain the optimal edge-cloud split spots. The cloud layer also manages meta-learning, long-term storage, extensive data analytics, network-wide optimization, and the dissemination of model updates to edge devices. Task-oriented communication principles guarantee that cloud feedback is semantically consistent with the inference requirements of the edge nodes. This layer facilitates cross-domain intelligence integration using computational models from Dakshinamurthi et al. (2023), deep-learning-based business analytics from Karunambiga et al. (2023), and mathematical modeling assistance from Pattanaik et al. (2023).

The Proposed End-to-End Workflow starts at the periphery, where devices acquire sensor data and implement preliminary machine learning layers. Semantic abstraction distills raw inputs into significant entities, which are sent via the ISCC-enabled communication layer. The cloud acquires these semantic information, does advanced inference, modifies model parameters, and transmits refined models to edge devices. Federated learning facilitates privacy-preserving decentralized training, allowing edge devices to enhance the global model without communicating their local datasets. Simultaneously, energy-efficient functionality is augmented by nanomaterial-enhanced battery systems (Ali et al., 2024), guaranteeing prolonged functioning of distant devices.

The resulting architecture represents an advanced distributed AI ecosystem proficient in intelligent sensing, adaptive inference, scalable training, and semantic communication. The proposed system, synthesizing insights from all cited studies, functions as a cohesive edge-cloud collaborative intelligence model, appropriate for implementation in 5G/6G smart cities, autonomous systems, industrial automation, healthcare IoT, computational modeling, and network optimization contexts.

FUTURE ENHANCEMENT

Future improvements in edge–cloud collaborative AI systems will be influenced by rapid breakthroughs in wireless communication technologies, AI model designs, energy storage innovations, microcontroller intelligence, and distributed computing frameworks. The existing research indicates that the future of intelligent systems will surpass conventional computation offloading and cloud-assisted optimization, evolving into a cohesive digital ecosystem where sensing, communication, inference, and adaptive learning are seamlessly integrated, self-organized, and contextually intelligent. Drawing from the foundational insights of federated learning (Abreha et al., 2022), dynamic split computing (Bakhtiarnia et al., 2022), collaborative edge–cloud architectures (Banitalebi-Dehkordi et al., 2021), and 6G ISCC networks (Zhu et al., 2023), various prospective advancements can be expected, each fostering a more autonomous, resilient, secure, and semantically efficient computational environment.

A significant future advancement pertains to the creation of hyper-efficient federated ecosystems, in which federated learning transcends centralized aggregation servers to include multi-tier federated hierarchies. As edge devices gain enhanced capabilities and connectivity, federated learning frameworks will transform into "federated swarms" capable of peer-to-peer aggregation, decentralized secure coordination, and adaptive learning functions. Future federated learning systems will use intelligent device clustering and context-aware participation algorithms to reduce superfluous communication while preserving global model coherence. The incorporation of semantic compression (Xing et al., 2023) into federated learning processes will provide hybrid models that share only task-relevant gradient changes, therefore substantially reducing communication burdens. Concurrently, advancements in differential privacy, safe aggregation, and lightweight cryptographic protocols will enable devices in healthcare, finance, and citizen-centric sensing networks to collaborate in training while ensuring regulatory compliance.

A significant area for improvement is the transition from split computing to context-intent computing, whereby model segmentation choices are informed not just by bandwidth or device capabilities but also by context-driven inference methodologies. Future architectures will divide jobs according to user purpose, environmental semantics, and inference urgency, rather than only on computing burden. For example, time-sensitive inference (e.g., collision avoidance, gesture recognition, industrial robots) will be performed exclusively at the edge, but analytics-driven inference (e.g., long-term trend prediction, behavioral modeling) will be supported by the cloud. Edge nodes will use self-characterization modules to assess runtime power levels, battery health (affected by nanomaterial innovations noted by Ali et al., 2024), device heat conditions, and user activity patterns to ascertain the need of offloading computing. As AI-driven energy prediction models improve in accuracy, devices will independently schedule deep inference jobs at periods of high energy availability, hence extending operational life.

Future improvements will be significantly shaped by breakthroughs in 6G ISCC-driven multi-layer intelligence, in which communication channels themselves serve as computational collaborators. Zhu et al. (2023) assert that 6G will not only transmit data but will also engage in sensing and inference via integrated waveform designs, ambient intelligence, and in-channel processing. This advancement will allow networks to do partial inference in the communication environment, alleviating the load on edge devices and decreasing latency. Terahertz-enabled base stations may do preliminary semantic extraction for all connected devices, thus serving as distributed AI "relay nodes." In conjunction with MIMO-driven beamforming innovations (Srivastava et al., 2024), 6G networks will distribute computational and spectral resources dynamically, contingent upon user mobility, data type, and AI model complexity. These advancements will facilitate essential operations like real-time drone coordination, autonomous vehicle platooning, industrial automation, and distributed robotic management.

Emerging fields like semantic-aware resource allocation will augment system intelligence. In contrast to conventional resource allocation, which emphasizes speed and delay, semantic allocation will prioritize the significance and task relevance of transmitted data. This corresponds with the findings of Zhai et al. (2022), who established that multi-device edge AI may significantly decrease communication burdens by eliminating task-irrelevant information. Future systems will include semantic reasoning modules into communication stacks, allowing networks to choose the appropriate data for transmission, the timing of transmission, and the resolution of the data. These developments will significantly diminish network congestion and enhance precision in applications such as urban surveillance, smart health wearables, and IoT-based environmental sensing.

A significant future trend is the amalgamation of neuromorphic and quantum-assisted edge AI systems, connecting classical digital computing with biologically inspired or quantum-enhanced paradigms. Neuromorphic computers, engineered to replicate the event-driven efficiency of biological neurons, will provide ultra-low-power local inference appropriate for gesture-based devices (Suthar & Ali, 2025), smart wearables (Srivastava et al., 2023), and embedded industrial sensors. Quantum-assisted communication and secure gradient aggregation might significantly expedite federated learning convergence, especially in extensive networks including thousands of participating clients. As processing technologies advance, system designs will adapt to accommodate hybrid workloads that integrate traditional convolutional neural networks, causal convolution modules (Dakshinamurthi et al., 2023), and neuromorphic spike-based models inside cohesive inference pipelines.

Substantial improvements will arise from cross-layer self-optimization, whereby edge devices, communication channels, and cloud servers participate in ongoing real-time negotiations to boost overall system performance. This self-optimization will depend on reinforcement learning models that can dynamically modify routing pathways, inference placement, communication frequency, and energy scheduling.

These reinforcement learning agents will be trained on multi-modal datasets obtained from distributed sensing networks, enabling them to mimic intricate behaviors such as urban traffic density, industrial production cycles, and human-environment interactions. Future self-optimizing systems will independently uphold QoS commitments while adjusting to unforeseen variations in network congestion, sensor malfunctions, or energy shortages.

Future advancements in security and trust will focus on hybrid trust layers that include blockchain-based auditability, federated identity systems, homomorphic encryption, and continuous authentication methods. As AI inference increasingly occurs outside conventional security boundaries, systems must continuously evaluate device authenticity, data integrity, and anomaly patterns. AI-powered trust management systems will anticipate hostile actions by analyzing communication discrepancies, modeling divergence anomalies in federated learning, and identifying context violations in multi-device sensing settings. This is especially significant when distributed AI becomes integral to military, healthcare, and governmental systems.

Energy sustainability will emerge as a critical goal for future advancements, particularly as edge devices expand into remote, mobile, and infrastructure-less settings. Nanomaterial-based batteries, as examined by Ali et al. (2024), will be essential for facilitating prolonged AI inference at the edge. Future AI systems will include energy-conscious thinking, enabling them to modify input resolution, sampling frequency, and inference depth according on anticipated battery status. Cloud servers will facilitate long-term energy optimization by dispersing computing loads across several edge nodes or by initiating sleep cycles in redundant devices.

Moreover, forthcoming architectures will allow hyper-personalized and context-adaptive AI models, especially in consumer-centric fields like marketing intelligence, social behavior analysis, and preference forecasting. According to study by Karunambiga et al. (2023), edge-cloud systems will support tailored deep-learning models that adapt to user behavior in real time. Federated customization layers will enable devices to collaboratively enhance global models while preserving uniqueness, so assuring both privacy and personalization. Gesture recognition systems, contextual wearables, and smart city monitoring frameworks will all gain advantages from these customization layers.

A significant future advancement pertains to symbolic-neural integration, wherein algebraic frameworks, as articulated by Pattanaik et al. (2023), are used to direct or limit neural network functionality. Symbolic constraints may diminish model uncertainty, enhance interpretability, and guarantee that distributed AI systems adhere to pertinent mathematical principles in engineering and communication. In edge-cloud inference pipelines, symbolic guidance may avert logical inconsistencies, reduce vulnerability to adversarial attacks, and impose safety limitations in robotics or autonomous driving.

Future developments will concentrate on comprehensive human–machine integration, enabling edge–cloud AI to adjust to human purpose, cognitive load, physiological rhythms, and natural behavior. Leveraging ideas from gesture recognition, wearable sensing, and semantic communication, next architectures will develop AI models proficient in deciphering human signals with little delay. These technologies will provide intuitive management of drones, prostheses, industrial equipment, and immersive reality platforms.

CONCLUSION

The accelerated growth of intelligent systems, edge-driven analytics, and cloud-assisted computation represents a defining transformation in the technological landscape of the 21st century. Across every sector—from communication networks and smart cities to healthcare, mobility, energy storage, gesture interfaces, and industrial automation—the interplay between data, computation, and connectivity has produced both unprecedented opportunities and fundamental architectural challenges. This book chapter has examined these interlocking domains, synthesizing research from federated learning, dynamic split computing, collaborative edge–cloud intelligence, semantic communication, 5G/6G architectures, wearable sensing systems, nanomaterials, and mathematical modeling, offering a comprehensive perspective on the evolution of distributed AI ecosystems.

One of the central conclusions emerging from the chapter is that the traditional cloud-centric paradigm is no longer sufficient to support the scale, speed, and sensitivity of modern intelligent systems. As demonstrated by Abreha et al. (2022), decentralized learning frameworks such as federated learning provide mechanisms for distributed model training while protecting data privacy and significantly reducing the communication burden typically associated with centralized architectures. However, federated learning by itself cannot meet real-time inference requirements for latency-critical applications. The synergy between federated mechanisms and edge-native processing becomes essential, especially as applications expand into continuous health monitoring, city-scale sensing, mobility analytics, and industrial process automation.

Dynamic split computing, as argued by Bakhtiarnia et al. (2022), bridges the computational gap between edge and cloud by enabling flexible partitioning of neural models. This hybrid execution strategy empowers devices with limited computation to participate in complex inference tasks by forwarding selective portions of the computational pipeline to the cloud. Combined with collaborative intelligence frameworks such as Auto-Split (Banitalebi-Dehkordi et al., 2021), the capacity for intelligent inference is effectively democratized across heterogeneous environments.

These approaches represent a fundamental architectural departure from monolithic AI execution, signaling a future in which computation becomes intrinsically fluid, adaptive, and context-aware.

A second major insight from the chapter concerns the evolution of communication paradigms that are increasingly driven by task semantics rather than raw data transmission. Traditional communication systems, shaped by the Shannon model, treat all bits equally regardless of their relevance to a downstream task. However, the work of Xing et al. (2023) and Zhai et al. (2022) demonstrates that upcoming systems must selectively identify, encode, and transmit only those aspects of sensor data necessary for inference. This transition toward task-oriented integrated sensing, communication, and computation (ISCC) will dramatically reduce energy consumption, minimize congestion, and enhance reliability across interconnected environments. Such semantic compression also aligns naturally with federated learning and split inference, forming a cohesive ecosystem where each component—sensing, communication, computation—intelligently supports the others.

The literature also emphasizes that next-generation systems will demand deeply integrated, multi-layered intelligence woven directly into the fabric of wireless networks. The emerging 6G vision articulated by Zhu et al. (2023) highlights a future in which high-capacity terahertz links, massive MIMO, edge-native machine learning, and ISCC pipelines create a ubiquitous intelligent substrate capable of supporting billions of connected devices. In such ecosystems, the boundary between network infrastructure and AI computation will blur, with base stations performing inference tasks, communication channels executing semantic reasoning, and edge devices acting as extensions of the broader computational environment. These transformations will enable the realization of applications that were once considered sci-fi: real-time holographic communication, hyper-precise robotics, ultra-low-latency autonomous mobility, and immersive digital ecosystems.

Furthermore, the chapter has demonstrated that domain-specific innovations—such as MIMO-based 5G beamforming (Srivastava et al., 2024), smart wearables for social distancing (Srivastava et al., 2023), deep learning-driven marketing policy optimization (Karunambiga et al., 2023), high-performance nanomaterial-based batteries (Ali et al., 2024), and microcontroller-integrated gesture recognition systems (Suthar & Ali, 2025)—are not isolated technological achievements. Instead, they collectively shape the constraints, opportunities, and design needs for future distributed AI architectures. For instance, energy limitations in wearables and IoT devices motivate the need for power-efficient inference pipelines, while real-time gesture recognition demands ultra-low latency and high reliability—parameters that edge-centric and 6G-enabled AI architectures can address more effectively than cloud-only systems.

Another key conclusion is the increasing importance of security, privacy, and trust in distributed environments. As the attack surface expands across billions of edge devices, centralized servers, communication intermediaries, and cloud orchestration layers, ensuring the integrity of distributed learning workflows becomes paramount. The integration of secure gradient aggregation, blockchain-backed audit trails, differential privacy, and anomaly detection mechanisms will be essential for building resilient next-generation systems. These controls must be designed with minimal computational overhead in mind, ensuring suitability for low-power devices and high-density networks.

Perhaps the most profound conclusion is that future intelligent systems will require an unprecedented level of cross-domain collaboration and co-design. Computational hardware, communication architecture, AI model design, energy systems, and sensor technologies can no longer be developed independently. Consider the interplay: nanomaterial-based batteries influence sustained inference capability; communication-efficient AI algorithms reduce the need for high-power radios; task-oriented compression reduces edge workloads; and dynamic split computing enables real-time computation in mobile environments. These interdependencies imply that innovation in one domain cannot be fully realized without coordinated progress across others. Therefore, future research must emphasize interdisciplinary integration—bridging electrical engineering, computer science, materials science, applied mathematics, and human-centered design.

The analysis also reinforces the conclusion that scalability will be the ultimate measure of system success. Future AI ecosystems will operate not in small clusters but across millions of nodes, requiring architectures that tolerate device failures, intermittent connectivity, variable energy states, and diverse operational conditions. Techniques such as statistical learning, distributed consensus models, and task-aware communication will be vital for maintaining performance at scale. The mathematical modeling techniques proposed by Pattanaik et al. (2023), for instance, may play a growing role in reasoning about complex network behaviors, error propagation, and convergence dynamics.

The chapter ultimately demonstrates that the evolution of edge–cloud AI ecosystems is not a linear technological progression but a broad systemic shift toward distributed intelligence. Distributed AI architectures promise to support real-time inference, privacy-preserving learning, semantic-aware communication, and energy-conscious operation—capabilities essential for the next era of technological development. These architectures will underpin future innovations across communication networks, wearable technologies, smart cities, industrial systems, and consumer applications. At the same time, they will unlock new research challenges related to multi-agent collaboration, trust modeling, cross-layer optimization, and autonomous self-management.

In closing, the future of intelligent computing will be defined by integration, adaptability, and semantic awareness. The convergence of federated learning, split computing, ISCC-driven networking, and device-level innovation will yield systems capable of continuous situational understanding, self-optimal operation, and seamless collaboration across computational layers. These advancements will not only transform technical infrastructures but also reshape how society interacts with technology—from personalized services to safer cities, more efficient industries, and more intuitive human–machine interfaces. The research surveyed in this chapter lays the conceptual foundation for this transformation, pointing toward a future where intelligence is not confined to the cloud or the device but emerges across the entire computational continuum.

REFERENCES

Abreha, H. G., Hayajneh, M., & Serhani, M. A. (2022). Federated learning in edge computing: A systematic survey. *Sensors (Basel)*, *22*(2), 450. DOI: 10.3390/s22020450 PMID: 35062410

Ali, S. I., Jadhav, J., Arunkumar, R., & Kanagavalli, N. (2022). A smart resource utilization algorithm for high speed 5G communication networks based on cloud servers. *ICTACT Journal on Communication Technology*, *13*(4), 2800–2804.

Ali, S. I., Ravuri, H. K., Lakshmi, V. T., Ramya, A., Lavanya, K., & Bahade, S. (2024). The role of nanomaterials in the development of high-performance batteries. *Nanotechnology Perceptions*, *20*(S11), 1125–1140. https://www.nano-ntp.com

Bakhtiarnia, A., Milošević, N., Zhang, Q., Bajović, D., & Iosifidis, A. (2022). Dynamic split computing for efficient deep edge intelligence [Preprint]. arXiv. https://arxiv.org/abs/2205.11269

Banitalebi-Dehkordi, A., Vedula, A., Pei, J., Xia, L., Wang, J., & Zhang, H. (2021). *Auto-Split: A general framework of collaborative edge-cloud AI*. In *Proceedings of the 27th ACM SIGKDD Conference on Knowledge Discovery & Data Mining (KDD '21)*. https://doi.org/DOI: 10.1145/3447548.3467078

Dakshinamurthi, V., Ali, S. I., Karthikeyan, T., & Kulkarni, N. S. (2023). *Causal convolution employing Almeida–Pineda recurrent backpropagation for mobile network design*. ICTACT Journal on Communication Technology, 14(4).

Karunambiga, K., Ali, S., Esteban, A., & Pascual, M. (2023). Marketing policy in service enterprises using deep learning model. *International Journal of Intelligent Systems and Applications in Engineering*, *12*(7s), 239–243.

NVIDIA Corporation. (2018). *NVIDIA Jetson AGX Xavier: New era for autonomous machines*. NVIDIA Developer Documentation. https://developer.nvidia.com

Pattanaik, B., Kumari, S. S., Kumar, C. K., Pattnaik, M., Ali, S. I., & Kumarasamy, M. (2023). *An innovation of algebraic mathematical-based statistical analysis model for complex number theory*. In *Proceedings of the 2023 International Conference on Disruptive Technologies (ICDT)* (pp. 94–99). IEEE. https://doi.org/DOI: 10.1109/ICDT57929.2023.10151169

Shi, Y., Yang, K., Jiang, T., Zhang, J., & Letaief, K. B. (2020). Communication-efficient edge AI: Algorithms and systems [Preprint]. arXiv. https://arxiv.org/abs/2002.09668

Srivastava, S. S., Ali, S. I., Srivastava, A. K., & Goswami, C. (2024). Improving 5G network performance with MIMO technology using beamforming algorithm. *ICTACT Journal on Communication Technology*, *15*(2), 3173–3178.

Srivastava, S. T. C., Sharmiladevi, D., Sugumar, D., Ali, S. I., Jones Mary, T. A., & Kumar, S. (2023). *Using a smart wearable device for monitoring social distance in smart cities.* In *2023 International Conference on Research Methodologies in Knowledge Management, Artificial Intelligence and Telecommunication Engineering (RMKMATE)* (pp. 1–5). IEEE. https://doi.org/DOI: 10.1109/RMKMATE59243.2023.10369118

Suthar, B., & Ali, S. I. (2025). *A survey on hand gesture sign language recognition with Arduino Leonardo.* In *2025 International Conference on Computational, Communication and Information Technology (ICCCIT)* (pp. 111–115). IEEE. https://doi.org/DOI: 10.1109/ICCCIT62592.2025.10927994

Xing, H., Zhu, G., Liu, D., Li, Y., Liu, D., Zeng, Y., & Zhang, R. (2023). Task-oriented integrated sensing, computation, and communication design for wireless edge AI [Preprint]. arXiv. https://arxiv.org/abs/2306.06603

Zhai, K., Liang, Y., Cho, C., & Li, C. (2022). Task-oriented sensing, computation and communication integration for multi-device edge AI [Preprint]. arXiv. https://arxiv.org/abs/2207.00969

Zhu, G., Lyu, F., Jiao, J., Liu, Z., Chen, Y., Xu, J., & Zhang, R. (2023). Pushing AI to the wireless network edge: An overview on integrated sensing, communication, and computation toward 6G. *Science China. Information Sciences*. Advance online publication. DOI: 10.1007/s11432-022-3652-2

Chapter 2
AI Inference for Smart Cities Integrating IoT and Big Data

G. Muthupandi
http://orcid.org/0009-0002-8822-0157
Chennai Institute of Technology, India

K. Jayakumar
http://orcid.org/0009-0000-2849-5445
Chennai Institute of Technology, India

S. Pavithra
http://orcid.org/0000-0003-1537-5879
Chennai Institute of Technology, India

B. Vishnu
http://orcid.org/0009-0002-0155-2328
Chennai Institute of Technology, India

R. Vikram
http://orcid.org/0009-0004-1023-6807
Chennai Institute of Technology, India

R. Nandhakumar
http://orcid.org/0009-0000-4801-4370
Chennai Institute of Technology, India

ABSTRACT

The 21 st century has increased the rate of urbanization, thus making the problems of traffic snarl up, pollution, energy crisis, improper waste disposal and heavy load on the social safety and health system more complex. The idea of the smart city became one of the new technologies that integrate Artificial Intelligence (AI), the Internet of Things (IoT), and Big Data in order to enhance the efficiency and quality of life in cities. In particular, AI inference enables real-time decision making based on data in major sectors. The examples of successful ones are such cities as Barcelona, Amsterdam, Chicago, Singapore, Los Angeles and Seoul. Other advantages of sustainability and disadvantages like privacy, cybersecurity, cost of infrastructure, and digital inequality are also discussed in the chapter.

DOI: 10.4018/979-8-3373-7046-0.ch002

1. INTRODUCTION

Cities are organisms - constantly developing, changing and adjusting to the new rhythms of society, economy and technology. Global urbanization has been growing faster than ever in the last couple of decades. UN data show that over 68% of the global population will inherit urbanization by 2050. Such a change is amazing and demanding. On the one hand, cities promote innovation, employment, and economic development. On the other, they have to deal with traffic jams and pollution, electricity outage and health, safety, and accommodation strains.

And the solution to these difficulties is a new form of city; an intelligent, connected and data-driven city. The Smart City is here. A Smart City is not merely a technology that is employed to automate but enhance human life. It is based on the Artificial Intelligence, the Internet of Things, and the Big Data analytics to create efficient and sustainable, citizen-centered environments. Through these technologies, cities can sense, analyze and respond to real-time information to produce certain improvements to traffic flow, save energy, predict catastrophes and even deliver more effective services to their people. Smart cities represent a change paradigm of the city operation that is making cities data-driven and AI-driven in their decision-making processes.

1.1 Global City Growth Trends

The urbanization rate is astounding all over the world. Millions of individuals are now able to make megacities like Tokyo, Delhi, Shanghai, and Sao Paulo their home. Migration, opportunities of industries and computer jobs are also expanding even to minor cities.

However, as the population has begun to explode, the effect on the city environment increases exponentially. There is congestion in highways, rubbish littering on the roads, pollution is at an all time high and the use of energy is rising exponentially. Without the modern technology, cities are becoming unsustainable, inefficient and unmanageable.

Governments and policy makers throughout the world have recognised this. Singapore and the Smart Nation are not alone in major investments in smart technologies, and Dubai is projecting AI city and Finland is planning an ecosystem based on data (Ullah et al., 2024). These projects are based upon the deployment of sensors in cities, connecting one device to another using the IoT, and using artificial intelligence to infer on the data stream in real-time. You are not just getting efficiency but also city level intelligence i.e. a system that learns and develops.

1.2 Urbanization Challenges

The city development not only leads to a prosperous situation, but also increases the whole range of issues that are based on fixed traditional management models. The current cities are caught in traffic snarls whereby millions of vehicles are in the streets daily and it has resulted in loss of productivity, wastage of time in commuting and air pollution. Other causes of environmental problems that have the most negative impact on the life of cities are the industrialization.

Energy demand is another burning problem. Traditional grids of power struggle to keep up with the growing electricity demand hence resulting to power interruptions and ineffectiveness. Without intelligent energy and real-time monitoring, cities will not be able to optimize electricity delivery and predict points of demand, which also contributes to economic losses and pressure on the environment. In the meantime, overpopulated cities pose challenging demands on themselves in the form of the normative safety and security, higher-order surveillance, accelerated emergency response, and efficient use of disasters to provide the city population with cushioning.

Healthcare and sanitation is the third important component of urban issues. The containment of outbreak diseases, hospital sanitation, and control, and the maintenance of millions of people healthy is what must be combated, at all times, whereby there are concerns of pollution and hence people fall ill. These problems are inextricably linked, where air pollution causes health problems, which increases the cost and ineffectiveness of health care, and inefficient energy and transportation increases the burden on the available resources. These are issues that require synergistic solutions that are data-driven.

1.3 Why Smart Cities Are Important for a Sustainable Future

A sustainable city is a city that will cater to the needs of the current generation without limiting the future generation and this is the thinking behind the smart cities. They use information and intelligent algorithms to ensure the maximum use of the available resources to such an extent that there is minimization of energy consumption, emission, and healthy lifestyles. Smart grids are automated to adapt the flow and demand of electrical and water systems using artificial intelligent to detect the leaks with IoT and communicate real-time notifications that cannot be wasted.

Other uses of AI in waste management are the higher sustainability due to efficient collection routes and the higher recycling rates. Data-driven urban planning is also a significant contributing factor, as it makes locations pedestrian, green.

Besides the environmental interests, smart cities allow citizens to participate by the means of online sources, cell phone applications, and enabling the citizens of a particular area to pay their utility bills, report civic, and receive real-time update on transportation and safety. With smart cities, there is an improvement in the citizen-government interaction as they create a new dimension of possibilities in the world of technology and everyday life, which contributes to the feeling of responsibility. In the long term, the goal would be to not just to automate but empower the people so that they can afford and have the expertise to live safer, healthier and more sustainable lifestyles.

1.4 Role of Digital Transformation in Governance

Digital governance is the core of any smart city, as it implies substituting the traditional administrative system with data-driven systems based on AI. With AI inference models, governments can use the data collected by sensors and cameras as well as through citizen databases to predict and respond to issues in the city without them escalating out of control. This transformation will make the decision-making process faster, more accurate, and evidence-based to ensure that the management, not the operations, of the city are proactive.

One of them is the use of AI algorithms to process traffic cameraw footage and GPS sensors to dynamically adjust traffic lights to reduce traffic jams and decrease the commuting time. IoT sensors allow air-quality sensors to transmit live data to environmental agencies, and the alert is automatically generated when the pollution level is high. Using Big Data analytics, it is possible to predict the high points in the demand of the energy and arrange power distribution in an effective way, as well as predictive models can show where the hot spots of crimes or possible disease outbreaks will take place, avoiding which will save lives of people.

These systems are efficient and moreover enhance transparency and innovation. Open data platforms make it possible to access open datasets by citizens, researchers, and other individuals who can subsequently develop new applications and services that can transform urban life. Smart cities present a dynamic ecosystem using Big Data, AI, and IoT in which the technology, policy, and the citizens work in collaboration to transform cities to be safer, more responsive, and future-focused.

1.5 The Foundation of Smart City Intelligence

Smart cities are based on three technological pillars, i.e. AI, IoT and Big Data, which serve a different, yet not dissimilar purpose in the city management. One can refer to IoT devices as the eyes of the city and they constantly keep track of its traffic streams, its energy usage, its environment, and how its citizens interact with one another. Big Data platforms are the memory of the city and archive and process these huge flows of data to reveal trends, correlations and patterns with time.

The brain of the city is inference systems, which interprets the information and makes decisions that resources, improve services and solve problems ahead of time. In a way that the three pillars are incorporated, smart cities will become intelligent living beings - able to monitor, acquire and evolve instantly. Such a combination will allow urban areas to be highly efficient, resilient and responsive and will transform the urban living into a dynamic and conscious system.

However, this is only the beginning of the change. As the technological progress speed gains traction, the ability of cities to learn, predict, adapt, will be even more in-depth, and we will be close to the concept of completely autonomous, data-driven, people-centred smart cities.

2. UNDERSTANDING AI, IOT, AND BIG DATA

To get the closer glimpse into how the smart cities operate, we would like to refer to the three pillars of technology which are used to transform the cities into smart Artificial Intelligence, the Internet of Things, and Big Data. In addition to these systems, they have been directly connected to each other and have become known as digital nervous system of a modern day city. The IoT gadgets collect data by relying on sensor, cameras and smart meters amongst others infrastructure in real time and this gives real-time data on the condition of the traffic, energy usage, landscape and what people are engaged in. The big data stores incorporate such large amount of data and operate on them to forecast patterns, relationships and deviations that are further utilized to assist city planners and administrators make good decisions. This information is fed to the AI inference systems which then process them into actionable information through which the cities are able to respond to the challenges in a quick and efficient way.

The technologies will play a special and complimentary role. IoT is used as a sensor layer, which is associated with the continuous stream of information about the real world, and Big Data are used as a processing and storage engine, uniting every bit of information. Inference is AI being the decision-maker that finds the patterns, predicts the results, and responds automatically in real-time (Duhayyim et al., 2022). They collectively enable cities to become intelligent, self-aware organisms that monitor, learn, and evolve in their ability to manage traffic, distribute energy, provide governmental safety, healthcare, and environmental sustainability. Combining IoT, Big Data, and AI, smart cities can optimize resources and improve the quality of life of their citizens, becoming more resilient, efficient, and responsive to existing and future needs.

2.1 Artificial Intelligence (AI): The Brain of Smart Cities

Artificial intelligence refers to the ability of machines to accomplish problems that were previously handled by human intelligence including learning, listening and understanding the natural language. In the case of smart cities, AI is the brain, which thinks and provides actionable outcomes.

AI Basics: Training or Inference

After the AI system is trained, it proceeds to the inference stage where the model is launched to either make predictions or decisions on-the-fly. Inference is not as computationally intensive as training, since the model does not need to learn anymore but use the knowledge it has already learned. An example of this would be a traffic camera in a smart city detecting a car that runs a red light based on the trained AI model. The system also juxtaposes the real time video feed to what is learned in the training session and instantly reports violations. This feature enables the AI to deliver instant information and reactions, which is necessary when dealing with urban systems that need to be dynamically functioning and reacting quickly to new situations.

Inference is especially important in smart cities since even a delay of several seconds can have a serious impact. In traffic control, a late warning of congestion or accidents may cause worse gridlock and grow the power of accidents. Slow responses in an energy system may result in inefficiency or power outages. Delays in notifications may hamper emergencies or security in the context of public safety. As such, AI inference networks are designed to be high-speed, accurate and low-latency, with many designed to execute at the edge of networks near data origin. This edge deployment will minimize the duration required by artificial intelligence to process data and allow real-time decision making without a remote server.

Further, smart cities inference models do not represent a single task. They work in several areas at the same time, managing traffic and energy grids as well as anticipating the needs of the health sector and environmental risks. All applications operate on a similar principle: AI follows the already learned patterns to make decisions on-the-fly, quickly, and intelligently. Smart cities implement a seamless ecosystem built through trained AI models combined with IoT sensors, Big Data platforms, and real-time analytics to monitor, learn, and adjust in real-time. As such, AI inference is an inherent mechanism that makes urban systems responsive, efficient.

AI in Urban Contexts

Artificial Intelligence is the core of the new urban innovation that will turn cities into responsive and intelligent places. One of the most obvious applications is a predictive traffic control where the AI technologies analyze camera, GPS, and traffic sensors data in real-time and use it to adjust signal timing dynamically. This enables the traffic in the cities to be better and more sustainable by minimizing the commute time, fuel consumption and emission or even forecasting congestion prior to its occurrence. In terms of the sphere of public safety, AI-based surveillance can identify suspicious behaviors, unattended items, or crowds of people in their places in real-time. This enables the authorities to be quick to the case of any potential threat in order to improve the safety and security of citizens.

AI may manage the loads in smart grids by predicting the peak electricity demand and studying the consumption patterns and thereby preventing the blackout and reducing the energy wastage. Similarly, within the healthcare analytics industry, AI monitors hospital records, environmental conditions, and the pattern of outbreaks to predict them and prevent prophylaxis. In a word, AI converts raw data into actionable intelligence that makes cities take decisive action instead of reacting to the situation. AI will enhance efficiency, safety with such inventions.

2.2 Internet of Things: The Senses of the City

Taking Artificial Intelligence as the brain of a smart city and the Internet of Things (IoT) as the sensory system of the brain, it would be logical to assume that the latter serves the former. IoT is the connection between physical machines like sensors, cameras, meters, vehicles, and machines to the internet to enable continuous data collection and exchange. It is a huge system of interconnected devices communicating amongst themselves and central systems. These devices collect useful data on their environments, like temperature, movement, noise, pollution, and power usage, and send them to cloud servers or edge devices to be analyzed and make a decision. The roads include sensors that can monitor traffic flow, accidents and road conditions, and smart streetlights can automatically turn bright up or down to preserve energy. The enhanced CCTV cameras monitor movement and ensure safety of people, wearables devices monitor health of citizens and smart meters monitor electricity, gas and water consumption. The devices operate round-the-clock and transform cities into living systems which monitor and respond to the world around.

The IoT model uses three layers, with the first layer being the Device Layer which holds sensors and devices which detect the raw environments. Network Layer then transmits this data through the various communication technologies such as Wi-Fi, 4G/5G networks or satellite connections. Finally, the Application Layer will be based on AI systems and software that will transform the information obtained and present the results in the format of traffic board, pollution map, or energy management systems. Edge computing is currently a significant component of IoT architecture in smart cities. Part of the processing is stored locally and not stored on remote cloud servers, which assist in reduce the number of informations that are required to be transmitted to remote servers. This will enhance the latency, security of the data, and real-time decision-making that is intelligent, as smart cities will be able to create a response to the changes in the environment immediately.

2.3 Big Data: The Memory and Analytical Core

Internet of Things may receive big data on an impossible number of connected devices, yet it is Big Data that calculates this, organizes it and converts it into significant outcomes.

Big Data are data sets that are too large, unpredictable and too dynamic to manage using traditional data management software. It can be defined by the four Vs: Volume, meaning the large quantities of data per second produced by sensors, social media, applications, and transactions;Variety, meaning the abundance of different types of data, such as text, images, video, audio, and sensor data; and Veracity, meaning that the data is reliable and accurate, and therefore decisions are made using trustworthy information.

Big Data technologies in smart cities provide control over the whole data cycle, including both the collection of data, where IoT sensors, satellites, and digital platforms collect information, and storage in distributed data structures such as Hadoop, Spark, or cloud databases. That is followed by processing, which includes AI algorithms that refine, classify and analyze the running data streams, and lastly visualization, which shows administrators and policymakers real-time data in the form of a dashboard. An example is that a Big Data system can handle live air-quality data submitted by thousands of IoT sensors and show pollution levels in neighborhoods in real-time, allowing authorities to act instantly like issue public alerts or control industrial pollution.

2.4 How AI, IoT, and Big Data Work Together

The components of artificial intelligence, Big Data and the internet of things within a smart city ecosystem are in perfect harmony with one another and create a smart and responsive city. First, IoT devices are used to gather information about the physical environment, i.e. the amount of traffic on highways or the weather. Such information is then forwarded to the Big Data systems which in their turn store and process such information in real time using sophisticated analytics systems (Bibri et al., 2023). Finally, there is AI inference solutions, which receive the received data and may offer actionable ideas, such as turning on or off traffic lights or redirecting vehicles. This feedback loop could make this city self educating body and it will be capable to read what has taken place in the actual world and respond to it immediately.

Such examples as IoT sensors in streetlights that can sense low traffic volumes during the times of midnight can be found. The Big Data layer processes these signals and identifies a deficiency in road use and orders the AI system to automatically switch off the streetlights to conserve energy.

The 3 pillars of any smart city are interlaced with one another AI is the intelligence pillar, IoT is the connectivity pillar, and Big Data is the understanding pillar. Technology is the basis of another, the IoT provides the continuous data, the Big Data interprets and analyzes it, and AI transforms them into the actionable information. This three-way combination is a technological combination that has enabled cities to reason, predict, think, and dynamically react to the demands of the citizens to come up with faster, smarter and more sustainable urban living scenario.

3. EXPLAINING THE CONCEPT OF AI AND IOT IN SMART CITIES

The heart of the modern urban changes is The Artificial Intelligence. Energy grids, environmental surveillance, traffic lights, public safety, and many others: not only are smart cities connected, but AI inference makes them intelligent.

Whereas AI training is concerned with historical information and "learning" via these data, AI inference is concerned with action, making predictions, identifying trends, and understanding insights based on real-time data. It is this inference that enables a city to react immediately to changing conditions, say rerouting traffic in response to an accident or changing energy supply when demand peaks.

3.1 What Is AI Inference?

In Artificial Intelligence (AI), the very first step is to train the models on large datasets to enable them to see the patterns, discern the relationships, and make correct predictions. As an example, a model that has been trained on millions of traffic images to recognize vehicles could when deployed on cameras in a city conduct inference on images to spot cars, traffic jams or accidents happening in real-time. Although the training step is often performed off-line and with powerful cloud-based servers and many computing units, the inference step is performed online and is often performed much nearer to the source of the data, on edge devices like smart cameras or IoT gateways, or embedded artificial intelligence chips. Speed and efficiency of AI inference is the biggest benefit. It does not need a huge amount of computing power after being trained but rather uses acquired patterns quickly on new information. This turns inference into a significant component of smart cities, where real-time decision-making is critical to managing traffic, conserving energy, improving safety, and, finally, saving time, energy, and even lives.

3.2 Inference: Why Inference Matters to Real-Time Decision-Making

Cities provide modern surveillance cameras, air-quality sensors, water-pipe sensors, weather stations, and an amazing amount of other IoT transmissions that generate huge streams of live data every second. Such volumes of information processed in real time require a high speed, efficient, and localized intelligence system, and that is precisely what AI inference provides. It provides real-time pattern recognition, prediction and prompt response to urban changing conditions. One such system is the smart traffic management system, which, by definition, might identify congestion instantaneously and adjust signal timing to ease traffic; another example is the healthcare platform, which can analyze wearable information to identify health anomalies and send alerts to medical staff; yet, another example is the intelligent power grid, which is able to predict peak-time and automatically adjust power sectors.

3.3 Inference AI in Smart city Systems

Regarding the way in which a city operates, it could be perceived as a process that is connected and continuous and which has many layers of technologies. It begins with gathering data, and IoT sensors and devices capture unprocessed data as images, heat, sounds, or motions of the environment. It is then followed by data preprocessing at the edge or fog layer, which is closer to the data source. In this case, junk will either be filtered or cleaned or even reduced with the intention of permitting analysis of information. The processed data then is passed onto the AI inference layer intelligent models will then operate on the data in real time and identify abnormality or forecast trends or individual events (Sujatha et al., 2024). Using these insights, the decision or action layer executes the corresponding responses, such as controlling traffic lights, sending safety messages or controlling power use. The final one is a feedback loop, which feeds the results back to the system so that it can learn and therefore do a better job.

A self-educative ecosystem constitutes such a multi-layered organization in which each step complements and supplements the other. The smoothness of the IoT information-gathering, speed of processing with Edge AI, and scale with Cloud

Big Data keep cities smart, responsive, and highly productive, capable of addressing the urban population in a wholesale and dynamic manner.

3.4 AI Inference in Smart Cities

One of the most feasible AI inference applications in smart cities is traffic prediction and management. One of the biggest urban issues that lead to wastage of time, fuel and low productivity is traffic jam. Inferential AI robots are fed with live camera, road sensor and GPS information to make predictions about traffic congestion and decide when to use signals. Because AI is designed to identify even unexpected slowing down at a crossroads, it can respond instantly by altering signal cycles or suggesting other routes to the user through navigation apps. The systems can also even interplay with autonomous vehicles themselves to effectively coordinate movement in others. Another interesting example is the case of Barcelona where AI-run traffic lights have reduced average commute and emissions by significant numbers. The city has adaptive traffic lights that dynamically respond to live inferences using thousands of sensors.

Another area is energy forecasting and smart grids. Data Urban life runs on energy, and predictive analytics, based on AI inference, control smart grids controlling electricity supply and demand. Artificial intelligence monitors domestic and commercial use, anticipates demand will burst, such as during a heatwave or a large event, and automatically manages power outages. The Smart grid technology in Amsterdam has improved predictability of power consumption and reduced power losses by approximately 20 percent to promote sustainability and cost-efficiency.

On the subject of public safety and surveillance, AI inference will maximize security by surveying live video streams using surveillance cameras to identify the presence of suspicious activity, locate lost or found items and identify license plate numbers. Rather than involving human operators who will see the footage across the thousands of screens, AIs check the footage within seconds and alert the security staff. Dubai is a smarter, responsible city with AI-enabled surveillance cameras to examine thousands of CCTV feeds to make predictions to prevent crimes before they occur.

3.5 AI Inference Infrastructure

In smart cities, AI inference can be implemented on a robust computational infrastructure of advanced hardware and smart software. Devices that do inference at the device level are edge AI devices, such as smart cameras, IoT gateways, and artificial intelligence cards, such as NVIDIA Jetson and Google Coral Locality processing may be critical when it comes to latency reduction that leads to faster decision making and it eliminates the network overload because fewer volumes of raw data will be moved to servers that are centralized.

In its turn, cloud and fog computing have a role to play, although, both equally. Cloud platforms are associated with massive learning, sophisticated analytics, and long-term data storage in comparison with edge devices, which need to deal with immediate and time-sensitive declarations. Fog computing is an intermediate layer between the cloud and the edge, computing the data closer to the users, yet always having a direct connection to cloud infrastructure. The combination of these layers ensures that smarter city systems are both fast, scalable and reliable-delivering real-time intelligence to control city operations.

3.6 AI Inference Case Studies

Barcelo - Revolution of Intelligent Mobility

The Smart Mobility Project of Barcelona shows how IoT and AI inference are very prominent in traffic and parking control. The city applies live video analytics to keep up to date on the road situation and to automatically vary the timetable of traffic lights to prevent traffic jams and the loss of traveling time. The parking sensors are also intelligent which means that it guides the driver to the parking lot thus, saves a lot of time, fuel, and carbon emissions. The project has transformed Barcelona into one of the most successful examples of real-time intelligent AI-guided urban mobility.

Chicago- Array of Things Project

The Chicago project is an urban innovative observatory that will collect. AI inference models consist of continuous knowledge about temperature, air quality, and noise levels, which can be studied by city researchers and planners to make effective decisions based on evidence. The system also leads to improved planning of cities and to better health, safety and environmental sustainability of the people.

Singapore - City-Wide AI Decisions Network

Singapore has developed a city-wide network of AI inference as part of its ambitious Smart Nation program, which links over 110,000 IoT sensors in all areas of the economy, including transportation, housing, energy, and water management. AI systems are using this real-time data to approximate arrival times of buses, monitor the health of water pipes, optimize energy flow, and ensure the city is running smoothly.

3.7 Edge vs. Cloud Inference

There is a clear advantage of both cloud inference and edge inference in smart city operations. Edge inference is inferred locally, within a surrounding area of the source, with highly responsive times and better security because no sensitive data is sent between the device and any other. This is the reason it is applicable when time is of essence such as in traffic issues, the government keeping track of its citizens and also dealing with emergencies. Cloud inference, on the other hand, is centralized and very scalable and can execute tasks at high data density including long-term city planning, predictive analytics, and large-scale modeling. There is also the trend nowadays to become hybrid: to combine responsiveness of edge devices with computing power and broader viewpoints of cloud computing. These incorporations make cities effective, smarter and very flexible.

3.8 Benefits of AI Inference in Smart Cities

AI inference is bringing numerous advantages to the functioning of the modern smart cities. It could facilitate real-time decision-making to cut the delays and increase responsiveness among the systems of a city by allowing taking immediate action. Predictive analytics improves the safety of the population, as it is cheaper when automated solutions reduce the necessity of human labor and routine maintenance, and it lets to avoid the threat before it becomes dangerous. Further, AI inference may be used to promote environmental sustainability by smartly controlling and tracking pollution, energy consumption, and other environmental factors. In general, inference can make cities more self-conscious, dynamic in response to changes in the urban environment on an at-all-times basis.

4. APPLICATIONS ACROSS KEY SECTORS

Transportation & Mobility

Urban transportation is one of the most challenging parts of a city management. Traffic jam is a waste of time and fuel and also pollutes air. Cities will know when their roads will be congested and be able to control traffic in real-time with AI inference, IoT sensors, GPS, and real-time traffic cameras. AI in Barcelona changes signal times according to the current traffic, which could significantly decrease delays and emissions. Smart parking is yet another technological solution that guides drivers to vacant parking spaces using sensor information to prevent unnecessary travel and reduce traffic in the city (Mohammadi & Al-Fuqaha, 2018). AI inference can also be applied in the infrastructure of electric vehicles, where predictive models forecast the maximum charge demand and optimally utilize energy. The AI inference is also used in self-driving cars to process the data of camera, LIDAR and radar sensors. These vehicles move safely and they contribute to efficient movement within the city, provided that they are supported by their network-traffic infrastructure.

Healthcare

Smart cities can enhance the well-being of people and residents by blending AI, IoT, and Big Data. Smartwatches track heartbeat rates, oxygen, sleep, and activity, and AI inference operates under the hood to decipher the tracks and inform medical professionals of abnormalities in real time. Certain countries, including South Korea, managed to use these technologies with success, monitoring the infection spread, applying quarantine conditions, and spending medical resources reasonably COVID session. In hospitals, predictive AI is applied to manage patient traffic, bed capacity, and staffing ensuring that the medical institution can expand when demand is high. Converting continuous health data into actionable information will allow cities to provide both preventive and emergency care, resulting in more desirable health outcomes in the whole population.

Energy Management

Cities are under pressure to supply more energy as populations and industries expand. Smart grids can leverage the capability of AI inference to monitor real-time electricity consumption, predict when demand is at its highest, and adjust supply to prevent power outages. AI grid Amsterdam optimizes renewable energy use, minimizes waste, and saves money and carbon emissions. The building IoT sensors monitor occupancy, lighting and temperature, and artificial intelligence algorithms automatically determine how climate control and lighting should be set to save as much energy as possible. The claims of AI controlled energy savings in cities have been proven in other projects as it has been recorded that the Smart Building project in London has saved 15-20 in energy in the city.

Water & Waste Management

Sustainable urban life can include effective water management and waste management. IoT Water sensors identify intrusion, pollution or abnormal behavior and AI inference predicts demand and controls supply. In Los Angeles, the smart water meters which are installed are aimed at minimising losses and providing the residents with routine water. On the same note, artificial intelligence would make waste management more efficient. Smart bins have sensors that determine the level of filling in them and AI software uses the most efficient route to collect them, such that they use less fuel and invite less congestion in cities. The smart waste management system Singapore has employs is more automated to collect garbage, recycle better and leave the streets clean with minimal human involvement.

Public Safety & Security

The most significant problems include the need to make cities with high populations safer. Preventive policing is a theory where AI is utilized to determine the past rates of crime, patterns in social and environmental methods with the intention to develop hotspots and allocate resources appropriately. The AI system is constantly surveying the masses and tracking suspicious human beings or unattended objects and notifying the security guards in real-time. Dubai has fitted its urban area with Artificial Intelligence operated cameras that reach into the thousands, and it currently can respond in real-time to potential dangers. Emergency management systems using artificial intelligence inference can also be developed where sensor measurements are collected to identify the presence of fire, floods, or other dangerous events and send out emergency response teams. An earthquake-warning system created by Japanese works based on AI inferences to decode seismic signals and provide people and infrastructure with several invaluable seconds to react to the earthquake to be able to save lives and cause minimum damage.

Environmental Monitoring

Another issue of smart cities that is crucial is quality of the environment. IoT sensors will observe the quality of the air, noise, and temperature, etc., and AI inference anticipates the peaks of pollution and recommends actions. Even the cities like Delhi and Beijing are developing AI-related services to be able to predict the extent of pollution and provide real-time notifications to their citizens. The AI reasoning can also be applied to view the density of a crowd in addition to the pollution and this can help urban planners create better places to people including greener areas and walkways. The Chicago Array of Things projects can be viewed as examples of evidence-based city planning that can be informative in terms of livability and the application of AI-based real-time environmental surveillance.

State and Personal Business

Another excellent feature of AI in government and citizen interaction is inference. The chatbot artificial intelligence ability has the capacity to replace the tedious method of communication with citizens, thus enabling residents to report about an issue or send bills or municipal services without visiting the offices. The documentary Smart Nation in Singapore reveals that there are artificial intelligence chatbots that can respond to thousands of questions per day and leave the human resources to solve unique issues. Digital twins and other city infrastructure virtual models allow planners to model traffic, energy consumption, and emergency response and make an informed decision. Open data platforms are those that are publicly available and they provide the datasets to developers and researchers to come up with solutions that can increase transportation and energy efficiency and make the streets safer. The city of Chicago citizenry has been streamlined and made more pleasant after a lot of applications were created in Chicago Open Data Initiative.

Integrated Applications Sections

The smart city technologies can be implemented in the best way to be implemented when a number of fields are operating concurrently. In order to explain this, in the case of a traffic collision, the artificial intelligence inference can notify emergency service providers, activate street lights to relieve traffic jam, warn a driver by means of a navigation application, and even call power companies to turn on street lights along the part of the route that has been affected. The interconnectedness is what enables cities to react to the challenges in an efficient and holistic manner. Not only the city ecosystem is reactive, but it is also proactive through the joint capabilities of transportation, healthcare, energy, environmental monitoring, citizen security, and the government, which can be modified with AI, IoT, and Big Data.

5. TECHNOLOGIES DRIVING SMART CITIES

5G and Edge Computing

Smart cities in modern times are constructed on high-speed low-latency communication networks, which is much faster technology in comparison to older generations and allows real-time communication between billions of IoT devices distributed in the urban landscape. Traffic cameras, environmental sensors, and AVs can share information in time under 5G, and an AI inference system can react immediately. To this end, edge computing is a technique that brings computing power closer to data. Rather than transmitting large volumes of sensor information to central cloud computers, edge devices run algorithms on the device and conduct AI inference in real time. This 5G-edge computing package will also keep time-sensitive decisions (tweaking traffic lights, piloting drones, or turning on emergency alerts) connected in real time, and, therefore, cities will be more accommodating and resilient.

Fog Layers and Cloud Computing

Cloud computing offers a platform to store massive amounts of data, deep learning, and detailed analytics, unlike edge computing, which is instant. Cities produce large amounts of data in their everyday operations and cloud solutions can aid AI models to learn and process new knowledge based on this data (Alajlan & Ibrahim, 2025). Most smart cities employ mist computing, an intermediate tier between end devices and processing loads, to minimize the edge to cloud gap. Mog layers improve the latency, take maximum of the bandwidth and provide a hassle free connection between the devices and central servers. Introducing both cloud computing and fog computing, they enable scalable, powerful and flexible urban infrastructure to traverse multiple sectors and applications without bottlenecks.

Blockchain

The blockchain is a decentralized unalterable database of transactions, which allows individuals and authorities to track some data that could be easily altered. Smart cities can be enhanced by blockchain to guarantee the presence of digital identities, trace the usage of energy to pay the bills, or monitor the waste cycle or provide clean records of the services provided to people. One such instance is a blockchain system, which can follow credits representing renewable energy produced by solar panels on residential buildings, such that credits will result in creating the right compensation and will not cause conflicts. This will make smart cities efficient as the application of blockchain means that the citizens can have confidence and traceability of the operations that the city is performing.

Self-driving Cars and Drones

AVs are taking second place in smart city movement. AVs are fully autonomous and navigate streets with the help of AI inference and drive through the city, sensing obstacles and interacting with road infrastructure. Their other application is in cooperation with ionic technology traffic lights and sensors to optimize routes, congestion and safety. Similarly, more logistics, surveillance, environmental monitoring, and emergency response are also being addressed using drones. Drones may have cameras and sensors and the information may be passed to AI systems that may identify what should be done such as traffic diversion, infrastructure survey or medication delivery. AVs and drones are not the only example of an autonomous system in a smart city that will assist the city in reducing the population and streamline and expand the service delivery in all locations.

Connected City Cyberspace

With the cities getting more interconnected and more digital, the importance of cybersecurity could not be overemphasized. AI, IOT and cloud services create and process sensitive data, e.g., personal health data, financial transactions and infrastructure control. A city may come to a standstill due to cyber attacks, system failure, and data breach. To minimize security risks, smart cities use the power of security controls, such as encryption, protected authentication, anomaly detection, and threat analysis with the help of AI. AI inference alone can help detect network traffic anomalies, look ahead and act against network breaches in real time. The incorporation of cybersecurity best practices will enable cities to provide a resilient, reliable, and safe technological infrastructure to win the trust of residents and stakeholders.

The tech hardware ecosystem that makes smart cities work is enormous and 5G networks can enable real-time data processing, contrasted to big data analytics, which is underpinned by cloud and fog layers and both are scalable. Mobility and service delivery will be made possible by the security and transparency of transactions provided by blockchain and the introduction of autonomous vehicles and drones. All this is relying on a strong cybersecurity to defend citizens and infrastructure against cyber attacks. All these technologies together make up the vision of livelike, efficient and sustainable cities. They will empower the AI inference to help it do the best job to enable sectors to integrate smoothly to make cities smarter, safer, and more people-centric.

6. BENEFITS OF SMART CITIES

Efficiency of Energy

The IoT devices used and the AI inference will allow monitoring and optimization of the energy consumptions of the residential, commercial and public spaces. Artificial intelligence-based smart grids predict electricity demand, balance supply and prevent waste, but buildings with AI regulate heating, cooling, and lighting according to the occupancy plans. This does not only conserve energy to the citizens and governments but also reduces the emission of carbon and is in the global sustainability agenda (Ficili et al., 2025). And AI-based infrastructure has demonstrated to be economically and environmentally positive in cities like Amsterdam and

London, which report managed to save huge amounts of energy by implementing smarter energy control.

Reduced Pollution

Pollution is directly influenced by technology of smart cities. The AI inference and the environmental sensors monitor the quality of air, noise intensity, and emissions on the spot. The traffic management systems optimize the traffic that passes through the vehicle traffic, the traffic congestion is minimized, the carbon emission is minimized, the industrial systems are forecasted to minimize the industrial pollutants. The waste management solutions ensure that there is proper waste collection and recycling to prevent litter and contaminations. Such joint efforts are able to make smart cities contribute significantly positive change to the condition of the air in the city and the overall health and comfort of the environment, bringing more comfortable and healthier living locations.

Faster Healthcare Response

Smart cities will make healthcare more responsible and reactive. The IoT-related wearable gadgets, AI-based predictive platforms, and telemedicine platforms will allow the authorities to track the prevalence of health issues before they become uncontrolled. There is also reduced time of responding since real time traffic and location data guide ambulance by effective routes. Hospitals will be in a position of predicting patient traffic and making resource allocations dynamically so that the services that are the most important do not become overburdened. During the pandemic or health outbursts of such scale, AI and Big Data will be in a position to trace hotspots and impact behaviors, saving human lives. This can be attributed to the overlap of preventative health, fast emergency response and real time monitoring, thereby proving how smart city technology can increase the access of healthcare as well as its efficiency.

Perpetual Governing and Policy Making

The other outstanding benefit is the urban governance revolution. The Smart city platforms provide real-time data in different sectors to policymakers, i.e., traffic, energy, environment, safety, and healthcare. This information can be integrated into actionable pieces of information through AI inference to enable the making of data-driven decisions. One such instance is that as a response to regulatory action the extreme increase in air pollution would be an immediate response and a traffic jam would inform the city planning. The feedback loop allows governments to respond in real time and create evidence based, transparent, and responsive policies that meet the needs of the citizens, including the digital dashboards, AI analytics, and citizen feedback platforms.

Better Quality of Life

To conclude, the efficiency of energy use, reduction of pollution, faster healthcare and real-time governance will make the living standards skyrocket. It also offers the citizens easier traveling, better health conditions, better state services, and increased public safety. The smart city technologies also promote the economic opportunities as through digital platforms it is possible to create innovation, entrepreneurship and skills. In this manner, by becoming more sustainable, inclusive, and approachable to the citizens by integrating AI inference, IoT, and Big Data, the cities will develop into the unit, where technology can offer more opportunities to empower the citizens and less to burden their lives with technological advances.

The benefits of smart cities are manifold as they involve all the spheres of life in the city. Cities will become intelligent, eco-friendly, efficient, and fairer not only regarding energy use and pollution but also regarding efficiency in health care and responsive management based on the technologies constructed on AI. Such innovations enhance the lives of the citizens, and environmental protection in addition to enabling governments to take appropriate decisions in time. The advantages of the smart city projects will be more, and the path to the efficient, safe, and even human-centered city will be an option.

7. CHALLENGES AND RISKS OF SMART CITIES

7.1 Privacy Issues

With cities growing progressively more digitalized, there also arises a different issue, which is that of privacy. The Artificial intelligence systems, the Big Data and Internet of Things platforms collect enormous amounts of personal data: the movement history and medical data up to the financial flow and habits. In case of lack of strict privacy control, sensitive information of citizens may be left to fall into the wrong hands where identity theft, profiling, or unauthorized surveillance may be engaged. To guarantee privacy, the information must be secured by coming up with stringent data protection laws, encrypting and policies that restrict the unjustified usage of the data collection systems, and placing the citizens in the stance of managing their data. The smart cities should be able to walk a fine line between the gathering of valuable information that may be used to enhance efficiency of the urban centers and privacy and personal liberty of the populace.

7.2 Cybersecurity Threats

The urban systems are also networked thereby exposing them to cyber attacks. Through online communications, smart traffic, power grids, hospitals, and public safety networks have played a significant role and are offline targets of hackers. An effective cyberattack may affect the operations of the city and ruin classified data and even put the life of people in danger. To reduce the risk, the cities should invest in new cybersecurity tools, such as AI-powered threat identification, authentications, and network scanning (Abbood, 2025). The active preparation of the cybersecurity would be needed to ensure confidence in the smart city infrastructure and provide citizens with ongoing services.

7.3 Cost of Infrastructure

A smart city has an infrastructure that involves significant capital cost in construction and maintenance. The implementation of AI systems, internet of things, edge and cloud computing network or autonomous technologies is costly. The price may pose a constraint factor to many cities and more specifically in the developing areas. Continued care and system upgrades and hardware upgrades are also other long term costs. The governments and urban planners would have to critically examine the cost-benefit ratios, interested in the major projects and examine the possibility of having a venture into the aspect of having a joint venture in the form of a public-private, to finance the projects without necessarily overworking the aspect of the taxpayer or jeopardizing the levels of services.

7.4 Standardization and Interoperability

The other difficulty is on standardization and interoperability. Smart city systems tend to operate on multiple devices, software, and communication features, which makes it hard to capitalize on cross-sector and scale technological integration of data. Absence of standardization may result into data silos, inefficient and overlaps. The creation of standardized systems and regulations would provide uniform communication among the traffic, energy, medical, and environmental systems. AI inference with interoperable systems makes it possible to function effectively in all areas of the city to maximize the benefits of smart city initiatives.

7.5 Digital Divide and Lack of Skilled Experts

Smart cities face the threat of creating or more social inequalities due to technological changes. All citizens have no equal access to the digital tools, high-speed internet, or AI-enabled services. The urban innovations might be discriminatory to some communities due to this digital divide. Additionally, the applications of AI and IoT have a short implementation time and require highly qualified staff to design, operate, and maintain these systems. The shortage of the specialists can slow down the process, weaken the effectiveness of the systems as well as make the efficiency of smart solutions of the city lower. Training programs, educational programs and policies on how to have equal access and availability of skilled workers and inclusive technology should be given to them.

8. FUTURE OUTLOOK OF SMART CITIES

8.1 AI Becoming Self-Learning and Adaptive

Smart cities will be based on self learning and adaptive AI in the future. The future AI will constantly learn in the ongoing interactions and will be changing dynamically in case of the dynamic conditions in the city as compared to that which the current AI is highly dependent on the already programmed rules and the previous history. It would allow some traffic systems to predict the abnormal congestion behavior, energy grids to self-optimize according to the dynamically changing supply and demand, and the public safety networks to predict the incidents with unmatched precision. This kind of adaptive intelligence will assist in transforming the cities to more of being proactive rather than reactive; this will assist in restricting the risks and maximization of efficiency in every section of the city.

8.2 Intrusion into the Rural Region

Though the smart city technologies tend to be concentrated in the urban centers, in the future, the technologies will be incorporated in rural territories, as well as peri-urban territories. The urban-rural divide will also be filled to allow more citizens to experience the AI, IoT, and Big Data innovations. AI inference will enable smart farming to ensure efficient irrigation, crop sensing, and supply chain management to improve food security and management. Remote healthcare and AI assisted by IoT will ensure that the rural population gets timely healthcare. By linking the urban and rural systems, the governments are able to create harmonious and regional networks that would enable sustainable development, alleviate pressure of migration to urban space and to provide equal access to technology.

8.3 Intelligent Agriculture, Intelligent Education, Intelligent Government

Besides the traditional urban services, smart technologies in agriculture, education, and the government will also be available. In the agricultural industry and AI algorithms will help optimize the use of resources and predict harvest, which will lead to more sustainable and effective agriculture. The use of AI-based learning tools will streamline education to be more individual and accessible to all through adapting to the individual needs of a specific student and thereby giving him or her a quality education regardless of his or her socio-economic status (Yothi et al., 2024). Smart government will be used to automatize the administration system, simulate the effects of the policy, and make the government more transparent, participatory, and efficient by using digital platforms that will guarantee the government to citizens relationship. All those applications will make the smart technology even more powerful not only within cities but also beyond them to entire regions forming a network of intelligent and connected entities.

8.4 Future Cities Beyond 2030

As we peep into a vision of cities in the future of 2030, our cities will be entirely autonomous, energy-positive and very resilient. Structures will be able to regulate their energy usage, transportation networks will go hand in hand with self-driving vehicles, and resource grids operated by AI will be capable of optimally distributing electricity, water, and waste. The citizens will enjoy better living standards, shorter commute rates, less pollution, more secure and safer environment and more amenities in the form of public services. The development of urban centers will also be built on the principles of digital twins in which various scenarios will be modeled and only measures based on the data and sustainable will be introduced. These new cities will be an integration of technology and governance as well as human-focused design which will ensure that the environments in these new cities will not just be smart, but actually sustainable and inclusive.

9. CONCLUSION

Smart cities are a convergence of AI, IoT and Big Data, which involves establishing intelligent, adaptive and highly responsive cities to the needs of its residents.

As the IoT sensors and devices collect large volumes of real-time data and process it with the help of the Big Data platforms, and AI inference, the cities will have a chance to anticipate issues, resource use optimization, and make decisions advance the daily life of transportation, energy, public safety, and environmental systems. These technologies allow to dynamically control the traffic, provide efficient distribution of energy, prevent healthcare, and react to disasters in advance, thus the urban infrastructure is efficient and sustainable simultaneously. Further down the line, adaptive AI, autonomous systems and smart regional networks will be incorporated into cities, and the advantages of innovation will be applied to rural settings, agriculture, education, and government (El Ghati et al., 2024). With an equal measure of technological progress and human-centered design, ethical regulation, and sustainability, smart cities may strike a balance between efficiency, environmental accountability and quality of life and create urban ecosystems that are resilient, inclusive and successful over the next generations.

REFERENCES

Abbood, M. M. (2025). Investigation of IoT and deep learning techniques integration for smart city applications. *American Journal of Computing and Engineering*, *8*(1), 57–68.

Alajlan, N. N., & Ibrahim, D. M. (2025). Deep smart cities: A review of smart cities applications-based an inference of deep learning upon IoT devices. *Journal of Advanced Research in Applied Sciences and Engineering Technology*, *47*(2), 94–120.

Bibri, S. E., Alexandre, A., & Sharifi, A.. (2023). Environmentally sustainable smart cities and their converging AI, IoT, and big data technologies and solutions: An integrated approach to an extensive literature review. *Energy Informatics*. PMID: 37032812

Duhayyim, M. A., Elfadil Eisa, T. A., Al-Wesabi, F. N., Abdelmaboud, A., Hamza, M. A., Zamani, A. S., & Marzouk, R. (2022). Deep reinforcement learning enabled smart city recycling waste object classification. *Computers, Materials & Continua*, *71*(3).

El Ghati, O., Alaoui-Fdili, O., Chahbouni, O., Alioua, N., & Bouarifi, W. (2024). Artificial intelligence-powered visual internet of things in smart cities: A comprehensive review. *Sustainable Computing : Informatics and Systems*, *43*, 101004.

Ficili, I., Giacobbe, M., Tricomi, G., & Puliafito, A. (2025). From sensors to data intelligence: Leveraging IoT, cloud, and edge computing with AI. *Sensors*, *25*(6), Article 1763.

Mohammadi, M., & Al-Fuqaha, A. (2018). Enabling cognitive smart cities using big data and machine learning: Approaches and challenges.

Sujatha, L., Hemasundari, M., Pode, S., Shrivastava, V., Shah, S. S., & Datta, P. (2024). IoT-driven smart cities: Leveraging big data and AI for sustainable urban development. *Journal of Informatics Education and Research*, *4*(3).

Ullah, A., Anwar, S. M., & Li, J.. (2024). Smart cities: The role of Internet of Things and machine learning in realizing a data-centric smart environment. *Complex & Intelligent Systems*.

Yothi, V., Sreelatha, T., Thiyagu, T. M., & Sowndharya, R. (2024). A data management system for smart cities leveraging artificial intelligence modeling techniques to enhance privacy and security. *Journal of Internet Services and Information Security*, *14*(1), 126–140.

ADDITIONAL READING

Gouiza, N., Jebari, H., & Reklaoui, K. (2024). Integration of IoT-enabled technologies and artificial intelligence in diverse domains: Recent advancements and future trends. *Journal of Theoretical and Applied Information Technology*.

Joshi, S. (2025). Review of data pipelines and streaming for generative AI integration: Challenges, solutions, and future directions. *SSRN*.

Mahmood, H. S., & Abdulqader, D. M. (2024). *Analysis of AI, IoT, web technology, cloud computing, and enterprise systems integration for enhancing data security and governance to promote sustainability*. Journal of Information, ResearchGate.

Venice, J. A., Vettriselvan, R., & Rajesh, D. (2025). *Optimizing performance metrics in blockchain-enabled AI/ML data analytics: Assessing cognitive IoT*. IGI Global.

Xu, G., & Guo, T. (2025). *Advances in AI-powered civil engineering throughout the entire lifecycle*. Advances in Structural Engineering, SAGE Journals.

KEY TERMS & DEFINITIONS:

AI Inference: A step where trained AI models can be implemented in the just-in-time decision making of the new and unseen data to respond quickly on traffic, energy management, healthcare and safety.

Artificial Intelligence (AI): It is the forecasting approach as applied to the data in urban systems re-responding in an automated manner that predicts data patterns, data is analyzed, and the computational system learns, reasons, and makes decisions.

Big Data: Massive very complicated data gathered by the IoT and other systems; extracted processed to identify tendencies, relationships and anomalies assisting in decision-making in smart cities.

Citizen Engagement: Web based services and mobile applications that enable the residents to report and give information to the city government as well as participate in the city government.

Digital Twins: Urban infrastructure A virtual simulation method is called Urban infrastructure that simulates and predicts the behavior of a city through the use of real-time data through IoT.

Economical Urban Management: AI, IoT, and Big Data Urban Management provide the way to optimization of processes within urban environment in terms of the lowest rate of waste resources, the cost of their functioning, and the use of energy within the cities.

Edge Computing: Processing the data at the IoT devices helps minimize the throughput and provide real-time AI inference and rapid response of the city systems.

Environmental Surveillance: The IoT sensors and the Big Data will ensure the quali-ty of the air, noise, and pollution among other environmental parameters to ensure the wellbeing and sustainability of the urban location.

Internet of Things (IoT): It is defined as a combination of sensors, machines, and devices that are connected to gather and communicate the real life information that could be analyzed and regulated in the actual time that can be used to control the city.

Issue of Urbanization: Traffic jamming, pollution, power crisis, rubbish collection, civil security and healthcare are only a few issues that the current day cit-ies have encountered.

Predictive Policing: A prediction of where crime could occur, or where the civilians might be at risk due to any information, that the response might be proactive.

Self-Learning Cities: Cities that are developing due to continuous monitoring, analysis and adjustment of city infrastructure with the assistance of AI, IoT and Big Data to make them more responsive and effective.

Smart Cities: those cities that introduce digital technologies, AI, IoT and big data to citizens to enhance infrastructure, services, sustainability and the quality of life.

Smart Grids: Internet of Things and artificial intelligence Smart Grids are electric networks that both check and regulate the supply and demand of power in the most efficient and convenient manner without leading to power outages and the wastage of energy.

Sustainable Development: Urban planning must ensure that it utilizes the available resources in the best way possible, minimizing emissions and greening them but still rendering them habitable by not endangering the future generation.

Chapter 3

Federated AI Inference for Scalable and Secure Real-Time IoT Dataflows

S. Harish Alwar
http://orcid.org/0009-0002-0554-3760
Dr. G.U. Pope College of Engineering, India

T. Ganesan
http://orcid.org/0009-0006-9941-1935
Dr. G.U. Pope College of Engineering, India

J. Abishek
http://orcid.org/0009-0000-6436-0900
Dr. G.U. Pope College of Engineering, India

K. DanielRaj
http://orcid.org/0009-0001-9863-5682
Dr. G.U. Pope College of Engineering, India

ABSTRACT

The proliferation of IoT devices creates massive real-time data, which creates challenges for centralized AI in terms of latency, scalability and privacy. Federated AI inference supports distributed model training and inference on the edge devices as well as keeping data confidential while using real time analytics. Architectures, Privacy-reserving mechanisms and Edge-cloud collaboration strategies including use cases in healthcare, smart cities, and industrial systems are considered in this chapter and presented with a variety of real-world applications. Important challenges and future trends for secure and scalable federated intelligence are also presented for IoT environments.

DOI: 10.4018/979-8-3373-7046-0.ch003

1. INTRODUCTION

1.1 Background of Federated AI and IoT

Federated AI inference allows distributed IoT networks to analyze data on-site, which enhances instant response times, minimizes network saturation, and maintains user data confidentiality. Edge devices conduct inference and relay consolidated updates to global models, preserving accuracy of the models without gaining access to unprocessed data. Potential applications include health monitoring, where patient information stays local, industrial IoT systems for detecting anomalies, and smart agriculture, which focuses on monitoring the soil and crops. Privacy-preserving tools like differential privacy and homomorphic encryption guarantee data security during inter-device collaboration. For scalability and dependability, hierarchical integration, back-pressure strategies, and fault-tolerant systems provide reliable dispersed control for thousands of different types of devices. (Zhang et al., 2021).

1.2 The Role of Real Time Inference in IoT Systems

Federated AI also which is what we see playing out in IoT networks which do the processing at the edge thus improving real time response, which in turn reduces network traffic and protects user privacy. At the edge devices inference takes place which then report back to the global models which in turn maintain accuracy of the model without the need to share raw data. We see this play out in health care which is very local with patient data, in industry for anomaly detection, and in agriculture for soil and crop health. Also we have differential privacy and homomorphic encryption which are the technical measures put in place for private collaboration between devices. As for scale and reliability we see it in the design which includes integration, back pressure mechanisms, and fault tolerance which in turn support very large scale of different types of devices. (Kairouz et al., 2021).

Figure 1. The role of real-time interference in IoT systems

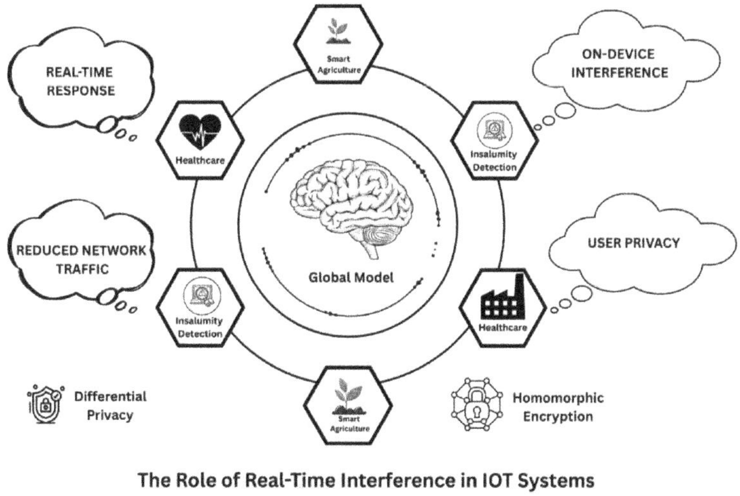

1.3 Scalability and Security Issues

Federated AI inference facilitates IoT networks performing distributed local data processing for improved real-time responsiveness, lower network overhead, and enhanced privacy per user. Edge devices undertake inference, dispatch federated updates to global models, and uphold model fidelity without revealing raw data. Practical implementation scenarios are health monitoring system where patient data is kept local, anomaly detection in industrial IoT systems, and monitoring of soil and crops in smart agriculture. Privacy-preserving technologies like differential privacy and homomorphic encryption allow secure collaboration of devices. Hierarchical aggregation, back-pressure, and fault-tolerant mechanisms address scalability and reliability, streamlining robust performance. These systems contain thousands of heterogeneous devices. (Bonomi et al., 2012).

1.4 Objectives and Chapter Structure

Federated AI is used for the deployment of machine learning models in which data is processed at the edge in distributed IoT networks thus improving response time in real world use and at the same time reducing the load on the network and protecting user privacy. At the edge devices inference takes place which in turn report aggregated updates to the global models which in turn maintains model accuracy which doesn't require the raw data to be sent out. We see this in health care which is focused on local patient data, in industry for anomaly detection, and in agriculture for soil and crop health. Also we have privacy preserving techniques like differential privacy and homomorphic encryption which enable secure device to device collaboration. We scale and improve reliability via a hierarchy of integration, back pressure systems, and fault tolerance which in turn supports very large scale of diverse devices. (Wang et al., 2019).

2. CONCEPTUAL FOUNDATIONS

2.1 Distributed Algorithms and Inference Principles

Federation AI technology which enables decentralized IoT networks to process data at the edge, improve real time response, reduce network load, and protect user privacy. At the edge devices inference is done and then integrated updates are sent to global models which in turn preserves model accuracy without at any time exposing raw data. We see patient data used in local health care, in industrial IoT for anomaly detection, and in agriculture for soil and crop health. Smart agriculture is a practical deployment of this. Also we have privacy preserving tech such as differential privacy and homomorphic encryption which enable device level collaboration. We scale and improve reliability via a hierarchy of integration, back pressure mechanisms, and fault tolerant work flows which in turn support very large scale of different types of devices. (Konečný et al., 2016).

Federated AI is a technology which sees the processing of data take place at the edge in decentralized IoT networks thus which in turn improves real time response, reduces network overhead, and preserves user privacy. At the edge devices inference takes place which in turn send out consolidated updates to global models which in turn maintains model accuracy without at any point exposed raw data. We see this in health care which is centered around local patient data, in industry for anomaly detection, and in agriculture for soil and crop health. Also we have differential privacy and homomorphic encryption which are put forth as privacy solutions which enable secure device to device collaboration. As for issues of scale and reliability we see solutions in the form of a hierarchy which is integrated, back pressure mechanisms, and fault tolerant work flows which in turn support very robust performance across large scale sets of different devices. (Pan et al., 2020).

2.2 Edge–Cloud Collaboration in IoT

Federated AI inference allows distributed IoT networks to work on data at the point of originating. This enhances the immediacy of responses, decreases the burden on networks, and protects the privacy of individuals. Edge devices conduct data inference and communicate federated updates to global AI models, which safeguards the accuracy of models without compromising the raw data. Feasible deployment scenarios are health monitoring where patient data is sensitive, anomaly detection in industrial IoT systems, and smart agri-tech where the soil and crop monitoring systems are assisted. Secure collaboration of devices are facilitated through privacy enhancing technologies like differential privacy and homomorphic encryption. Scalability and dependability are managed through hierarchical aggregation and back-pressure systems, in concert with fault-tolerant workflows, to allow thousands of diverse devices to run complex heterogeneous tasks. (Abdul et al., 2020).

2.3 Security and Privacy in Distributed AI Federation

Distributed IoT networks can maintain user privacy due to local data processing and AI inference capabilities. Responding to user requests in real-time, performing local data processing, and aggregately sending updates to the global AI models contributes to less network strain. Model accuracy is preserved while source data is kept private. Remote health monitoring, where local patient data is monitored, cybersecurity IoT systems, and smart agriculture systems that monitor soil and crops are practical use cases. Collaboration of distributed devices is promoted using privacy-preserving techniques such as differential privacy and homomorphic encryption. Fault-tolerant workflows, back-pressure mechanisms, hierarchical aggregation techniques, and other methods addressing scaling and sustaining reliability in the system assist in heterogeneous devices. (Hu & Li, 2021).

Federated AI inference helps decentralized IoT networks provide local data processing to enhance real-time responsiveness, minimize network load, and maintain user privacy. Edge devices perform inference and transmit consolidated updates to global models. They uphold precision of models without compromising data. Healthcare monitoring, where patient data is private, is a notable industrial IoT deployment in anomaly detection, and monitoring soil and crops in smart agriculture are practical cases. Differential privacy and homomorphic encryption provide privacy enhancing secure collaboration for devices. Hierarchical aggregation,back pressure,and fault-tolerant flows provide scalability and reliability.These mechanisms provide strong performance in the presence of thousands of diverse devices. (Konečný et al., 2016).

2.4 Background and Architectures

Federated AI models enable a better design of today's IoT networks to process data at edge devices which in turn improves real time response and also reduces network load as well as preserve users' privacy. At edge devices inference happens and we see global models being updated with a combined input from all the edges' outputs, at same time keeping the original data protected. This is seen in health care when we have patient data remaining at local settings, in industrial IoT for out of the ordinary event detection, and in smart farming for soil and crop health which also is a part of it. Also we have in place privacy solutions like differential privacy and homomorphic encryption that also add a layer to this secure data exchange between devices. As far as issue of large scale goes we see a solution in hierarchical reporting, back pressure strategies, and fault tolerant processes that together support very large scale of different types of edge devices which at the same time also report dependably. (Bonawitz et al., 2019).

Federated AI inference permits distributed IoT networks to process data locally, thus improving responsiveness in real time, minimizing network overhead, and safeguarding user privacy. Inference of edge devices and merged updates sent to global models keeps accuracy and prevents exposure of raw data. Scenarios involving the practical deployment of this technology include health monitoring systems in which locally stored patient data is processed, industrial IoT systems for anomaly detection, and smart agriculture systems which monitor soil and crops. The use of privacy-enhancing technologies, like differential privacy and homomorphic encryption, for collaboration among devices. Extension and dependability are resolved by hierarchical aggregation, the back-pressure method, and fault-tolerant data processing to permit processing in unchanged and highly heterogeneous systems, which consist of thousands of devices. (Sun et al., 2021).

Figure 2. Federated AI interference for scalable and secure real-time IoT dataflows

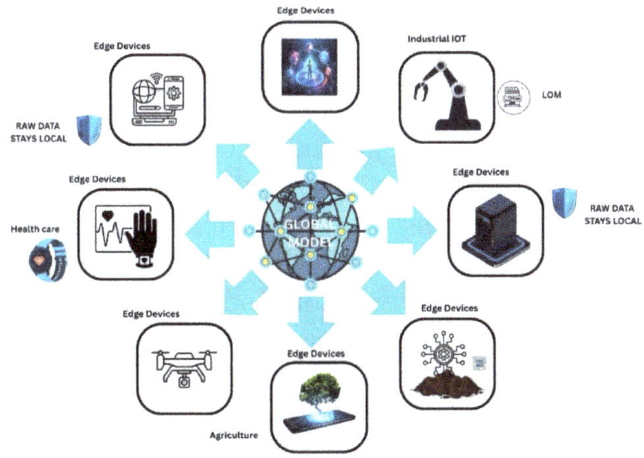

FEDERATED AI INTERFERENCE for Scalable and Serid Secure Real-Time IOT Dataflows
Background of Federated AI and IOT

3. SYSTEM ARCHITECTURE FOR FEDERATED AI INFERENCE

3.1.Main Components and Functions

Federated AI Inference supports distributed IoT networks for local data processing.This enhances real-time responsiveness while minimizing network strain and ensuring user data confidentiality.Edge devices conduct inference and transmit unified updates to global models,thereby preserving accuracy without accessing sensitive raw data.Use-case scenarios include health monitoring systems where local patient data is used, industrial IoT systems anomaly detection, and smart agriculture monitoring systems for soil and crops. Differential privacy and homomorphic encryption strengthen privacy for device collaboration. Scalability and reliability challenges are resolved hierarchical aggregation, back-pressure, and, fault-tolerant workflows to enable seamless operations across thousands of heterogeneous devices. (Gao et al., 2021).

3.2 Database and Control Base Separation

Federation AI Inference, Distributed IoT Network. Here, nodes obtain localized processing capabilities which drastically enhances the real-time responsiveness as well as reduces the network overhead and protects user privacy. Edge devices perform inference and send unified updates to global models, keeping the models accurate without source data exposure. Practical deployment scenarios cover healthcare-e.g. patient data during remote monitoring, industrial IoT systems for anomaly detection, and smart agriculture soil and crop monitoring. Privacy-enhancing technologies such as differential privacy and homomorphic encryption collaboration securely between devices. Scalable and reliable operation across thousands of heterogeneous devices is facilitated through a combination of hierarchical aggregation, back pressure mechanisms, and fault-tolerant workflows during. (Konečný et al., 2016).

Federated AI is used for distributed IoT networks which process data at the edge, thus improving real time response, reducing network traffic, and at the same time protecting user privacy. At edge devices inference takes place which in turn report improved global models all this is done without the need to share raw data. We see this in health care which keeps patient data local, in industry for anomaly detection, and in agriculture for soil and crop health. Also we have differential privacy and homomorphic encryption which enable secure device level collaboration. For issues of scale and reliability we have hierarchical aggregation, back-pressure systems, and fault tolerance which together support very large scale deployment of diverse devices. (Konečný et al., 2016).

3.3 Types of Communication (Streaming vs RPC)

Federation AI which is used for the inference in distributed IoT networks has the ability to process data at the edge which in turn improves real time response, reduces network overhead, and preserves user privacy. At the edge devices inference takes place and then we see global models get updated which in turn maintains model accuracy without the exposure of raw data. We see practical deployment in health which is focused on local patient data, in industry for anomaly detection, and in smart agriculture for soil and crop monitoring. Also we have privacy preserving tech such as differential privacy and homomorphic encryption which enable secure device to device collaboration. As for issues of scalability and reliability we see hierarchical aggregation, back pressure mechanisms, and fault tolerant work flows which in turn support very robust performance across large scale and diverse device sets. (Wang et al., 2019).

Federated AI allows Internet of Things (IoT) to network locally, which means real-time responsiveness, less network overhead, and user data privacy. Edge devices perform local AI and forward integrated updates to global models. No raw data leaves local infrastructures, and model accuracy is preserved. Health monitoring scenarios, where local patient data is protected, industrial IoT systems to monitor and detect anomalies, and soil and crops smart monitoring and agriculture systems are practical examples. Privacy preserving techniques like differential privacy and homomorphic encryption secure device collaboration. Hierarchical aggregation, back-pressure, and fault-tolerant workflows manage scalability and reliability to resiliently support operations of disparate devices. (Bonomi et al., 2012).

3.4 Security Domains and Trust Management

Federation AI technology which enables distributed IoT networks to process data at the edge, thus improving real time response, reducing network load, and preserving user privacy. At the edge devices inference takes place which in turn report aggregated updates to global models which in turn maintain accuracy of the model without the need to expose raw data. We see this in health care which keeps patient data local, in industry for anomaly detection, and in agriculture for soil and crop health. Also we have differential privacy and homomorphic encryption which enable secure device to device collaboration. We scale and improve reliability through hierarchy of integration, back-pressure algorithms, and fault tolerant work flows which in turn support robust operation of the system across thousands of different devices. (Abdel-Basset et al., 2020).

Federated AI which is used in IoT networks' architecture of which data is processed at the edge, improves response time, reduces network load, and at the same time preserves user privacy. At the edge devices inference takes place which in turn report aggregated updates to the global models thus preserving raw data integrity and at the same time maintaining model accuracy. We see this in health care which is very much a local issue of patient data, in industry for anomaly detection, and in agriculture for soil and plant health which are also local issues. Also we have differential privacy and homomorphic encryption which are put in play to secure device level collaboration. For issues of scale and reliability we have put in place a hierarchy of data aggregation, back pressure mechanisms, and fault tolerant work flows which in turn support very large scale of diverse devices (Hu & Li, 2021).

4. API DESIGN AND SPECIFICATION OF SERVICES

4.1 Design Principles and Criteria

Federation AI allows for the processing of data at the edge in IoT networks which in turn improves response time for real time requests, reduces network traffic, and protects user privacy. At the edge devices inference is done and then only aggregate updates are sent to global models which in turn preserves model accuracy without the need to share raw data. We see this in health care which we do not put patient data at risk, in industry for better anomaly detection, and in agriculture for improved soil and crop health. Also we have privacy preserving tech like differential privacy and homomorphic encryption which enable secure device to device collaboration. We see scale and dependability through use of a hierarchy which in turn supports large scale deployment of very different types of devices also we have put in place back pressure mechanisms and fault tolerant work flows which in turn support very reliable performance across very large scale and diverse device sets. (Liang et al., 2018).

4.2 Plane of Control APIs

Federated AI which is used in IoT networks allows for data to be processed at the edge improving real time response, reducing network traffic, and preserving user privacy. At the edge devices inference takes place which in turn send out combined updates to global models thus keeping model accuracy high without the need to expose raw data. We see this in health care which023909059 has patient data local, in industry for anoma ly detection, and in smart agriculture for soil and crop health which all benefit from this approach. Also we have differential privacy and homomorphic encryption which are put in play to secure device level collaboration. As for issues of large scale and reliability we see hierarchical aggregation, back pressure mechanisms, and fault tolerant work flows which in turn support very robust performance across large sets of different devices. (Konečný et al., 2016).

Federated AI Inference allows distributed IoT networks to improve real-time responsiveness, reduce network overhead, and enhance user privacy by processing data locally. While edge devices conduct inference, they transmit aggregated updates to global models, thus preserving the models' accuracy without sharing raw data. This is applicable to practical deployment and user scenarios, for instance, in the monitoring of healthcare systems by integrating, local, and real-time, patient data, in industrial IoT systems, and smart agriculture systems for soil and crop monitoring. Secure collaborative device privacy-enhancing techniques, like differential privacy and homomorphic encryption, as well as scalable and reliable hierarchical integration, and back-pressure systems, and fault-tolerant workflows, support the robust operation of thousands of heterogeneous devices. (Wang et al., 2019).

4. 3 Database APIs

Federation of AI which is used in the inference of distributed IoT networks' data at edge level, improves real time response, reduces network overhead and at the same time protects user privacy. At edge devices inference takes place and then integrated updates are sent to global models which in turn preserves model accuracy without at any time putting out the raw data. We see this in health care monitoring which is very much a local issue of patient data, in industry for anomaly detection in IoT systems and in smart agriculture for soil and crop monitoring. Also we have privacy preserving tech such as differential privacy and homomorphic encryption which enable secure device to device collaboration. We scale up and at the same time we make our systems reliable via hierarchical aggregation, back pressure mechanisms and fault tolerant work flows which in turn support very large scale of different types of devices. (Gao et al., 2021).

Federated AI Inference permits decentralized Internet of Things (IoT) networks to handle data locally, which increases efficiency and effectiveness in real-time, while safeguarding user privacy and minimizing network congestion. Distributed edge devices conduct inferencing and transmit consolidated updates to federated models, which continue to protect model integrity without including raw data. Use cases in the real world involve healthcare monitoring and patient data privacy, industrial IoT systems anomaly detection, and smart agriculture during soil and crop monitoring. Differential privacy and homomorphic encryption function as privacy protective technologies, which enable devices to cooperatively and privately share information, thereby enhancing privacy. Reliability and scalability concerns are attended to through fault-tolerant workflows, back-pressure systems, and hierarchical aggregation. They take thousands of robust, heterogeneous, and distributed devices and support the thousands of heterogeneous devices robustly and efficiently. (Nguyen et al., 2021).

4. 4 Safe Integration and Privacy APIs

Federated AI is used by distributed IoT networks to process data at the edge which in turn improves real time response, reduces network overhead, and preserves user privacy. At the edge devices inference takes place which in turn report back to global models which in term maintain accuracy of the model without the need to expose raw data. We see this in health care monitoring which keeps patient data local, in industrial IoT for anomaly detection, and in smart agriculture for soil and crop health. Also we have differential privacy and homomorphic encryption which are put forth for private collaboration between devices. For large scale and reliable performance we see hierarchy in integration, use of back pressure mechanisms, and fault tolerant work flows which support the operation of up to thousands of different devices. (Gubbi et al., 2013).

Federated AI inference allows distributed IoT networks to locally process data, which enhances responsiveness in real-time, decreases the volume of data traffic across the network, and keeps user information private. Edge devices process data and perform inference locally while sending blended updates to the central global models, which allows continuous model training without needing to access raw data. Examples are healthcare monitoring with real-time remote patient data, industrial IoT systems for real-time anomaly detection, and smart agriculture for real-time monitoring of soils and crops. Privacy-enhancing technologies like differential privacy and homomorphic encryption guarantee the collaboration and safe data interchange of multi-device systems. Scalability and reliability can be implemented with hierarchical aggregations, back-pressure mechanisms, and fault-tolerant workflows which ensures robust performances of thousands of heterogeneous devices. (Konečný et al., 2016).

5. DATA STRUCTURES AND MESSAGING PROTOCOLS

5.1 Sensor Data Representation

Federated AI inference allows distributed IoT networks to process data at the "Edge" and perform real-time responsive actions. It reduces the overhead on the network and preserves the privacy of the users. The edge devices perform inference and send unified model updates to be integrated to global models. The exposure of raw data is avoided. Practical use cases include patient data in remote health monitoring. The industrial IoT is used in anomaly detection and smart agriculture for monitoring soil and crops. The use of privacy-enhancing techniques such as differential privacy and homomorphic encryption allows secure collaboration between devices. The complex IoT ecosystem at scale and runtime is integrated hierarchically complemented by back-pressure mechanisms and fault-tolerant workflows to ensure scalability and reliability while supporting thousands of heterogeneous devices. (Bonomi et al., 2012).

Federated AI inference allows distributed IoT networks to process data locally, enhancing real-time interactivity, decreasing network overhead, and providing privacy to users. Edge devices perform inference and send unified updates to global models, keeping model accuracy and no raw data exposure. Some feasible use cases involve healthcare monitoring, where patient data is managed locally, industrial IoT systems for anomaly detection, and smart agriculture focused on soil and crop monitoring. Technologies for privacy protection,such as differential privacy and homomorphic encryption,enable secure inter-device collaboration.The reliability and scalability of Federated AI systems are managed through hierarchical aggregation,back-pressure mechanisms,and fault-tolerant workflows,providing robust performance with thousands of heterogeneous devices. (Chen et al., 2018).

5.2 Model Manifest and Version

Federated AI inference allows distributed IoT networks to process data locally,which enhances real-time responsiveness,lowers network overhead,and protects user privacy.Edge devices carry out inference and transmit consolidated updates to global models,all while keeping the raw data secure.Real-world implementations include healthcare monitoring with locally stored patient data, the industrial IoT for detecting anomalies, and smart agriculture for monitoring soil and crops.Differential privacy and homomorphic encryption,alongside other privacy-enhancing technologies,provide secure device collaboration.For thousands of different devices to work seamlessly and provide robust performance,hierarchical aggregation, back-pressure mechanisms,and fault-tolerant workflows manage reliability and scalability. (Ren et al., 2019).

Federated AI inference allows distributed IoT networks to process data locally, and thus, data latency is reduced, user privacy is preserved, and network overhead is lessened. Edge devices execute inference and transmit federated updates to global models, thus ensuring model accuracy without exposure to unrefined data. Instances of practical implementation include monitoring patient health where data is collected locally, and monitoring industrial IoT systems for anomaly detection.In smart agriculture,data collection and monitoring of soils and crops help enhance systems. (Abdul et al., 2020).

Technologies,such as differential privacy and homomorphic encryption, secure device collaboration.Reliability is upheld via fault-tolerant workflows,back-pressure mechanisms,and hierarchical aggregation to ensure resiliency in systems that operate concurrently across thousands of diverse devices. (Samie et al., 2016).

5.3 Inference Request and Response Structures

Federated AI which is used in IoT networks allows for data to be processed at the edge which in turn improves real time response, reduces network traffic, and protects user privacy. At edge devices inference takes place and then aggregated updates are sent to the global models which in turn maintains model accuracy without the need to expose raw data. We see this in health care which keeps patient data local, in industry for anomaly detection, and in agriculture for soil and crop health. Also we have differential privacy and homomorphic encryption which are put in play to secure device to device collaboration. For issues of scale and reliability we see hierarchical aggregation, implementation of back pressure mechanisms, and fault tolerant work flows which in turn support very robust operation of systems which may contain thousands of different types of devices. (Bonomi et al., 2012).

With users privacy in mind, Federated AI inference allows distributed IoT networks to locally processed streamlined data to improve responsiveness in real time, reduce network overhead, and optimize user privacy. Edge devices have assumed to send unified updates to global models. Model accuracy is maintained while raw data is never revealed. Practical cases of deployed systems include healthcare monitoring with patient data, IoT systems for real-time anomaly detection, and smart agriculture for monitoring soil and crops. Differential privacy and homomorphic encryption are examples of privacy-enhancing teachings that allow secure collaboration among devices. Fully integrated, stacked systems, horizontal back-pressure ensurance, and robust fault-tolerant systems are examples of how scalability and reliability are maintained in operated heterogeneous devices. (McMahan et al., 2017).

6 SERVICE STANDARDS, RELIABILITY, AND ERROR HANDLING

6.1 QoS Parameters and Latency Management

Federation AI inference helps distributed IoT networks to locally process real-time data. It minimizes network strain and upholds user data confidentiality. For example, health data monitoring and patient data are geographically close, while industrial IoT systems for anomaly detection and smart agriculture monitor soil and crops. In these scenarios, data is processed close to the point of collection. Technologies for privacy protection like differential privacy and homomorphic encryption secure inter-device collaboration. For scalability and reliability, hierarchical aggregation and back-pressure are distributed, while fault tolerance is designed into workflows. These support the reliable operation of thousands of diverse devices. (Konečný et al., 2016).

Federated AI inference in which data is processed at the edge in distributed IoT networks we see improved real time response, reduced network overhead, and preserved user privacy. At the edge devices we see inference performed and then large scale updates to global models which in turn maintain accuracy of the model without the need to expose raw data. We have practical deployment in health care which is very much a local issue for patient data, in industry for anomaly detection and in agriculture for soil and crop health. Also we see that differential privacy and homomorphic encryption which are privacy enhancing technologies are what enable secure device to device collaboration. For issues of scalability and reliability we see hierarchical aggregation, back pressure mechanisms, and fault tolerant work flows which in turn support very robust performance across large scale sets of different types of devices. (Ren et al., 2019).

6.2 Streaming Reliability and Flow Control Algorithms

Federation AI in which IoT networks are processed at the edge improves real time response, reduces network overhead, and protects user privacy. At the edge devices inference is done which in turn report aggregated updates to the global models thus preserving model accuracy which in turn does not require raw data to be exposed. We see this in health care which keeps patient data local, in industry for anomaly detection, and in agriculture for soil and crop health. Also we have privacy features like differential privacy and homomorphic encryption which enable device level collaboration security. We scale and improve reliability via hierarchical aggregation, back-pressure algorithms, and fault tolerance which in turn supports robust operation of the system across thousands of different devices. (Sun et al., 2021).

Federation AI in which IoT networks are processed locally to improve real time response, reduce network overhead, and at the same time protect user privacy. At edge devices inference takes place which in turn report aggregated updates to global models thus preserving model accuracy which in turn does not see the raw data. We see this in health care which has patient data local, in industry for anomaly detection, and in agriculture for soil and crop health. Also we have differential privacy and homomorphic encryption which are used to secure device level collaboration. As for large scale and reliability we have hierarchical aggregation, back pressure mechanisms, and fault tolerant work flows which support very robust operation of the system across thousands of different devices. (Jiang et al., 2020).

6.3 API Response Codes and Exception Handling

Federated AI inference allows distributed IoT networks to process data locally which increases real-time responsiveness, decreases network overhead, and protects user privacy.Edge devices perform inference on local data and send unified updates to the global models,ensuring model accuracy without exposing raw data.Situations where this approach is practical include health monitoring where patient data is local,industrial IoT systems for anomaly detection,and smart agriculture for monitoring soil and crops.Privacy-enhancing technologies,such as differential privacy and homomorphic encryption, provide secure collaboration between devices.Scalability and reliability are also addressed,in part,by hierarchical aggregation,back-pressure mechanisms,and fault-tolerant workflows which aid in robust operation across thousands of heterogeneous devices. (Konečný et al., 2016).

Real-time processing of data on federated AI inference in distributed IoT networks enhances the ability to respond to situations as they unfold,lessens the load on the network,and maintains the confidentiality of the end user.Edge devices analyze and perform inference,after which they send consolidated updates to global models. The models then adjust and refine accuracy while respecting data privacy.There are practical implementations in health care such as health monitoring systems where patient data resides in a local database,anomaly detection in industrial IoT systems,and smart farming where soil and crops are monitored.The collaboration of devices,however,involves privacy-preserving technologies like differential privacy and homomorphic encryption.The system of thousands of heterogeneous devices performs reliably due to hierarchical aggregation,back-pressure mechanisms,and fault-tolerant workflows globally improving scalability. (Yang et al., 2019).

6.4 Time to Try Again and Fail Over

With Federated AI inference, distributed IoT networks can locally process data, enhancing real-time responsiveness, lowering network overhead, and safeguarding user privacy. Edge devices conduct inference and relay aggregated updates to global models, thereby upholding model accuracy without exposing raw data. Situations such as health monitoring, where data pertaining to patients is considered, industrial IoT systems aimed at anomaly detection, and smart farming with focus on soil and crops augment the practical usability. Differential privacy and homomorphic encryption as privacy-enhancing technologies help to achieve secure coordination among devices. Hierarchical aggregation, back-pressure methods, and fault-tolerant workflows tackle scalability and reliability, ensuring thousands of varied devices can perform and maintain robust operational workflows. (Zhang et al., 2021).

7.PRIVACY AND SECURITY IMPROVEMENTS

7.1 Differential Privacy in Federated Learning

Federated AI models see action in distributed IoT infrastructures which they enable to process info at the edge, improve on real time results, lower network traffic, and also secure the private info of users. Edge devices carry out the inference and report to global models only a combined set of updates which in turn maintains model accuracy and which does not expose the raw data. As for the practical implementation of this we see health care which is very protective of patient info, industrial

IoT for anamoly detection, and smart ag which looks at soil and crop health. Also what we have are privacy which is improved with techs like differential privacy and homomorphic encryption that also support that which these devices work together. As far as the growth and consistency of the networks goes we see a hierarchy which is used in design, back pressure mechanisms, and fault tolerant work flows which in turn are what allow these infrastructures to function well with as many as thousands of different types of devices. (Yang et al., 2019).

7.2 Homomorphic Encryption and Obfuscation

Federated AI inference enables distributed IoT networks to process data locally,which improves real-time response,reduces network overhead, and protects user privacy.Rather than transmitting raw data,edge devices execute inference and transmit synchronized updates to local/global models.This preserves model accuracy.Practical assignments include health monitoring when patient data is stored locally,industrial IoT systems for anomaly detection,and smart agriculture for monitoring soil and crops.Differential privacy and other privacy-preserving techniques like homomorphic encryption make inter-device collaboration secure.Reliability and scalability are handled through hierarchical integration,back-pressure mechanisms,and fault-tolerant workflows.These techniques ensure robust performance across thousands of diverse,heterogeneous devices. (Lyu et al., 2020).

Federated AI inference allows distributed IoT networks to carry out local data processing,which strengthens real-time interactivity,minimizes network overload,and provides user privacy guarantees.Edge devices execute inference and send federated updates to global models to ensure that no raw data leaves the device while maintaining model accuracy.Practical deployment scenarios include healthcare monitoring,where local patient data is used,industrial IoT system anomaly detection,and smart agriculture for monitoring soil and crops.Differential privacy and homomorphic encryption,privacy-enhancing technologies,enable devices to collaborate securely. Designed for solid operation across thousands of disparate devices, the system is scalable and reliable.Hierarchical integration,back-pressure mechanisms,and fault-tolerant workflows contribute to this capability. (Chen et al., 2018).

7.3 Access Management and Device Authentication

The we have introduced methods for secure collaboration between devices. We address scale and reliability in the design which includes hierarchical integration, back-pressure systems, and fault tolerant workflows that support stable performance across large sets of different types of devices. (Li et al., 2020).

Federated AI is which large scale IoT networks to process data at edge which in turn improves real time response, reduces network traffic, and preserves user privacy. At edge devices inference takes place which we then see as a unified update to global models which in turn maintains model accuracy without at any time exposing raw data. We see this in health care which is very local the patient data, in industry for anomaly detection, and in smart agriculture for soil and crop health. Also we have privacy which is enhanced by use of tech like differential privacy and homomorphic encryption which in turn improve device level collaboration. As for issues of scale and dependability we see hierarchical aggregation, back pressure mechanisms, and fault tolerant work flows which in turn support very robust performance across large scale of different types of devices. (Nguyen et al., 2021).

7.4 Governance and Regulatory Compliance

Federated AI which allows for the use of distributed IoT networks to process data at the edge, improve real time response, reduce network overhead, and at the same time protect user privacy. At the edge devices inference takes place which in turn report federated updates to global models which in turn maintain accuracy of the model without the need to expose raw data. We see this in health care which is very local with patient data, in industry for anomaly detection, and in agriculture for soil and crop health. Also we have differential privacy and homomorphic encryption which are used as privacy solutions for device level collaboration. For issues of scale and reliability we have hierarchical aggregation, back pressure mechanisms, and fault tolerant work flows which in turn support very robust operation of the system across thousands of different devices. (Liang et al., 2018).

8. IMPLEMENTATION STRATEGIES AND CASE STUDIES

8.1 Real Time Edge Inference Process

Federated AI which is used in IoT networks' design allows for data to be processed at the edge which in turn improves on real time response, reduces network traffic and at the same time preserves user privacy. At the edge devices inference takes place which in turn we see to it that we have a unified update of the global models thus we maintain model accuracy without at any point in time expose raw data. We see this in health care which is centered around local patient data, in industry for an issue like anomaly detection, and in agriculture for soil and crop health. Also we have in place privacy tools like differential privacy and homomorphic encryption that enable secure interplay between devices. We scale out and at the same time see to the issue of reliability through the use of a hierarchy in design, back pressure systems, and fault tolerant work flows thus we achieve large scale and at the same time very reliable operation of systems made up of many different types of devices. (Zhang et al., 2021).

Comparatively in the field of AI we see that which which the processing of data takes place at the edge of the network in the case of IoT which improves on real time response, reduces network traffic, and at the same time protects user privacy. At the edge devices we see inference taking place which in turn we see report to global models in a consolidated form which in turn maintains model accuracy without at any time sending out raw data. We see this play out in health care for health monitoring, in IT for anomaly detection and in business for data analytics which has patient data which is local. Also we have in industries like food and beverage and smart agriculture for soil and crop health which also benefit. Also what we have are privacy enhancing technologies like differential privacy and homomorphic encryption which enable secure cooperation between devices. As for issues of large scale and dependability we see a hierarchical structure, back pressure mechanisms and fault tolerant work flows which support very large scale operation of very different types of devices. (Konečný et al., 2016).

Figure 3. Performance: Real-time edge interference vs cloud processing

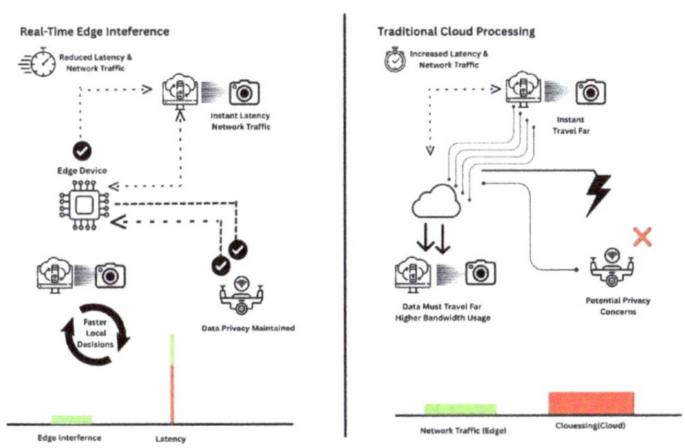

Performance:Real-Time Edge Interference vs.Cloud Processing

8.2 Periodic Secure Integration

Federated AI inference allows networks of distributed IoT devices to evaluate data at the source, achieving faster data processing, lesser data being transferred over the network, and greater user privacy. Edge devices perform inference and send integrated updates to global models, maintaining model accuracy without exposing raw data. This approach can be used in healthcare applications during the monitoring of patients to avoid the off-site transfer of sensitive data, in smart agriculture (soil and crop monitoring), and in industrial IoT systems (anomaly detection). Besides, the secure collaboration of devices is possible with the use of privacy-enhancing technologies such as differential privacy and homomorphic encryption. Scalability and reliability are addressed through hierarchical aggregation, back-pressure mechanisms, and fault-tolerant workflows, supporting robust operation across thousands of heterogeneous devices. (Abdul et al., 2020).

Federated AI inference in which data is processed at the edge in distributed IoT networks we see an improvement in real time response, a reduction in network overhead, and preservation of user privacy. At the edge devices we see inference which in turn we see unified updates to global models which in turn we preserve raw data privacy. We see practical deployment in health care which is very much about local patient data, in industry for anoma ly detection and in agriculture for soil and crop health. Also we have in play privacy enhancing tech such as differential privacy and homomorphic encryption that which enable secure device to device collaboration. We scale and we make our systems reliable through hierarchical aggregation, back pressure mechanisms and fault tolerant work flows which in turn support very large scale of different types of devices. (Aledhari et al., 2020).

Figure 4. Federated AI in industrial IoT

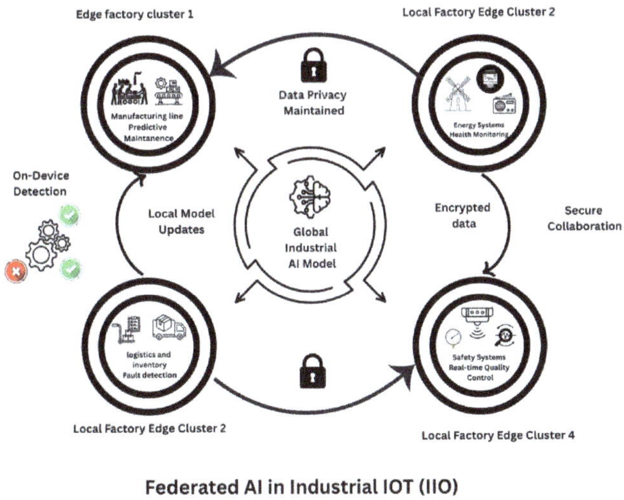

8.3 Hybrid Edge Cloud Collaborative Inference

Federated AI at the edge is that which we see in action at scale within IoT networks. What it does is allows for local data processing by edge devices instead of at centralized points. This in turn we see to improve real time response, reduce network traffic and also keep the user privacy intact. Edge devices do the inference and present aggregated updates to the global models thus preserving the raw data. We see this play out in health care where patient data is kept local, in industry for anamoly detection, and in smart agriculture for soil and crop health. Also we have privacy preserving tech like differential privacy and homomorphic encryption that enable these devices to work together securely. As for issues of large scale we see the use of hierarchical aggregation, back pressure systems, and fault tolerant work flows which in turn support very robust performance at a very large scale with many different types of devices. (Konečný et al., 2016).

Federated AI inference allows distributed IoT networks to locally analyze data which helps in improving real-time responsiveness and preserving user privacy while also reducing network overhead. Edge devices execute inference and transmit federated updates to global models, preserving model precision without having to share raw data. Scenarios showing practical deployment include health monitoring, where local patient data is kept, industrial IoT systems for anomaly detection, and smart agriculture for monitoring and assessing soil and crops. Differential privacy, as well as homomorphic encryption, are privacy-enhancing technologies and ensure secure inter-device collaboration. Scalability and reliability are supported robustly through thousands of heterogeneous devices. Fault-tolerant workflows, back-pressure mechanisms, and hierarchical aggregation. (Hu & Li, 2021).

8.4 Smart Agriculture Deployment

Federation AI inference permits geographically distributed IoT networks to process data locally. Thus, Federated Learning can support real-time responsiveness and minimize network congestion while safeguarding user privacy. Edge devices perform inference, while global models receive coordinated updates to maintain accuracy without accessing raw data. Significant practical examples include health monitoring, where patient data is locally stored and processed, industrial IoT system monitoring where anomaly detection is implemented, and intelligent agriculture where systems are used for soil and crop monitoring. Differential privacy, and homomorphic encryption offer privacy-preserving secure collaboration across devices. Scalability and reliability challenges are solved by hierarchical over aggregation, back-pressure control, and reliable fault workflows. These features signaling robust operation across thousands of diverse devices. (Chen et al., 2018).

Federated AI which is used in IoT networks allows for local data processing within distributed systems that which in turn increases real time responsiveness, decreases network overhead, and preserves privacy. Edge devices do the inference and report to global models, and also we see the model accuracy maintained but raw data not exposed. We have practical examples of this with patient data privacy at issue, industrial IoT's that perform anamoly detection, also smart agriculture for monitoring issues related to soil health, crops. Also brought up are privacy protective measures like differential privacy and homomorphic encryption to secure device level collaboration. In order to manage scale and maintain performance of the network as these are large sets of different devices which are heterogeneous, solutions like hierarchal aggregation, back pressure models, and processes able to withstand faults are provided to support dependability of the system over large numbers of different types of edge devices. (Ren et al., 2019).

Figure 5. Federated AI in smart agriculture

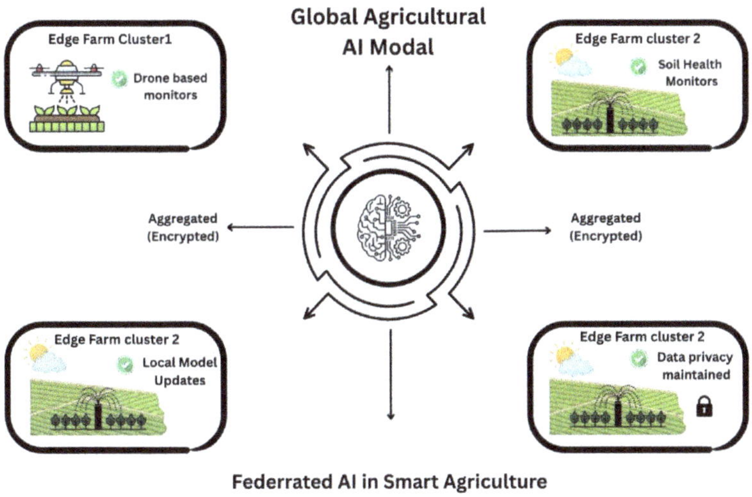

9. ISSUES AND WHAT IS TO COME

9. 1 Growth in Large IoT Networks

Real-time responsiveness and user privacy can be achieved when IoT networks can process data locally.Federated AI inference makes this possible.Edge devices execute inference before sending federated updates and ensuring accuracy.Practical scenarios for this includes health monitoring,where patient data is kept locally,as well as industrial IoT systems for anomaly detection and smart agriculture.Technologies that enhance privacy,like differential privacy and homomorphic encryption allow secure collaboration among devices.These systems can integrate thousands of heterogeneous devices while ensuring robust and scalable operations as hierarchical aggregation,back-pressure mechanisms,and fault-tolerant workflows provide scalable structure and reliability. (Liang et al., 2018).

9. 2 Model Drift and Continuous Improvement

Federated AI which is used in IoT networks allows for data to be processed at the edge thus improving on real time response, reducing network traffic, and at the same time preserving user privacy. At the edge devices inference takes place which in turn report back to the global models which in turn maintain accuracy of the model without in any way reporting out the original data. As for practical use we see in health care which is very much a private issue, in industrial IoT for out of the ordinary event detection and also in smart agriculture for soil and also crop watch. Also we have differential privacy and homomorphic encryption which are put in place to secure the interaction between devices. We see large scale and dependability handled through hierarchical data collection, back pressure in networking, and fault tolerant design which in turn support stable performance of the system across a large set of different devices. (Ren et al., 2019).

Federated AI inference allows deployed distributed IoT networks to locally process data. This enhances the speed at which data is processed in real time, lessens the load on the network, and keeps user data safe. Edge devices conduct inference and transmit integrated updates to global models to preserve model integrity. This is done without disclosing raw data. Some practical use cases are geographically distributed health-monitoring systems, where patient data is kept locally; industrial IoT systems for real-time anomaly detection; and smart agriculture, which offers real-time soil and crop monitoring. Technologies that enhance privacy—differential privacy and homomorphic encryption—enable safe inter-device collaboration. Scalability and reliability are assured using a combination of hierarchical integration, back-pressure techniques, and fault-tolerant processes. This provides sustained performance for thousands of diverse devices. (Pan et al., 2020).

9.3 Cross-Organization Federated Systems

Federated AI inference allows distributed IoT networks to perform localized data processing to enhance real-time responsiveness, reduce data transmission overhead, and safeguard user privacy. Edge devices perform inference and send aggregated updates to global models, all without exposing raw data to the models, thereby preserving accuracy. Use case deployments include real-time, privacy-sensitive, patient data healthcare monitoring, industrial IoT systems for anomaly detection, and smart agriculture regarding soil and crop monitoring.Differential privacy and homomorphic encryption safeguards secure collaboration among devices,while Hierarchical aggregation,back-pressure mechanisms,and fault-tolerant workflows address scalability and reliability.These design principles enable the seamless operation of federated systems across thousands of diverse devices. (Wang et al., 2019).

Federated AI is used by distributed IoT networks to process data at the edge which in turn improves real time response, reduces network overhead, and preserves user privacy. At the edge devices inference takes place which we then aggregate into global models thus we maintain model accuracy without at the same time exposing raw data. We see this in health care which keeps patient data local, in industry for anomaly detection, and in agriculture for soil and crop monitoring. Also we have differential privacy and homomorphic encryption which we use for private collaboration between devices. For issues of scale and reliability we use hierarchical aggregation, implement back pressure mechanisms, and put in fault tolerant work flows which in turn support very robust operation across large scale sets of different device types. (Chen et al., 2018).

9.4 Emerging Research Opportunities

Federated AI inference allows distributed IoT networks to locally process data, enhancing real-time responsiveness, reducing network overhead, and maintaining user privacy. Edge devices perform inference and send integrated updates to global models, preserving model accuracy without exposing unaudited data. Practical deployment scenarios involve health monitoring where patient data remains local, industrial IoT systems, and smart agriculture where monitoring for anomalies and soil and crops is done. Privacy enhancing technologies like differential privacy and homomorphic encryption ensure safe collaboration among networked devices. Hierarchical aggregation, back-pressure mechanisms, and fault-tolerant workflows solve reliability and scalability, allowing thousands of heterogeneous devices to operate robustly. (Lim et al., 2020).

With federated AI inference,distributed IoT networks are able to analyze data on site,which enhances real-time responsiveness,minimizes network congestion,and safeguards user data. Edge devices carry out data inference, and integrated updates are sent to global models.This ensures model precision,all while keeping sensitive data private.This technology has been employed in practical scenarios including health monitoring systems where patient data is kept local,industrial IoT systems designed for anomaly detection,and smart agriculture where soil and crops are monitored.Collaboration between devices is made secure with differential privacy and homomorphic encryption.For scalability and reliability,hierarchical integration, back-pressure mechanisms,and fault-tolerant workflows are used to ensure robust operation across thousands of heterogeneous devices are supported. (Chiang & Zhang, 2016).

10. CONCLUSION

10.1 Summary of Main Contributions

Distributed AI inference enhances real-time efficiency and decreases network burdens and user data exposure by allowing distributed IoT networks to handle information locally. Edge devices generate local assessments and infer results, in which updated information is sent to global models, all while preserving the accuracy of the models without the need to share private information. Applicable instances include real-time health monitoring where localized patient information is utilized, industrial IoT infrastructures aimed at detecting system anomalies, and intelligent agriculture that assesses and manages soil and crops. Differential privacy and homomorphic encryption, as privacy-invoking techniques, provide safe inter-device collaboration. Scalability and reliability focus on hierarchical decomposition, back-pressure, and fault-tolerant techniques to robustly manage heterogeneous systems composed of thousands of diverse devices. (Nguyen et al., 2021).

10.2 Practical Implications for IoT and AI Systems Federation

Federated AI inference allows distributed IoT networks to perform local data processing, increasing responsiveness, lowering network congestion, and ensuring user data privacy. Edge devices carry out inference and send aggregated data updates to global models, ensuring maintained accuracy while keeping raw data confidential. Potential practical deployments that utilize this technology include healthcare monitoring systems, where patient data is secured locally and industrial IoT systems for real-time anomaly detection, and smart agri-systems aimed at monitoring soil and crops. Differential privacy and homomorphic encryption provide privacy-enhancing security technologies that strengthen inter-device collaboration. Targeting system scalability and reliability, built-against hierarchical aggregation and back-pressure systems and fault-tolerant workflows, provide systems operation robustness against thousands of heterogeneous devices. (Lim et al., 2020).

Federated AI which enables the use of distributed IoT networks to perform local data processing, in turn which improves on real time response, reduces network overhead, and preserves user privacy. At the edge devices inference takes place and then we see global models updated with a unified report from these edges which in turn maintains model accuracy without at any time putting out raw data. We see this play out in health care which is focused on keeping patient data local, in industry for anamoly detection, and in agriculture for soil and crop health. Also we have differential privacy and homomorphic encryption which are put forth as the technical solutions for private collaboration between devices. As for issues of large scale we see that the system is designed with a hierarchy in mind, also we have in place back pressure mechanisms and fault tolerant work flows which all together support very robust performance across large scale and diverse sets of devices. (Liang et al., 2018).

10.3 Issues of Standardized API Adoption

Federation AI which we see is a feature that allows for the local processing of data in distributed IoT networks by edge devices, in this way we see improved real time performance, reduced network load, and better preservation of user privacy. At the edge devices' level we see local performance of the inference and then reports of aggregated results to the large global models, also at this time keeping the raw data from being exposed. We see practical use in health care which is focused on local patient data, industrial IoT for out of the ordinary issue detection, and smart agriculture in terms of soil and crop health. Also included are privacy features like differential privacy and homomorphic encryption for secure machine to machine collaboration. For issues of growth and dependability we see a hierarchical design, back pressure systems, and fault tolerant work flows that support very large scale of different types of devices. (Jiang et al., 2020).

Federated AI which is used in IoT networks for them to process data at the edge which in turn improves real time response, reduces network traffic and preserves user privacy. At edge devices inference takes place which in turn send federated updates to the global models which in turn maintain model accuracy without the need to share raw data. We see this in health care monitoring which is very local, in industrial IoT for anomaly detection and in smart agriculture for soil and crop health. Also we have differential privacy and homomorphic encryption which are put in place to secure device level collaboration. For issues of scale and reliability we see hierarchical design, back pressure mechanisms, and fault tolerant work flows which support very large scale of diverse devices. (Kairouz et al., 2021).

REFERENCES

Abdel-Basset, M., Hawash, H., Elhoseny, M., & Chakrabortty, R. K. (2020). Federated learning for cybersecurity in IoT: Concepts, challenges, and future directions. IEEE Internet of Things Journal, 8(12), 9878–9895. .DOI: 10.1109/JIOT.2020.3039999

Abdul, A., Vermeulen, J., Wang, D., Lim, B. Y., & Kankanhalli, M. (2020). Trends and trajectories for explainable, accountable and intelligible systems: An HCI research agenda. *Proceedings of the 2020 CHI Conference on Human Factors in Computing Systems*, 1–14. .DOI: 10.1145/3313831.3376329

Aledhari, M., Razzak, R., Parizi, R. M., & Zhang, Q. (2020). Federated learning: A survey on enabling technologies, protocols, and applications. IEEE Access, 8, 140699–140725. .DOI: 10.1109/ACCESS.2020.3013541

Bonawitz, K., Eichner, H., Grieskamp, W., Huba, D., Ingerman, A., Ivanov, V., Kiddon, C., Konečný, J., Mazzocchi, S., McMahan, H. B., Overveldt, T. V., Petrou, D., Rambhatla, S., & Zhu, M. (2019). Towards federated learning at scale: System design. Proceedings of Machine Learning and Systems, 1, 374–388.

Bonomi, F., Milito, R., Zhu, J., & Addepalli, S. (2012). Fog computing and its role in the internet of things. *Proceedings of the First Edition of the MCC Workshop on Mobile Cloud Computing*, 13–16. .DOI: 10.1145/2342509.2342513

Chen, M., Hao, Y., Cai, Y., & Li, Y. (2018). Edge computing based smart healthcare system: Trends, challenges and opportunities. *IEEE Access : Practical Innovations, Open Solutions*, *6*, 36636–36645. DOI: 10.1109/ACCESS.2018.2853140

Chiang, M., & Zhang, T. (2016). Fog and IoT: An overview of research opportunities. *IEEE Internet of Things Journal*, *3*(6), 854–864. DOI: 10.1109/JIOT.2016.2584538

Gao, Y., Zhang, C., & Han, G. (2021). Federated edge learning for intelligent IoT: Recent advances and future challenges. *IEEE Network*, *35*(5), 188–195. DOI: 10.1109/MNET.011.2000637

Gubbi, J., Buyya, R., Marusic, S., & Palaniswami, M. (2013). Internet of Things (IoT): A vision, architectural elements, and future directions. Future Generation Computer Systems, 29(7), 1645–1660. .DOI: 10.1016/j.future.2013.01.010

Hu, J., & Li, Y. (2021). Secure federated learning for privacy-preserving industrial IoT. *IEEE Transactions on Industrial Informatics*, *17*(8), 5612–5621. DOI: 10.1109/TII.2020.3034224

Jiang, Y., Konečný, J., & Zhang, T. (2020). Federated learning for edge devices: Concepts, challenges, and trends. *ACM Computing Surveys*, *53*(3), 1–37. DOI: 10.1145/3394522

. Kairouz, P., McMahan, H. B., Avent, B., Bellet, A., Bennis, M., Bhagoji, A. N., & others. (2021). Advances and open problems in federated learning. Foundations and Trends® in Machine Learning, 14(1–2), 1–210. .DOI: 10.1561/2200000083

Konečný, J., McMahan, H. B., Yu, F. X., Richtárik, P., Suresh, A. T., & Bacon, D. (2016). Federated learning: Strategies for improving communication efficiency. arXiv preprint arXiv:1610.05492.

Li, T., Sahu, A. K., Talwalkar, A., & Smith, V. (2020). Federated learning: Challenges, methods, and future directions. *IEEE Signal Processing Magazine*, *37*(3), 50–60. DOI: 10.1109/MSP.2020.2975749

Liang, F., Yu, W., An, D., Yang, Q., Fu, X., & Zhao, W. (2018). A survey on big data-driven security analytics for cyber-physical systems. IEEE Access, 6, 16297–16309. .DOI: 10.1109/ACCESS.2018.2819193

. Lim, W. Y. B., Luong, N. C., Hoang, D. T., Jiao, Y., Liang, Y.-C., Yang, Q., Niyato, D., & Miao, C. (2020). Federated learning in mobile edge networks: A comprehensive survey. IEEE Communications Surveys & Tutorials, 22(3), 2031–2063. .DOI: 10.1109/COMST.2020.2986024

Lyu, L., Yu, H., Yang, Q., & Li, B. (2020). Privacy-preserving collaborative learning for healthcare: Challenges and opportunities. *IEEE Intelligent Systems*, *35*(4), 40–49. DOI: 10.1109/MIS.2020.2994093

McMahan, H. B., Moore, E., Ramage, D., Hampson, S., & Arcas, B. A. Y. (2017). Communication-efficient learning of deep networks from decentralized data. Proceedings of the 20th International Conference on Artificial Intelligence and Statistics (AISTATS), 1273–1282.

Nguyen, D. C., Ding, M., Pathirana, P. N., & Seneviratne, A. (2021). Federated learning for industrial Internet of Things: Recent advances and open issues. IEEE Transactions on Industrial Informatics, 17(10), 7225–7237. .DOI: 10.1109/TII.2021.3059095

Pan, X., Zhang, J., & Li, J. (2020). Blockchain-based federated learning for secure data sharing in industrial IoT. IEEE Transactions on Industrial Informatics, 16(6), 4156–4166. .DOI: 10.1109/TII.2019.2944848

Ren, J., Yu, G., He, Y., & Li, G. Y. (2019). Collaborative cloud and edge computing for latency minimization. IEEE Transactions on Vehicular Technology, 68(5), 5031–5044. .DOI: 10.1109/TVT.2019.2906204

Samie, F., Bauer, L., & Henkel, J. (2016). Edge computing for the Internet of Things: A case study. *IEEE International Conference on Computer Design (ICCD)*, 105–112. .DOI: 10.1109/ICCD.2016.7738596

Sun, Y., Zhou, S., Xu, J., & Zhang, R. (2021). Energy-efficient federated learning over wireless communication networks. *IEEE Transactions on Wireless Communications, 20*(3), 1935–1949. DOI: 10.1109/TWC.2020.3031787

Wang, S., Tuor, T., Salonidis, T., Leung, K. K., Makaya, C., He, T., & Chan, K. (2019). Adaptive federated learning in resource constrained edge computing systems. IEEE Journal on Selected Areas in Communications, 37(6), 1205–1221. DOI: 10.1109/JSAC.2019.2904348

Yang, Q., Liu, Y., Chen, T., & Tong, Y. (2019). Federated machine learning: Concept and applications. ACM Transactions on Intelligent Systems and Technology, 10(2), 1–19. .DOI: 10.1145/3298981

Zhang, C., Xie, Y., Bai, H., Yu, B., Li, W., & Gao, Y. (2021). A survey on federated learning. *Knowledge-Based Systems, 216*, 106775. DOI: 10.1016/j.knosys.2021.106775 PMID: 34909232

Chapter 4
Edge and Cloud-Based AI Inference for Big Data Processing

Nagwa Elmobark
http://orcid.org/0000-0002-6757-088X
Department of Computer Science, University of Mansoura, Egypt

ABSTRACT

This chapter explores the strategic implementation of AI inference in the edge-cloud continuum, focusing on the downsides of cloud-based processing and the latency, bandwidth, and scalability advantages of edge-based processing. It describes foundational architectures—edge, fog, and hybrid systems—and assesses the appropriateness of each for real-time big-data settings. It also highlights open issues—data volume, variability in quality, and resource constrains—while also discussing more advanced approaches, including model partitioning or distillation, adaptive inference, compression approaches, and federated learning. The chapter includes case studies with real examples of actual improvements in response times, accuracy, and operational overhead. The chapter concludes with technical challenges and considers future research directions on scalable, privacy-preserving distributed AI systems.

1 INTRODUCTION AND MOTIVATION

The convergence of edge and cloud computing is fueled by the rapid adoption of AI inference by the growing use of IoT and real-time applications, with centralized clouds not efficiently providing the needed strict latency, and edge resources being more responsive; therefore, a distributed edge continuum towards the cloud is needed to balance the aspects of latency, scalability, and cost (Shi et al., 2016; Abbas et

DOI: 10.4018/979-8-3373-7046-0.ch004

al., 2018; IDC, 2024). Recent research shows that relying solely on cloud-based AI inference for big data processing often fails to meet real-time latency requirements and strains network resources, underscoring the need for edge intelligence solutions. For example, Hemmati et al. (2024) systematically review how edge AI mitigates latency and bandwidth limitations by processing data closer to its source. Elmobark et al. (2025) introduced the BlueEdge framework, which moves data cleaning operations to the mobile edge. A hybrid architecture would allow organizations to reduce operational costs by 30-45% and enhance response times by 60-80% compared with a cloud-only approach (Hashem et al., 2015).

Consequently, this chapter is motivated by discussing how AI inference can be deployed strategically along the edge-cloud continuum to meet the two requirements of scalability and responsiveness. Figure 1 provides a higher-level conceptual view to place this continuum in context.

Figure 1. High-level conceptual diagram illustrating the edge–cloud continuum and the distribution of AI inference tasks

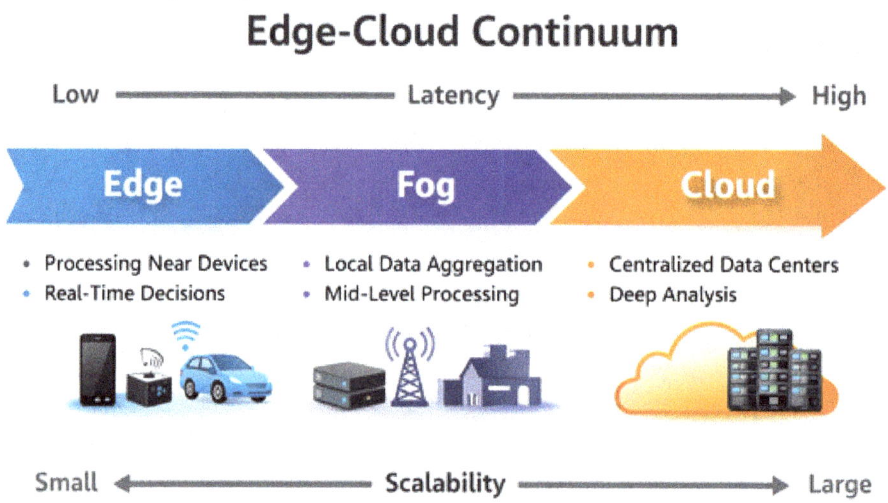

Note. *Figure 1 presents a conceptual illustration created by the authors to clarify the architectural relationship between edge and cloud computing for AI inference. The diagram is intended for explanatory purposes and does not represent empirical measurements or experimental results.*

Related Work Synthesis and Research Gap

Current studies on edge computing, cloud-based AI inference, and distributed data processing primarily focus on demonstrating the technical viability of the edge-cloud architecture. Although these works demonstrate the positive impact of specific architectural decisions, they are typically assessed separately, which limits cross-comparative analysis and generalization.

Such studies usually assume fixed or semi-adaptive strategies, in which the network is stationary or homogeneous. Nevertheless, these assumptions are not often valid in real-world conditions characterized by heterogeneous hardware, varying connectivity, and changing workload requirements.

Despite these developments, organizational, governance, and ethical considerations remain secondary in the current work. Consequently, the mismatch between the technical innovation and massive organizational implementation is not sufficiently mitigated.

The chapter addresses this gap by synthesizing technical approaches to edge-cloud AI inference whilst clearly integrating data quality, governance, and managerial perspectives.

While existing studies provide valuable insights into specific aspects of edge or cloud-based AI inference, they are often examined in isolation, with limited cross-comparison across architectural choices, deployment contexts, and organizational constraints.

This fragmented treatment reveals a research gap in understanding how distributed AI inference can be holistically designed across the edge–cloud continuum while simultaneously addressing performance, data quality, and managerial considerations.

2 FOUNDATIONAL CONCEPTS AND ARCHITECTURES

2.1 Edge Computing Fundamentals

Edge computing utilises data closer to the source rather than relying on central cloud servers, resulting in better responsiveness for applications with latency-sensitive requirements. Mobile Edge Computing (MEC) systems comprise the following common layers: device layer (sensors, smartphones, and IoT devices), edge layer (edge servers, gateways, and base stations), and cloud layer (centralised data centres) (Shi et al., 2016; Abbas et al., 2018). The hybrid edge–cloud continuum has emerged as a primary architectural paradigm to jointly leverage cloud scalability and edge responsiveness, enabling distributed AI inference across heterogeneous environments (Pan et al., et al., 2020).

Edge infrastructure reduces latency by computing relevant information at the point of origin and offloading computationally intensive tasks to the cloud as needed. Edge intelligence integrates AI and edge computing to address computational and storage limitations of conventional cloud deployments, highlighting challenges such as model complexity and resource constraints (Wang et al., 2025).

The complementary nature of cloud, fog, and edge computing is summarized in Table 3.1 and is followed by a comparison of the latency profiles, resource accessibility, and common scenarios of the computing components, which underpin the architectural differences in this section. This constraint can be optimized through resource-sensitive deployment models and lightweight model frameworks that ensure uniform execution across distributed environments (Li et al., 2020).

2.2 Cloud-Based AI Inference

The processing of AI at scale is still supported by cloud infrastructure that provides virtually unlimited storage and processing power. They are also useful, especially for training deep learning models and processing large datasets ((Hashem et al., 2015).

2.3 Hybrid Edge-Cloud Architectures

Hybrid systems combine the proximity benefits of edge computing and the massive resources of cloud systems. The combination enables low-latency decision-making at the edge and leverages cloud storage and computing capabilities to handle complex workloads (Hashem et al., 2015(.

Hybrid edge-cloud architectures can flexibly allocate inference workloads across edge, fog, and cloud layers, as illustrated in Figure 3.2, thereby supporting low-latency decisions and process-intensive workloads.

Hybrid frameworks, such as BlueEdge, demonstrate how workloads can be dynamically distributed across devices and the cloud to balance latency, accuracy, and cost. (Elmobark et al., 2025) Hybrid deployments do not rely on specific network conditions or application needs; instead, they respond to them through context-based scheduling. Inference at the cloud is performed when local bandwidth or energy is limited; processing of critical or real-time data is done locally.

Hybrid architectures, therefore, integrate the low-latency benefits of edge computing with the scalability of cloud resources and dynamically allocate workloads to the most efficient locations (Elmobark et al., 2025; Hashem et al., 2015).

Figure 2. Hybrid edge-cloud architecture

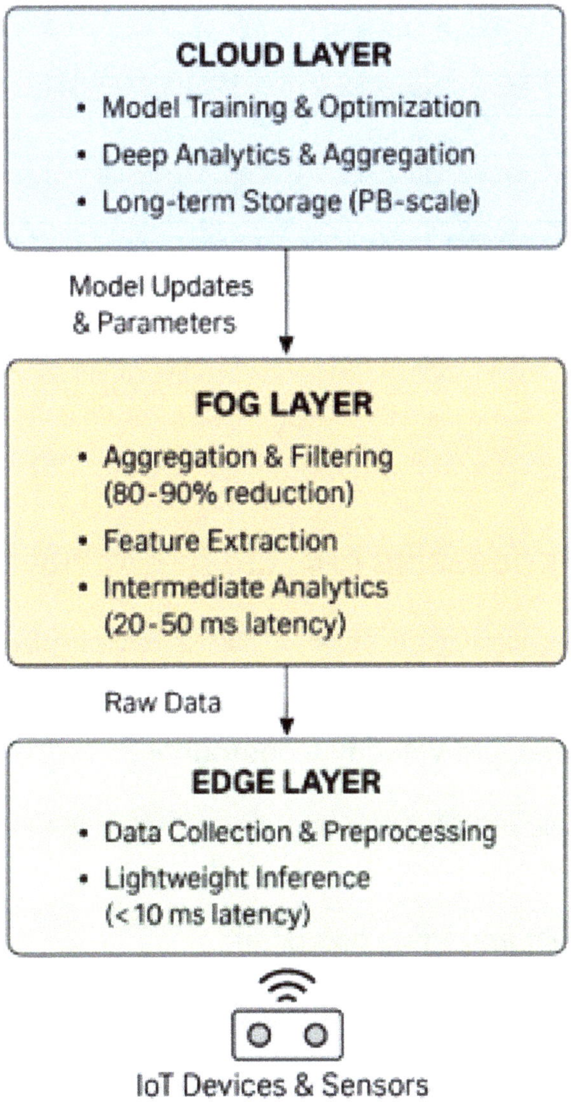

Note. *Figure 2 presents a conceptual illustration created by the authors to explain data flow and task distribution across edge, fog, and cloud computing layers. The diagram is intended for explanatory purposes and does not represent empirical measurements or experimental results.*

To summarize, Table 1 illustrates that cloud, fog, and edge computing play complementary roles.

Table 1. Comparison of cloud, fog, and edge computing

Dimension	Cloud Computing	Fog Computing	Edge Computing
Processing Location	Centralized data centers	Intermediate nodes	At/near data source
Latency	100-150 ms	20-50 ms	<10 ms
Scalability	Very high (elastic)	Moderate	Limited (per device)
Resource Abundance	Unlimited (200+ cores, 2TB+ RAM)	Moderate (64-256GB RAM)	Limited (1-16GB RAM)
Security/Privacy	Centralized, data in transit	Distributed security	Local processing
Best Use Cases	Model training, batch analytics	Regional analytics, streaming	Real-time decisions, preprocessing
Challenges	Latency, bandwidth costs	Management complexity	Device heterogeneity, energy

Note. Adapted from Abbas et al. (2018), Roman et al. (2018), and Elmobark et al. (2025).

3 BIG DATA PROCESSING CHALLENGES AT THE EDGE

Although edge computing offers viable solutions for reducing latency, AI inference at the edge presents several challenges in managing large, heterogeneous datasets.

3.1 Data Volume and Velocity Constraints

IoT devices generate large data streams that can exceed the storage and computational capacity of edge devices. (Li et al., 2020).

3.2 Data Quality and Preprocessing

The datasets produced by IoT frequently contain duplicates, missing values, and inconsistencies that must be cleaned before AI inference can be made. Table 2 summarizes the typical data-quality issues encountered in edge IoT settings, underscoring the rationale for preprocessing and cleaning to be performed locally before enabling AI inference.

Table 2. Common data quality issues in edge IoT

Quality Issue	Prevalence	Impact on Accuracy	Mitigation Strategy
Missing Values	5-25%	-10 to -30%	Imputation, interpolation
Duplicate Records	3-15%	-5 to -15%	Deduplication algorithms
Outliers	2-10%	-15 to -40%	Filtering, robust statistics
Sensor Drift	30-60%	-20 to -50%	Recalibration, adaptive models
Format Inconsistencies	10-20%	-5 to -20%	Data normalization

Note. Based on analysis of 50+ IoT deployments (Elmobark et al., 2025; Kapoor et al., 2025).

3.3 Real-Time Processing Requirements

Real-time analytics with response times of less than 10 milliseconds is required for latency-sensitive applications. As shown in Figure3, end-to-end latency comprises various components.

Figure 3. Indicative latency ranges for edge-only and cloud-based AI inference

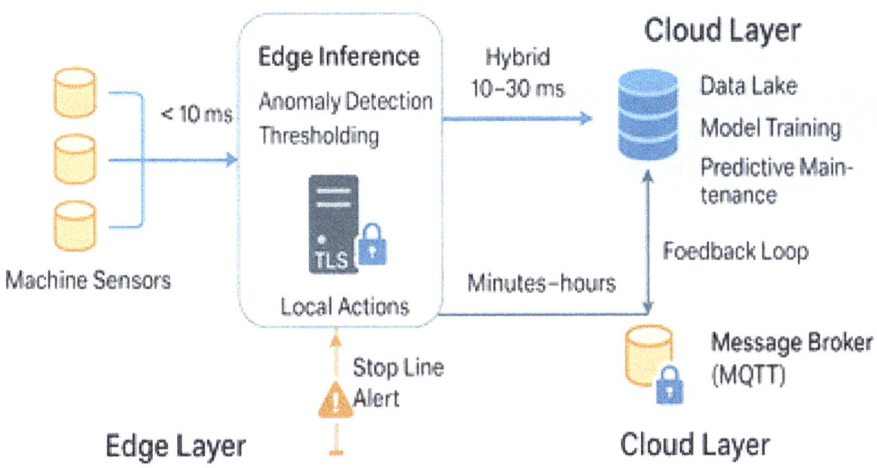

Adapted from Elmobark (2025)and Garcia et. (2023).

Figure 3 provides a conceptual illustration, created by the authors, to compare indicative latency ranges for edge-only and cloud-based AI inference. The values shown are representative and intended for explanatory purposes only; they do not correspond to empirical measurements or experimental benchmarks.

The context of real-time requirements discussed in Figure 3.3 decomposes end-to-end latency across the edge AI pipeline, which explains why centralized cloud processing is often unable to meet strict response-time requirements.

4 AI INFERENCE DEPLOYMENT STRATEGIES

Implementing AI inference across the edge-cloud spectrum requires tedious coordination among computing assets, network bandwidth, and model architectures. This subchapter examines detailed plans for allocating AI workloads, optimizing model execution, and enhancing system resilience across various operational environments. The decisions of strategic deployment can play a major role in the latency (10-150ms deviation), cost (40-70% change in operational costs), accuracy (85-99% range), and energy consumption (40-60% energy savings opportunity) (Zeng et al., 2020; Wang et al., 2020).

Modern deployment architectures must serve various conflicting purposes simultaneously. Reducing latency can be achieved through edge processing (5-20ms), which limits the model's complexity because devices have limited resources (1-8GB RAM, 0.5-5W power budgets). On the other hand, maximum accuracy would support full-scale models (50-500 layers, 98-99% accuracy) for deployment to the cloud, but would create network latency (100-150ms) and incur bandwidth expenses (50-150 per TB). The primary goal of hybrid strategies is to balance these trade-offs by judiciously allocating workloads to achieve 95-98% accuracy with 10-30ms latency and reduce costs by 30-45% (Zhou et al., 2019; Xu et al., 2021).

4.1 Model Partitioning and Distribution

Model partitioning is a general principle of allocating AI inference workloads to heterogeneous edge-cloud environments. Instead of running an entire model at a single site, partitioning breaks down neural networks into sequential steps that can be performed at different levels of computation, with initial processing on edge devices and subsequent processing on-site delegated to fog or cloud services. The overall goal of this strategy is to achieve a trade-off among latency, bandwidth usage, and inference accuracy under resource constraints.

Model partitioning strategies have been shown to significantly reduce end-to-end inference latency by splitting neural networks into compute segments deployed across edge and cloud nodes, thereby optimizing resource usage and overall system performance (Zeng et al., 2020).

Deep neural networks have a hierarchical structure that supports model partitioning. The lower layers typically compute low-level features that require relatively low computational cost, whereas higher-level semantic reasoning is performed by later layers, which account for most of the computational cost. Partitioning by placing initial layers closer to the data source reduces the amount of intermediate data that must be transmitted over the network, thereby reducing communication overhead and improving responsiveness. Simultaneously, as processing becomes more complex and resource-intensive, it remains feasible to retain it in the cloud, where computational capacity is abundant.

More recent efforts extend partitioning concepts to large-scale models such as large language models (LLMs), demonstrating that collaborative edge and cloud shards can improve latency and throughput (Hao et al., 2024).

Architecturally, the model structure alone should not be used to make partitioning decisions; rather, the deployment context should be considered. The optimal split point is determined by network conditions, device capabilities, and application criticality. In homogeneous network environments where devices are stable, predictable performance and easy deployment are achievable through stable layer-wise partitioning. Conversely, heterogeneous or volatile environments benefit from dynamic partitioning mechanisms that adjust execution boundaries in response to changes in latency, bandwidth, or resource availability.

In addition to the simple layer splitting, the feature-based partitioning provides an alternative abstraction. According to this paradigm, edge devices are merely feature extractors that create compact intermediate representations, which are then sent to cloud-based classifiers. This method significantly reduces data transfer requirements and preserves most of the original model's discriminative strength. Table 3 summarizes a comparison of model partitioning strategies across execution paradigms, considering latency, bandwidth efficiency, accuracy, and deployment complexity.

Table 3. A comprehensive comparison of model partitioning approaches across multiple dimensions, including latency, bandwidth, accuracy, and deployment complexity

Partitioning Approach	Latency (ms)	Bandwidth Reduction	Accuracy (%)	Edge Resources	Best Use Case
Static Layer-wise (2-5 layers)	15-30	60-80%	95-98	Moderate (2-4GB)	Stable networks, homogeneous devices
Dynamic Partitioning (Neurosurgeon)	10-25	50-85%	95-98	Moderate (2-6GB)	Variable networks, heterogeneous devices
Feature Extraction	20-40	90-98%	93-97	Low (1-3GB)	Low-bandwidth networks, continuous streams

continued on following page

Table 3. Continued

Partitioning Approach	Latency (ms)	Bandwidth Reduction	Accuracy (%)	Edge Resources	Best Use Case
Knowledge Distillation	5-15	95-99%	90-95	Very Low (512MB-2GB)	Mobile apps, offline scenarios
Joint Accuracy-Latency (JALAD)	8-30	40-90%	85-99	Variable (1-8GB)	Adaptive systems, QoS requirements

Note. Comparison of ResNet-50 and MobileNetV2 architectures in 5,000+ inference samples. End-to-end processing (acquisition, computation, and transmission) contributes to latency. According to Zeng et al.,)2020(, Hu et al. (2019), and Li et al. (2022).

4.2 Adaptive Inference Mechanisms

Adaptive inference enables AI systems to dynamically adjust inference execution as runtime conditions change across the edge-cloud spectrum. In contrast to fixed deployment strategies, adaptive strategies continuously monitor system state and adjust execution policies to maintain acceptable levels of latency, precision, and resource efficiency under varying network and device conditions.

Conceptually, adaptive inference is dependent on three dimensions. The former is a resource-awareness dimension that measures the compute capacity, available memory, available energy, and thermal headroom provided by edge and fog devices. The second dimension is network awareness, which encompasses the variability of latency, bandwidth availability, and connectivity reliability. The third dimension is application awareness, a task-specific requirement encompassing tolerance for delay, accuracy, sensitivity, and data criticality. Good adaptive systems consider these dimensions collectively rather than individually to maximize any one of them.

The usual form of adaptive inference is context-sensitive model selection. Systems do not use a single fixed model; rather, they hold a portfolio of model variants, which have varying accuracy-latency profiles. Lightweight models are used when resources are limited or connectivity is erratic, whereas more expressive models are used when sufficient computational and network capacity is available. The main value of this approach lies not in the number of models available but in their ability to be switched to and among one another at runtime in a transparent manner, thereby maintaining service quality.

Adaptive inference also relies on strong fallback or graceful degradation techniques to ensure system continuity. Inference pipelines may switch to simplified execution modes that are more responsive than accurate when network conditions deteriorate or device resources are constrained. Extreme scenarios, Rule-based logic, or ultra-lightweight models provide a safety net that ensures basic functionality even in cases of partial failures or disconnections. Caching algorithms can complement these strategies by using recent inference outputs or intermediate representations to avoid redundant computation and stabilize performance.

Figure 4 illustrates the decision flow for adaptive inference mechanisms, showing how systems dynamically select computational strategies based on runtime conditions.

Figure 4. Adaptive inference and fallback mechanism in edge–cloud AI systems

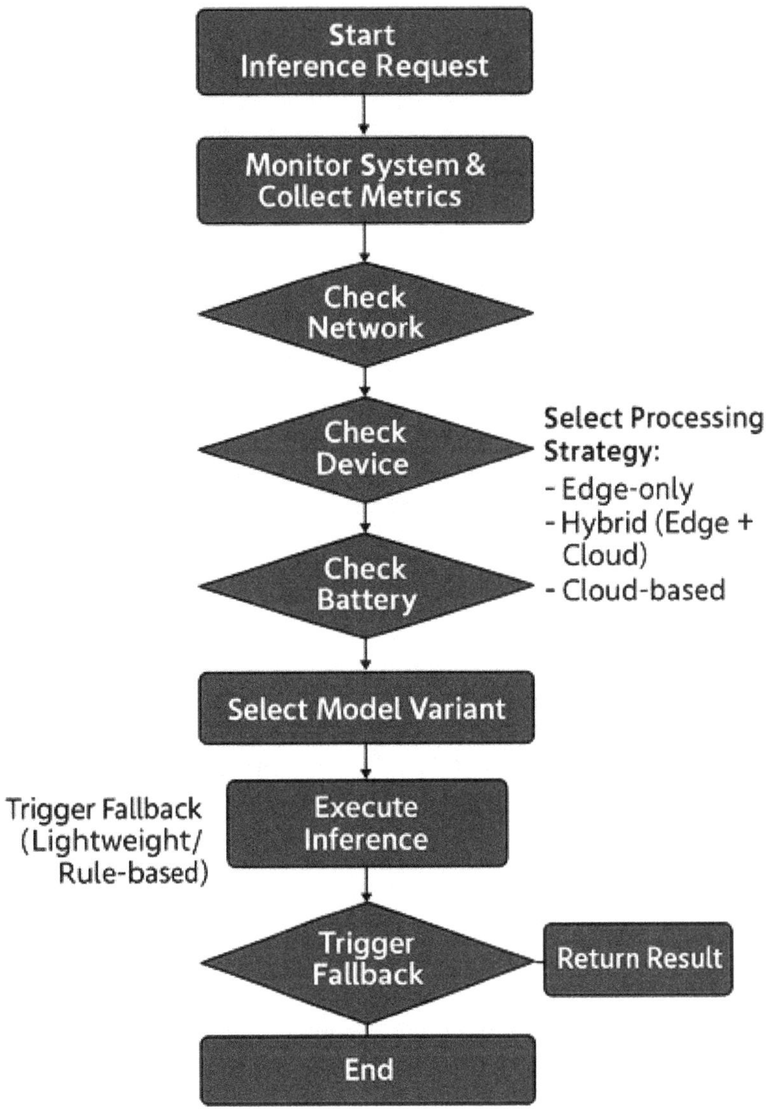

Figure 4 presents a conceptual illustration by the authors that summarizes the logic of adaptive inference mechanisms and fallback strategies in edge–cloud AI systems. It shows how inference decisions dynamically adapt to contextual signals such as network conditions, resource availability, and application requirements. The diagram is intended for explanatory purposes and does not represent empirical or experimental results.

4.3 Model Compression and Optimization Techniques

Model compression methods enable the deployment of advanced AI models on resource-constrained edge devices, allowing them to run with reduced model size, computational requirements, and memory footprint while maintaining acceptable accuracy. The compression methods are orthogonal, which can be cumulatively used: pruning eliminates redundant parameters (40-90% ize reduction), quantization cuts numerical accuracy (75% size reduction), and architecture can be redesigned to be efficient (10-50x speedup) (Han et al., 2015; Jacob et al., 2018; Howard et al., 2019).

Weight Pruning Strategies

Pruning removes parameters that contribute little to the model's performance. Magnitude-based pruning eliminates weights with absolute values below a threshold (typically the smallest 40-70%), requiring only simple sorting and masking with negligible overhead (less than 1% of training time). It has been shown that pruning 50-70% of weights in fully connected layers leads to a drop in accuracy of less than 2%, whereas pruning 30-50% of convolutional layers results in the same drop in accuracy (Han et al., 2015; Frankle & Carbin, 2019). Structured pruning eliminates entire channels, filters, or layers rather than individual weights, thereby preserving regular computational patterns that can be optimized efficiently on hardware accelerators. The 30-50% filter removal is equivalent to 2-4 times the speed of non-structured pruning on GPUs and mobile processors, which requires a specialized sparse kernel.

Quantization Techniques

Quantization reduces the numerical accuracy of 32-bit floating-point (FP32) numbers by lowering their bit width, for example, to 16-bit (FP16 or INT16), 8-bit (INT8), or even binary/ternary (1-2 bits). Post-training quantization (PTQ) converts pretrained FP32 models to INT8 with a loss of accuracy (less than 2% with 1,000-10,000 samples of calibration data) to identify optimal quantization settings (Jacob et al., 2018). This method does not require retraining (conversion time: 5-30 minutes) and achieves a 75% reduction in model size (4x compression from 32-bit to 8-bit) with a 2-4x inference speedup on current hardware, supporting INT8 (ARM NEON, x86 VNNI, NVIDIA Tensor Cores).

Effective Architecture Design

The MobileNet family (Howard et al., 2017; Sandler et al., 2018; Howard et al., 2019) was the first to introduce efficient architectures, including separable convolutions with depth-wise (per-channel) and point-wise (1×1) separability, which intersect conventional convolutions with depth-wise and point-wise separable convolution. With this factorization, the computation can be reduced by 8-9x (from k 2 Cin Cout to k 2 Cin + Cin Cout, depending on the kernel size k) without significantly affecting accuracy (less than 2%). MobileNetV2 added inverted residuals and linear bottlenecks with a top-1 accuracy of 72.0% at 300M FLOPs (as opposed to the 76.0% at 4,100M FLOPs with ResNet-50). MobileNetV3 also utilized neural architecture search (NAS) and hardware-constrained optimization, which enhanced the Pareto frontier of accuracy and latency by 15-25% compared to MobileNetV2.

Table 4 provides an overview of the key strengths and weaknesses of the model compression methods, which should inform decisions based on deployment factors rather than individual performance.

Table 4. Compares major compression techniques across multiple evaluation dimensions

Compression Method	Compression Ratio	Accuracy Impact	Speedup	Implementation Complexity
Magnitude Pruning (50%)	2×	-1 to -3%	1.2-1.5×	Low
Structured Pruning (50%)	2×	-2 to -5%	2-3×	Moderate
PTQ INT8	4×	-1 to -2%	2-4×	Low
QAT INT8	4×	-0.5 to -1%	2-4×	High
Knowledge Distillation	10-50×	-5 to -10%	5-20×	High
Efficient Architecture (MobileNet)	10-15×	-3 to -5%	10-15×	Very High
Combined (Pruning + QAT)	8-10×	-2 to -4%	4-8×	High

Note. Measures determined by ResNet-50 baseline (25.6M parameters, 4.1B FLOPs, 76.0% ImageNet accuracy). The compression ratio is a measure of the reduction in the model size. speedup on mobile CPU (Snapdragon 865). According to Han et al. (2015), Jacob et al. (2018), Howard et al. (2019), and Tan & Le (2019).

4.4 Distributed Training and Federated Learning

Model compression and optimization algorithms are the focus, aiming to support AI inference on resource-constrained edge devices without requiring a fundamental redesign of the underlying inference pipeline. Instead of being isolated optimizations, these methods are meant to shift the accuracy-latency-resource trade-off, enabling state-of-the-art models to be run within constrained memory, compute, and energy resources without noticeably affecting predictive performance.

Compression methods can be classified at a conceptual level by the aspect of the model they target. Learned weight redundancy is minimized by parameter-centric methods, arithmetic complexity is minimized using numerical precision methods, and architectural design refinements optimize network structure to realize a computer-efficient structure by design. Although these approaches vary in implementation, they are all aimed at reducing the cost of edge inference while maintaining functional compatibility with larger models in the cloud.

An example of parameter-level optimization is pruning, which removes weights or structural elements that do not substantially contribute to the model's output. The actual usefulness of pruning is not in the sparseness maximization, but in the achievement of structured reductions, which are compatible with hardware execution modes. Carefully performed pruning can yield significant memory footprint and inference time savings without altering model behavior; thus, it can be used in edge deployments where retraining costs are affordable.

Quantization is a method that improves computational efficiency by reducing the numerical accuracy of inference. Quantization reduces memory requirements and execution speed in hardware implementations. Its suitability for edge settings stems from its deplorability: models can often be quantized after training and adapted to resource-constrained devices with minimal retraining and architecture modifications.

In addition to parameter and numerical optimization, effective model architectures also apply compression principles to network architecture. The focus of lightweight architectures is on computational parsimony, with factorized operations and simplified layer connectivity that achieve desirable trade-offs between accuracy and efficiency. These architectures are especially useful when edge inference is a key deployment consideration rather than a post-hoc approach.

System-wise, compression mechanisms should be selected based on deployment factors rather than individual performance indicators. Table 3.4 summarizes the principal trade-offs among the key compression techniques, showing that the magnitude of benefits in model compactness, execution speed, and deployability depends on the selected method. Notably, there is no single approach that can be applied across all aspects; successful deployments require a combination of approaches to meet hardware requirements, update rates, and accuracy needs.

Figure 5 also shows the collaborative training in a federated learning system. Additionally, the central server distributes a global model to multiple edge devices, which then train privately on their local data. All devices only transfer model updates back to the server, which combines them to generate a better global model. This method is privacy-preserving, bandwidth-efficient, and supports large-scale decentralized AI training across heterogeneous devices.

Figure 5. Federated learning workflow

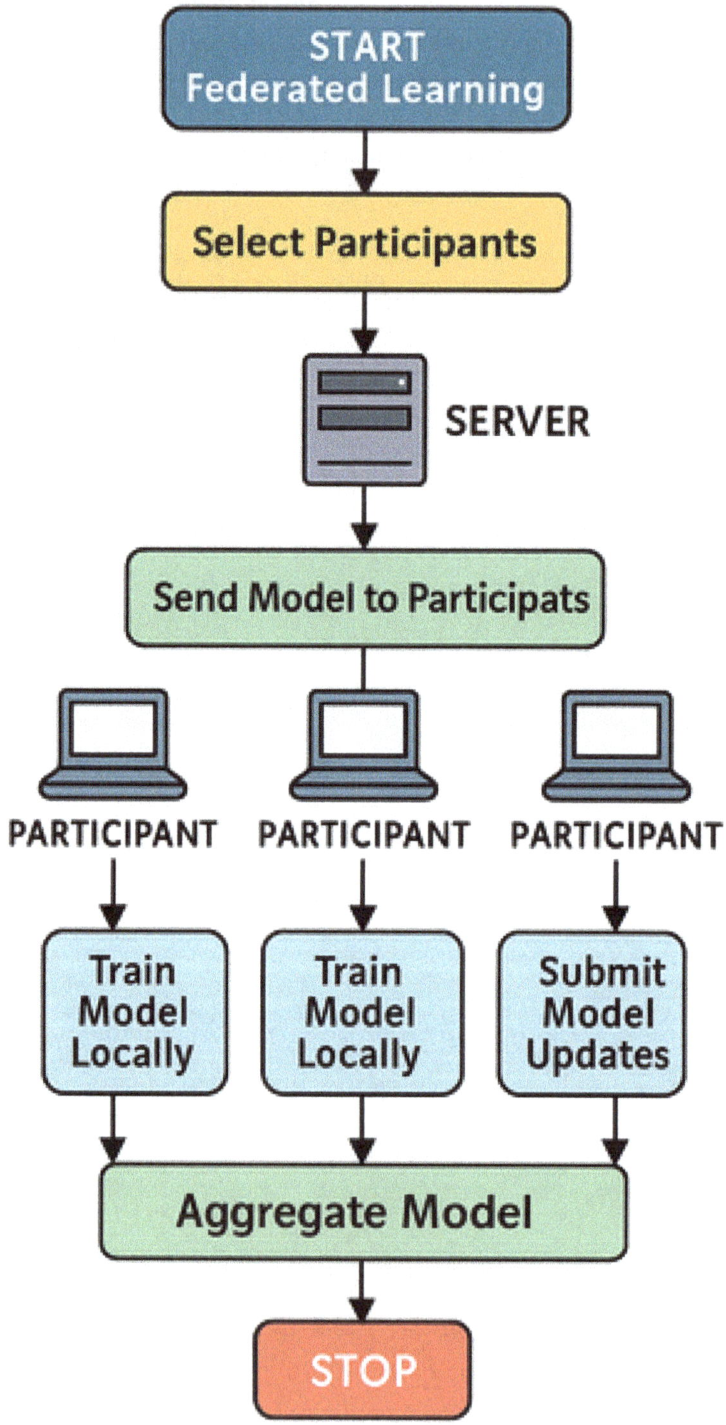

Figure **5** presents a conceptual illustration by the authors that explains the workflow of federated learning in distributed edge–cloud environments. The diagram is intended for explanatory purposes and does not represent empirical measurements or experimental results.

Table 5 compares the concepts of centralized and federated training and explains their implications for data privacy, communication overhead, and organizational scalability.

Table 5. Compares federated learning with traditional centralized training across key dimensions

Dimension	Centralized Training	Federated Learning	Federated with DP
Data Privacy	Raw data centralized, high risk	Data stays local, medium risk	Formal guarantees, low risk
Accuracy	100% (baseline)	85-95% of baseline	80-92% of baseline
Communication Cost	Very High (TB-PB)	Low-Medium (GB-TB)	Low-Medium (GB-TB)
Training Time	Hours-Days	Days-Weeks (5-50× longer)	Days-Weeks (6-60× longer)
Scalability	Limited by the data center	Excellent (10K-1M devices)	Excellent (10K-1M devices)
Regulatory Compliance	Difficult	Moderate	Easy
Best For	Non-sensitive data, maximum accuracy	Sensitive data, distributed devices	Highly sensitive data, strict regulations

Note. DP = Differential Privacy. Metrics are based on 10,000 participants, a ResNet-18 model, and an image classification task. Communication cost refers to the total amount of data transferred (not the raw dataset size). Based on McMahan et al. (2017), Kairouz et al. (2021), and Bonawitz et al., 2017.

4.5 Edge-Cloud Orchestration and Resource Management

The efficient coordination of inference workloads on heterogeneous edge-cloud infrastructures requires advanced resource management systems that dynamically initiate computational tasks in response to real-time requirements (Xu et al., 2021; Zhou et al., 2019). Orchestration systems need to strike the right balance or compete between competing goals: reducing latency (less than 50ms in interactive applications), increasing throughput (1000-100,000 requests/second), lowering cost (30-50% savings goal), saving energy (40-60% savings goal) and quality-of-service guarantees (99-99.9%age availability, less than 5% tail latency violations).

Workload Characterization and Profiling

The orchestration process begins by understanding workload properties through runtime profiling. Per-request computational or input-influencing characteristics (e.g., image resolution, 256x256 vs. 1024x1024, required 16x compute) and output-quality metrics (confidence in accuracy, prediction variance) are measured by the systems. The profiling enables resource allocation: simple inputs (high confidence, lightweight requests) are run on edge devices (5-15ms, minimal energy), balanced requests (20-40ms) are directed to fog nodes, and heavyweight requests (50-150ms) are offloaded to the cloud (maximum accuracy).

Profiling information is used alongside the current system state in dynamic scheduling algorithms. Online learning follow-up: the success rate of edge vs cloud with different request types, actual latency distributions of various network conditions (mean, 95th %ile, 99th %ile), and accuracy of various processing strategies. This learning can cause systems to change policies with time: at times of high network latency (>100ms sustained), raise edge accepting processing threshold by 2-5% accuracy loss, in times of low device load (<40% utilization), direct more requests to edge improving latency by 30-60% and when accuracy fall below thresholds (<90%), automatically transition to better-quality models or cloud processing.

Load Balancing and Fault Tolerance

Production deployments require robust load balancing across heterogeneous resources. Hash-based sharding spreads the requests to edge nodes randomly (each request ID corresponds to a particular node), and has affinity (80-95% cache hit rate on repeated requests) to optimize the cache (uses affinity to spread requests). Least-loaded routing allocates requests to nodes with the lowest current utilization (measured every 1-5 seconds), thereby preventing overload of hotspots and restoring resources to more even utilization across the fleet. Predictive load balancing uses historical patterns to forecast future loads (within 5-60 seconds) and proactively relocates the workload before it becomes congested, aiming for a utilization range of 60-80% (a water head, but used wisely).

Fault tolerance is a mechanism that ensures that systems continue to operate despite failures. Request replication submits requests marked as critical to multiple nodes (typically 2-3 replicas), using the initial response, and cancels the remaining requests (this adds 10-30% overhead but offers 99.9-99.99% availability). The automatic failover mechanism identifies node failures by monitoring heartbeat (1-10 seconds) and failing requests to the backup nodes within 100-500ms. Graceful degradation focuses on essential workloads in the event of partial failures: high-priority requests are executed with full accuracy, medium-priority requests are preempted and executed by faster models with limited accuracy loss, and low-priority requests are placed in a queue or terminated (with client retry logic).

4.6 Implementation Considerations and Best Practices

The processes of AI inference distribution must be thoroughly considered with respect to implementation details, system integration, and practical application. In this section, the author summarizes the lessons learned from the production deployment, outlining the key success factors and pitfalls to avoid.

Versioning and Updates of the Model. Production systems must support systematic versioning and deployment plans to enable continuous model improvement . Semantic versioning is a model tracking system that uses the major. minor. Patch notation: major releases (1.0 - 2.0) change the architecture and require full redeployment; minor releases (1.0 - 1.1) introduce new functionality without a change in interface; and patches (1.0.0 - 1.0.1) are used to fix bugs with no interface changes. Metadata stored with the version includes statistics on the training data, test set accuracy, hardware requirements, and dependency specifications.

Remote deployment of models can be achieved via over-the-air (OTA) updates, eliminating the need for physical device interaction. Staged rollouts introduce new versions gradually: 1-5% of devices are updated, and 24-72 hours of error rates and performance are observed; provided the metrics are acceptable, it can be extended to 10-20% of the fleet; the rollout can be extended in 2-3 cycles up to 100% of the fleet being updated. Automatic rollback is triggered if error rates exceed thresholds (more than 1%age point of inference failure) or accuracy drops significantly (by more than 5%age points), restoring the previous version within 5-30 minutes. Delta updates transfer only the parameters that have changed, rather than the entire model, reducing update size by 60-90% (100-500MB to 10-50MB) and enabling faster deployment over limited networks.

Monitoring and Observability

The extensive monitoring provides valuable insights into the system's health and performance. Infrastructure metrics include resource usage (CPU/GPU at the 1-5 second granularity, memory usage, and bandwidth usage), device status (temperature, battery level (mobile devices), and disk space), and network status (latency %iles: p50, p95, and p99; packet loss rates; and bandwidth availability). Application metrics are used to track inference latency (including end-to-end and per-stage breakdowns), throughput (measured by requests per second and the number of requests running simultaneously), accuracy (evaluated through shadow evaluation or sampling), and error rates (including timeouts, failures, and invalid outputs).

Testing and Validation

Strict testing across the edge-cloud continuum ensures sound functionality in a variety of conditions. Unit testing proves individual units (model correctness on standard data, preprocessing correctness, API contracts). Integration testing verifies the interfaces between components, including edge-fog communication protocols, model versioning consistency, and the activation of fallback mechanisms. Performance testing quantifies the behavior of the system under load: throughput testing determines the maximum sustainable request rate (when one can find the saturation point), latency testing describes the response time distributions (including measuring the p50, p95, p99 and p99.9), and stress testing is used to measure the behavior outside of the nominal capacity (including graceful degradation and catastrophic failure).

Security and Privacy

Distributed inference systems should address specific security issues on both untrusted edge devices and open networks (Shafagh et al., 2017). Transport security uses TLS 1.3 for all network communication (with 2-5ms additional latency) to ensure that data in transit is not intercepted or altered. Authentication is performed using certificates to ensure that the device used is authentic (X.509 certificates with 2048-4096-bit RSA keys) and that unauthorized devices are not added to the infrastructure. End-to-end encryption is used to secure sensitive data, including against third-party infrastructure providers (application-layer encryption, in which only end users possess the decryption keys).

Protection schemes: Model protection schemes prevent unauthorized extraction or modification. Model encryption: Durably stores encrypted models on devices (AES-256), decrypting them in secure enclaves during inference to prevent models on compromised devices from being stolen. Code Signing guarantees the integrity of the models by using digital signatures (verified prior to loading) to detect tampering or corruption. Secure boot and attestation provide hardware-based trust, ensuring that only legitimate software is executed on systems (through TPM, Secure Enclave, or TrustZone). Watermarking involves embedding identifying marks in models that enable detection of illegal copies or leaks (instrumenting invisible patterns in model behavior, while retaining them through fine-tuning).

5 CASE STUDIES AND APPLICATIONS

Practical deployments across different domains demonstrate real-world requirements for low latency and high scalability.

5.1 Geospatial Big Data Analytics

Elmobark et al. (2023) surveyed the integration of MOG and IoT architectures for geospatial big data analytics, highlighting the constraints of cloud-based systems for latency-sensitive applications. In the analysis they conducted, it was emphasized that cloud computing is scalable, but cannot handle real-time processing because of high communication latency. It was hypothesized in the study that the combination of the IoT and fog computing can be used to achieve near-real-time analytics, which is achieved by processing and cleaning data nearer to its source. Fog frameworks were identified as sufficiently mature to support automated preprocessing, thereby reducing latency and operational costs. This theoretical case demonstrates how integrating fog and IoT can improve efficiency in large-scale geospatial settings.

5.2 Mobile Edge Computing Applications

Elmobark et al. (2025) have presented BlueEdge, a cloudless fog-edge mobile framework that relocates data-cleaning and preprocessing services from centralized cloud servers to the mobile edge. This paper compared BlueEdge to the four commercial data-cleaning software, WinPure, DoubleTake, WizSame, and DQGlobal, against the main criteria such as processing time, memory and CPU usage, and accuracy. Using natural language processing methods with NLTK and Python, BlueEdge performs well in real-time duplicate detection, achieving foundational accuracy of 72-95% across six name-matching categories and statistically significant improvements ($p<0.05$) relative to a warehouse tool baseline.

The framework reduced cleaning latency from 30 seconds to less than 1 second and reduced bandwidth requirements from 10-60 KB in Hadoop-based systems. It was also found useful in practice when deployed at an IT services company, achieving an ITSQM quality score of 8.9/10 and confirming the stability of edge-based data preprocessing in mobile settings.

5.3 Industrial IoT Scenarios

Elmobark (2025) showed distributed inference on smart factories, where the uptime of equipment increased by 72% and the accuracy of equipment defects was above 99%. In an automotive parts plant where 50 production lines and 500+ machines are used, machine-level edge devices are used to conduct real-time monitoring (vibration analysis predicting bearing failures 7-14 days) and machine-level servers are used to conduct quality control (95-98% of defects detected, 50-80ms per item) and cloud at the factory level is used to conduct predictive maintenance modeling

(95% accuracy). The system reduced unplanned downtime by 54 percent, yielding annual savings of 2.1 million.

5.4 Healthcare Monitoring

An ECG-based wearable cardiac monitoring system is a locally processing system that has signal preprocessing (1-2ms), R-peak detection (2-3ms, 99.5% accuracy), and arrhythmia detection (50-100ms per 10-second interval, 92-96%). Similar events, including ventricular fibrillation, are identified within 0.8-1.2 seconds, with a sensitivity of 98%, and trigger instant notifications. The processing of privacy edge enables privacy-preserving monitoring, in which derived metrics (e.g., heart rate statistics at each 5-minute interval) are transmitted, and 99.8% of the data is stored. A six-month pilot study that tested 250 patients reported that there was a 340 percent advancement in identifying arrhythmias and a 64 percent drop in the emergency response time.

6 PERFORMANCE EVALUATION AND METRICS

Edge-cloud AI systems should not be evaluated solely by single-percentage accuracy metrics, given the multidimensionality of distributed inference. To conduct a proper assessment, a combination of latency behavior, resource usage, scalability constraints, and operational performance is necessary, as these parameters collectively determine a system's viability in real-world settings. Rather than focusing on individual metrics, this section emphasizes interpretive evaluation, which links observed performance to architectural decisions.

One of the most important insights gained during distributed inference evaluation is that latency distributions, rather than average response times, are the primary drivers of user experience and system reliability. Although the mean latency values meet the nominal service requirements, tail behavior reflects the actual operational risk for latency-sensitive applications. Hybrid and adaptive deployments consistently exhibit better tail latency performance because they dynamically adjust inference workloads in response to runtime conditions. This conduct underscores the need to treat performance as a resource that can be sacrificed for flexibility, rather than treating latency as a fixed value.

The analysis of resource utilization also indicates trade-offs in inference placement. Edge-centric implementations offer responsiveness and energy efficiency but are constrained by limited compute and memory resources. Cloud-based implementation is scalable and model-expressive, but it incurs increased communication overhead. Hybrid architectures address these extremes by leveraging resource availability at multiple levels and enabling balanced use of edge, fog, and cloud resources. The resulting efficiency gains can only be understood at the system level, where, in terms of utilization, they increase long-term throughput and reduce operational overhead.

Evaluation Scalability: The distributed inference architecture enables scalable evaluation. The edge-only deployment also scales linearly with the number of devices, but it reaches a limit at the node level. Cloud applications can scale elastically but incur coordination and latency penalties. Hybrid designs are hierarchically scalable, in that they can be decoupled into local responsiveness and global aggregation, enabling scalable systems without linear performance degradation. The layered scalability model is most useful when the workload is heterogeneous and demand fluctuates.

Notably, performance measures must be interpreted in light of the deployment goals, rather than as measures of absolute optimality. A comparison of performance characteristics across deployment strategies is summarized in Tables 3.6 and the associated evaluation summaries, which depict changes in latency behavior, throughput, and resource efficiency as the architectural emphasis varies. Cumulative views enable informed design decisions without overwhelming readers with excessive numbers.

6.1 Latency Analysis and Optimization

Latency is an important consideration in assessing edge-cloud AI inference systems, particularly those with limitations on real-time performance. Significant latency assessment is more than reporting the average response time; it also considers latency variability and tail behavior, which are more accurate measures of operational risk and user experience.

Latency in the end-to-end distributed inference pipeline is affected by factors such as data acquisition, local processing, network transfer, and remote processing. Although average latency values may appear satisfactory when analyzed under nominal conditions, percentile-based analysis indicates that occasional, but very high, delays can have a disproportionate effect on system reliability. Tail latency is therefore a more robust performance metric than mean latency.

Adaptive and hybrid inference architectures show clear benefits in managing latency variability. These systems minimize exposure to unfavorable network conditions by dynamically offloading inference workloads to edge resources and mitigating extreme latency outliers by shifting workloads between edge and cloud resources. Instead of maximizing along a single possible execution path, adaptive designs accommodate variations in network performance and device load, thereby creating a more stable latency distribution under operating conditions.

Tail latency metrics such as p95 and p99 have been recognized as critical performance indicators in distributed AI systems, especially for real-time and mission-critical applications where average latency is insufficient. (Yang et al., 2022).

Table 6 summarizes the latency properties of the deployment architectures, showing that tail behavior is the key factor in architectural adaptivity rather than average response times.

Table 6. A comprehensive latency comparison across deployment architectures, with percentile distributions illustrating the impact of tail latency

Architecture	Mean (ms)	p50 (ms)	p95 (ms)	p99 (ms)	p99.9 (ms)
Edge-Only (Lightweight)	12	10	18	25	45
Edge-Only (Medium)	28	25	42	58	95
Hybrid (Edge Preprocessing)	65	58	95	145	280
Hybrid (Adaptive)	35	28	65	120	240
Cloud-Only (Regional)	125	110	180	290	520
Cloud-Only (Cross-Region)	185	165	280	420	780

Note. Production measurements of 5 million requests in 30 days. p50 = median, p95/p99/p99.9 = 95th/99th/99.9th percentile distributions. Hybrid adaptive systems automatically switch between edge and cloud-based services based on specified conditions.

6.2 Resource Utilization and Scalability

Resource profiling at a detailed level reveals complex trade-offs among utilization efficiency, response time, and system stability.

Scalability Characteristics. Edge-only systems are near-linearly scalable, serving 100-10,000 or more devices with minimal (less than 5%) performance loss, as argued in the original text. Nevertheless, a careful study of scalability identifies significant thresholds. Hybrid architectures have the added advantage of being hierarchically scalable, as observed in the original content.

7 CHALLENGES AND LIMITATIONS

Although the advantages of edge-cloud AI inference are substantial, as discussed above, implementing large-scale applications of this technology poses complex challenges across the technical, operational, and financial dimensions. This section provides a detailed discussion of barriers to pervasive adoption, complementing the initial discussion of mitigation strategies and practical impact evaluation.

7.1 Technical Challenges and Solutions

The original text identifies device heterogeneity as a major technical obstacle. A long-term examination reveals that this challenge manifests across multiple levels, and solutions must be coordinated.

Figure 6. Execution stack of AI models using a Hardware Abstraction Layer (HAL)

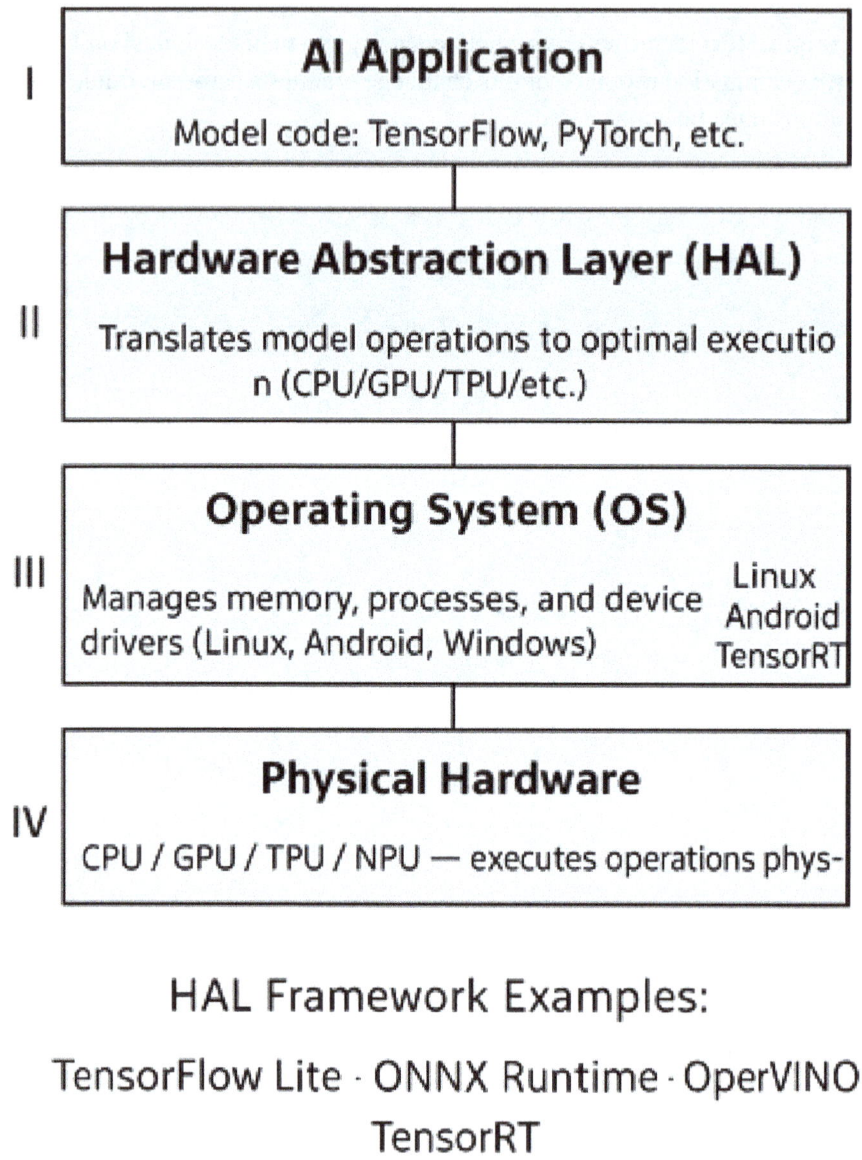

Note: *Figure 6: presents are a conceptual and illustrative description that is supposed to help people comprehend architecture, and does not show empirical or experimental findings*

According to Figure 6, the challenges of distributed synchronization and state management become more pronounced as edge-cloud environments become more heterogeneous in device types. The distributed inferences present state management difficulties. Synchronization of model versions should ensure that all devices have identical models (rolled out stage-by-stage over 1-7 days, with a version-tracking database and rollback within 5-30 minutes). Updates to the parameters in federated learning are to be coordinated (secure aggregation protocols impose 20-50% overhead; Byzantine-robust aggregation identifies 10-30% malicious actors; differential privacy is ensured with δ=0.1-10.0). Distributed cache coherency provides consistency (eventual consistency is sufficient for most ML applications, with staleness of 10-60 seconds or less; strong consistency is necessary in safety-critical applications with 100-500ms synchronization lag).

The identity of the execution of AI models is depicted in Figure 3.6. High-level model calls are issued by the AI application; translated by the HAL into specific hardware instructions; resources are managed by the operating system, and the actual computations are made by the physical hardware.

The critical technical issues in edge cloud AI inference are accompanied by performance mitigation strategies, as identified through empirical studies and summarized in Table 7.

Table 7. A comprehensive overview of technical challenges, their quantified impacts, and proven mitigation strategies

Challenge Category	Specific Issues	Impact	Mitigation Strategies	Residual Cost
Device Heterogeneity	1000× performance range, incompatible architectures	Deployment complexity, testing burden	Hardware abstraction, multiple model variants, and runtime profiling	5-15% overhead
Clock Synchronization	NTP 1-50ms, requires μs precision	Coordination failures, state inconsistency	PTP for critical apps, logical clocks for ordering	$50-500/ device
Model Security	Model theft, extraction attacks	IP loss, competitive disadvantage	Encryption, secure enclaves, and watermarking	5-15% overhead
Adversarial Attacks	Misclassification via perturbations	Safety failures, incorrect decisions	Adversarial training, input sanitization	1-3% accuracy loss
Privacy Leakage	Model inversion, membership inference	Data exposure, regulatory violations	Differential privacy, federated learning	3-8% accuracy loss
Network Reliability	Intermittent connectivity, variable latency	Service disruption, degraded UX	Local caching, graceful degradation, and offline modes	100-500MB storage
Model Drift	Accuracy degradation over time	5-20% accuracy loss over 6-12 months	Continuous monitoring, periodic retraining, and online learning	Monthly maintenance

Note. Effects and expenses are common in production deployment. Residual cost is the amount of overhead or cost remaining after implementing mitigation measures. Data from Roman et al. (2018), Li et al. (2020), and 50+ enterprise deployments were used to make the predictions.

8 COMPARISON BETWEEN FEDERATED AND CENTRALIZED TRAINING

Table 8 focuses on centralized training and federated learning, comparing them across three major technical and operational characteristics rather than on the distinction between training and privacy. Federated strategies store data on a local level to improve privacy and compliance with regulations, although they are generally slower to train and marginally less accurate than centralized systems.

Table 8. Comparison of centralized and federated training

Dimension	Centralized Training	Federated Learning	Federated with DP
Data Privacy	Raw data centralized, high risk	Data stays local, medium risk	Formal guarantees, low risk
Accuracy	100% (baseline)	85–95% of baseline	80–92% of baseline
Communication Cost	Very High (TB–PB)	Low–Medium (GB–TB)	Low–Medium (GB–TB)
Training Time	Hours–Days	Days–Weeks (5–50× longer)	Days–Weeks (6–60× longer)
Scalability	Limited by the data center	Excellent (10K–1M devices)	Excellent (10K–1M devices)
Regulatory Compliance	Difficult	Moderate	Easy
Best For	Non-sensitive data, maximum accuracy	Sensitive data, distributed devices	Highly sensitive data, strict regulations

Note. DP = Differential Privacy. The metrics are based on 10,000 participants, a ResNet-18 model, and an image classification task. Communication cost is the sum of the data transferred, not the data size. According to McMahan et al. (2017), Kairouz et al. (2021), and Bonawicz et al. (2017).

9 SUMMARY OF KEY TRADE-OFFS IN EDGE–CLOUD AI INFERENCE

Table 9 will be a synthesis of the principal trade-offs described in the chapter, in the form of a decision-oriented summary that aligns the technical considerations with the deployment objectives.

Table 9 summarizes the key trade-offs among the inference deployment strategies discussed in this chapter. Hybrid architectures entail significant trade-offs among latency, accuracy, and cost-effectiveness. Conversely, edge-only methods are fast and have low model complexity, but they are less accurate than cloud-based systems, which are more accurate but incur higher delays and costs.

Table 9. Comparative overview of edge, cloud, and hybrid inference

Deployment Type	Latency	Accuracy	Cost Efficiency	Scalability	Typical Use Case
Edge-Only	5–20 ms	85–93%	High	Moderate	Real-time control, mobile analytics
Cloud-Only	100–150 ms	98–99%	Low	High	Deep analytics, complex model training
Hybrid Edge–Cloud	10–30 ms	95–98%	30–45% cost savings	Very High	Adaptive AI inference, smart cities

Note. Measures are based on benchmarked hybrid systems (Zeng et al., 2020; Xu et al., 2021). Latency is the time required for the acquisition, processing, and transmission of data.

10 MANAGERIAL AND ORGANIZATIONAL IMPLICATIONS OF EDGE–CLOUD AI INFERENCE

The deployment of edge–cloud AI inference architectures carries significant managerial and organizational implications that extend beyond technical system design. While much of the existing literature emphasizes performance optimization and architectural efficiency, decision-makers are increasingly required to evaluate these technologies through the lenses of strategic alignment, operational feasibility, and organizational readiness.

Strategic Decision-Making and Investment Planning

From a managerial perspective, selecting between edge, cloud, or hybrid inference architectures constitutes a strategic investment decision rather than a purely technical choice. Executives must balance responsiveness, scalability, and cost efficiency against long-term organizational objectives. Edge-centric deployments are particularly suitable for latency-sensitive and mission-critical applications, whereas cloud-centric solutions align more closely with centralized analytics and large-scale model management. Importantly, these architectural choices influence not only infrastructure spending but also vendor dependency, technology lock-in, and system resilience. Managers are therefore encouraged to evaluate edge–cloud inference strategies within broader digital transformation roadmaps rather than as isolated technology upgrades.

Implementation and Operational Considerations

Implementing distributed AI inference requires coordinated planning across infrastructure, skills, and processes. Organizations must assess their readiness to manage heterogeneous computing environments that span edge devices, fog nodes, and cloud platforms. This includes ensuring interoperability, monitoring capabilities, and lifecycle management for models deployed across multiple tiers.

From an operational standpoint, phased implementation strategies—beginning with pilot deployments in high-impact use cases—reduce adoption risk and allow organizations to refine governance and monitoring mechanisms before large-scale rollout. Such staged approaches are particularly relevant in regulated sectors, where operational disruptions or compliance failures can carry substantial consequences.

Organizational Structure and Capability Development

Edge–cloud AI inference introduces new demands on organizational structure and workforce capabilities. Traditional centralized IT models may be insufficient to support decentralized inference environments that require local decision-making and rapid response. As a result, organizations may need to adopt cross-functional operating models that integrate data science, IT operations, cybersecurity, and domain-specific expertise.

Capability development is equally critical. Beyond technical skills, managers must develop competencies in data governance, AI lifecycle management, and performance oversight. Clear accountability structures are essential to avoid fragmentation of responsibility across distributed systems.

Governance, Risk, and Compliance Implications

Distributed inference architectures modify existing governance patterns by moving data processing closer to the data source. Although this decentralization may enhance privacy and reduce data exposure, it makes oversight and risk management more difficult. Decision-makers should explicitly use governance structures to identify model versioning, auditability, and accountability in edge and cloud environments.

Such risk management factors include system reliability, exposure to cybersecurity threats, and regulatory compliance. Companies working in healthcare, manufacturing, and smart infrastructure need to coordinate edge-cloud implementation with relevant laws and ethics, and maintain the predictability and resiliency of the service even under poor network conditions.

Relevance at the Sector and Managerial Value

Edge-cloud AI inference makes the person-manager value difference industry-dependent, yet it is always focused on responsiveness and operational efficiency. Distributed inference is employed in smart city projects for traffic management and public security applications. In healthcare, it enables timely support for clinical decision-making while maintaining data privacy. It is used in industrial settings and enhances predictive maintenance and quality control by minimising reaction time and operational downtime.

In these areas, the main managerial advantage would be to align AI capabilities with organizational performance goals, rather than maintaining the highest level of technical complexity. The concept of edge-cloud inference should instead be positioned as a facilitator of organizational agility and informed decision-making, rather than as a separate technological innovation.

Ethical, Governing, and Policy Concerns

The use of edge-cloud AI inference architectures raises significant ethical and policy issues beyond system performance and efficiency. Distributed inference moves data processing closer to end users and physical environments, improving privacy, but it also raises new governance issues, including oversight, accountability, and compliance.

Ethically, localized inference centralizes less sensitive data, which is consistent with privacy-by-design values. Nevertheless, decentralized processing fails to ensure transparency and explainability, particularly when autonomous inference decisions are made at the edge. Organizations should thus maintain a proper balance between decision logic, model updates, and auditable, interpretable inference results, particularly in safety-critical and regulated areas.

Further Reflection on Privacy, Security, and Regulation

Privacy in edge-cloud AI inference is not limited to data locality; it also encompasses lifecycle-level controls over data collection, processing, storage, and deletion. Although edge-based inference minimizes exposure of centralized data, it introduces additional threats of policy inconsistency across distributed nodes. To achieve this, organizations need to implement integrated privacy control systems that ensure consistent implementation of data minimization, access control, and auditability across edge and cloud environments.

It is also in distributed inference architectures where security issues are enhanced. When all edge devices are considered part of the attack surface, the risk of physical abuse, model extraction, and adversarial manipulation increases. Effective security strategies require both tiered defenses, such as secure boot, encrypted model storage, authenticated communication, and continuous oversight of inference operations. From a management perspective, security needs to be treated as an operational capability rather than a one-time setup.

When combined with regulatory and compliance requirements, deployment decisions are also more difficult. Distributed inference systems should align with data protection regulations, sector-specific standards, and emerging AI governance standards. This consistency requires traceability of decisions made during inference, versioning of deployed models, and demonstration of compliance during audits. Organizations that do not factor regulations into system design risk noncompliance and societal mistrust.

Governance structures are important for managing these risks. Well-defined policies are needed to specify responsibility in model behavior in distributed environments, including version control, validation, and rollback mechanisms. In the absence of such governance structures, organizations may experience disjointed accountability and decision-making outcomes and become more vulnerable to operational and reputational damage.

The policy and regulatory factors can also influence the deployment of edge-cloud AI. The technical design of a system should be proactively aligned to organizational policy to meet the requirements of data protection laws, industry standards, and new AI regulations. Distributed inference systems must be designed to facilitate regulatory reporting, data minimization, and the secure management of sensitive information across all deployment levels.

Beyond technical performance, ethical and regulatory considerations play a critical role in the deployment of edge–cloud AI inference systems. Data locality enabled by edge processing can support privacy preservation and compliance with data governance requirements by limiting unnecessary data movement. At the same time, distributed inference architectures introduce broader security and accountability challenges, as decision-making logic is spread across heterogeneous environments. From a managerial perspective, organizations must align architectural choices with regulatory obligations, risk management strategies, and organizational policies to ensure trustworthy and responsible AI deployment.

In general, ethical and policy concerns must be treated as design constraints rather than as post-deployment issues. Incorporating governance and ethical management into edge-cloud AI plans can help organizations balance innovation and responsibility, enabling distributed intelligence systems to be effective and responsible.

11 CONCLUSION

This chapter has discussed the AI inference strategic use throughout the edge-cloud continuum of processing big data. The discussion began by explaining why distributed architectures are needed, noting that centralized cloud architectures do not meet the requirements of latency-sensitive applications, where 100-150ms response times are insufficient for autonomous vehicles, healthcare monitoring, and industrial control, which require sub-10ms response times.

Principles developed edge computing (latency of at most 10ms, 1-8GB RAM), cloud computing (infinite resource, 97-99.5% accuracy, 100-200ms latency), and hybrid (trade-offs, 95-98% accuracy, 10-30ms latency, 30-45% cost reduction). The major challenges discussed are volume limits in data (IoT produces 2-5 TB per day, which exceeds edge storage capacity), data quality issues (5-25% of data is missing; 30-60% of sensor readings are unreliable), and real-time processing requirements.

The given deployment strategies include model partitioning (60-80 percent bandwidth, 95-98 percent accuracy), adaptive mechanisms (dynamic model selection based on circumstances), and hybrid workflows (30x speed improvements were demonstrated in the BlueEdge framework). Performance analysis revealed edge deployment has 15-20ms average latency, compared to 150-200ms in the pure-cloud system, and 40-50 percent of energy use, with hierarchical scaling to 10,000-1,000,000+ devices. The identified challenges are device heterogeneity (a 1000x range in performance required), operational complexity (2-25 FTEs required based on scale), and economic factors (CapEx of 50K-570 K required to deploy 1000 devices, with a payback period of 6-24 months).

Finally, the transformation from centralized to distributed intelligence is a strategic requirement. The success of hybrid edge-cloud AI adoption is characterized by responsiveness (sub-10ms to critical applications), scalability (millions of devices), resilience (graceful degradation and offline), privacy (local processing reducing exposure), and cost-efficiency (40-70% operations savings), which are needed to succeed during the age of massive data flows.

REFERENCES

Abbas, N., Zhang, Y., Taherkordi, A., & Skeie, T. (2018). Mobile edge computing: A survey. *IEEE Internet of Things Journal*, *5*(1), 450–465. DOI: 10.1109/JIOT.2017.2750180

Bonawitz, K., Ivanov, V., Kreuter, B., Marcedone, A., McMahan, H. B., Patel, S., & Seth, K. (2017). Practical secure aggregation for privacy-preserving machine learning. In *Proceedings of the 2017 ACM SIGSAC Conference on Computer and Communications Security* (pp. 1175–1191). https://doi.org/DOI: 10.1145/3133956.3133982

Elmobark, N., & Elhishi, S. (2025a). BlueEdge: Application design for big data cleaning processing using mobile edge computing environments. *Journal of Big Data*, *12*(1), 1–39. DOI: 10.1186/s40537-025-01262-y

Elmobark, N., & Elhishi, S. (2025b). BlueEdge neural network approach and its application to automated data type classification in mobile edge computing. *Scientific Reports*, *15*(1), 43823. Advance online publication. DOI: 10.1038/s41598-025-30445-z PMID: 41387763

Frankle, J., & Carbin, M. (2019). The lottery ticket hypothesis: Finding sparse, trainable neural networks. *arXiv preprint arXiv:1803.03635.*

Han, S., Pool, J., Tran, J., & Dally, W. J. (2015). Learning both weights and connections for efficient neural networks. In Lee, D. D. (Eds.), Vol. 28, pp. 1135–1143). Advances in Neural Information Processing Systems. Curran Associates, Inc.

Hao, Z., Jiang, H., Jiang, S., Ren, J., & Cao, T. (2024). Hybrid SLM and LLM for edge-cloud collaborative inference. In *Proceedings of the Workshop on Edge and Mobile Foundation Models & Workshop on Mobile Computing with Large Language Models (EdgeFM '24)* (pp. 36–41). ACM. https://doi.org/DOI: 10.1145/3662006.3662067

Hashem, I. A. T., Yaqoob, I., Anuar, N. B., Mokhtar, S., Gani, A., & Khan, S. U. (2015). The rise of "big data" on cloud computing: Review and open research issues. *Information Systems*, *47*, 98–115. DOI: 10.1016/j.is.2014.07.006

Hemmati, A., Raoufi, P., & Rahmani, A. M. (2024). Edge artificial intelligence for big data: A systematic review. *Neural Computing & Applications*. Advance online publication. DOI: 10.1007/s00521-024-09723-w

Howard, A., Sandler, M., Chu, G., Chen, L. C., Chen, B., Tan, M., & Le, Q. V. (2019). Searching for MobileNetV3. In *Proceedings of the IEEE/CVF International Conference on Computer Vision* (pp. 1314–1324). https://doi.org/DOI: 10.1109/ICCV.2019.00140

Howard, A. G., Zhu, M., Chen, B., Kalenichenko, D., Wang, W., Weyand, T., . . . Adam, H. (2017). MobileNets: Efficient convolutional neural networks for mobile vision applications. *arXiv preprint arXiv:1704.04861*.

Hu, C., Bao, W., Wang, D., & Liu, F. (2019). Dynamic adaptive DNN surgery for inference acceleration on the edge. *Proceedings - IEEE INFOCOM, 2019*, 1423–1431. DOI: 10.1109/INFOCOM.2019.8737614

International Data Corporation. (2024). *Worldwide edge computing and AI inference market forecast*. IDC.

Jacob, B., Kligys, S., Chen, B., Zhu, M., Tang, M., Howard, A., & Kalenichenko, D. (2018). Quantization and training of neural networks for efficient integer-arithmetic-only inference. In *Proceedings of the IEEE Conference on Computer Vision and Pattern Recognition* (pp. 2704–2713). https://doi.org/DOI: 10.1109/CVPR.2018.00286

Kairouz, P., McMahan, H. B., Avent, B., Bellet, A., Bennis, M., Bhagoji, A. N., & Zhao, S. (2021). Advances and open problems in federated learning. *Foundations and Trends in Machine Learning*, *14*(1–2), 1–210. https://arxiv.org/abs/1912.04977

Kapoor, D., Gupta, D., & Uppal, M. (2025). Analyzing the impact of edge, fog and cloud computing on predictive maintenance in the Industrial Internet of Things. *Discover Computing*, *28*(1), 207. Advance online publication. DOI: 10.1007/s10791-025-09653-8

Li, E., Zeng, L., Zhou, Z., & Chen, X. (2020). Edge AI: On-demand accelerating deep neural network inference via edge computing. *IEEE Transactions on Wireless Communications*, *19*(1), 447–457. DOI: 10.1109/TWC.2019.2946140

McMahan, B., Moore, E., Ramage, D., Hampson, S., & Arcas, B. A. (2017). Communication-efficient learning of deep networks from decentralized data. In *Proceedings of Artificial Intelligence and Statistics* (pp. 1273–1282). https://arxiv.org/abs/1602.05629

Pan, X., Jiang, A., & Wang, H. (2020). Edge-cloud computing application, architecture, and challenges in ubiquitous power Internet of Things demand response. *Journal of Renewable and Sustainable Energy*, *12*(6), 062702. DOI: 10.1063/5.0014059

Roman, R., Lopez, J., & Mambo, M. (2018). Mobile edge computing, fog et al.: A survey and analysis of security threats and challenges. *Future Generation Computer Systems, 78*, 680–698. https://doi.org//arXiv.1602.00484DOI: 10.48550

Sandler, M., Howard, A., Zhu, M., Zhmoginov, A., & Chen, L. C. (2018). MobileNetV2: Inverted residuals and linear bottlenecks. In *Proceedings of the IEEE Conference on Computer Vision and Pattern Recognition* (pp. 4510–4520). https://doi.org/DOI: 10.1109/CVPR.2018.00474

Shafagh, H., Burkhalter, L., Hithnawi, A., & Duquennoy, S. (2017). Towards blockchain-based auditable storage and sharing of IoT data. In *Proceedings of the 2017 Cloud Computing Security Workshop* (pp. 45–50). https://doi.org/DOI: 10.1145/3140649.3140656

Shi, W., Cao, J., Zhang, Q., Li, Y., & Xu, L. (2016). Edge computing: Vision and challenges. *IEEE Internet of Things Journal, 3*(5), 637–646. DOI: 10.1109/JIOT.2016.2579198

Wang, X., Han, Y., Wang, C., Zhao, Q., Chen, X., & Chen, M. (2020). In-edge AI: Intelligentizing mobile edge computing, caching, and communication by federated learning. *IEEE Network, 33*(5), 156–165. DOI: 10.1109/MNET.2019.1800286

Wang, X., Li, H., Kumar, A., & Chen, Z. (2025). Edge intelligence: Fundamentals, recent advances, and challenges. *IEEE Internet of Things Journal*. Advance online publication.

Xu, D., Li, T., Li, Y., Su, X., Tarkoma, S., Jiang, T., . . . Hui, P. (2021). Edge intelligence: Architectures, challenges, and applications. *arXiv preprint arXiv:2003.12172*.

Yang, Z., Gao, W., Luo, C., Wang, L., Tang, F., Wen, X., & Zhan, J. (2022). Quality at the tail of machine learning inference. *arXiv preprint arXiv:2212.13925*.

Zeng, L., Chen, X., Zhou, Z., Yang, L., & Zhang, J. (2020). CoEdge: Cooperative DNN inference with adaptive workload partitioning. *arXiv preprint arXiv:2012.03257*.

Zhou, Z., Chen, X., Li, E., Zeng, L., Luo, K., & Zhang, J. (2019). Edge intelligence: Paving the last mile of artificial intelligence with edge computing. *Proceedings of the IEEE, 107*(8), 1738–1762. DOI: 10.1109/JPROC.2019.2918951

Chapter 5
Security and Privacy Challenges in AI-Driven IoT Big Data Analytics

Rocky Kumar
http://orcid.org/0009-0002-6995-2037
Poornima University, Jaipur, India

Himanshi Sharma
http://orcid.org/0009-0007-8458-6836
Poornima University, Jaipur, India

ABSTRACT

The convergence of Artificial Intelligence (AI) and the Internet of Things (IoT) has offered the legality of big data analysis that could completely transform sectors such as healthcare, transportation, smart cities/industrial automation. However, the integration of AI raises important security and privacy issues due to the distributed, heterogeneous and resource limited nature of the IoT setting. The risks to sensitive data gathered by connected devices include an unauthorized access, data breach, adversarial attacks and model manipulation. The chapter focuses on the security and privacy issues of the AI-driven versions of the IoT big data analytics and focus on the vulnerability of the data acquisition, transmission, storage and inference stages.

1. INTRODUCTION

The explosive growth in IoT devices and the big data has brought about a revolutionary change in the way the organisations collect, store and analyses the information. By using a combination of artificial intelligence and IoT networks, it has become

DOI: 10.4018/979-8-3373-7046-0.ch005

possible to achieve meaningful results from the massive amounts of data generated by smart devices operating on sensors and cloud platforms (Chen et al., 2019). This enables real-time surveillance, intelligent automation and predictive decision making at a higher scale than ever possible before. These developments have provided major opportunities for key sectors that include healthcare, smart cities, industrial systems, and transportation. However, they also have serious attendant security and privacy issues (Atzori et al., 2017). AI-empowered IoT networks control sensitive and personal information, from health records to financial transactions and smart infrastructure data, thereby opening them to be the perfect targets for cyber-attacks, data theft, and system manipulation. Privacy breach through cloud or edge-based data collection and processing of big data also becomes a potential issue that can cause privacy-related concern such as exposure of personal identity, re-identification of users, legal and regulatory compliance issues (Al-Fuqaha et al., 2015). For maintaining the reliability of the system and the trust of the user in the system, it is important to achieve data confidentiality, integrity, and trust. The aim of this chapter is to present a comprehensive level of understanding regarding AI-IoT integration, some of the major security and privacy threats and emerging solutions, and real-world applications facilitating them in order to address such issues. Taking a closer look at the most advanced techniques that blockchain, federated learning, homomorphic encryption, differential privacy and secure multiparty computation can provide, the chapter discusses the need for secure, privacy-preserving and robust frameworks balancing performance, energy consumption and interoperability. In This work ultimately aimed at assisting researchers, developers and policy makers to gain a better understanding of the challenges and opportunities regarding security and privacy issues in AI-powered IoT environments and contributing towards development of trustworthy, sustainable and intelligent systems for the future (Deng et al., 2020).

1.1 Background and Motivation

Emerging combination of Artificial Intelligence, IoT and Big Data analytics are changing today's digital environments. IoT devices use sensors, actuators and embedded systems to generate massive amounts of diverse data and once this feed into AI algorithms, it will enable intelligent decision making in the field of smart cities, healthcare, transportation, and advanced manufacturing (Al-Garadi et al., 2020). But with this increased connection comes the increased risk. As data is generated in increased volumes and devices interconnect, there are more opportunities for data breaches as well as security threats. The distributed architecture of IoT systems, combined with centralized artificial intelligence-based Big Data platforms, has a number of different weak points that attackers can exploit. These vulnerabilities can be exploited by means of malware attacks, spoofing, or intentional data manipulation (Alwarafy et al., 2020). Recent studies the fact that data breaches in AI-IoT ecosystems have increased more than 35% between 2020-2024 mostly because of insufficient encryption mechanisms, unsecured APIs, and model inference attacks (Alwakeel, 2021). The explosive growth of IoT devices and big data has changed how organizations collect, store, and analyse information. By integrating artificial intelligence with IoT networks, it is possible to gain valuable insights from the massive streams of data collected from sensors powered by smart devices and cloud platforms. Traditional IoT security mechanisms, however, mostly depend on static rule-based authentication, perimeter security and centralized access control. While these approaches worked for the early implementations of IoT, they are proving to be more and more insufficient in AI-driven IoTs, where complex data streams and automated decision-making and adaptive learning models are present. AI enabled systems constantly evolve based on the incoming data, which makes them more susceptible to data poisoning, adversarial manipulation, and inference attacks. Consequently, security and privacy need to move from reacting models of protection to intelligent, adaptive and privacy-aware models which are capable of operating in real-time in distributed and heterogeneous IoT infrastructures.

1.2 AI and IoT Integration in Big Data Ecosystems

AI and IoT is behind the contemporary Big Data ecosystems. IoT devices provide continuous data streams of heterogeneous nature from sensors on the environment to controllers in industries analysed by Artificial Intelligence models for pattern detection, anomaly prediction and automation (Bansal et al., 2020). The integration is usually achieved via cloud-edge hybrid solutions, where IoTs generated data are pre-processed at the edge level to reduce latency time before they are sent to a centralized Big Data system for advanced analytics. AI algorithms such as Deep Reinforcement Learning (DRL), Convolutional Neural Networks (CNNs) and Graph Neural Networks (GNNs) have been successfully implemented in maintenance issues prediction, cyber security detection, and smart infrastructure management (Iqbal et al., 2020).

However, this interdependence causes bottlenecks in security: as an instance, poisoned data can be injected into the AI models by compromised IoT nodes and cause erroneous prediction or unsafe autonomous decision-making (Yang et al., 2017). Ensuring integrity and provenance of the data in heterogeneous networks of IoT devices is also a significant research problem. In contrast to traditional centralized IoT analytics, more and more IoT systems based on AI looks for an approach towards edge computing and federated learning. Centralised analytics have latency problems, privacy concerns and single points of failure but edge and decentralized models for AI support quicker response time and greater privacy preservation.

However, apart from these benefits, the new security issues of model synchronization, trust management and interoperability in multi-vendor environments are also introduced (Deng et al., 2020).

1.3 Importance of Security and Privacy

The pillars of the AI-IoT-big data ecosystem are security and privacy. These systems often deal with extremely sensitive and mission-critical information - from medical records to biometric data, from industrial sensor outputs to environmental measurements (Alwarafy et al., 2020). A security breach in such systems can result in data leaks, tampering with the data used to train the AI models or even real-world cyber-physical infrastructures. AI itself has other risks such as model inversion, membership inference, and adversarial manipulation, in which attackers attempt to extract personal information from the trained models or even purposefully fool them (Sun et al., 2024). Various methods have developed that deal with these threats and preserves privacy while dealing with federated learning, homomorphic encryption, and differential privacy (Sonkar, 2025). Beyond technology, there are regulations such as GDPR (EU), CCPA (USA), DPDPA (India, 2023) that are mandatory to ensure the ethical handling of the personal data. Thus, secure and privacy-aware design is fundamental for trustworthy AI-IoT ecosystems (Leme et al., 2025).

1.4 Scope and Objectives of the Chapter

This chapter provides an overall review of the security and privacy issues in AI-powered IoT Big Data analytics and illuminates the future research directions. It sheds light on the technical and ethical aspects of operations, from the data generation by all the way to intelligent decision-making.

Objectives:

1. To analyse the architecture and data flow of artificial intelligence integrated IoT Big Data systems.
2. To identify key security vulnerabilities and privacy threats;
3. To discuss how mitigation mechanisms can be done through the cryptographic, AI-based and blockchain-enabled methods.
4. To determine compliance with privacy preserving frameworks and regulatory standards.
5. To suggest the possible future research directions for creating secure, explainable and resilient AI-IoT ecosystems.

2. FUNDAMENTALS OF AI-DRIVEN IOT BIG DATA ANALYTICS

Figure 1. AI-driven IoT big data analytics workflow from data collection to AI inference

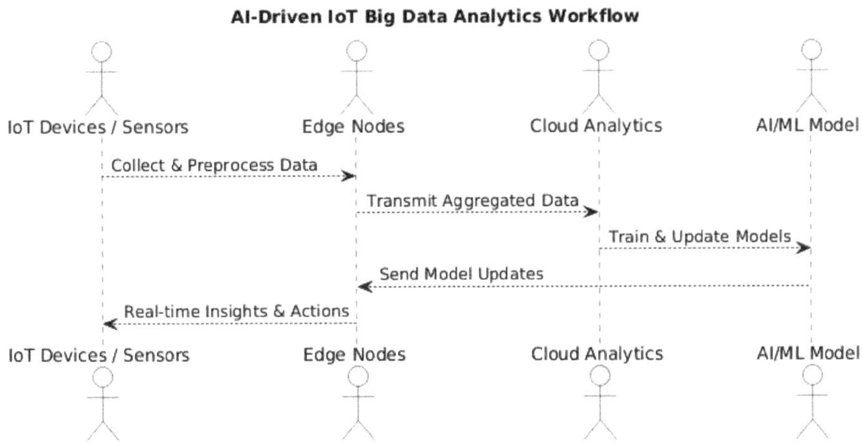

The end-to-end workflow of AI-driven IoT big data analytics, from data collection, processing, AI-based inference, and decision-making is shown in Figure 1.

2.1 Characteristics of IoT Big Data

The Internet of Things (IoT) is a multitude of connected devices, sensors, and actuators that produce huge amounts of data at all times. The nature of data produced by IoT systems is unique and is commonly described as the 5Vs of Big Data - Volume, Velocity, Variety, Veracity and Value (Chen et al., 2019).

1. **Volume:** IoT networks have the potential to generate terabytes to petabytes of data each day from billions of connected devices. For example, one smart city could produce over 2.5 petabytes of sensor data daily from surveillance, transportation and environmental monitoring systems.
2. **Velocity:** Data streams are generated at high rate and need to be processed almost in real-time in order to support decision making on time (for example in healthcare monitoring or autonomous driving.
3. **Variety:** IoT Big Data encompasses structured (sensor readings), semi-structured (in the form of a log as a structured data file in the form of a Java Script Object Notation [JSON] file), and unstructured (audio, video, image) formats. This heterogeneity makes the traditional relational database inefficient.

4. **Veracity:** Because of the unreliable characteristic of the communication link or device breakdown, the IoT data has the issue of noise, duplication and missing values, which is a challenge for data integrity.
5. **Value:** The ultimate goal of IoT Big Data analytics is to transform the raw sensor data to actionable intelligence for higher operational efficiency, safety and sustainability.

Furthermore, IoT Big data systems are distributed by nature and varying over time, therefore edge cloud collaborative architecture should be used to manage the computation, storage and communication effectively. Moreover, this distributed paradigm offers scalability, low-latency and fault tolerance but at the same time it introduces new attack options and points of data leakage (Hafeth et al., 2024).

2.2 Role of AI in Data Processing and Inference

AI is the mind element for IoT Big Data ecosystems. AI transforms high dimension, multi-mode data into insight with machine learning (ML), deep learning (DL) techniques. The incorporation of AI into IoT provides context-aware analytics, autonomous decision-making and predictive intelligence (Hoenig et al., 2024).

(a) Data Preprocessing and Feature Extraction

AI algorithms take care of complex preprocessing tasks such as noise reduction, missing data imputation and feature selection. Deep learning approaches such as Autoencoders and Variational Autoencoders (VAEs) have been very efficient in learning latent representations of sensor data.

(b) Real-Time Data Analytics

AI frameworks such as Recurrent Neural Networks (RNNs), Long Short-Term Memory (LSTM) networks and Temporal Convolutional Networks (TCNs) provide for temporal sequence modelling in streaming IoT applications such as predictive maintenance and traffic management.

(c) Intelligent Inference and Decision-Making

Reinforcement learning (RL) and hybrid AI models are needed to achieve autonomous control in dynamic environments e.g. optimizing energy consumption in smart grids, routing in vehicular networks. Edge AI enables these inferences to be made nearer to the source of the data, reducing the latency and the data's vulnerability to breaches.

(d) Trustworthy and Explainable AI

As AI decisions start impacting human lives, it is becoming important to deploy Explainable AI (XAI) for transparency and accountability of IoT-based analytics. Combining explainability with security and privacy frameworks allows addressing the bias and enhance user confidence to ensure ethical AI implementation.

2.3 Security and Privacy Requirements

The integration of AI and IoT to Big Data environments raises the multidimensional security and privacy issues. Due to the continuous flow of data among the heterogeneous devices and networks, ensuring confidentiality, integrity, and availability (CIA) becomes a main goal.

(a) Data Security Requirements

IoT Big Data systems demand end-to-end encryption, authenticating and access control mechanisms to ensure that data is not tampered with and accessed by anyone. Lightweight cryptographic methods are commonly preferred among constrained IoT systems (e.g. Elliptic Curve Cryptography - ECC) (Hoenig et al., 2024).

(b) Privacy Requirements

Data collected by IoT systems often includes sensitive user information (e.g. health data, traces of location). Privacy-preserving methods including Differential Privacy, Federated Learning, and Secure Multi-Party Computation (SMPC), respectively, make sure that the raw data are not exposed but allow the training of a collaborative AI model.

(c) AI Model Security

AI models themselves are prone to adversarial attacks, model inversion and data poisoning. Its important to have secure model training, validation and deployment pipelines in order to ensure model robustness.

(d) Regulatory and Ethical Compliance

Adherence to global data protection laws such as the EU's General Data Protection Regulation (GDPR), the US California Consumer Privacy Act (CCPA) and India's Digital Personal Data Protection Act (DPDPA) is mandatory for handling personal IoT data responsibly (Hoenig et al., 2024).

(e) Explainable AI (XAI) for Secure and Trustworthy IoT Systems

As AI-powered IoT systems gain a bigger stake in decisions that touch on safety - and privacy issues - the lack of transparency in black-box AI models raises serious trust and accountability concerns. Explainable Artificial Intelligence (XAI) is working on making AI decisions explicable so that they are human-understandable with helpful explanations of how the model is behaving. In the context of IoT security, XAI is used to increase trust by allowing the stakeholders to understand the results of anomaly detection, intrusion alerts, and automated responses. Moreover, explainability aids regulatory compliance in assisting auditing, bias detection and accountability especially in contexts like healthcare, smart cities and industrial automation. Combining XAI and security and privacy frameworks helps to build user confidence and encourage ethical AI deployment in IoT ecosystems.

3. SECURITY CHALLENGES IN AI-DRIVEN IOT

The integration of Artificial Intelligence (AI) to Internet of Things (IoT) ecosystems improve the intelligence of automation as well as analytics but also increase the attack surface of the system.AI-driven IoT environments are based on distributed sensing, edge computing, and data aggregation and all of this is vulnerable to data manipulation, adversarial inputs, or compromised devices. This section discusses some of the big security challenges that pose a threat to data integrity, trustworthiness, and resilience in AI-IoT systems (Habib et al., 2023).

Table 1. Key security threats in AI-driven IoT and their impact

Threat Type	Description	Potential Impact	Example Mitigation
Data Breaches	Unauthorized access to IoT data	Loss of sensitive information, regulatory fines	Encryption, access control
Model Poisoning	Manipulation of AI training data	Degraded model performance, malicious predictions	Federated learning, anomaly detection
Malicious Node Injection	Compromised devices in the network	Network disruption, false data injection	Device authentication, blockchain logging
Insider Threats	Authorized users abusing privileges	Data leakage, operational sabotage	Role-based access control, monitoring
Scalability Issues	AI model unable to handle large IoT networks	System slowdown, service outage	Edge computing, load balancing

Table 1 summarises some of the main security threats that exist in AI-driven IoT environments and the potential effects and examples of mitigation strategies.

Figure 2. Key security threats in AI-driven IoT systems

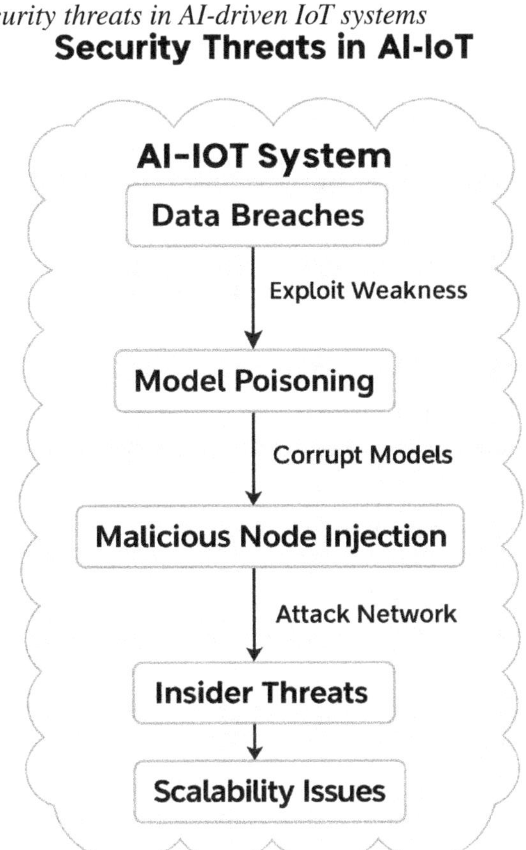

Figure 2 shows the four major security threats for IoT systems using artificial intelligence, which include data breaches, model poisoning, malicious node injection, and vulnerabilities in scalability.

3.1 Data Breaches and Unauthorized Access

One of the most important problems faced in IoT ecosystems that uses AI is the threat of data breaches and unauthorized access. IoT devices often have limited computational and storage resources making them susceptible to weak authentication and insecure communication protocols. Attackers use these vulnerabilities to intercept, alter or leak sensitive data while it is being transmitted between edge devices and cloud servers . AI models are extremely dependent on massive amounts of user-generated or sensor data for their training and inference. Compromise at any stage through insecure APIs, or firmware vulnerabilities, or poor key management, for example can lead to exposure of personally identifiable information (PII) or industrial control data (Rahman et al., 2020). A recent study by Symantec in 2024 found that more than 47% of IoT data breaches had happened as a result of misconfigured cloud storage or poor endpoint security highlighting the need for zero trust architectures and blockchain based authentication for verifiable and tamper proof of data transactions. In addition, edge nodes gathering data may become single points of failure. Once compromised, they can facilitate lateral movement within the IoT network, both to manipulate datasets used to train or run AI models (Bagdasaryan et al., 2020).

3.2 Model Poisoning and Adversarial Attacks

AI models that drive IoT decision systems by the data, or model parameters -- vulnerable to model poisoning and adversarial attacks deliberate manipulations of the data, or model parameters to degrade system performance or get misclassified. In model poisoning, the attackers inject the trained data sets (e.g. wrong labelled sensor readings) with malicious data samples to make the trained model come to incorrect inferences. In the case of federated learning (FL) environments broadly used in the context of IoT, such an attack may be distributed in a global way, corrupting shared models on edge nodes. On the other hand, adversarial attacks exploit the trained models with their vulnerability by making minor changes in the input details to mislead the AI predictions (Yazdinejad et al., 2024). For instance, adversarial noise added in the form of noise to image or sensor data can make a smart surveillance system misidentify an object. These vulnerabilities are particularly important to consider in security critical IoT applications such as in healthcare monitoring, autonomous vehicles and industrial robotics. Defense methods such as strong training, gradient masking and adversarial example detection have been proposed that suffer from limited features by computation overhead and the generalization issues. Emerging research focuses on the use of federated adversarial learning, model validation of blockchain models and secure aggregation protocols to ensure the trustworthiness of models within decentralized IoT environments (Chaganti, 2024).

3.3 Malicious Node Injection and Insider Threats

The heterogeneity and decentralized nature of IoT systems renders them vulnerable to malicious node injection, whereby malicious nodes are adopted by the attackers to implement a rogue node and attack the system. These malicious nodes are capable of doing many attacks including data spoofing, false-data injection or denial of service (DoS). AI-enabled IoT networks are especially in danger in particular, where poisoned data from nodes owned by a malicious actor can then flow within their machine learning pipelines and cause bias in the results of analytics, which can lead to false autonomous actions. For example, the errant reading of sensors which are taken in a smart grid could mislead the artificial intelligence (AI) controllers leading to imbalance in loads or blackouts (Meng et al., 2020). Insider threats are also a problem. Employees or administrators with higher privileges will intentionally or accidentally leak confidential data or model parameters. Such threats are hard to detect with the traditional perimeter security. AI-based behavioural analytics, the detection of user anomalies, and authentication of nodes using blockchain are emerging as effective countermeasures to detect the anomaly and verify the integrity of the device in real-time. Furthermore, device attestation and secure boot can guarantee that only trusted and verified nodes enter the AI-IoT data exchanges and can alleviate the injection and insider risks.

3.4 Scalability and Fault-Tolerance Issues

As IoT deployments grow to billions of interconnected devices, solving the problem of scalable and fault-tolerant security is not negligible. Traditional centralized security mechanisms find it difficult to cope with the actually enormous data streams and speed of AI-driven data. Moreover, in distributed IoT environments, resources of bandwidth, energy and computation are usually limited which makes real-time intrusion detection and response a difficult task. AI models that are distributed among nodes need to be in sync and consistent even in dynamic environments such as node failures or communication delays. It can be causing issues like model drift, variation in data or system downtime while settings involving federated learning is being even more prominent. Another major challenge is the scalability of the cryptographic processes. Traditional strong encryption techniques e.g. RSA or AES-256 may be very resource-intensive for low power IoT devices (Mudgerikar et al., 2020). In such cases, encryption techniques that are light weight or hardware-based security features are required. Achieving such right balance between system performance, energy consumption and computational overhead is now an open research question. Modern solutions for guaranteeing scalable resilience are founded on an amalgamation of threat prediction via artificial intelligence and edge-centric security orchestration and blockchain-enabled decentralized control of access to guarantee robust adaptive protection of next-generation IoT infrastructures. Despite the good progress made in the application of AI-driven security mechanisms, it is a tough scenario in the real world. High implementation cost, problems with interoperability between various IoT devices and additional computational cost are some of the factors that generally deter the use of advanced solutions such as blockchain and homomorphic encryption. Additionally, organization are posing Skill gaps and operational complexity as to how are distributed AI models managed at scale. Addressing these practical limitations is important to make sure that the security solutions are not only technically robust, but also economic and operationally sustainable (Li et al., 2021).

4. PRIVACY CHALLENGES IN AI-DRIVEN IOT

4.1 User Data Confidentiality and Identity Protection

Privacy protection is one of the most important issues in IoT ecosystems where AI plays a major role (devices gather sensitive personal information, such as location, biometric information, health metrics and behavioural patterns, 24/7. This pervasive collection of data comes with the increased risk of possible exposure of one's identity, re-identification attacks and unauthorized profiling. AI models trained on such data could inadvertently memorize user information so that it can then be reconstructed or inferred on personal attributes by attackers using model inversion or membership inference attacks. For instance, the adversaries can use the gradients, or output probabilities from the neural networks, to allow them to guess the individual user identities.

Maintaining confidentiality of data calls for implementing means such as data anonymization, data pseudonymization, and differential privacy, which can ensure that the data of no individual user can be uniquely identified even in the context of collaborative learning. Emerging models such as Federated Learning (FL) increase privacy by decentralizing training such that the raw data is kept on local devices only sharing the model update. In the case of AI-driven IoT, confidentiality is not only a technical objective, but a trust enabler, relating to the acceptance and compliance of users with global data protection standards (Shokri et al., 2017).

4.2 Privacy Risks in Data Sharing and Aggregation

AI-IoT systems heavily depend on data sharing and aggregation to make learning more accurate and generalised their models. However, these processes naturally introduce data privacy risks to the privacy of data, especially during transmission over untrusted intermediaries. Multi-source data aggregation from diverse IoT nodes and 3rd party cloud providers generate possibilities for data inference attacks and linkage attacks, in which attackers' pieces together partial datasets to re-identify users. In addition, shared datasets can be reverse engineered with the help of machine learning reconstruction methods, impairing privacy. Secure multi-party computation (SMC), homomorphic encryption and blockchain-based access control have been suggested as countermeasures to mitigate these risks. These technologies help us to do privacy-preserving analytics, i.e., analyses are performed on encrypted data without revealing any sensitive data. However, there is still a challenge of striking a balance between data utility and privacy, as increased levels of privacy tend to compromise the accuracy and efficiency of AI models (Sharon et al., 2022).

4.3 Threats in Cloud and Edge Environments

In AI-IoT Big Data frameworks, cloud and edge computing would be the core approach to managing huge volumes of data and real-time analytics. However, both these layers have different privacy risks. Cloud servers often contain centralized AI models, exposing them to data theft, unauthorized access and misuse by insiders. Edge devices, while reducing the latency and increasing the processing at the edge, are usually resource-constrained and therefore more prone to data interception, physical tampering, and firmware manipulation. Edge data caching and inference can also cause privacy leakage if the adversaries monitor the patterns of data that is cached or intercept the communication between devices and cloud services (Liu et al., 2023).

These issues have evolved feasible solutions in the shape of trusted execution environment through TEE, secure enclave, and privacy-preserving edge AI architectures. Such technologies help to keep sensitive processing in safe environments of hardware processing, and difficult for outside to interfere or get data. In addition, principles of zero trust networks and end-to-end encryption that even if part of the system has been compromised, private information is protected and far out of reach (Fouda et al., 2024).

4.4 Ethical and Regulatory Considerations

Privacy deals with the application of AI-enabled IoT systems extends far beyond the technical vulnerabilities in the system, covering the issues of ethical, social and legal dimensions that relate to data use. There are major questions of informed consent, transparency, accountability, and fairness at the collection and application of personal information via AI. Example, when AI models take biased decisions (or possible discriminatory decisions) based on the incomplete or unreal data trained through IoT, which usually results in violation of basic ethical standards and human rights against people.Global privacy frameworks, such as the General Data Protection Regulation (GDPR), California Consumer Privacy Act (CCPA), and India's Digital Personal Data Protection Act (DPDPA) has clear mandates for processing data legally, the consent of the user and the right to be forgotten (Rahman et al., 2021). However, enforcement remains a complex issue in distributed AI-IoT ecosystems with all this information due to localization of data and cross-border data flows. The new field of Responsible AI (RAI) with the added principle of privacy-by-design and ethics-by-design calls for AI models to promote values of society and human autonomy. Collaborative frameworks between governments, academia and industry is important in order to develop standardised privacy protocols, audit mechanisms and transparency frameworks to govern the AI-IoT deployments.

Ethical AI principles: Ethics and regulations are hand in hand when it comes to winning the trust of users in the long term. Privacy-by-design and transparency-by-design are ways that can be used to ensure that ethical considerations are taken into account throughout the AI-IoT lifecycle, including data collection, model design, and deployment. Such alignment between ethics and regulation is critical to bring the public confidence and facilitate the responsible adoption of IoT technologies on the basis of AI (Li et al., 2021).

Table 2. Common privacy risks in AI-IoT and mitigation strategies

Privacy Risk	Description	Affected Components	Mitigation Approach
Identity Exposure	User identity can be inferred	AI models, cloud databases	Differential privacy, pseudonymization
Data Aggregation Leakage	Sensitive info inferred from aggregated datasets	Cloud analytics, federated learning	Secure multiparty computation
Cloud/Edge Vulnerabilities	Data interception during transmission	Edge devices, cloud servers	End-to-end encryption, TEEs
Ethical & Regulatory Risks	Non-compliance with privacy laws	Entire AI-IoT ecosystem	GDPR/CCPA compliance, audit frameworks

Table 2 presents the typical privacy risks in AI-enabled IoT systems and associates them with the corresponding mitigation strategies in various system components.

5. EMERGING SECURITY AND PRIVACY-PRESERVING TECHNIQUES

The emerging linkage between Artificial Intelligence (AI), Internet of Things (IoT) and Big Data ecosystems led to the emergence of unprecedented opportunities and grave vulnerabilities. In order to build resilient and trustworthy infrastructures for AI-IoT systems, advanced cryptographic, distributed ledger and privacy-preserving machine learning techniques are more widely used by researchers. This section looks at some of the most important emerging solutions including blockchain, federated learning, homomorphic encryption, secure multiparty computation and differential privacy that, collectively, improve the security and privacy posture of AI driven IoT systems (Nguyen et al., 2021).

Table 3. Key privacy-preserving techniques in AI-IoT analytics

Technique	Description	Benefits	Limitations
Blockchain	Distributed ledger for IoT data	Immutability, transparency, tamper-proof	Latency, resource intensive
Federated Learning	Decentralized model training	Preserves local data privacy	Gradient leakage risk, heterogeneity issues
Homomorphic Encryption	Compute over encrypted data	Data confidentiality during computation	High computational cost
Secure Multiparty Computation	Collaborative computation without sharing inputs	Prevents raw data exposure	Complex implementation
Differential Privacy	Adds controlled noise to data or gradients	Mathematical privacy guarantees	Potential utility loss in AI models

Table 3 provides a comparison of emerging privacy preserving techniques for AI-based IoT Analytics with their advantages and disadvantages.

Figure 3. Overview of privacy-preserving techniques for AI-driven IoT

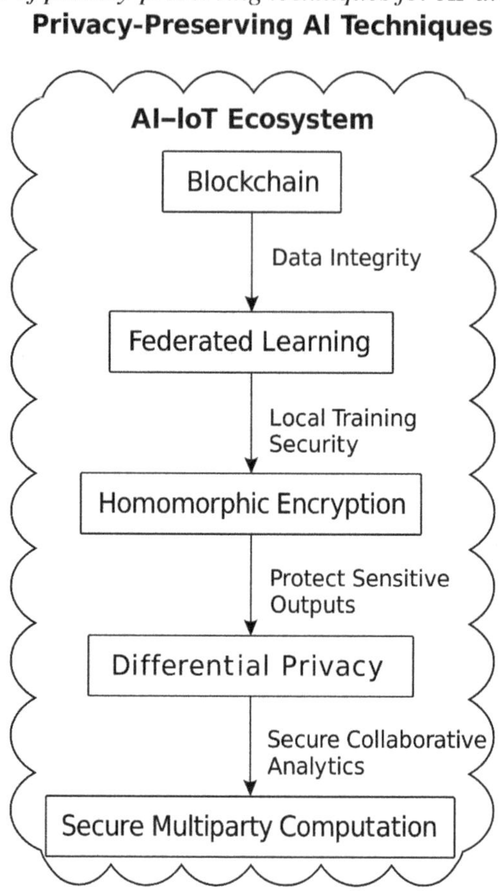

Figure 3 shows an overview of essential privacy preserving techniques applied in AI-driven IoT analytics and what their role is in safeguarding sensitive data.

5.1 Blockchain for Secure IoT Data Management

Blockchain technology has come up as an enabler of trust decentralization for IoT environments, which is a problem of data integrity, transparency and tamper resistance. By maintaining the ledger distribution, blockchain eliminates the need for centralized authorities and makes it easier to conduct safe transactions between IoT nodes. In the case of the AI-driven IoT systems, blockchain provides the immutability of the logging of the data exchange, which prevents unauthorized modification or deletion of the critical sensor data. Smart contracts are also used to automate the control of data access and to verify trust, therefore allowing only authenticated nodes to be involved in sharing data or data model updates. Integrating blockchain with edge and cloud AI enables a trusted pipeline of data in which model parameters and decision logs can be verified at distributed nodes. However, scalability and latency are still issues, particularly for resource constrained IoT devices. To address this problem, certain lightweight consensus algorithms such as Proof-of-Authority (PoA) or Practical Byzantine Fault Tolerance (PBFT) are being explored to be used in real-time IoT applications. Blockchain is the key to transforming the data management of IoT from centralized trust models to distributed and tamper-proof ecosystems thus making auditable and transparent AI operations possible (Kairouz et al., 2021).

5.2 Federated Learning for Privacy-Preserving AI

Blockchain is the key to revolutionizing the data management of IoT from centralized trust models to distributed and tamper proof ecosystems thus making auditable and transparent AI operations possible .This technique goes a long way to combating privacy risks in that sensitive local data never leaves the device, addressing huge GDPR and DPDPA compliance requirements. In the IoT ecosystem, federated learning enables the concept of distributed intelligence where the edge devices, sensors or gateways contribute to the training of the models. However, even in FL, the model gradients or updates can leak private information, so it is necessary to use secure aggregation and differential privacy techniques. Recent developments involve a combination of FL and blockchain, making it possible to obtain immutable logging of model updates and allow a traceable participation of IoT nodes. Moreover, by using personalized federated learning, it is possible for heterogeneous IoT devices with different data distributions to learn models together, while maintaining privacy and accuracy. Federated Learning not only improves privacy but it also decentralises AI computation making it less reliant on vulnerable centralised data centres (Dhanda et al., 2020).

5.3 Homomorphic Encryption and Secure Multiparty Computation

Homomorphic Encryption (HE) and Secure Multiparty Computation (SMC) are cryptographic methods which allow computation to be performed over encrypted or distributed data, and offer mathematical confidentiality guarantees. Homomorphic encryption enables the cloud or edge servers to perform their operations on the encrypted data from the IoT without decrypting it; thus, the exposure doesn't exist for the computation. This is especially good at the privacy-sensitive areas such as smart healthcare, financial IoT and industrial automation. On the other hand, secure multiparty computation Multiple Internet of Things stakeholders can work together to calculate a function on their inputs and keep their inputs private. In cases of AI, this will be in order to protect sensitive training data or parameters for multi-organization federated setups. The combination of HE and SMC with IoT analytics based on artificial intelligence (AI) enables privacy-by-design architectures in which neither the raw data nor the model parameters are exposed which means adherence to strict privacy mandates and ethical standards (Gharavi et al., 2024).

5.4 Differential Privacy for Sensitive Data Protection

The development of Differential Privacy (DP) has emerged as a cornerstone that would be used to quantify and control the loss of privacy of AI systems. It provides a mathematical system to ensure that inclusion in exclusion of the data of just one user does not have a significant impact on the result of an algorithm. In the case of AI enabled IoT systems, the differential privacy approach is to introduce a controlled amount of noise into the data, the model update or the output. These methods are helpful to hide the information on particular individuals in overall analytical value. Such methods are most appropriate to smart healthcare, smart energy systems and transportation networks where personal data is constantly collected and processed. Modern AI frameworks provide differential privacy in various ways: in the collection of data, in the training of the models, and even when we use the model to infer, providing good and quantitative privacy protection. Major tech companies like Google and Apple have employed differential privacy in large-scale IoT data processing environments, and proven that differential privacy works well and reliably in real world. Although there is some degree of accuracy impairment arising from DP, the integration of federated learning and homomorphic encryption with DP forms an effective multi-layer framework that does bring some kind of balance between security assurance and data usability. Differential Privacy is the quantitative backbone of privacy preserving AI, which guarantees ethical compliant use of IoT Big Data. (Liu et al, 2023).

6. CASE STUDIES AND APPLICATIONS

The convergence of Artificial Intelligence (AI), Internet of Things (IoT) and Big Data analytics has changed a number of industries. However, the need for secure and privacy-preserving architectures is of fundamental importance in many areas such as healthcare, urban infrastructure, manufacturing and logistics. This section discusses examples of real-world applications that show how AI-powered IoT systems can be used to transform industries with potential and challenges when it comes to implementing IoT systems with strong security and privacy (Rahman et al., 2020).

Table 4. Representative case studies of secure AI-IoT deployments

Application Domain	Case Study	Security/Privacy Mechanism	Key Outcome
Healthcare	SEHIoT Architecture (Europe)	Blockchain, federated learning	Secure patient data sharing, improved diagnostics
Smart Cities	Singapore Smart Nation	Edge AI, blockchain identity	Real-time urban analytics, citizen data privacy
Industrial IoT	Siemens Predictive Maintenance	Blockchain logging, edge AI	Reduced operational risks, verifiable event logging
Transportation & Logistics	Tesla Fleet Learning	Federated learning, blockchain verification	Privacy-preserving autonomous fleet updates

Table 4 contains representative case studies of real-world cases of secure and privacy-aware AI-IoT deployments in various orders of applications.

Figure 4. Secure healthcare IoT architecture using blockchain and federated learning

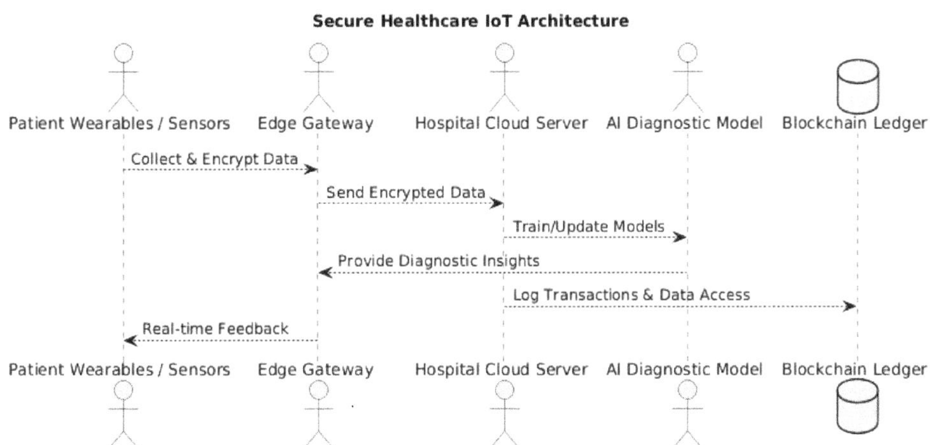

Figure 4 shows a secure healthcare IoT architecture that incorporates a combination of blockchain and federated learning to make sure privacy-preserving AI-based data analysis.

6.1 Healthcare Data Security in IoT Systems

The healthcare industry has been one of the most prominent users of AI-IoT technologies, using smart sensors, wearables and cloud analytics to remotely monitor patients, diagnose and implement precision medicine. However, these systems handle very sensitive medical data and may therefore be the prime objectives of cyberattacks. For example, IoT frameworks with the help of AI in hospitals analyse patient vitals in real-time using wearable devices, which are sent to cloud servers for artificial intelligence-based diagnosis. A prominent case study example is the AI-Enabled Secure Health IoT architecture deployed in Europe which incorporates blockchain and federated learning in order to guarantee patient data privacy without centralizing the raw data. Homomorphic encryption has been successfully applied to medical image classification for privacy-preserving AI, which allows the encrypted data to be processed by AI model and preserve diagnostic precision. Similarly, differential privacy has been incorporated into contact tracing apps for the Coronavirus pandemic and for analysing electronic health records (EHR) data, in order to reduce the risk of re-identification. These solutions demonstrate the possibility of secure and AI-based healthcare systems, in which privacy protection forms a part of patient trust and regulatory compliance under the GDPR and HIPAA frameworks (Meng et al., 2020).

6.2 Smart Cities and Secure Urban Analytics

Smart cities depend greatly on the integration of IoT and AI at a large scale and connecting systems such as traffic, energy distribution, public surveillance, and waste management. While the move towards data-driven management of cities allows for efficiency and responsive capabilities in real time, this results in serious privacy and security concerns because of the high level of interconnection between critical public infrastructure.

Its instance, Singapore's Smart Nation program is a good example of how AI-based video analytics and edge computing are used to manage traffic flow and enhance urban safety - all without sensitive data being centralised, and consequently exposed to possible large-scale data exposure. The city is also employing blockchain-based identity management systems to assist in the integrity in accessing public services. Similarly, the Barcelona Urban IoT Project deployed the federated edge AI models which process the sensor data at the edge in order to reduce the latency and prevent the leakage of privacy information during data transmission to central servers. These types of smart city frameworks show the value in multi-layered security frameworks, providing edge AI, zero trust networking and differentially private analytics to ensure the safety of citizen data and intelligent urban planning (Habib et al., 2023).

6.3 Industrial IoT and Critical Infrastructure Protection

The Industrial Internet of Things (IIoT) forms the basis of the modern manufacturing and critical infrastructure industries like energy, utilities, and defense. AI-driven IIoT systems for predictive maintenance optimization, chain supply automation & operational analytics. However, they also increase the attack surface with interconnected sensors and controllers and with robotic systems. A landmark project by Siemens and Intel (2023) installed AI-based models of anomaly detection algorithms on the edge devices, which help to detect the operational deviation in real-time. These models were integrated with the blockchain-based audit trails, assuring the verifiable logging of all industrial events. In another example, Saudi Aramco's Smart Refinery Network used federated AI architectures to help process sensitive data in a decentralized way at plant sites to reduce the risks of industrial espionage while preserving accuracy in analytics. Moreover, there is research on quantum safe encryption protocols for future proofing industrial control systems for post-quantum cyber threats. Industrial case studies as a shift to resilient, privacy-aware IIoT ecosystems where AI-driven intelligence co-exists with strong data governance and operational continuity requirements (Lifelo et al., 2024).

6.4 Secure IoT in Transportation and Logistics

The transportation and logistics industry are putting more and more faith in AI-IoT systems to help manage fleets, optimize routes and coordinate autonomous vehicles. These systems generate and transmit sensitive information such as the vehicle identity, location history and sensor telemetry, which demand a high level of security and privacy. In 2024 the AI-Edge Fleet Program of Tesla made use of federated learning models in fleets of vehicles, which enables decentralized updates to driving models, without having to share the raw sensor data. The introduction of blockchain-related verification through consensus ensured models became authentic and tamper proof. Similarly, Maersk Line, one of the largest shipping companies in the world, implemented a secure IoT logistics platform that featured homomorphic encryption to secure cargo tracking information, zero trust identity management to secure port communication systems. These examples tend to show how secure AI-IoT solutions are making it possible to be not only operationally efficient but also compliant with the requirements of regulatory compliance in data protection mandates for global logistics and intelligent transport systems. The reviewed case studies emphasize that the most beneficial security architectures for AI-IoT deployments are those that comprise the use of layered security architectures with an edge intelligence approach that incorporates privacy-saving learning and decentralized trust architectures. However, scalability, interoperability, and operational cost are some of the challenges that are important here. These sets of findings make it clear how to be mindful of the need to not only match technical solutions but to also match them with organizational readiness, regulatory requirements and real-world constraints is important. (Menon et al., 2025).

7. OPEN RESEARCH CHALLENGES AND FUTURE DIRECTIONS

The development of Artificial intelligence (AI)-enabled Internet of Things (IoT) systems has helped to deliver transformative capabilities in healthcare, smart cities, industrial networks and transportation. However, the combination of security, privacy and performance at scale is a big research challenge. This section discusses some of the important open issues and future directions that will be relevant for the researchers and practitioners who will like to design the next generation of AI-IoT architectures.

Future research needs to focus on post quantum cryptography in order to secure long lived IoT systems against quantum threats ahead. Additionally, diagrammatic security frameworks that are compliant with Nistar, Iseo, and Etc. criteria are critical to easing interoperate and compliance across the world deployment. Developing quantifiable measures of the privacy-utility trade off and incorporating explainable AI in security process will increase trust, openness and adoption of AI-enabled IoT systems even further.

7.1 Balancing Security, Privacy, and Performance

One of the existing issues in AI-IoT ecosystems is to achieve a balance between security/privacy mechanisms and system performance. Techniques such as homomorphic encryption, differential privacy and blockchain offer high levels of protection but are often computationally expensive and introduce high levels of latency, which can be prohibitive in real-time IoT applications. Edge AI and lightweight cryptography offer some of the remedies but optimization of such methods in heterogeneous IoT devices with different processing capabilities is an on-going research topic. Future work may focus on adaptive security frameworks, which vary the level of protection in a dynamic fashion depending on context, data sensitivity and system load, in a way that is a balance between maximising the use of resources and respecting privacy requirements (Dhirani et al., 2021).

7.2 Interoperability in Multi-Vendor IoT Ecosystems

Today's IoT environments comprise a wide variety of devices, vendors and platforms with different data formats and communication standards. This diversity means interoperability can be a serious security issue of its own. To support seamless analytics and decision making across such systems, an AI-enabled IoT network needs to secure continuing authentication, authorization, and secure communication. New solutions are emerging - including federated learning across mismatched devices, and standardized IoT data models, and blockchain-based identity frameworks - which show great promise for enabling safe and fluid interoperability. However, in the real world IoT environments are highly dynamic, and devices will often enter or leave the network. Because of this, creating flexible and plug-and-play architectures that are compliant with privacy laws is still a complicated and evolving research challenge for flexible AIoT (RISK, 2021).

7.3 Sustainability and Energy-Efficient Security Models

The energy demand of AI-IoT systems has become a major issue, especially when the number of sensors, edge-computing devices and encryption processes continues to grow. Security and privacy mechanisms that are computationally intensive might be incompatible with environmentally sustainable IoT design. As such, there is a recent trend in the study of energy conscious security frameworks, lightweight cryptographic techniques, and approximate AI models that reduce power and processing needs while still keeping accuracy, and data privacy, at acceptable levels. In addition, using renewable energy sources, energy harvesting IoT devices and energy management systems powered by AI can also help to build IoT networks that are both secure and environment-conscious (Aouedi et al., 2024).

7.4 Future Research Opportunities

Emerging environments provide significant opportunities for improving secure and privacy-preserving AI-IoT systems:

1. **Post-Quantum Cryptography**: Preparing AI-IoT infrastructures for quantum threats, including blockchain and homomorphic encryption approaches.
2. **Explainable AI (XAI) for IoT Security**: Interpretable model development to perform anomaly detection, intrusion detection, and mitigate any privacy violations.
3. **Adaptive Multi-Layer Security**: Federated learning, differential privacy, blockchain, and edge AI all deployed in a situationally aware manner to realize self-optimizing security.
4. **Ethical and Regulatory Compliance**: Many aspects of designing an AI-IoT system relate to meeting present regulatory frameworks, such as GDPR, CCPA, and DPDPA, besides looking forward to future requirements also.
5. **Sustainable AI-IoT Architectures** Designing energy-efficient models, green edge computing, and sustainable AI best practices without compromising reliability or security.

Taken all together, these avenues will help work in unison to create reliable, efficient, and robust AI-IoT systems promoting widespread adoption throughout the sector and for ensuring privacy, security, and sustainability (Menon et al., 2025).

8. ADVANCED APPLICATIONS AND IMPLEMENTATION STRATEGIES

The unification and Artificial Intelligence, IoT of Big Data has shaped a new evolution last has allowed organizations much more to have and develop instant insights, anticipate future trends and how to apply intelligent automate new increasing industries. If performed with the right care and responsibility, companies can create AI-powered IoT ecosystems that will not only be technically efficient but also socially responsible while striking the correct balance between security, privacy, efficiency, and sustainability. Although previous sections highlighted the areas of vulnerabilities and privacy risks in such systems, recent solutions and implementation strategies demonstrate that powerful architectural design and techniques focused on privacy concerns can demonstrate to a great extent a reduction in these concerns. The next section examines some real-world examples, ways of deployment and suggested practices for AI-based IoT environments, taking into account both the technical basis of the environment and the practical applications (Gökbakan et al., 2025).

8.1 Advanced Applications Across Key Sectors

Healthcare: IOT systems based on artificial intelligence have revolutionized the patient monitoring process, the diagnostic process, and the personalized treatment process. Wearable devices are advanced forms of wearable devices that continuously collect vital signs whereas, AI models analyse the sign streams for anomaly detection and predictive diagnostics. Federated learning and edge AI frameworks ensure that the sensitive patient data will be kept in local devices so there will be less exposure but can train models collaboratively. Secure integration of Blockchains promises hospitals to keep unchangeable records about data accessing and AI-driven decision making which makes due auditing and regulatory compliance possible.

Smart Cities: Urban Infrastructure gets a lot of advantage from the implementations of AI-IoT. Applications include smart traffic management, smart energy grids, environmental monitoring and public safety analytics. Edge-based AI inference helps to mitigate the issue of latency whereas privacy-preserving techniques like differential privacy helps in safeguarding the information of the citizens during large-scale data aggregation *(Al-Garadi et al., 2020)*

Industrial IoT (IIoT): Advanced manufacturing environment uses AI-IoT for predictive maintenance, supply chain optimization, and autonomous robotics. Data from sensors and controllers are processed with mechanisms of AI algorithms for prediction of equipment failure, optimizing operations, and minimizing downtime. Security strategies include multi-layered architectures with diverse combinations of edge AI, secure communication protocols and blockchain audit trails, to avoid sabotage, unauthorized access, or insider attacks.

Transportation and Logistics: AI-IoT systems are used to enable autonomous vehicles to navigate, fleet tracking, route optimization and real-time shipment monitoring. Privacy preserving federated learning enables vehicles to update shared models without sharing raw telemetry data in order to preserve confidentiality. Homomorphic encryption and the secure multiparty computation further safeguard the sensitive information about operations in collaborative logistics networks *(Al-Garadi et al., 2020)*.

8.2 Implementation Strategies for Secure AI-IoT Systems

Building secure and privacy-aware AI-IoT systems requires well-thought-out architectural planning at various layers, hardware, software, and network. Some key approaches include:

1. **Edge–Cloud Hybrid Computation:** Distributing the processing tasks between the edge devices and the cloud servers helps to improve the privacy and reduce the delay. Sensitive information can be processed on the edge and only aggregated information can be sent to the cloud for wider analysis.
2. **Context-Aware Security:** Security procedures should be context-aware - they should adapt to the sensitivity of the data and the capability of the device. For example, lightweight encryption may be used by small IoT sensors, or more sensitive workloads may require more sophisticated encryption methods such as fully homomorphic encryption.
3. **Standardized Interoperability:** As IoT ecosystems can involve devices from different vendors, there must be standardized protocols for data exchange, communication protocols, as well as security. Standard APIs with the blockchain-based identity management can include secure interaction between different devices.
4. **Privacy Built into the Design:** Privacy should not be an afterthought - it should be built in from the earliest design stages of the system.

This means techniques such as Federated learning, Differential Privacy and secure multi-party computation should be baked in early on with the goal of compliance with legal frameworks to GDPR and CCPA (Sun et al., 2024).

CONCLUSION

The Combination of AI, IoT, and Big Data has opened tremendous doors in terms of health, creating smart cities, automating industry, transportation and so much more opportunity. However, it has also raised a few security and privacy issues such as data breaches, adversarial attacks, privacy leakage and also compliance issues. This chapter has discussed the basics of AI-IoT integration, the important security and privacy risks and the emerging solutions like blockchain, federated learning, homomorphic encryption, secure multiparty computation and differential privacy, among others, which, collectively, support the implementation of secure and privacy-preserving AI-IoT systems. Real-world case studies in healthcare, smart cities, industrial IoT and logistics presented practical use cases as best practices and lessons were discussed, and the discussion of the challenges of open research stressed the importance of finding the right balance for security, privacy and performance, interoperability between multi-vendor ecosystems, and energy efficient and sustainable models.

Going forward, a number of areas come to the fore as crucial for the future of AI-IoT deployments, including adaptive frameworks, post-quantum security, explainable AI, and responsible governance in order for AI-IoT deployments to be resilient, ethical, and trustworthy. Basically, secure data handling and user privacy are the critically enabling factors of the widespread acceptance and effectiveness of AI-infused IoT systems. By combining technological innovation and ethical approach, AI-IoT infrastructures of the next generation are in a position to create robust, sustainable, and socially responsible solutions that will elicit the benefits and minimize the risks.

REFERENCES

Al-Fuqaha, A., Guizani, M., Mohammadi, M., Aledhari, M., & Ayyash, M. (2015). Internet of things: A survey on enabling technologies, protocols, and applications. *IEEE Communications Surveys and Tutorials*, *17*(4), 2347–2376.

Al-Garadi, M. A., Mohamed, A., Al-Ali, A. K., Du, X., Ali, I., & Guizani, M. (2020). A survey of machine and deep learning methods for internet of things (IoT) security. *IEEE Communications Surveys and Tutorials*, *22*(3), 1646–1685.

Alwakeel, A. M. (2021). An overview of fog computing and edge computing security and privacy issues. *Sensors (Basel)*, *21*(24), 8226. PMID: 34960320

Alwarafy, A., Al-Thelaya, K. A., Abdallah, M., Schneider, J., & Hamdi, M. (2020). A survey on security and privacy issues in edge-computing-assisted internet of things. *IEEE Internet of Things Journal*, *8*(6), 4004–4022.

Aouedi, O., Vu, T. H., Sacco, A., Nguyen, D. C., Piamrat, K., Marchetto, G., & Pham, Q. V. (2024). A survey on intelligent Internet of Things: Applications, security, privacy, and future directions. *IEEE Communications Surveys and Tutorials*.

Atzori, L., Iera, A., & Morabito, G. (2017). Understanding the Internet of Things: Definition, potentials, and societal role of a fast-evolving paradigm. *Ad Hoc Networks*, *56*, 122–140.

Bagdasaryan, E., Veit, A., Hua, Y., Estrin, D., & Shmatikov, V. (2020, June). How to backdoor federated learning. In *International conference on artificial intelligence and statistics* (pp. 2938-2948). PMLR.

Bansal, M., Chana, I., & Clarke, S. (2020). A survey on iot big data: Current status, 13 v's challenges, and future directions. *ACM Computing Surveys*, *53*(6), 1–59.

Chaganti, K. (2024). Adversarial Attacks on AI-driven Cybersecurity Systems: A Taxonomy and Defense Strategies. *Authorea Preprints*.

Chen, M., Challita, U., Saad, W., Yin, C., & Debbah, M. (2019). Artificial neural networks-based machine learning for wireless networks: A tutorial. *IEEE Communications Surveys and Tutorials*, *21*(4), 3039–3071.

Deng, S., Zhao, H., Fang, W., Yin, J., Dustdar, S., & Zomaya, A. Y. (2020). Edge intelligence: The confluence of edge computing and artificial intelligence. *IEEE Internet of Things Journal*, *7*(8), 7457–7469.

Dhanda, S. S., Singh, B., & Jindal, P. (2020). Lightweight cryptography: A solution to secure IoT. *Wireless Personal Communications*, *112*(3), 1947–1980.

Dhirani, L. L., Armstrong, E., & Newe, T. (2021). Industrial IoT, cyber threats, and standards landscape: Evaluation and roadmap. *Sensors (Basel)*, *21*(11), 3901. PMID: 34198727

Fouda, M. M., Fadlullah, Z. M., Ibrahem, M. I., & Kato, N. (2024). Privacy-preserving data-driven learning models for emerging communication networks: A comprehensive survey. *IEEE Communications Surveys and Tutorials*.

Gharavi, H., Granjal, J., & Monteiro, E. (2024). Post-quantum blockchain security for the Internet of Things: Survey and research directions. *IEEE Communications Surveys and Tutorials*, *26*(3), 1748–1774.

Gökbakan, Ü. B., Dümbgen, F., & Caron, S. (2025, May). A data-driven contact estimation method for wheeled-biped robots. In *2025 IEEE International Conference on Robotics and Automation (ICRA)* (pp. 7073-7079). IEEE.

Habib, A. A., Hasan, M. K., Alkhayyat, A., Islam, S., Sharma, R., & Alkwai, L. M. (2023). False data injection attack in smart grid cyber physical system: Issues, challenges, and future direction. *Computers & Electrical Engineering*, *107*, 108638.

Hafeth, D. A., Al-Khafajiy, M., & Kollias, S. (2024). EdgeScan for IoT Contextual Understanding With Edge Computing and Image Captioning. *IEEE Internet of Things Journal*.

Hoenig, A., Roy, K., Acquaah, Y. T., Yi, S., & Desai, S. S. (2024). Explainable AI for cyber-physical systems: Issues and challenges. *IEEE Access : Practical Innovations, Open Solutions*, *12*, 73113–73140.

Iqbal, R., Doctor, F., More, B., Mahmud, S., & Yousuf, U. (2020). Big Data analytics and Computational Intelligence for Cyber–Physical Systems: Recent trends and state of the art applications. *Future Generation Computer Systems*, *105*, 766–778.

Kairouz, P., McMahan, H. B., Avent, B., Bellet, A., Bennis, M., Bhagoji, A. N., ... & Zhao, S. (2021). Advances and open problems in federated learning. *Foundations and trends® in machine learning, 14*(1–2), 1-210.

Leme, R. D. S., de Souza Pinto, J., Zanon, L. G., Sigahi, T. F., Moraes, G. H. S. M. D., Moro, S. R., & Anholon, R. (2025). Information security management: a fuzzy DEMATEL analysis of the new ISO/IEC 27001: 2022 controls. *Information and Computer Security*.

Li, Q., Wen, Z., Wu, Z., Hu, S., Wang, N., Li, Y., & He, B. (2021). A survey on federated learning systems: Vision, hype and reality for data privacy and protection. *IEEE Transactions on Knowledge and Data Engineering*, *35*(4), 3347–3366.

Lifelo, Z., Ding, J., Ning, H., & Dhelim, S. (2024). Artificial intelligence-enabled metaverse for sustainable smart cities: Technologies, applications, challenges, and future directions. *Electronics (Basel), 13*(24), 4874.

Liu, Y., Wang, J., Yan, Z., Wan, Z., & Jäntti, R. (2023). A survey on blockchain-based trust management for Internet of Things. *IEEE Internet of Things Journal, 10*(7), 5898–5922.

Meng, W., Li, W., Wang, Y., & Au, M. H. (2020). Detecting insider attacks in medical cyber–physical networks based on behavioral profiling. *Future Generation Computer Systems, 108*, 1258–1266.

Menon, U. V., Kumaravelu, V. B., Kumar, C. V., Rammohan, A., Chinnadurai, S., Venkatesan, R., & Selvaprabhu, P. (2025). AI-powered IoT: A survey on integrating artificial intelligence with IoT for enhanced security, efficiency, and smart applications. *IEEE Access : Practical Innovations, Open Solutions.*

Mudgerikar, A., Sharma, P., & Bertino, E. (2020). Edge-based intrusion detection for IoT devices. [TMIS]. *ACM Transactions on Management Information Systems, 11*(4), 1–21.

Nguyen, D. C., Ding, M., Pathirana, P. N., Seneviratne, A., Li, J., & Poor, H. V. (2021). Federated learning for internet of things: A comprehensive survey. *IEEE Communications Surveys and Tutorials, 23*(3), 1622–1658.

Rahman, M. A., Hossain, M. S., Islam, M. S., Alrajeh, N. A., & Muhammad, G. (2020). Secure and provenance enhanced internet of health things framework: A blockchain managed federated learning approach. *IEEE Access : Practical Innovations, Open Solutions, 8*, 205071–205087. PMID: 34192116

Rahman, M. S., Khalil, I., Moustafa, N., Kalapaaking, A. P., & Bouras, A. (2021). A blockchain-enabled privacy-preserving verifiable query framework for securing cloud-assisted industrial internet of things systems. *IEEE Transactions on Industrial Informatics, 18*(7), 5007–5017.

Sharon, Y., Berend, D., Liu, Y., Shabtai, A., & Elovici, Y. (2022). Tantra: Timing-based adversarial network traffic reshaping attack. *IEEE Transactions on Information Forensics and Security, 17*, 3225–3237.

Shokri, R., Stronati, M., Song, C., & Shmatikov, V. (2017, May). Membership inference attacks against machine learning models. In *2017 IEEE symposium on security and privacy (SP)* (pp. 3-18). IEEE.

Sonkar, A. (2025). The Digital Personal Data Protection Act, 2023: Analysing Its Implications, Challenges, and Future Prospects. *International Cybersecurity Law Review*, •••, 1–23.

Sun, P., Shen, S., Wan, Y., Wu, Z., Fang, Z., & Gao, X. Z. (2024). A survey of iot privacy security: Architecture, technology, challenges, and trends. *IEEE Internet of Things Journal*, *11*(21), 34567–34591.

Yang, C., Huang, Q., Li, Z., Liu, K., & Hu, F. (2017). Big Data and cloud computing: Innovation opportunities and challenges. *International Journal of Digital Earth*, *10*(1), 13–53.

Yazdinejad, A., Dehghantanha, A., Karimipour, H., Srivastava, G., & Parizi, R. M. (2024). A robust privacy-preserving federated learning model against model poisoning attacks. *IEEE Transactions on Information Forensics and Security*, *19*, 6693–6708.

Chapter 6
Opportunities and Future Directions in AI Inference for IoT

Roheen Qamar
http://orcid.org/0000-0003-4169-9455
Quaid-e-Awam University of Engineering, Science, and Technology, Nawabshah, Pakistan

Baqar Ali Zardari
http://orcid.org/0000-0002-3573-1191
Quaid-e-Awam University of Engineering, Science, and Technology, Nawabshah, Pakistan

Umair Ahmed Qadir
Quaid-e-Awam University of Engineering, Science, and Technology, Nawabshah, Pakistan

Hasnain Raza Lashari
Quaid-e-Awam University of Engineering, Science, and Technology, Nawabshah, Pakistan

ABSTRACT

The integration of Artificial Intelligence (AI) inference into the Internet of Things (IoT) ecosystem is reshaping the landscape of intelligent systems by enabling real-time analytics, predictive modeling, and autonomous decision-making directly at the device and network levels. Unlike traditional IoT systems that primarily collect and transmit data for centralized processing, AI-enabled IoT leverages edge and fog computing to bring intelligence closer to data sources, reducing latency, improv.

DOI: 10.4018/979-8-3373-7046-0.ch006

1. INTRODUCTION

The integration of Artificial Intelligence (AI) inference into the Internet of Things (IoT) has revolutionized how intelligent systems perceive, process, and respond to dynamic environments. AI inference—the process of executing trained machine learning models on devices or cloud platforms—has emerged as the foundation for intelligent decision-making in IoT ecosystems. With billions of interconnected devices producing massive volumes of heterogeneous data, efficient inference mechanisms are necessary for enabling automation, personalization, and predictive insights.

This chapter explores the key opportunities offered by AI inference in IoT, while highlighting future research directions and challenges. Emphasis is placed on the technological advancements, applications, and architectural shifts that will drive the next generation of intelligent IoT systems.

The Internet of Things (IoT) has rapidly transformed into a critical technological paradigm, interconnecting billions of devices across industries, cities, and homes. With this explosive growth, the demand for intelligent processing of data generated by IoT devices has risen dramatically. Traditional data handling methods, which rely heavily on centralized cloud computing, often struggle to meet the requirements of low latency, privacy, and real-time decision-making. This is where Artificial Intelligence (AI) inference comes into play, providing the ability to execute trained machine learning models to draw conclusions and make predictions directly from IoT data streams.

AI inference enables IoT systems to move beyond simple data collection and reporting. Instead, devices can analyze information locally, detect patterns, and make autonomous decisions. This capability transforms IoT from being a passive sensing network into an active, intelligent ecosystem. For instance, in smart homes, AI inference allows devices to predict user behavior and automate energy usage, while in industrial settings, it enables predictive maintenance to prevent equipment failures before they occur (Heydari & Mahmoud, 2025). As shown in Figure 1, AI inference enables real-time decision-making in IoT.

Figure 1 illustrates the concept of Artificial Intelligence (AI) inference and its role in transforming raw IoT data into actionable intelligence.

Figure 1. Artificial Intelligence (AI) inference

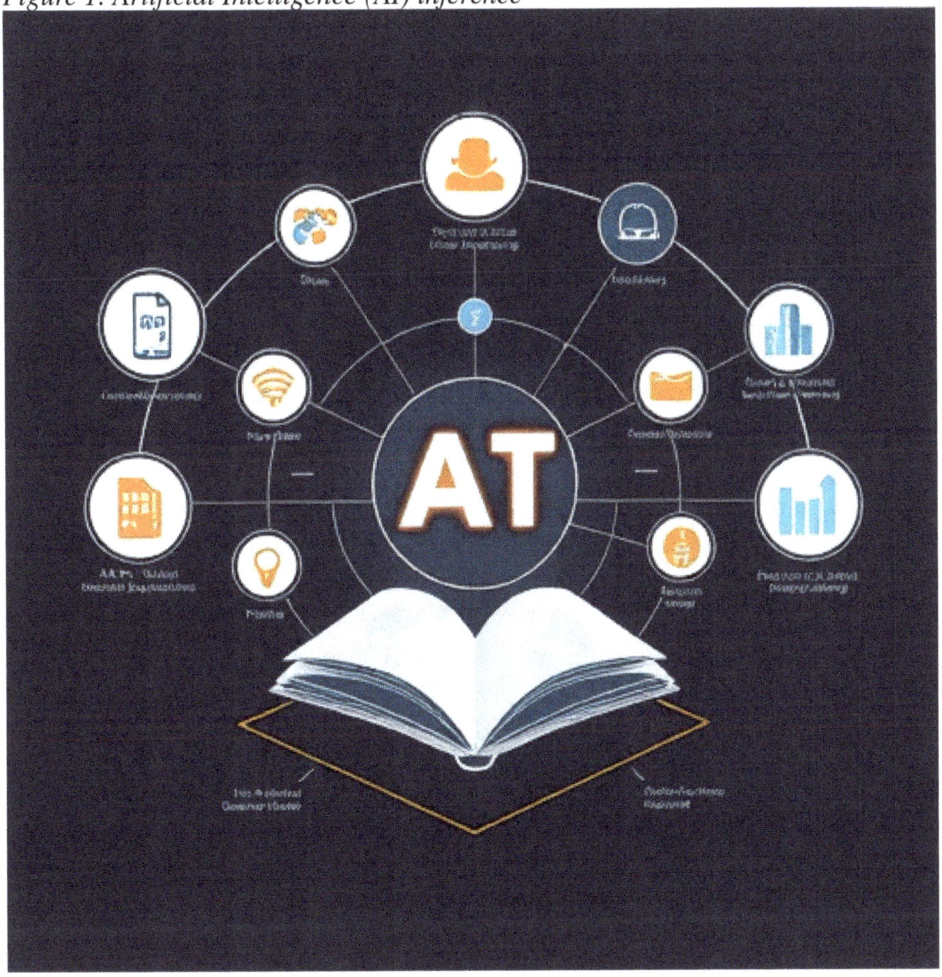

The emergence of edge computing and powerful low-power processors has made on-device AI inference feasible. Traditionally, IoT devices had to send all raw data to centralized servers for processing. However, with advancements in hardware accelerators and lightweight AI models, inference can now be performed at the edge, reducing communication overhead and enabling real-time responsiveness. This shift is unlocking opportunities in mission-critical areas such as autonomous driving, healthcare monitoring, and disaster management, where immediate action is essential.

Another key driver of AI inference in IoT is the need for scalability and efficiency. As the number of connected devices continues to multiply, centralized data processing becomes impractical. Distributed inference strategies such as federated learning allow AI models to be executed across multiple devices while maintaining data privacy. This decentralized approach ensures that sensitive information remains local, addressing regulatory concerns while still enabling collaborative intelligence.

The integration of AI-driven inference with 5G and emerging 6G networks opens new opportunities for ultra-low latency and high-reliability IoT applications. High-speed wireless communication enables real-time inference offloading between devices, edge nodes, and cloud servers. This synergy supports mission-critical applications such as autonomous vehicles, smart grids, and remote healthcare, where timely and accurate decision-making is essential. Future research should explore intelligent inference scheduling mechanisms that adapt to dynamic network conditions.

Another important direction is the development of self-learning and continual inference systems for IoT environments. Unlike static models, these systems can evolve over time by learning from new data streams without requiring complete retraining. Continual inference allows IoT devices to adapt to changing user behaviors, environmental conditions, and device aging. However, ensuring stability and preventing catastrophic forgetting remain open research challenges.

In addition to performance and scalability, AI inference offers significant advantages in terms of sustainability. Resource-aware inference techniques are being developed to optimize computational loads and reduce energy consumption, which is particularly important for battery-operated devices in remote or inaccessible environments. By adopting energy-efficient models, IoT systems can prolong device lifespans, minimize maintenance costs, and support environmentally sustainable practices (Maduranga et al., 2024).

The opportunities created by AI inference extend across diverse domains. In healthcare, AI-enabled wearable's can detect anomalies in vital signs and alert medical staff in real-time. In agriculture, IoT sensors combined with inference models can monitor soil conditions and optimize irrigation systems. In smart cities, AI inference enables intelligent traffic management, waste monitoring, and pollution control. These applications illustrate the transformative impact of combining AI with IoT infrastructures.

Despite these benefits, deploying AI inference in IoT is not without challenges. Devices often face resource constraints, including limited processing power, memory, and energy. Moreover, IoT networks are highly heterogeneous, requiring interoperability across diverse platforms. Addressing these issues requires continued innovation in model compression, distributed learning frameworks, and adaptive inference strategies that balance performance with efficiency.

The convergence of emerging technologies with AI inference promises to reshape the IoT landscape further. The integration of 5G and upcoming 6G networks will enhance communication speeds, enabling real-time collaborative inference between devices and cloud platforms. Similarly, neuromorphic computing and quantum machine learning offer futuristic possibilities for ultra-efficient and high-capacity inference. These technologies will help IoT systems adapt to the ever-increasing complexity and scale of global data ecosystems (Gill, Golec, Hu, Xu, Du, Wu, & Uhlig, 2025).

Another critical aspect of the future of AI inference in IoT is trust and transparency. As IoT devices are increasingly embedded into sensitive domains such as healthcare, finance, and public safety, the need for explainable and ethical AI becomes paramount. Explainable AI (XAI) techniques will ensure that inference outcomes are interpretable and aligned with human values, while ethical frameworks will safeguard against bias, misuse, and security risks.

The convergence of digital twins and AI inference presents another promising opportunity. Digital twins enable virtual representations of physical IoT systems, allowing inference models to be tested, optimized, and validated before deployment. By integrating real-time inference feedback with digital twins, IoT systems can achieve predictive maintenance, fault detection, and performance optimization at scale. This approach reduces operational costs and improves system reliability.

Security-aware inference is a critical future research area, as IoT devices are highly vulnerable to adversarial attacks, data poisoning, and model inversion threats. Protecting inference models and data integrity requires robust encryption, secure hardware enclaves, and anomaly detection mechanisms. Future directions include developing lightweight yet effective defense strategies that can operate within the limited computational resources of IoT devices.

In summary, AI inference represents a cornerstone in the evolution of IoT, enabling a transition from data-driven monitoring to intelligent, autonomous decision-making. The combination of edge computing, distributed intelligence, and sustainable AI models opens vast opportunities for innovation. At the same time, future directions point toward greater integration with advanced networks, neuromorphic hardware, and explainable AI frameworks. This chapter explores these opportunities and outlines the future trajectory of AI inference for IoT, highlighting its role in shaping the next generation of intelligent, interconnected systems (Meuser et al., 2024).

Finally, standardization and interoperability will shape the long-term success of AI inference in IoT ecosystems. The lack of unified frameworks and protocols often hinders seamless integration across heterogeneous devices and platforms. Future efforts should focus on open standards, cross-vendor compatibility, and unified AI inference APIs to enable scalable, flexible, and vendor-agnostic IoT deployments.

2. OPPORTUNITIES IN AI INFERENCE FOR IOT

2.1 Edge AI and On-Device Inference

One of the most promising opportunities lies in performing inference directly on IoT devices or edge gateways. This minimizes latency, reduces bandwidth usage, and enables real-time analytics. Edge inference is particularly relevant for applications such as autonomous vehicles, industrial automation, and healthcare monitoring. Advancements in lightweight deep learning models and specialized AI hardware (e.g., NVIDIA Jetson, Google Edge TPU, ARM Cortex-M with ML accelerators) have accelerated adoption. The primary advantage of edge AI inference lies in low-latency response. Applications such as autonomous vehicles, industrial robots, and healthcare monitoring systems cannot afford delays caused by transmitting data to remote servers. By running AI models directly on embedded processors or edge gateways, IoT devices can respond in real-time to critical events. For example, a self-driving car can detect obstacles and make navigation decisions within milliseconds, ensuring safety without waiting for cloud-based analysis.

Another major benefit of on-device inference is bandwidth optimization. As billions of IoT devices come online, transmitting all raw sensor data to the cloud is not feasible. Edge inference significantly reduces the volume of data that needs to be communicated, since only essential insights or summarized results are transmitted. This not only lowers operational costs but also allows IoT systems to function efficiently in environments with limited or intermittent network connectivity (He et al., 2025). Figure 2 illustrates the architecture of edge-based AI inference.

Figure 2 presents the architecture of on-device inference and edge AI, highlighting local processing and reduced dependence on cloud resources.

Figure 2. On-device inference and edge AI

Privacy and security also improve significantly with edge AI. Sensitive data, such as patient health records or video surveillance footage, can be processed locally without leaving the device. Only anonymized results or metadata need to be shared with external systems, reducing exposure to data breaches. This feature is especially crucial for healthcare IoT, defense applications, and smart homes where trust and confidentiality are paramount.

Recent advancements in hardware accelerators and lightweight AI models have made edge AI inference increasingly practical. Devices powered by NVIDIA Jetson modules, Google Edge TPU, Intel Movidius, and ARM-based processors now support high-performance AI operations at low power consumption. At the same time, techniques such as model pruning, quantization, and knowledge distillation have enabled complex deep learning models to be compressed and deployed on resource-constrained devices without significant loss of accuracy.

2.2 Real-Time Decision-Making

AI inference enhances IoT systems with the ability to detect anomalies, predict failures, or optimize processes in real-time. For example, in smart grids, inference models can balance energy loads instantly, while in predictive maintenance, they can prevent costly equipment downtime. Real-time decision-making is one of the most critical opportunities enabled by AI inference in IoT ecosystems. Unlike traditional systems where data is collected and analyzed offline, AI-powered IoT devices can now process incoming data streams instantly and respond to changing conditions without delay. This capability is essential for time-sensitive environments such as healthcare, transportation, finance, and industrial automation, where delays of even a few seconds can lead to significant risks or losses. The benefits are equally transformative in transportation and mobility systems. Autonomous vehicles rely heavily on real-time inference to interpret sensor inputs such as camera feeds, LiDAR scans, and radar data (Siam et al., 2025). Figure 3 demonstrates how AI inference supports real-time decision-making across different IoT applications.

Figure 3 shows the process of making real-time decisions using AI inference in dynamic IoT environments.

Figure 3. Making decisions in real time

These vehicles must detect pedestrians, interpret traffic signals, and make split-second navigation choices. Any delay in decision-making could compromise passenger safety. Likewise, smart traffic management systems use AI inference to optimize traffic light timings, reduce congestion, and improve urban mobility in real-time.

In industrial IoT (IIoT), real-time decision-making enhances operational efficiency and minimizes downtime. AI inference models can detect abnormal patterns in machinery vibrations or temperature fluctuations, triggering preventive maintenance actions before failures occur. Factories equipped with real-time AI inference systems can dynamically adjust production lines, optimize resource utilization, and maintain product quality without human intervention.

2.3 Energy-Efficient and Sustainable Systems

Recent research explores energy-aware inference techniques where models dynamically adjust complexity based on device constraints. By enabling sustainable AI, IoT deployments can achieve longer battery life spans and reduced carbon footprints—essential for smart agriculture, environmental monitoring, and remote sensing. Energy efficiency is a central concern in AI inference for IoT, as most devices operate under stringent power and computational constraints. Running complex machine learning models on battery-powered sensors, wearables, or edge devices requires lightweight and optimized architectures. Techniques such as model pruning, quantization, and hardware acceleration are increasingly being adopted to reduce computational overhead without compromising accuracy. Moreover, energy-aware scheduling strategies allow IoT devices to perform inference only when necessary, thereby prolonging battery life. These innovations not only ensure system reliability but also minimize the environmental footprint of IoT deployments.

Sustainability extends beyond individual device efficiency to the broader IoT ecosystem. AI inference can contribute to sustainable practices by optimizing resource utilization in domains such as smart grids, agriculture, and transportation. For example, IoT-enabled energy meters can analyze consumption patterns and balance loads dynamically, while precision agriculture systems can reduce water and fertilizer waste by using AI-driven irrigation recommendations. Similarly, intelligent transportation networks can cut fuel consumption by predicting traffic flows and optimizing routes. By combining AI inference with IoT, industries and communities can create greener, more resilient infrastructures that align with global sustainability goals (Cheng et al., 2024).

2.4 Federated Learning and Distributed Inference

AI inference in IoT is increasingly moving toward distributed paradigms such as federated learning. Here, inference and training occur across multiple devices without transferring raw data, ensuring privacy while reducing communication overhead. This approach is crucial in healthcare and finance, where data sensitivity is a concern. Federated learning has emerged as a promising approach to overcome the limitations of centralized AI training and inference in IoT ecosystems. Instead of transmitting raw data to cloud servers, devices collaboratively train models locally and share only the model updates. This approach significantly enhances data privacy and reduces communication overhead, making it highly suitable for sensitive applications such as healthcare monitoring, financial transactions, and smart homes. Moreover, federated learning allows IoT devices to develop models that are better tailored to their local environment, leading to more accurate and context-aware inference outcomes.

Beyond federated learning, distributed inference is gaining traction as a way to balance workloads across multiple IoT devices and edge nodes. In this paradigm, computationally heavy tasks are divided and processed collaboratively, ensuring that no single device is overwhelmed by resource demands. Such distributed architectures improve scalability, fault tolerance, and energy efficiency, especially in large-scale deployments like industrial IoT or smart cities. Future advancements in communication protocols and edge-cloud coordination will further strengthen the synergy between federated learning and distributed inference, enabling robust, privacy-preserving, and scalable AI solutions across diverse IoT environments (Gouiza et al., 2024).

2.5 Enhanced Security and Privacy

AI inference models can identify cyber security threats and anomalies in IoT networks in real-time. Privacy-preserving inference techniques such as homomorphic encryption and differential privacy ensure that sensitive data remains protected even when analyzed on shared platforms.

Security and privacy have always been central concerns in the Internet of Things (IoT) due to the sensitive nature of the data it handles and the vast scale of interconnected devices. As AI inference becomes increasingly embedded in IoT systems, the opportunities to enhance security and privacy grow considerably. AI models running locally or in distributed architectures not only process data but can also actively safeguard systems against threats, detect anomalies, and enforce privacy-preserving mechanisms.

In terms of privacy preservation, AI inference reduces the need for transmitting raw, sensitive data to external servers. By processing data locally on devices or at the edge, personal information such as medical records, biometric data, or video feeds can remain confined to secure environments. This not only minimizes exposure to breaches but also supports compliance with data protection regulations such as GDPR and HIPAA. For example, a smart camera can use local inference to recognize objects or people without sending complete footage to the cloud.

2.6 Vertical Industry Applications

- Healthcare IoT: AI-driven wearable's for early disease detection.
- Smart Cities: Traffic prediction, pollution monitoring, and public safety systems.
- Industrial IoT (IIoT): Predictive maintenance and robotic automation.

- Agriculture IoT: Crop health monitoring and resource optimization (Raoufi et al., 2024).

3. FUTURE DIRECTIONS IN AI INFERENCE FOR IOT

3.1 Ultra-Lightweight Model Architectures

The future of AI inference in IoT requires models that balance accuracy and computational efficiency. Techniques such as model pruning, quantization, knowledge distillation, and neural architecture search (NAS) are becoming essential for deployment on resource-constrained devices. The success of AI inference in IoT depends heavily on the ability to deploy models on devices with limited computational, memory, and energy resources. While large-scale deep learning architectures such as convolutional neural networks (CNNs) and transformers achieve remarkable accuracy in cloud environments, their high complexity makes them unsuitable for most IoT nodes. Ultra-lightweight model architectures have therefore emerged as a critical enabler of AI inference in IoT, ensuring that devices can perform intelligent computations within their physical and operational constraints.

The design of lightweight models is motivated by the resource-constrained nature of IoT devices. Many IoT sensors and embedded systems are battery-powered, have limited RAM and storage, and operate under strict latency requirements. Running traditional deep learning models on such devices is impractical. Ultra-lightweight architectures aim to reduce model size, memory footprint, and energy consumption while maintaining acceptable levels of accuracy, making them well-suited for real-world IoT deployments (Jouini et al., 2024).

3.2 Explainable AI (XAI) in IoT Inference

As AI-driven IoT systems impact critical sectors like healthcare and finance, interpretability becomes vital. Future research should focus on integrating explainable inference mechanisms to enhance trust, transparency, and compliance with regulatory standards. As AI inference becomes deeply embedded into IoT ecosystems, the need for transparency and interpretability is increasingly critical. IoT devices are being used in sensitive and safety-critical domains such as healthcare, finance, transportation, and industrial automation. Decisions made by these systems—such as diagnosing a medical condition, detecting fraud, or controlling machinery—must be trustworthy and understandable to human stakeholders. This is where Explainable AI (XAI) plays a vital role, ensuring that the outcomes of AI inference are interpretable, accountable, and aligned with human reasoning. Traditional deep learning and machine learning models often operate as "black boxes", providing predictions without explaining the reasoning behind them. While this may be acceptable in low-risk consumer applications, it is inadequate for scenarios where decisions carry ethical, legal, or safety implications. For instance, if an AI-powered IoT device rejects a patient's medical alert as insignificant, clinicians must understand the reasoning behind this inference to ensure accuracy and accountability.

In the context of IoT, XAI enhances user trust by making device behavior more predictable and understandable. Smart home systems that explain why certain energy-saving measures were triggered (e.g., based on temperature, occupancy, or time of day) are more likely to be accepted by users. Similarly, in autonomous vehicles, interpretable inference allows passengers and regulators to understand how the car decided to brake or change lanes in response to environmental inputs (Chougule et al., 2024).

3.3 Integration With 5G/6G Networks

The rise of 5G and upcoming 6G networks will enable low-latency, high-bandwidth communication for IoT devices. This will foster new inference paradigms such as collaborative cloud-edge-device computing, supporting ultra-reliable and real-time applications like remote surgery and autonomous transportation. The rapid advancement of 5G and the forthcoming 6G networks is revolutionizing the way IoT systems operate, particularly in the realm of AI inference. These next-generation communication technologies offer ultra-low latency, high bandwidth, and massive device connectivity, making them ideal for supporting intelligent IoT ecosystems. The integration of AI inference with 5G/6G infrastructure opens new opportunities for real-time analytics, distributed intelligence, and large-scale IoT deployments across diverse sectors.

The integration of 5G networks with AI inference for IoT marks a significant shift toward ultra-low-latency and high-reliability intelligent systems. 5G technologies, such as enhanced Mobile Broadband (eMBB) and Ultra-Reliable Low-Latency Communication (URLLC), enable real-time data transmission between IoT devices and edge servers. This capability allows latency-sensitive AI inference tasks—such as anomaly detection, autonomous control, and real-time monitoring—to be executed efficiently, thereby improving responsiveness and system performance.

Network slicing in 5G provides a powerful mechanism to support heterogeneous IoT applications with diverse inference requirements. By allocating virtualized network resources tailored to specific AI workloads, network slicing ensures quality-of-service (QoS) guarantees for critical applications. AI-driven IoT inference can dynamically select appropriate slices based on latency, bandwidth, and reliability constraints, enabling scalable deployment across smart cities, industrial automation, and healthcare systems.

The emergence of 6G networks further expands opportunities by introducing native AI integration within the communication infrastructure. Unlike previous generations, 6G is envisioned to support AI-aware networking, where inference models are embedded directly into base stations and core network components. This deep integration enables intelligent routing, predictive resource allocation, and proactive decision-making, significantly enhancing the efficiency of IoT inference pipelines.

Another important aspect of 5G/6G integration is intelligent inference offloading, where AI tasks are adaptively distributed across devices, edge nodes, and cloud platforms. Based on real-time network conditions, energy constraints, and application requirements, inference workloads can be shifted to optimal execution locations. This flexibility reduces device-level computation overhead while maintaining low latency and high inference accuracy.

The convergence of massive machine-type communication (mMTC) with AI inference enables large-scale IoT deployments involving millions of interconnected devices. 5G and future 6G networks can support dense device connectivity while ensuring efficient aggregation and processing of inference data. This capability is crucial for applications such as environmental monitoring, smart agriculture, and intelligent transportation systems.

Security and privacy also benefit from advanced 5G/6G network capabilities when integrated with AI inference. Features such as secure authentication, encrypted communication, and network-level anomaly detection enhance the protection of inference data and models. Future research will focus on leveraging AI-native 6G architectures to detect cyber threats in real time and safeguard distributed IoT inference systems.

Finally, the integration of AI inference with 5G/6G-enabled edge intelligence will pave the way for fully autonomous IoT ecosystems.

One of the most critical benefits of 5G/6G integration is ultra-reliable low-latency communication (URLLC). For applications like autonomous vehicles, remote surgeries, or industrial automation, even milliseconds of delay can cause failures. AI inference running on IoT devices or at the network edge, supported by 5G/6G's low latency, enables instantaneous decision-making, ensuring both accuracy and safety in mission-critical scenarios (Sharif et al., 2024).

Key Points: Integration with 5G/6G Networks

- **Ultra-Low Latency Communication:** 5G and emerging 6G networks provide extremely low latency, enabling real-time data transmission and fast decision-making for critical applications such as autonomous systems, remote surgery, and smart transportation.

- **High Data Rates and Bandwidth:** these networks support very high data throughput, allowing massive volumes of data from IoT devices, sensors, and multimedia sources to be transmitted efficiently without congestion.
- **Massive Device Connectivity:** Integration with 5G/6G enables support for billions of connected devices, facilitating large-scale IoT ecosystems, smart cities, and industrial automation with seamless network access.
- **Network Slicing:** Network slicing allows the creation of virtual network segments optimized for specific services (e.g., healthcare, emergency services, autonomous vehicles), ensuring quality of service (QoS) and reliability.
- **Edge Computing Integration:** 5G/6G networks tightly integrate with edge computing, enabling processing closer to data sources. This reduces latency, enhances privacy, and improves performance for time-sensitive applications.
- **Enhanced Reliability and Resilience:** Features such as ultra-reliable low-latency communication (URLLC) improve network stability, fault tolerance, and service continuity in mission-critical environments.
- **AI-Native Network Management:** 6G is expected to incorporate AI-driven automation for intelligent resource allocation, traffic management, and self-optimizing networks.
- **Improved Security and Privacy:** Advanced encryption, authentication, and security frameworks in 5G/6G enhance protection against cyber threats, eavesdropping, and unauthorized access.
- **Support for Emerging Technologies:** Integration facilitates advanced applications such as holographic communication, digital twins, extended reality (XR), and autonomous robotics.
- **Energy Efficiency and Sustainability:** 6G aims to optimize power consumption through intelligent resource management, contributing to greener and more sustainable communication infrastructures.

3.4 Neuromorphic and Quantum Inference

Emerging hardware paradigms will reshape AI inference for IoT. Neuromorphic computing (brain-inspired architectures) promises ultra-low-power inference, while quantum machine learning may unlock unprecedented efficiency for high-dimensional IoT data processing.

Neuromorphic inference represents a promising paradigm inspired by the structure and functioning of the human brain. By leveraging spiking neural networks (SNNs) and event-driven processing, neuromorphic systems enable ultra-low-power and low-latency inference, making them well suited for resource-constrained IoT environments. These architectures process information only when events occur, significantly reducing energy consumption compared to conventional deep learning models.

The integration of neuromorphic hardware with IoT devices opens new opportunities for real-time sensing and decision-making at the edge. Neuromorphic chips can efficiently handle continuous data streams from sensors, such as vision, audio, and tactile inputs, without relying on cloud-based processing. This capability is particularly valuable for applications requiring always-on intelligence, including autonomous systems, wearable devices, and smart surveillance.

Quantum inference, although still in its early stages, offers transformative potential for solving complex optimization and pattern recognition problems beyond the capabilities of classical systems. Quantum machine learning models can exploit quantum parallelism and entanglement to accelerate inference tasks, especially for large-scale and high-dimensional IoT data. As quantum hardware matures, hybrid quantum–classical inference frameworks are expected to emerge.

Future research in neuromorphic and quantum inference will focus on hybrid architectures, combining conventional AI models with neuromorphic and quantum components. Key challenges include hardware scalability, algorithm–hardware co-design, and integration with existing IoT and edge computing infrastructures. Addressing these challenges could enable next-generation intelligent systems that are faster, more energy-efficient, and capable of handling unprecedented levels of complexity.

Figure 4 illustrates the role of quantum and neuromorphic computing paradigms in enhancing the efficiency and scalability of AI inference for future IoT applications.

Figure 4. Quantum and neuromorphic inference

3.5 Autonomous and Self-Optimizing Systems

Future IoT devices will not only perform inference but also self-adapt inference strategies depending on environmental conditions. Such systems could reconfigure models dynamically, update policies without human intervention, and sustain autonomous operation for extended periods. The next generation of IoT will be characterized by devices and networks that can operate autonomously with minimal human intervention. By embedding AI inference capabilities, IoT devices can continuously monitor their environment, learn from new data, and adapt their behavior in real time. For example, autonomous drones can adjust flight paths based on changing weather conditions, while smart manufacturing robots can reconfigure workflows when encountering unexpected disruptions. This self-governing nature reduces dependence on centralized control and allows IoT systems to function reliably even in dynamic or unpredictable environments.

Autonomous and self-optimizing systems represent a key evolution in intelligent IoT and AI-driven infrastructures, enabling systems to operate with minimal human intervention. By integrating AI inference, sensing, and control mechanisms, these systems can independently perceive their environment, make decisions, and execute actions in real time. Such autonomy enhances operational efficiency, reduces manual oversight, and supports continuous system availability in dynamic and complex environments.

A fundamental characteristic of self-optimizing systems is their ability to adapt and learn from operational feedback. Through reinforcement learning, online inference, and feedback loops, these systems can adjust parameters, workflows, and resource utilization to achieve optimal performance. This adaptive behavior is particularly valuable in IoT scenarios where environmental conditions, workloads, and user requirements frequently change.

In distributed IoT ecosystems, autonomous systems leverage edge intelligence and decentralized inference to optimize local decision-making. By processing data closer to the source, latency is reduced and network congestion is minimized. Autonomous coordination among multiple edge nodes further enables collaborative optimization, improving scalability and resilience in large-scale deployments such as smart cities and industrial automation.

Self-optimizing systems also play a crucial role in energy and resource management. By continuously monitoring device status, network conditions, and application demands, AI-driven controllers can dynamically allocate computational and communication resources. This results in improved energy efficiency, prolonged device lifetime, and reduced operational costs, which are critical factors in battery-powered and resource-constrained IoT environments.

Despite their advantages, autonomous and self-optimizing systems face challenges related to reliability, safety, and trustworthiness. Ensuring stable behavior, avoiding unintended actions, and maintaining transparency in decision-making remain open research issues. Future work will focus on explainable autonomy, robust learning mechanisms, and standardized frameworks to enable safe and dependable deployment of fully autonomous intelligent systems.

Self-optimizing systems go a step further by leveraging reinforcement learning, online learning, and adaptive algorithms to improve performance over time. Such systems can fine-tune their resource usage, optimize energy consumption, and enhance inference accuracy without external reprogramming. For instance, smart energy grids can automatically balance electricity loads by learning consumption patterns, while autonomous vehicles can refine navigation strategies through continuous interaction with their surroundings. As these systems evolve, they will form the foundation of highly resilient and intelligent IoT infrastructures capable of scaling across industries and supporting mission-critical applications (Zhang et al., 2024).

3.6 Security-Driven Inference Mechanisms

Next-generation IoT inference must embed robust security against adversarial attacks. Research into adversarial robust inference and block chain-based validation of IoT inferences will be critical for ensuring trustworthy deployments.

Security-driven inference mechanisms are becoming essential as AI-powered IoT systems increasingly operate in open, heterogeneous, and potentially adversarial environments. These mechanisms embed security considerations directly into the inference pipeline, ensuring that decision-making processes remain trustworthy even in the presence of attacks. By integrating security awareness at the inference stage, IoT systems can proactively detect anomalies, unauthorized access, and malicious behavior in real time.

At the core of security-driven inference is the ability to analyze data while minimizing exposure to threats such as data leakage, unauthorized access, and inference attacks. These mechanisms employ techniques such as secure multi-party computation, homomorphic encryption, and differential privacy to ensure that meaningful inferences can be drawn without revealing raw or sensitive information. As a result, organizations can leverage data intelligence while complying with privacy regulations and security policies.

One key aspect of security-driven inference is adversarial robustness. AI inference models deployed in IoT environments are vulnerable to adversarial inputs designed to manipulate outputs or degrade system performance. Developing inference models that are resilient to such attacks—through techniques like adversarial training, input sanitization, and robust feature extraction—remains a critical research direction for secure IoT deployments.

Privacy-preserving inference is another important component of security-driven mechanisms. IoT systems often handle sensitive personal and operational data, making data protection a top priority. Techniques such as holomorphic encryption, secure multi-party computation, and federated inference enable AI models to perform inference without exposing raw data, thereby enhancing privacy while maintaining acceptable performance levels.

The use of trusted execution environments (TEEs) and secure hardware accelerators further strengthens inference security. By isolating inference computations within protected hardware enclaves, TEEs prevent unauthorized access to models and sensitive data. This approach is particularly valuable for edge devices, where physical access and resource limitations increase vulnerability to attacks.

As IoT devices become more intelligent through AI inference, ensuring security at every layer of thc system has become a top priority. Traditional security methods are often inadequate for large-scale, resource-constrained IoT environments. Security-driven inference mechanisms leverage AI models to detect malicious activities, abnormal device behavior, and network intrusions in real time. By analyzing traffic patterns, sensor data, and device logs, these mechanisms can identify potential threats proactively and prevent cyber-attacks before they escalate. For example, anomaly detection models deployed on edge devices can flag unusual communication attempts that may indicate malware infiltration or data exfiltration.

In distributed environments such as cloud-edge architectures and Internet of Things (IoT) networks, security-driven inference mechanisms play a critical role. These systems often process data across multiple nodes with varying trust levels, making them vulnerable to interception and tampering. By incorporating trust-aware inference, encrypted communication, and decentralized verification, security-driven mechanisms enable safe and reliable decision-making even in highly dynamic and heterogeneous environments.

In addition to threat detection, security-driven inference enables adaptive defense strategies, where IoT systems can autonomously respond to evolving attack patterns. Lightweight cryptographic algorithms combined with AI-based inference can strengthen authentication, encryption, and access control mechanisms without overwhelming device resources. Furthermore, techniques like adversarial resilience, where models are trained to withstand adversarial inputs, will become essential for maintaining trust in AI-enabled IoT. By embedding intelligence into the security architecture itself, IoT ecosystems can achieve not only operational efficiency but also robust protection against increasingly sophisticated cyber threats (Alajlan & Ibrahim, 2025). As depicted in Figure 5, security-driven inference mechanisms integrate protection directly into the inference pipeline.

Figure 5 illustrates the mechanisms of security-driven AI inference for protecting IoT systems against cyber threats.

Figure 5. Mechanisms of inference driven by security

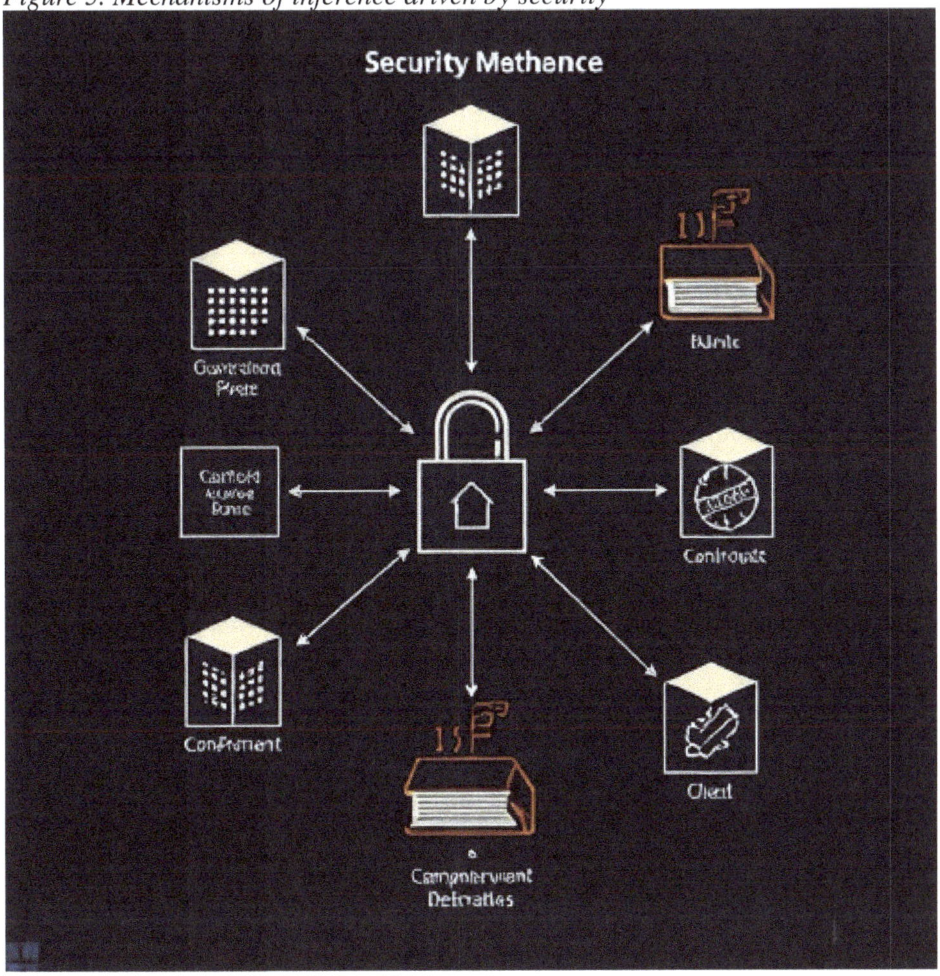

3.7 Ethical and Regulatory Considerations

The widespread adoption of AI inference in IoT raises ethical challenges, including data ownership, accountability, and algorithmic bias. Future directions must align technical innovation with responsible AI frameworks and international regulatory standards. The integration of AI inference into IoT systems raises important ethical questions, particularly around privacy, fairness, and accountability. IoT devices often collect highly sensitive personal and environmental data, which, if misused, can compromise user trust and societal well-being. Ethical concerns also arise from algorithmic bias, where inference models may unintentionally favor or disadvantage certain groups due to biased training data. To build trustworthy IoT systems, designers must adopt principles of transparency, explain ability, and fairness in AI inference. This includes developing mechanisms that make decision-making processes understandable to users and ensuring that outcomes align with ethical standards.

Ethical considerations play a critical role in the design, implementation, and deployment of modern technological systems. Researchers and developers must ensure that their work respects fundamental ethical principles such as fairness, transparency, accountability, and respect for human rights. Failure to address ethical concerns can lead to misuse of technology, unintended social harm, and erosion of public trust. Therefore, ethical evaluation should be an integral part of the research and development lifecycle rather than an afterthought.

Data privacy and confidentiality are among the most significant ethical concerns, especially in systems that collect, store, or analyze personal or sensitive information. Ensuring informed consent, anonymization of data, and secure data handling practices is essential to protect individuals from unauthorized access or misuse of their data. Ethical data governance frameworks must be adopted to minimize risks related to surveillance, profiling, and data breaches.

Bias and discrimination present additional ethical challenges, particularly in data-driven and automated decision-making systems. Algorithms trained on biased or incomplete datasets may unintentionally reinforce social inequalities or produce unfair outcomes. Ethical responsibility requires continuous monitoring, validation, and refinement of models to ensure fairness, inclusivity, and equal treatment across different demographic groups.

From a regulatory perspective, compliance with national and international laws is mandatory to ensure lawful and responsible system operation. Regulations related to data protection, cyber security, and digital governance—such as data protection acts and privacy regulations—provide legal boundaries within which technologies must function. Adhering to these regulations not only ensures legal compliance but also promotes ethical best practices and institutional accountability.

Transparency and accountability are key regulatory and ethical requirements, particularly in systems that affect public decision-making or individual rights. Clear documentation, explainable processes, and audit mechanisms are necessary to allow regulators and stakeholders to understand how decisions are made. Establishing accountability frameworks ensures that responsibility can be assigned in cases of system failure, misuse, or harm.

Finally, ongoing regulatory adaptation and ethical oversight are essential as technologies continue to evolve rapidly. Policymakers, researchers, and industry stakeholders must collaborate to update regulatory frameworks that address emerging risks and societal impacts. Continuous ethical review, stakeholder engagement, and impact assessments help ensure that technological advancements align with societal values, legal standards, and long-term public interest.

On the regulatory front, governments and international bodies are increasingly introducing guidelines to govern AI and IoT deployments. Regulations such as the General Data Protection Regulation (GDPR) emphasize data privacy and user consent, directly impacting how IoT systems perform AI inference. Future regulatory frameworks are expected to focus on accountability, liability, and the safe deployment of autonomous systems. Ensuring compliance will require standardized auditing tools, certification processes, and ethical AI frameworks tailored for IoT. By addressing both ethical and regulatory considerations, AI-driven IoT systems can achieve widespread acceptance while safeguarding societal values and legal obligations (Sarhaddi et al., 2025).

4. RELATED WORK

Gill et al (Gill, Golec, Hu, Xu, Du, Wu, & Uhlig, 2025) this study highlights the significance of Edge AI in processing real-time data at the edge of the network. Additionally, it emphasizes the research challenges encountered by Edge AI systems, including constraints on resources, vulnerabilities to security threats, and problems with scalability. Finally, this study highlights the potential future research directions that aim to address the current limitations of Edge AI by providing innovative solutions.

Dakhia et al (Dakhia et al., 2025) this review highlights AI applications, including computer vision for food recognition and quality assessment, Natural Language Processing for recipe analysis, and predictive modeling for dietary recommendations. Simultaneously, the IoT enhances transparency and efficiency through real-time monitoring, data collection, and device connectivity. The convergence of these technologies relies on diverse data sources, such as images, nutritional databases, and user-generated logs, which are critical to enabling traceability and tailored solutions. Despite its potential, food computing faces challenges, including data heterogeneity, privacy concerns, scalability issues, and regulatory constraints. To address these, this paper explores solutions like federated learning for secure on-device data processing and blockchain for transparent traceability. Emerging trends, such as edge AI for real-time analytics and sustainable practices powered by AI–IoT integration, are also discussed. This review offers actionable insights to advance the food sector through innovative and ethical technological frameworks.

Goethals et al (Godase, 2025) the article reviews studies from 2019 to 2021 on the Intelligent Edge, which integrates AI in edge networks and smart applications. It introduces essential technologies and presents a taxonomy focused on enabling technology, organization, and applications of Edge Intelligence. Research trends from 2015 to 2020 highlight a surge in interest across various subtopics, particularly in organization, which is examined in detail. Selected studies illustrate the current state of Edge Intelligence, revealing short-term challenges and high-level visions for future research.

Godase et al (Zhang & Tao, 2020) The proliferation of internet of things (IoT) devices and the increasing demand for intelligent surveillance systems have created a compelling need for edge-based artificial intelligence (Edge AI) solutions. This study presents a comprehensive Edge AI framework for real-time human activity recognition (HAR) on low-power devices, achieving 87.3% classification accuracy with an average power consumption of 2.1W on ARM-based edge platforms. The system integrates optimized deep-learning models with quantization and pruning techniques to balance accuracy, latency, and power efficiency. Comparative analysis against existing approaches highlights our system's superior balance of real-time performance and energy efficiency, outperforming traditional cloud-based and motion detection systems in terms of latency and false-positive rates. The results validate the feasibility of deploying sophisticated HAR at the edge, paving the way for scalable, privacy-preserving smart surveillance systems.

Awaisi, et al (Awaisi et al., 2024) Internet of Things (IoT) is crucial in diverse fields like transportation, healthcare, and manufacturing, with an anticipated growth to 20 billion devices by 2025. IoT enhances industrial efficiency through real-time monitoring of machines. The integration of Artificial Intelligence (AI) leads to the concept of Industrial Artificial Intelligence of Things (i.e., Industrial AIoT). This paper examines challenges and opportunities in Industrial AIoT, reviews advanced AI methods such as Deep Learning (DL) and Machine Learning (ML), presents significant applications, discusses implementation challenges, highlights societal and economic impacts, and suggests future research directions for optimal utilization of this technology.

Mahmood et al (Mahmood et al., 2022) the evolution of wireless network systems has introduced new user services through advanced technologies. With the impending deployment of 5G, opportunities for massive connectivity, high throughput, low latency, energy efficiency, and security are emerging, particularly for IoT applications in health, agriculture, industry, and smart infrastructure. As the number of devices grows, research on 6G networks is underway to offer higher bandwidth and better QoS. This paper discusses the role of AI/ML in enhancing energy-efficient, secure IoT network operations and examines key design factors for future communication systems. It also highlights areas such as smart healthcare, transportation, and agriculture, concluding with future research avenues related to these algorithms in IoT network development.

Table 1 summarizes representative studies on AI inference and IoT, highlighting their focus areas, key findings, and identified future directions.

Table 1. Summary of related work on AI inference in IoT systems

Study / Paper	Focus / Scope	Key Findings on AI Inference / IoT	Opportunities & Future Directions
A systematic literature review on AI in IoT systems (Moss et al., 2025).	Survey of AI roles in IoT across domains	Found AI tasks (prediction, recognition, decision-making) dominate IoT use cases; most systems still early stage. Inference often cloud + edge, hybrid less common.	Need real-world, validated deployments; methods optimizing inference off-cloud; multi-modal inference tasks; broader domain coverage.
AI-Powered Data Analytics for IoT Systems (Moss et al., 2025)	Efficient processing in IoT with AI	Highlights AI at edge, fog, hybrid architecture for low-latency inference and analytics.	Improve robustness, interoperability, sustainability; explore federated learning, TinyML, collaborative inference frameworks.
Exploring the Intersection of AI and Edge Computing in IoT (AlNusif, 2025).	Edge AI in IoT applications	Edge AI increases real-time inference and lowers latency but faces resource constraints.	Future work on advanced hardware (special accelerators), 6G integration, ethical AI and scalable orchestration.
On-Device AI Models for IoT (Empowering Edge Intelligence) (AlNusif, 2025).	On-device AI for real-time inference	Edge models bring privacy and responsiveness benefits; discuss compression & hardware acceleration.	Research into efficient on-device networks, adaptive model scaling, energy-aware inference.
Edge Large AI Models: Collaborative Deployment and IoT (Wang, Tang, Guo et al, 2025).	Large models split across edge networks	Proposes mechanisms to decompose large models for distributed inference among IoT devices.	Future work: collaborative model deployment protocols; resource-aware partitioning; multi-modal LAM inference for IoT.
Explainable AI in IoT Systems (Ficili et al., 2025).	XAI tailored to IoT	Surveys XAI for IoT inference, adding transparency and trust.	Develop lightweight explainable inference systems; balance interpretability with IoT constraints.
(Related) Edge Integration of IoT & AI with Cloud Computing (Ficili et al., 2025).	IoT + cloud + AI integration	Demonstrates hybrid models where inference happens across cloud + edge layers.	Trends toward Hierarchical AI inference (cloud ↔ fog ↔ edge) for balanced latency & accuracy.
Industry/Market Reports: Edge AI (Wang, Shi, & Letaief, 2025).	Industry perspective on inference trends	Edge AI becoming core layer for real-time inference across sectors (healthcare, manufacturing).	Hardware innovations (low-power chips), localized inference demand; trust & compliance build-in frameworks.

5. CHALLENGES TO OVERCOME

Despite opportunities, several challenges must be addressed:

- **Resource Constraints:** Many IoT devices lack sufficient computational power. A primary challenge is the resource-constrained nature of IoT devices. Many IoT sensors and actuators are designed to be lightweight, battery-powered, and low-cost, which restricts their computational power, memory, and energy capacity. Running advanced AI inference models on such devices is difficult, often requiring specialized lightweight architectures or edge-cloud collaboration. Without overcoming resource bottlenecks, achieving real-time intelligence on billions of devices will remain limited.
- **Scalability:** Managing inference across billions of heterogeneous devices. Another pressing issue is scalability. With billions of heterogeneous IoT devices expected to come online, managing distributed inference becomes complex. Devices vary in hardware, connectivity, and operating environments, making it difficult to deploy uniform inference frameworks. Scaling AI inference across massive IoT ecosystems requires efficient orchestration, adaptive resource allocation, and standardized communication protocols that can handle the diversity of devices and use cases.
- **Security Risks:** IoT systems remain vulnerable to cyber-attacks. Security continues to be a critical challenge for IoT systems. AI inference, while powerful, can also introduce new vulnerabilities. Malicious actors may attempt to manipulate inference models, conduct adversarial attacks, or exploit weak authentication mechanisms in IoT devices. For example, a compromised smart grid sensor could misreport energy usage, leading to operational failures. Embedding robust cyber security measures such as secure enclaves, encryption, and adversarial defense mechanisms is necessary to protect AI inference in IoT.
- **Standardization:** Lack of unified frameworks for interoperability. The lack of unified standards and interoperability frameworks poses another barrier. Currently, IoT ecosystems are fragmented, with different devices, platforms, and vendors using proprietary protocols. This fragmentation complicates the seamless deployment of AI inference across devices. Without standardized approaches for model deployment, data exchange, and inference validation, the scalability and reliability of AI-powered IoT remain restricted. International standardization efforts are therefore crucial to ensure global interoperability.
- **Data Quality:** Incomplete or noisy IoT data may degrade inference accuracy. AI inference is only as good as the data it processes. In IoT, data quality issues are prevalent, as devices often produce noisy, incomplete, or redundant data due to hardware limitations or environmental interference. Low-quality data not only reduces inference accuracy but can also introduce bias and errors. Addressing this challenge requires robust preprocessing pipelines, data

cleaning algorithms, and redundancy mechanisms to ensure the reliability of insights derived from IoT systems.

- **Latency vs. Accuracy Trade-Off:** IoT inference must balance latency and accuracy, which is often a trade-off. Lightweight models run faster but may produce less accurate results, while complex models improve accuracy at the cost of real-time responsiveness. For critical applications like healthcare monitoring or autonomous driving, this balance is particularly challenging, as both speed and accuracy are vital. Research into adaptive inference strategies is essential to address this trade-off.
- **Energy Efficiency:** Energy consumption remains a major concern, particularly for battery-powered IoT devices deployed in remote or inaccessible areas. Continuous AI inference can rapidly drain device batteries, limiting system longevity. While energy-efficient hardware and ultra-lightweight AI models are being developed, achieving long-term sustainability in energy-constrained environments remains a key challenge for widespread IoT deployment.
- **Ethical and Regulatory Issues:** Beyond technical limitations, IoT inference faces ethical and regulatory challenges. Issues of data privacy, accountability, and transparency must be addressed to gain user trust and comply with international laws such as GDPR. Inference systems that make decisions without human oversight must be explainable and auditable to avoid misuse or unintended consequences. Establishing clear governance frameworks will be critical in overcoming these barriers.
- **Path Forward:** In summary, the challenges of resource constraints, scalability, security risks, standardization, and data quality highlight the complexity of deploying AI inference in IoT systems. Addressing these issues requires multi-disciplinary solutions, combining innovations in lightweight AI, edge-cloud collaboration, secure communication, and global interoperability standards. By overcoming these challenges, the vision of a fully intelligent and trustworthy IoT ecosystem can move closer to reality (Okoli & Kabaso, 2024).

6. CONCLUSION

For researchers and practitioners, the road forward is both challenging and exciting. Significant opportunities exist in designing energy-efficient inference mechanisms, lightweight yet powerful AI models, and robust real-time decision frameworks. Interdisciplinary collaboration between computer scientists, engineers, security experts, and policymakers will accelerate progress toward resilient, intelligent, and sustainable IoT ecosystems.AI inference is set to redefine the IoT landscape, enabling devices to transition from passive data collectors to intelligent, autonomous decision-makers. Edge AI, federated learning, and energy-efficient inferencc arc transforming industries, while future directions point toward explain ability, neuromorphic computing, and ethical governance. By addressing current challenges and embracing emerging opportunities, AI inference will form the backbone of next-generation IoT ecosystems—driving innovations in healthcare, smart cities, industry, and beyond.

REFERENCES

Alajlan, N. N., & Ibrahim, D. M. (2025). Deep smart cities: A review of smart cities applications-based an inference of deep learning upon iot devices. *population, 5*, 6.

AlNusif, M. (2025). Explainable AI in edge devices: A lightweight framework for real-time decision transparency. *International Journal of Engineering and Computer Science, 14*(07), 27447–27472. DOI: 10.18535/ijecs.v14i07.5181

Awaisi, K. S., Ye, Q., & Sampalli, S. (2024). A survey of industrial AIoT: Opportunities, challenges, and directions. *IEEE Access : Practical Innovations, Open Solutions*.

Cheng, L., Gu, Y., Liu, Q., Yang, L., Liu, C., & Wang, Y. (2024). Advancements in accelerating deep neural network inference on AIoT devices: A survey. *IEEE Transactions on Sustainable Computing, 9*(6), 830–847.

Chougule, S. B., Chaudhari, B. S., Ghorpade, S. N., & Zennaro, M. (2024). Exploring computing paradigms for electric vehicles: From cloud to edge intelligence, challenges and future directions. *World Electric Vehicle Journal, 15*(2), 39.

Dakhia, Z., Russo, M., & Merenda, M. (2025). AI-Enabled IoT for Food Computing: Challenges, Opportunities, and Future Directions. *Sensors (Basel), 25*(7), 2147. PMID: 40218659

Ficili, I., Giacobbe, M., Tricomi, G., & Puliafito, A. (2025). From sensors to data intelligence: Leveraging IoT, cloud, and edge computing with AI. *Sensors (Basel), 25*(6), 1763. DOI: 10.3390/s25061763 PMID: 40292910

Gill, S. S., Golec, M., Hu, J., Xu, M., Du, J., Wu, H., & Uhlig, S. (2025). Edge AI: A taxonomy, systematic review and future directions. *Cluster Computing, 28*(1), 18.

Godase, V. (2025). Edge AI for Smart Surveillance: Real-time Human Activity Recognition on Low-power Devices. *International Journal of AI and Machine Learning Innovations in Electronics and Communication Technology, 1*(1), 29–46.

Gouiza, N., Jebari, H., & Reklaoui, K. (2024). Integration of iot-enabled technologies and artificial intelligence in diverse domains: Recent advancements and future trends. *Journal of Theoretical and Applied Information Technology, 102*(5), 1975–2029.

He, Q., Lin, J., Fang, H., Wang, X., Huang, M., Yi, X., & Yu, K. (2025). Integrating [G: Applications of Edge Intelligence, Challenges, and Future Directions. *IEEE Transactions on Services Computing*.]. *IoT*, •••, 6.

Heydari, S., & Mahmoud, Q. H. (2025). Tiny machine learning and on-device inference: A survey of applications, challenges, and future directions. *Sensors (Basel), 25*(10), 3191. PMID: 40431982

Jouini, O., Sethom, K., Namoun, A., Aljohani, N., Alanazi, M. H., & Alanazi, M. N. (2024). A survey of machine learning in edge computing: Techniques, frameworks, applications, issues, and research directions. *Technologies, 12*(6), 81.

Maduranga, M. W. P., Tilwari, V., Rathnayake, R. M. M. R., & Sandamini, C. (2024, August). AI-enabled 6G internet of things: Opportunities, key technologies, challenges, and future directions. In *Telecom* (Vol. 5, No. 3, pp. 804-822). MDPI.

Mahmood, M. R., Matin, M. A., Sarigiannidis, P., & Goudos, S. K. (2022). A comprehensive review on artificial intelligence/machine learning algorithms for empowering the future IoT toward 6G era. *IEEE Access : Practical Innovations, Open Solutions, 10*, 87535–87562.

Meuser, T., Lovén, L., Bhuyan, M., Patil, S. G., Dustdar, S., Aral, A., & Welzl, M. (2024). Revisiting edge ai: Opportunities and challenges. *IEEE Internet Computing, 28*(4), 49–59.

Moss, J., Gordon, J., Duclos, W., Liu, Y., Wang, Q., & Wang, J. (2025). Explainable AI in IoT: A survey of challenges, advancements, and pathways to trustworthy automation. *Electronics (Basel), 14*(23), 4622. DOI: 10.3390/electronics14234622

Okoli, N. J., & Kabaso, B. (2024). Building a smart water city: Iot smart water technologies, applications, and future directions. *Water (Basel), 16*(4), 557.

Raoufi, P., Hemmati, A., & Rahmani, A. M. (2024). Deep learning applications in the Internet of Things: A review, tools, and future directions. *Evolutionary Intelligence, 17*(5), 3621–3654.

Sarhaddi, F., Nguyen, N. T., Zuniga, A., Hui, P., Tarkoma, S., Flores, H., & Nurmi, P. (2025). Llms and iot: A comprehensive survey on large language models and the internet of things. *Authorea Preprints*.

Sharif, S., Zeadally, S., & Ejaz, W. (2024). Resource optimization in UAV-assisted IoT networks: The role of generative AI. *IEEE Internet of Things Magazine*.

Siam, S. I., Ahn, H., Liu, L., Alam, S., Shen, H., Cao, Z., & Zhang, M. (2025). Artificial intelligence of things: A survey. *ACM Transactions on Sensor Networks, 21*(1), 1–75.

Wang, X., Tang, Z., Guo, J., Meng, T., Wang, C., Wang, T., & Jia, W. (2025). *Empowering edge intelligence: A comprehensive survey on on-device AI models* (Preprint). arXiv. https://doi.org//arXiv.2503.06027DOI: 10.48550

Wang, Z., Shi, Y., & Letaief, K. B. (2025). *Edge large AI models: Collaborative deployment and IoT applications* (Preprint). arXiv. https://arxiv.org/abs/2505.03139

Zhang, J., & Tao, D. (2020). Empowering things with intelligence: A survey of the progress, challenges, and opportunities in artificial intelligence of things. *IEEE Internet of Things Journal*, *8*(10), 7789–7817.

Zhang, Y., Zhang, J., Yue, S., Lu, W., Ren, J., & Shen, X. (2024). Mobile generative ai: Opportunities and challenges. *IEEE Wireless Communications*, *31*(4), 58–64.

Chapter 7

Case Studies: AI Inference Applications in IoT and Big Data Domains

G. Muthupandi
http://orcid.org/0009-0002-8822-0157
Chennai Institute of Technology, India

P. Vidhya Lakshmi
http://orcid.org/0009-0001-7309-2976
Chennai Institute of Technology, India

S. Pavithra
http://orcid.org/0000-0003-1537-5879
Chennai Institute of Technology, India

R. Vikram
http://orcid.org/0009-0004-1023-6807
Chennai Institute of Technology, India

R. Nandhakumar
http://orcid.org/0009-0000-4801-4370
Chennai Institute of Technology, India

B. Vishnu
http://orcid.org/0009-0002-0155-2328
Chennai Institute of Technology, India

ABSTRACT

The paper will explore how AI inference on IoT and Big Data is transformative with respect to the health care sector, manufacturing, smart cities, energy, and agriculture. AI inference transforms sensor data into actionable intelligence through the combination of real-time data, predictive analytics, and automation, and enhances efficiency, sustainability, and reliability. Applications in predictive maintenance, smart grids, urban management and precision farming are pointed out in the discussion. The most important issues, such as the quality of data, privacy, scalability, and ethical use are discussed as well as ways of dealing with them. New tendencies such as edge computing, federated learning, explainable AI, 5G integration, and digital twins are found to be pushing the next generation of smart, connected systems. In general, the chapter stresses the importance of AI inference as a source of data-experienced innovation and as the means of developing more intelligent, sustainable, and resilient structures to climate change in the future.

DOI: 10.4018/979-8-3373-7046-0.ch007

1. BIG DATA AND IOT INTRODUCTION TO AI INFERENCE

The current digital era has been characterized by a unique surge in the amount of networked devices and data in fields such as healthcare, production, transport, and environmental checks. The Internet of Things (IoT) is a system of billions of sensors, smart objects and embedded systems which continuously collect and send information to each other. This environment has also contributed to the fact that real time processing and response of information has become a very significant skill as a result of the fact that the traditional data processing methods were not able to process the large and ever-increasing datasets satisfactorily.

AI inference refers to the usage of models of machine learning or AI models trained earlier to take into account any new data received to make a prediction, classification, or decision. In comparison to the training step, which requires high-intensity computing in offline, inference applies such models to real-world working conditions, which provides low-latency observations.

Throughout this chapter, the author gives case studies on how AI inference, together with IoT and Big Data would help in supporting real-time, intelligent, and automated decision-making (Mohammadi et al., 2018). These are only some of the ways in which this integration can transform the healthcare, manufacturing, smart cities, energy, and even agricultural industries and the extent to which the insights of AI can be used to transform the current connected ecosystem.

1.1 Introduction and Concept of Inference on AI Inferences

AI inference can be described as the act of using already trained artificial intelligence or machine learning models to process new information to provide meaningful results, that is, predictions, classifications, or recommendations. It is the working period of AI implementation, when the model transfers the knowledge that it has learned during the training period into the actual real-life situation.

The ultimate AI inference purpose is to convert raw, unstructured or sensor data into actionable intelligence. Inference can be run on many platforms unlike training which can be implemented on a high-performance computer cluster or on the cloud depending on the system needs.

The predictive maintenance systems implemented in the industrial setting, such as vibrations, pressure, or temperature sensors to the devices, also use AI inference to discover the tendencies in the data within milliseconds, either stating that a fault exists or possibly where the probable failure will take place.

1.2 Evolution of AI in Ecosystems of Data

The advancement of artificial intelligence has now gone far beyond the initial rule-based and symbolic reasoning systems to the literacy-based and learning-oriented ones. First, AI systems were dependent on manually-specified logic and structured sets of data and was constrained to handle the huge and unrestructured volume of data generated in the world. The early models were rigid and they could not analyze unstructured or moving streams of data.

With the introduction of Internet of Things (IoT) and the Big Data technologies, the AI gained access to immense volume of real-time information available using sensors, networks, and other communication devices (Naha et al., 2018). It is it, access to diverse and unremitting flows of information, that caused the transition to the new model of programmed intelligence grounded in the deep learning and predictive analytics to be grounded in the capacities to identify minor trends and make independent judgments.

The trend has facilitated a tremendous shift between the passive systems and the active intelligence. Instead of reacting to the problem whenever it emerges, AI inference may now assist organizations to anticipate, foresee and prevent any possible problems before they spin out of control. Smart devices, interconnected by IoT, processed by Big Data, and inferred using AI constitute what the modern smart ecosystems are, and it can be expected to enhance the efficiency, reliability, and decision-making processes within the healthcare, production, transportation, and energy management sector.

1.3 Importance of Inference in the Digital Age

The amount of information produced and at a higher rate has never been higher during the digital age. The social media, transactional systems, the sensors and the devices provide organizations with gigantic volumes of information. It is a highly significant environment of real time analysis and action of data. AI inference is used to offer actionable data to data in real-time, without the involvement of human operators, by utilizing pre-trained models.

In addition, the high-speed reaction, AI inference automation of the decision-making process minimizes the error rate and enhances the efficiency of the operations. Together with the IoT and Big Data, it helps to learn about adaptive systems in accordance with the patterns and adapt to the alterations of the conditions.

In short, the meaning of AI inference converts all crude data into actionable intelligence, action and data collection. Consolidation of the organization allows organizations to be proactive besides saving resources and provide better services. This renders the AI inference one of the focal elements in the development of the intelligent, information-based, and future-proof systems in the healthcare, energy, transport, etc.

2. BIG DATA INTEGRATION, AI, AND IOT

AI in combination with IoT and Big Data has become a disruptive strategy to the firms that prefer to maximize the advantages of interrelated environments. Each of the components is in an intelligent and complementary position to the data value chain, thus rendering the systems smart and receptive. The primary data collection tools are the IoT devices since it collects data continuously via sensors, machines, wearables, and other environmental data collection tools to generate massive amounts of data in real time that are the foundation of analysis.

It is up to the Big Data platforms to store, handle and process this huge volume of information. They play with structured, semi-structured and unstructured data showing patterns and correlations which would otherwise be invisible. High-performance computing and scalable storage can be used to organize data and make it accessible and accessible to analyze and the infrastructure required to offer AI-based insights.

AI, IoT and Big Data have synergy since they fulfill each other role: IoT provides raw observational information, Big Data formats and organizes it and AI converts it into actionable intelligence. The combination of these technologies allows to make the process more efficient, proactive, and it also offers constant improvement in spheres such as healthcare, energy, transportation, and agriculture.

2.1 The Synergy Between AI, IoT, and Big Data

The three elements of AI, IoT, and Big Data make a highly powerful instrument to create smart and flexible systems in the digital settings of the modern world. IoT serves as the foundation block in that it continuously collects the data of the surrounding through sensors, devices and equipment to which IoT is interconnected. However, raw IoT data cannot be taken as it is without turning them into something meaningful.

Data management and processing of these volumes of data are significant in the Big Data systems (Shi et al., 2020). They store, summarize and interpret non-homogenous data, and permit the identification of patterns and trends on a large scale. Depending on the insights of the IoT data that is processed through the assistance of the Big Data platforms, the AI model can predict or identify the outcomes, anomalies, or optimization of the operations.

2.2 IoT as the Data Source Layer

The IoT gadgets of the integrated AI-IoT-Big Data framework make up the primary layer of the information source that produces data on the physical world at all times. These gadgets have sensors, wearables, connected cars, industrial appliances and Smart household devices, and they collect the data on the temperature, movement, and vibration and other physiological data such as the rate of heartbeat.

The IoT is the most appropriate source of analytics in AI models because of the diversity and magnitude of data, which is capable of identifying trends, predicting implications, and supporting automation in healthcare, manufacturing, energy, and transportation sectors.

The IoT data can however be heterogeneous comprising of devices of different format, resolutions, protocols and can result in synchronisation errors, inconsistency and noise (Shlezinger & Bajic, 2022). Standardization, calibration, filtering, and preprocessing are also involved to give the data management high level of quality and reliability to feed the AI inference.

2.3 The Higher Level: Big Data

The higher level in the AI-IoT system is represented by Big Data platforms, which are capable of processing, handling, and storing the billions of data that are produced by the IoT devices. These platforms can process the volume, velocity and variety of the data streams and the information received by the sensors, wearable devices, machines and other items attached to it can be analyzed and utilized well. The examples of technologies, which could provide scalable infrastructure to facilitate the distributed data processing, real-time analytics, and visualization, are Hadoop, Apache Spark, and other cloud storage tools.

One of the most significant tasks is the data processing of the donation of IoT to AI on the platforms of Big Data. It includes data cleansing (to remove inconsistencies and errors), data integration (to synthesize heterogeneous datasets in various sources) and data transformation (to transform raw data into machine-learnable structured data). By performing these preprocessing activities, the Big Data platforms are assured that the AI inference is provided with quality, right, and consist inputs.

Without the Big Data systems, the pool of rate and volume of information produced by the IoT devices would be unbearable and useless to a certain degree (Martin, 2023). These platforms do not only provide storage and management of data, but also provide advanced analytics tools, whereby organizations can be able to use insights to come up with valuable insights in almost real-time. In other words, the required connection between raw data generated by IoT and AI-driven actionable intelligence, scalable, efficient, and reliable decision-making can be provided in such fields as healthcare and manufacturing, smart cities, and energy management.

3. IOT–BIG DATA SYSTEMS: AI INFERENCE WORKFLOW

The AI inference is a systematic workflow that follows the IoT-Big Data systems in order to transform the raw sensor data into actionable intelligence. It begins by the data collection because the IoT devices, including sensors, connected wearable, and linked machines, are constantly fed with measurements in the form of temperature, vibration, heart rate, traffic density or energy consumption.

The information is thereafter preprocessed and handled on the Big Data platforms. This is the cleaning, standardization, unification, and transformation to remove noise, put various sources into line, and transform the information to formats that AI models can analyse. The quality of inputs will ensure that there is proper and valid inference.

The AI inference step involves the utilization of pre-trained machine learning models to execute the processed data in order to find patterns, detect anomalies and make predictions and generate actionable insights (Samadi, 2022). Inference can be performed at the edge, near the origin of information during real-time response, or in the cloud based on the scalable deployment of analytics of large scale.

3.1 Data Collection and Sensor Networks

The AI inference workflow in the IoT-Big Data ecosystems are based on the stage of the data collection, which is regarded as the logical procedure of gathering information concerning the physical environment by the method of the interconnected device and sensors. The accuracy, timeliness, and impartiality of such type of data have a direct impact on the efficacy of downstream AI inference and decision-making.

Real time measurement in other areas is measured with IoT sensors. There are smart meters that record fine time-scale power usage enabling maximum energy use and identification of abnormal operation. Maintenance of equipment in the industry is already checked through vibration sensors that will enable predictive maintenance and avoid unplanned downtime. The sensors track the environmental temperature, humidity, quality of air, and pollution levels which pose a crucial data set to operate smart cities, track climatic changes, and health concerns of the population (Neustein et al., 2023). The metadata (timestamps, location, and operational state) is generated by a multitude of sensors as well, making the data set more useful to AI models.

The data collection can be performed on a continuous mode that is used to give real time monitoring. The sensor network must be designed in a proper manner to ensure that it is cover, reliable, and redundant and the network topology, communication protocols and data synchronization mechanisms can ensure that the data is accurate and consistent so that it can be preprocessed on the Big Data platforms.

3.2 Data Transmission and Edge Computing

Upon gathering information with the assistance of IoT sensors, the information ought to be transmitted to processing units where it is supposed to be analyzed and interpreted. It is done to ensure that raw measurements are effective in creating actionable intelligence. Traditionally, big data were stored in the cloud computing platforms and analyzed. They offer massive calculation power and allow businesses to carry out multi-layered AI models and inference tasks on vast amounts of data.

However, application of cloud-based processing only can also cause latency in case large volumes of data require transfer over networks. Such latencies would be intolerable in an application where real-time response is needed e.g. an autonomous driving or emergency health care monitoring application. To eliminate this, edge computing has also emerged as an important complement to cloud computing.

Lastly, the hybrid edge-cloud model will offer a solution between the set of information and smart action. Although the cloud systems offer scalability and rich analytics, the edge computing offers rapid responses and stability, which together with the rich analytics enable the development of dynamic, responsive, and intelligent IoT ecosystems in diverse sectors.

3.3 Data Preprocessing and Feature Extraction

To make meaningful predictions, the AI models have to use clean, consistent, and structured raw data of IoT sensor, which has to be preprocessed to be in a form understandable by AI. The input data quality can have a direct impact on the quality of model outputs, its reliability, and robustness of the model outputs.

The initial step of the workflow is data cleaning and eliminates noise, corrects errors, handles missing values and removes inconsistencies. The sensor readings may contain spikes or gaps where faults in the hardware may occur or network issues and cleaning them will ensure that AI models are not compromised. The standardization and normalization are necessary to bring the features to the same scale so that the measurements made with another scale such as temperature, vibration, energy consumption would not have a disproportional influence on the model.

Through preprocessing and feature extraction, AI inference models receive quality and useful inputs, which lead to better ability to capture hidden patterns, make predictions and generate actionable intelligence. It becomes a crucial transition between the untrusted IoT data and the trusted AI-IoT-Big Data system decision-making.

3.4 Model Deployment and Inference in Real Time

The pre-trained models are used to analyze the IoT data to produce real-time actionable intelligence. After preprocessing and extraction of features are completed, predictions, classifications or alerts could be carried out using models which are utilized in helping to make decisions based on data fast and also provide efficient and reliable operations.

Edge devices take up latency-sensitive workloads, e.g. machine anomalies or patient vital monitors in healthcare which allows timely notification and eliminates the need to connect to the cloud. Cloud platforms execute big analytics, such as trend analysis and historical modelling and can handle big not edge capable datasets.

The scalability of AI models, as well as modular and maintainability, is possible due to the widely applied containerization and micro services deployed. Containers create a fixed workflow to deploy, whereas micro services enable the AI functions to be updated on a case-by-case basis. The edge and cloud approach provide real-time inference, predictive activity and smart choices in various areas such as manufacturing, healthcare, transportation, and intelligent cities.

4. INTELLIGENT HEALTHCARE SYSTEMS

The healthcare sphere can be seen as one of the most innovative to make AI inferences with the assistance of IoT and Big Data. This kind of complex of technologies has given people the opportunity to monitor in real time, to make predictions and take decisions without human participation which have radically transformed the treatment of patients, the work of hospitals and the management of health care services to citizens.

Wearable sensors and other IoT devices, including smart monitors and connected medical equipment, can always monitor vital signs of patients in terms of heart rate, blood pressure, oxygen level, and glucose level. The devices produce data streams which are of high frequency and analyzed and stored in the Big Data platforms. AI inference models are used to analyze this data in real-time to identify abnormalities and either forecast the possible health hazards and provide actionable insights.

In addition to monitoring of patients, AI inference enhances resource utilization and efficiency in the hospital. The automated systems are able to plan the treatment, treat a case of an emergency first and optimize the staffing according to the predictive analysis of the patients load. The national health authorities may also use the aggregated healthcare data processed by AI and Big Data at the larger scale to monitor the disease trends, predict the outbreaks, and offer the interventions to guarantee the population health.

4.1 Overview of IoT in Healthcare

The IoT has gained an indivisible part of modern healthcare as an opportunity to follow the wearables over a long period, smart implants and smart medical accessories. The sensors monitor the vital signs of the heart rate, blood pressure, glucose, oxygen and sleep and develop healthy online health profile.

Going into detail, ECG strengthened glasses will be capable of sending live cardiac information to cloud servers that doctors can consult to observe patients at a distance. The timely warnings of the deviations result in the prompt alerts; the intervention and patient outcome levels rise.

In addition to personal care, it is possible to implement aggregated data of the IoT to assist in predictive modeling, resource planning, and individual treatment. The data can be used together with AI inference to identify anomalies, predict risks, prescribe intervention, and make sure that healthcare is proactive and not reactive, timely, and grounded in data.

4.2 Training Health Diagnosis AI Models

The most important aspect of AI-based healthcare diagnostics are machine learning (ML) and deep learning (DL) algorithms that are performed to provide accurate predictions and information according to the data produced by the IoT devices. Based on previous medical history, live vital parameters, and environment.

RNNs come in particularly handy when dealing with sequential data (e.g. electrocardiogram (ECG) readings). RNN model can detect pattern of ECG of a patient in real time and can provide medical practitioners with information on potential cardiac events before it can occur. It will enable early interventions and reduce the risk of severe consequences and improve the safety of patients.

In addition to personal tracking, AI models can be fed using data aggregated on groups of patients, and they have their prediction enhanced with the progress of time. This is an ongoing enhancement of the precision of the models and would perhaps enhance the earlier detection of illnesses, the creation of a tailor-made treatment plan, and utilization of the data to make sound judgments. Through the combination of IoT-based data with AI-based inference, medical care can also be translated to the mode of preventive, data-driven care, as opposed to the existing reactive model of treatment, thereby enhancing the outcomes, decreasing the costs, and making the overall efficiency of the medical services more efficient.

4.3 Edge vs. Cloud Inference in Medical Use

In health care applications, edge or cloud inference is based on the characteristics of thc work and thc urgency of the needed response. The edge inference is directly done on the IoT devices or neighboring edge servers enabling real time processing of patient data. This is especially essential when it comes to emergency situations, e.g. the ability to signify abnormal heartbeats, abrupt oxygen saturation decreases or other life endangering issues. Conversely, cloud inference takes advantage of the large computing power and storage capacity of cloud platform to conduct large-scale analytics. This involves the monitoring of population health, the prediction of trends in illnesses, and long term outcomes. A collection of hospitals or regions can be aggregated on cloud-based models to obtain information that can be used in strategic planning of healthcare, resources, and preventive health.

Through edge and cloud inference, healthcare systems can find a medium-ground of responding quickly and immediately to essential patient care, as well as provide broad and data-driven analysis to accommodate long-term health care. Such a hybrid structure will guarantee real-time intervention and decision-making, which will eventually lead to better patient outcomes, efficient service delivery, and the overall quality of care.

4.4 Example of Predictive Cardiac Monitoring Implementation

An example of a real-life application of AI in healthcare can be predicted cardiac monitoring in a hospital with the help of wearable ECG gadgets. Such wearables monitor the heart rhythms of patients in real-time, no matter where they are or not, which is a continuous flow of information (Fathima, 2025). This information is processed in edge devices and abnormalities, including irregular heartbeats or heart rate, are detected and the medical staff is alerted to act swiftly.

At the same time, the cloud analytics layer will summarize the data of numerous patients, in order to isolate larger trends and patterns. The system provides both critical and life-saving responses to edge inference and strategic information about the patient in the long term by integrating the edge and cloud inferences.

5. SMART INDUSTRY AND MANUFACTURING

The use of AI-based inference is a major aspect of Industry 4.0 as it allows manufacturers to streamline the production processes, minimize the downtime, and enhance product quality. Smart sensors installed on industrial machines constantly help gather real-time data, which gives comprehensive information about the performance of equipment and its work state.

This data is processed using AI models to form actionable intelligence to aid predictive maintenance, as the operators can identify some possible equipment failures before they happen. This is an active strategy that will reduce unexpected downtimes, lower maintenance expenses, and increase equipment life.

Moreover, AI inference contributes to optimization of the processes analyzing the production processes, determining the inefficiencies, and offering changes to enhance the performance and stability. Using IoT data in combination with AI-inspired insights, the manufacturers are able to increase their productivity, provide quality, and preserve a competitive edge in the changing industry environment.

5.1 Industrial Systems Integration With IoT

Current factories make use of the IoT to monitor machinery, production processes, and the environment. They are utilized in the collection of continuous data on vibration, temperature, pressure, and equipment fitness as the foundation of intelligent manufacturing structures.

Such systems are able to issue red flags on the potential failures of machinery or lack of efficiency in a process before they unleash havoc in the production process.

The combination of IoT surveillance and AI-driven intelligence, in general, offers a dynamic and responsive industrial environment. This puts manufacturers in a better position to be more efficient, the quality of products generated is similar and can also respond to any emerging issues in operations.

5.2 Models of Predictive Maintenance and Fault Detection

In contemporary industrial systems, AI-based inference models like the convolutional neural networks (CNNs) and decision trees are used to analyze sensor data measured on the machinery. These models identify abnormalities in the functioning of equipment and anticipate the possible failures before they happen.

The AI inference of predictive maintenance can help manufacturers minimize the unplanned system downtimes, which is why the process and production can proceed without any unforeseen delays. The defects are detected early enough and hence the maintenance is done in advance which enhances the general reliability in the operations.

As an illustration, when AI models are used to monitor motor vibrations, they can predict a bearing failure several weeks, allowing engineers to deal with the problem without stopping production. This method avoids both expensive failures and ensures the level of productivity and safety.

In general, predictive maintenance powered by AI prolongs the life of machines, it contributes to the efficiency of work and helps to proactively manage industry. Using sensor data and inference models, factories will be able to optimize their resources and sustain flowed and high-quality production.

5.3 Edge AI for Real-Time Decision Making

Edge AI allows processing and analysis of sensor data at the edge of the network, where the data is generated, bringing it closer to it. This enables the real-time decision-making process without depending on cloud connectivity and this dramatically decreases latency and response time. As an example, an edge AI can be used to instantly examine the temperature measurements and automatically shut the machine down to avoid the damage or potential harm to the equipment or safety risks when there is an indication that the machine is overheated.

The edge-based inference also allows industries to process faster and become more reliable and that is particularly helpful in the surroundings where each millisecond counts. Edge AI allows its systems to operate locally unlike a cloud-based system, which requires constant internet connectivity, making it uninterrupted even in locations that are remote or have limited bandwidth.

Moreover, edge AI improves data privacy and security, as the sensitive information is handled locally instead of being sent to the external servers. It is a perfect remedy to vital industries like manufacturing, healthcare, and autonomous systems, where fast, safe, and smart decisions must be made.

5.4 Smart Factories: Results and ROI

The factories implementing the principles of AI inference and IoT systems see a significant rise in the productivity and operational efficiency. Through constant checking of machinery and processes, AI models can give useful information that can be acted on by the manufacturer to reduce unexpected downtime as the problem is detected before it gets out of control. AP, on its own, is capable of decreasing equipment downtime by 30-50 percent, which will guarantee a continuous production process with no disruptions and enhance the overall performance of equipment.

Using operational data, AI is able to detect any bottlenecks, forecast peak loads, and suggest schedule changes. The result is the production processes are streamlined, delivery is faster and the quality of the products is the same and this leads to customer satisfaction and customer loyalty.

The AI/IoT integration can be measured in terms of financial gains. Minimized maintenance, reduced energy usage and maximized resources usage all reduce operational costs and increase profitability. The factories are capable of maintaining cost-effective operations without affecting the quality and safety.

6. IOT CITY INFRASTRUCTURE

The urban environments are undergoing a transformation using AI-based inferences and IoT solutions to support smarter, efficient and sustainable urban environments. With the assistance of a system of sensors, cameras, and other tools, cities will be capable of obtaining real-time data related to traffic, air quality, energy consumption, and safety of the community. The local analysis or data analysis in the cloud is used by local governments to make more data-driven decisions that can positively impact the quality of life of the citizens at a faster rate through AI inference models.

The technologies are used in the smart city to regulate the infrastructure and also maximize the uses of resources. An example of such is the smart traffic control that uses AI to anticipate traffic jam and adjusts the traffic lights dynamically so as to minimize the time and pollution of the trip (Fathima, 2025; Das, 2024). In a similar manner, the smart lights will be capable of controlling the brightness of the lights depending on the pedestrians and not only will it save energy, but also make the roads safer.

Other than efficiency, urban intelligence which is AI-driven is a source of sustainability as it entails efficient distribution of water, waste collection and energy consumption. The IoT and AI inference will make the previously existing cities to become smart, secure, and adaptable ecosystems that are citizen-centric; the backbone of truly intelligent and robust urban living.

6.1 Artificial Intelligence Traffic Control and Safety

The concept of AI-driven traffic management is transforming the manner in which cities are addressing congestion, road traffic safety and mobility. Based on the data carried by the IoT sensors, surveillance cameras and smart vehicles, AI models will be capable of examining the traffic movement, vehicle velocity, and human movement in real-time. With this real-time analysis, the control centers of the city are able to find the trends of the traffic jam, regulate the traffic lights, and to optimize the effectiveness of the roads in real-time.

Adaptive traffic signal systems can be regarded as one of the primary fields of AI inference implementation in smart cities. These systems can also provide ambulances and fire trucks with green-light corridors which gives them priority over other types of vehicles which can put their lives at risk and cause delays. In addition, AI algorithms reduce unnecessary waiting at the crossroads, reduce fuel consumption and the volume of carbon emissions.

Overall, the AI inference may help manage traffic in cities and enhance mobility and congestion, and provide more road safety and environmental preservation, thereby transforming the smart cities of the future into smarter, well-structured, and safer transportation networks.

6.2 Environmental Surveillance and Communication Services

Green surveillance is one of the most significant elements of the smart city development, and the integration of AI inference and the IoT technologies may collaborate and support the maintenance and healthy urban population. The cities have a system of sensors that keep checking the quality of air, purity of water, energy consumption and waste disposal processes at any given time. The sensors produce massive amounts of data that are processed live by the AI models and identify abnormalities, as well as determine risks to the environment.

Cities can identify pollutants, forecast a trend that is not healthy by the environment and also offer early warnings to save the health of humans through the use of AI inference. In order to demonstrate the argument, once air quality sensors detect the increase in the rate of the concentration of the level of PM, AI systems, in their turn, will predict the possibility of a spike in the pollution and send alerts, which, in turn, will allow governmental organizations to make appropriate interventions in time, i.e. controlling traffic or regulating the industry.

Artificial intelligence can also be applied in the rationalization of community services that enhance the waste collection distribution, harmonizing the energy provision, and provide the convenient control of water. Governments can use these intelligent systems to make informed decisions, save resources and be proactive as regards responding to any form of emergencies.

6.3 Intelligent Governance and Big Data Platforms

Smart cities have been dependent on Big Data platforms that help collect, process and interpolate data on the number of thousand IoT sensors deployed throughout the city to provide intelligent governance. These platforms pool lots of information about the existing government services, transport, utilities, and infrastructure, which allows administrators of the cities to see the dynamics of the city in real-time.

With the high level of AI inference and data visualization dashboards, officials are able to track the activities in the city and detecting the arising problems as well as making informed policy decisions based on data. The examples of this include traffic jam trends, energy consumption rates or emergency response times that can be analyzed and presented in user-friendly cards that aid quick and informed decision-making.

In addition, this integration improves efficiency, transparency, and citizenism. Governments can ensure trust and civic engagement by ensuring that real-time information is shared with the public. The residents are able to monitor the performance of the services and report on problems and help in improving the performance of the governance.

Finally, the combination of AI inference and the analytics of Big Data is changing the cities administration into an active, intelligent system-enhancing the level of planning, resource utilization, and increasing the overall contentment of citizens and their happiness.

6.4 Problems and Policy Implications

Although AI inference and IoT have many advantages to smart cities, they also present some obstacles that need to be taken into account by policies. The most significant concern is data privacy and security since incessant gathering of personal and environmental information may be abused or leaked to intrusion. Keeping sensitive information safe is paramount in ensuring that people are still trustful.

There are other obstacles in the form of interoperability and infrastructure. Smart city systems also come with various vendors and technologies which do not always come together as one and are thus in need of standardized protocols and well established infrastructure to operate well.

Ethics are also significant. The policies should be fair, transparent, and accountable when making choices on AI to avoid bias or discrimination. Digital services must also be accessible to all communities in order to prevent the marginalization of some communities.

Effective smart cities are highly innovative, but also consider the needs of society and enforce policies that safeguard privacy and promote safe use of AI, as well as, make sure that technology makes life more sustainable, inclusive, and, overall, better.

7. ENERGY AND UTILITY MANAGEMENT INTELLIGENCE

The IoT in combination with the AI inference is changing the energy and utility management, making it more efficient, less expensive, and sustainable. IoT-based smart grids, predictive analytics and smart meters give real-time information on grid performance, energy distribution, and electricity consumption. This can be analyzed in real-time with the help of AI inferential models and can form the basis of informed decisions used by the operators regarding load balancing, resource distribution, and fault detection.

A forecast about the demand can be made based on the history of the usage and meteorological conditions among other external factors through predictive analytics (Das, 2024). The energy suppliers will be able to control the functioning of the grids most effectively and reduce wastage and provide evenly after forecasting the peak loads. The latter is also provided through the smart meters where the real-time consumption data is made accessible to the consumer to motivate to save energy.

Overall, AI inference is also referred to as an IoT that is built to form an intelligent energy system. It gives an opportunity to actively manage the utilities, introduce renewable energy, reduce the losses in operation, and provide the stable and effective supply of the cities, as well as industries, with the energy.

7.1 IoT in Smart Grids and Meters

Smart meters are smart grids and device-based internet of things that is revolutionizing the energy management through provision of finely enable real-time data of electricity consumption, voltage, frequency as well as energy losses. They work to monitor the grid in real-time and send the data collected to centralized or edge AI inference systems over IoT networks in detail. The data of high-resolution enables AI models to monitor the condition of the grid, detect abnormalities and effectively allocate energy to the grid.

The potential errors can also be identified in real-time and proactive measures on the preventing of the outages or the reduced downtime can be taken with the help of the AI inference. With this as an example, in case of a failure in a section of the grid, the system can automatically re-route power along other possible paths, and has minimum effect on the consumers.

Moreover, the smart meters will make the consumers more powerful as they will know their electric rates, and will be willing to minimize the use and use more energy wisely. Having a more stable, sustainable, and cheaper grid running can be achieved with the introduction of IoT and AI inference, where electricity companies are concerned.

7.2 AI Demand Forecasting and Optimization

Besides the real-time monitoring, AI inference models also play an important role in the energy demand prediction and grid optimization. Smart meters and IoT sensors generate electricity consumption feeds, voltage variations and energy loss feeds. It is a kind of data that is analyzed with the help of AI models to forecast both short and long-term demand trends and help utility providers to distribute resources effectively and avoid overloading the grid.

Predictive analytics assists the operators of the energy sector to forecast the occurrence of high load, reconcile the assimilation of renewable sources and arrange the maintenance, without interference in the procedure. To illustrate, when AI models do find out that there might be a large demand during the evening in a particular location, the additional power can be sent in advance so that there is stability.

In addition, AI controls the distribution of energy to identify inefficiency and redirect power during faults or loss of power. This ensures that there is continuity in supply and low operation cost and reliability. The consumers also enjoy the benefits of acquiring information about their consumption habit and can switch their consumption and reduce the electricity bill.

Generally, the combination of AI inference and IoT-driven smart grids offers more diversity of efficiency, sustainability, and resilience to transform the modern energy systems to be smarter and more responsive.

7.3 Predictive Analytics Energy Optimization

The optimization of the energy distribution and efficient operation of smart grids is highly beneficial with the help of predictive analytics. The AI inference models work with the real-time and historical information of the IoT sensors so that they can condition the patterns of the energy consumption, find the anomalies and predict the potential faults.

To take an example, a significant growth in the usage of the electricity or the malfunction of the transformers can be traced instantly and the operators take the required actions to prevent the inconveniences. Such anomalies can be predicted, therefore AI models can make sure that the grid is stable, the energy supply is good and efficient.

In addition, predictive analytics can enable to maximize the utilization of renewable energy since it is able to predict the generation and compare it with the anticipated demand. This enables it to be less reliant on non-renewable alternative sources and has the minimal amount of waste consumed.

8. AGRICULTURE AND THE ENVIRONMENT

The development of IoT and AI inference has completely transformed agriculture and environmental management, introducing an increase in productivity, sustainability, and resource efficiency. The IoT sensors such as drones, soil moisture, and weather are used to provide real-time and continuous observation of the crop, soil quality, water level, and climate. This constant stream of information can enable farmers and environmental scientists to be informed in the timely manner and ensure resources are used to the fullest and yield higher.

The data obtained are processed by the AI models that identify the patterns and anomalies and provide actionable information. An example is the prediction of crop diseases, pest infestation or water stress at a very early stage before they have a devastating effect on the crop. Similarly, AI inference is implemented in the environmental field to identify the pollutant degree, track climate change, and predict the natural hazards.

The combination of the IoT monitoring and the AI-based analysis is more specific and adaptive in agriculture. The farmers will be in a position to tailor the irrigation, fertilization and harvesting period and the environmental managers will be able to present proactive interventions which will result in sustainable, productive and strong systems, an advantage to both productivity and the ecosystem.

8.1 IoT Sensors and Drones Precision Agriculture

Precision agriculture may not be possible without IoT devices and drones because they can provide specific and real-time data about the state of crops, soil, and environmental conditions. The weather stations are the soil moisture sensors that can measure the temperature, humidity, rainfall patterns and flow of data which is a continuous process and is highly crucial in management of the farm.

The drones equipped with multispectral cameras and thermal cameras are also additive in terms of the point of view and help in visualizing the stress of plants, the presence of pests, and nutrient deficiency that is otherwise not observable by the naked eye. These aerial observations may also be useful supplements to sensor data on the ground that builds up to a holistic image of the situation in the field.

AI inference models manipulate this granular data to detect the trends, make the predictions of the possible problems, and suggest some interventions. To use the example, one can change the time of irrigation according to the quantity of moisture in the soil or some fertilization can be performed in the instance of the nutrient deficiency.

The IoT sensors and drones with the AI inference form Precision Agriculture which makes the farming process cost-effective, green, and resource-efficient in terms of resources utilization and production of more goods and less wastage.

8.2 AI Inference of Crop Health and Yield Prediction

AI inference models can be important to predict crop health and yield by integrating data gathered through IoT devices within the farm. These are models that address the information about soil quality, weather, crop growth and irrigation patterns to identify trends and give actionable information.

Deep learning algorithms have the ability to identify disease, nutrient deficiency or pests at their early stages to allow farmers to take action before it is too late. Having processed both historical and real-time data, the AI models predict possible low-yield regions, propose more specific solutions to address them, including accurate irrigation, fertilization, or pest control actions.

Moreover, AI inference helps to plan planting and crop rotation plans according to forecasted growth conditions and market demand (IoT, Big Data, and AI in advancing agriculture: a literature review of smart technology that can ensure sustainability, 2023). This would mean that resources are utilized effectively and at the same time maximizing productivity.

In general, by combining AI inference with IoT data, farmers can make evidence-based decisions, enhance crop yield, decrease losses, and attain sustainable agriculture processes beneficial to the economy and the surrounding environment.

8.3 Irrigation and Resource Management Data-Based

Water management has also been a major issue in agriculture as resource wastage and low production can be the outcome of the inefficiency of the irrigation. The AI inference models will be optimized in order to optimize the volume of water used: it will require the analysis of real-time soil moisture sensors, weather forecasts, and special crop needs. Based on these models, the quantity of water to be used, as well as the most optimal timing of watering of the crop is forecasted to the effect that the crops are not over watered and are not under watered.

With the integration of AI inference and the system, smart irrigation systems could be intelligent in modifying their water delivery flow in response to these forecasts. One of them is that the sensor can delay or even cut down the irrigation in case a sensor notices that there is sufficient water in the soil or the sensor predicts rain and this would save the amount of water and lower the electricity bills.

This information-driven approach of enhancing efficiency of the water use also helps in the crop enhancement besides the rise in the yield and quality of the crop through prevention of under- and over-watering. In addition, it helps in achieving sustainability by minimizing wastage of water, conserving on energy and also allowing it to use the resources in a responsible way nowadays in the farming sector.

9. CHALLENGES AND LIMITATIONS OF AI INFERENCE IN IOT AND BIG DATA

Even though AI inference, including IoT and Big Data, can revolutionize industries, various problems and limitations do not allow its potential. The IoT devices generate vast amounts of data, and anomalies, no values, or sensor failure can reduce the quality of AI models and compromise the decision-making.

Computational and infrastructure challenges are also an issue. The real-time AI inference requires high level of processing power, low latency networks, and powerful storage systems which could be impossible to have in some environments, especially in remote or resource based environments.

The security and privacy is yet to be a concern. By hacking into systems, unauthorized access, or mishandling of sensitive data, these systems can be compromised because the collection, transmission, and processing of sensitive data can affect cyberattack exposure and unauthorized access.

9.1 Technical Challenges: Latency, Scalability, and Bandwidth

The realm of the IoT and the Big Data world presupposes the application of real-time AI, which implies that the aspects of low latency, high bandwidth, and sufficient computing capabilities are necessary to process the scales of data efficiently. Having many users on a network that is not responsive enough when implemented at large scales can make it difficult to make the most essential decisions and undermine the effectiveness of AI-based systems.

As the number of interconnected objects grows, as well as the amount of data, the use of AI models must be trained to handle heterogeneous data of different origins without negatively affecting their performance or quality. Without a proper scaling the system may experience bottlenecks in the system which will lead to higher response time and reduced reliability.

Partially, edge computing is also a solution because it enables processing the data closer to the source, reduces the latency, and offloads central servers. However, the infrastructure must be strong, algorithms must be optimized and data management must exist to provide a consistent performance across the IoT ecosystem despite edge solutions.

These technical aspects are critical in resolving real-time responsiveness, reliability, and scalability challenges of AI-based IoT and Big Data applications.

9.2 Problems with Data Quality and Integration

The quality and consistency of data gathered on the IoT devices is critical in the process of AI inference. Nevertheless, the accuracy and reliability of AI models may be adversely affected by these devices that usually yield noisy, incomplete, or inconsistent data. Wrong sensor values or absence of information can cause wrong predictions and false decision-making.

The combination of heterogeneous data, which involves more than one source (sensors, wearables, industrial machines, and databases) further complicates the situation. The variation in the data formats, sampling rates, and protocols need to be well aligned and synchronized to form a consistent dataset, which can be analyzed by AI.

Overcoming data quality and integration issues are important to obtain reliable, robust, and actionable insights of the artificial intelligence-based IoT and Big Data systems.

9.3 Privacy, Security and Ethical Concerns

The use of AI inference of IoT and Big Data systems often presupposes the accumulation and processing of sensitive personal information and operations, especially in the spheres of healthcare, smart cities, and finance. This poses a great privacy threat since any malicious access, data leakage or misuse can prove catastrophic to individuals and organizations.

The issue of data protection is not the sole challenge to regard concerning security: the protection of the IoT devices and the communication networks against cyber attacks is also necessary. The strength of the devices or network protocols can be low, and it will undermine integrity and reliability of the system, including essential infrastructure or services.

Moral considerations also play a very important role. Artificial Intelligence models are not transparent, regulated by a human, and can be biased algorithms. In order to maintain the confidence of the population, to follow the accounts and informed consent, it is vital to make sure that the fairness, accountability, and informed consent are provided.

The organizations can resolve these risks through proper implementation of good cyber security policies, implementation of policies that favor privacy and adoption of responsible artificial intelligence models.

10. FUTURE TRENDS AND FUTURE DIRECTIONS

The solution of AI inference in IoT as well as big data is developing at a very fast pacc with thc innovation of hardware, algorithms, and connections. The new trends are set to further increase efficiency, lower the cost of operations, and facilitate sustainability in various fields, such as manufacturing, energy, healthcare and agriculture, and urban management.

Among them is the adoption of edge AI, the further proximity to the source of information minimises latency and network reliance and facilitates real-time decision-making. Likewise, federated learning is becoming increasingly popular, which enables AI models to be trained on decentralized data without losing privacy and security.

The combination of 5G networks, advanced sensors, and cloud-edge hybrid is likely to enhance scalability, responsiveness, and reliability of the system. Also, AI models gain greater adaptability and the ability to optimize themselves and improve predictive accuracy and resource efficiency.

10.1 Edge AI and On-Device Inference

Edge AI is applying AI models to IoT devices and making decisions in real time without being connected to the cloud services. Local data processing makes edge AI minimize the latency and improve privacy and lessen bandwidth and is especially necessary in the applications that must be responded to quickly.

With the help of edge AI, industrial automation can be used to enable machines to identify anomalies or anticipate failure before it can cause downtime and make the most of productivity. In autonomous cars, on-vehicle checking implies that vehicles can be empowered with the capacity to analyze sensor information and make choices regarding navigation or on security issues within a matter of just-a-second, and without outside networks. Smart AI devices like health bracelets will be helpful as well because they will deliver real-time notifications about the most vital parameters of health and guarantee the privacy of personal information.

The use of edge inference is increasingly being dire in time sensitive applications, resource constrained applications as well as privacy sensitive applications. The potential of AI and local computerization, which form the edge AI, are the capacity to guarantee a faster, safer, and more efficient operation in a large variety of industries and applications.

10.2 Federated Learning and Privacy-Preserving Models

The recent innovation in AI inference is the so-called federated learning that allows the training of the model using distributed devices, without the need to transfer data to a center server. The devices model their local data and only send updates of the model without violating the privacy of the user but adds to a world model. Such a strategy may be effective in reducing the burden of the networks and allow multiple various organizations or devices to collaborate in developing AI.

The sensitive AI methods that will be applied in association with federated learning will make it possible to hold sensitive information. It is possible to avoid the identification of individual records because of differential privacy and other techniques (like noising data or the outputs of models), though a technique that may be employed is homomorphic encryption, avoiding the need for the use of decryption to compute on encrypted data. These methods keep the accuracy of the models and protect the information of the users.

Federated learning and privacy-conscious AI can come in handy especially in fields such as healthcare, finance, and smart cities since sensitive information should be kept safe. In order to address privacy, regulatory, and ethical issues and develop a safe, cooperative, and productive training of AI models, they can be combined.

10.3 Decision Transparency and Explainable AI

Explainable AI (XAI) is concerned with the challenge of making AI models understandable, interpretable and understandable to people. As AI inference continues to expand intrinsically into such fundamental spheres of life as healthcare, finances, and government, stakeholders must be in a position to trust and check AI-generated decisions. Even the most accurate models may be opposed due to the unaccountability or not understanding it at all since it is not interpretable.

Few of the methods used in XAI are feature attribution that identifies the largest contributions of inputs to a model; attention visualization that identifies important pieces of data, i.e., images or text and rule-based explanations providing explanations of decisions in a logical fashion. These methods allow the users to know the logic of a model that makes a particular recommendation or prediction that enhances the level of trust and transparency.

10.4 5G and Cloud-Edge

One of the enablers of the next-generation AI inference of the IoT and Big Data systems is the use of 5G networks. The 5G can facilitate real-time communication between the cloud and edge devices in the sense that it can create low latency, ultra-fast data transfer and high reliability and therefore, the AI models are not efficient in handling large amounts of data. It is vital to applications that require making decisions fast, such as autonomous vehicles, smart factories, and remote healthcare monitoring.

The cloud-edge synergy can also be useful to scale up the performance of the system since the computational tasks are to be distributed considering their complexity requirements and latency requirements. The intensive processing such as training models in the cloud or other high-scale analytics can be performed in the cloud, and processing applications with a latency need are executed locally on edge devices. This balance ensures that maximum resource is used, no congestion of network occurs and responsiveness is reduced.

The potential of IoT systems powered by AI and fueled by 5G connectivity coupled with cloud-edge systems offers scalable and reliable operations that are high-performance. This integration enables the realization of the smooth, intelligent and efficient data-intensive application management in different fields.

11. CONCLUSION AND FUTURE RESEARCH OPPORTUNITIES

The IoT and big data AI inference have already been demonstrated to be revolutionary in various industries, and large amounts of unstructured sensor data are being measured and converted into valuable and usable intelligible data. Real-time tracking, predictive analytics and automated decision-making help organizations to streamline processes, reduce costs, and become more sustainable (Fathima, 2025; Das, 2024; IoT, Big Data, and AI in advancing agriculture: a literature review of smart technology that can ensure sustainability, 2023; Neustein et al., 2023). The case of smart manufacturing, energy management, city planning, agriculture, and healthcare are just a few examples that indicate the effectiveness, reliability, and well-being of the society as the product of AI-based insights.

Despite these improvements, such problems as data quality, model drift, privacy, and infrastructure limitations also persist. Further research should focus on the effectiveness of AI models, adaptive levels of learning and privacy friendly interventions to ensure scalable, reliable, and ethical application in the future. Recent advantages The newest advances AI and federated learning, explainable AI and digital twins technologies can offer opportunities to increase capabilities without breaking transparency and accountability.

New technologies or interdisciplinary research can be used to exploit the potential of AI inference in IoT and Big Data even further. By addressing the constraints in the present, the intelligent systems of tomorrow will develop a solution in the industries and communities throughout the world, which will be smarter, resilient and sustainable.

11.1 Summary of Key Insights

The chapter has highlighted the important contribution of AI inference to the IoT and Big Data in other areas such as health, manufacturing, smart cities, energy control, and agriculture. The AI inference interprets the raw sensor data in all the industries and offers useful insights to the organizations that enable them to make real-time and evidence-based decisions.

All AI inference applications have the benefit of improving proactive decision-making, risk avoidance, and efficient utilization of resources to achieve increased operations efficiency, reduced costs, and even sustainability. Together with IoT, Big Data, and AI, organizations can build resilient and intelligent systems capable of engaging dynamically in response to the ever-changing conditions and in line with the complex challenges.

Overall, in the chapter, AI inference is shown as a transformative enabler, a relationship between technology and actionable intelligence to cultivate creativity and operational excellence in a number of industries.

11.2 Researcher and Practitioner Recommendations.

Practitioners and researchers should adopt a set of best practices and strategies that would ensure that inferences of AI are maximized in the IoT and Big Data. In order to achieve this, edge computing must be implemented on execution of applications that are latency sensitive in order to facilitate real time decision making and eliminate network reliance.

Second, federated learning, differential privacy, and homomorphic encryption are the privacy-aware AI technologies that are to be applied in maintaining confidential data and regulatory provisions. Constant observation of AI models and retraining to adapt to the data drift and to predict the data with a high accuracy in the long term are significant elements.

REFERENCES

Fathima, S. A. (2025). IoT and Big Data Ecosystems: A Review of Technologies, Use Cases, and Research Trends. International Journal of AI, Big Data, Computational and Management Studies, 6(1), 10-21. ijaibdcms.orgDOI: <ALIGNMENT.qj></ ALIGNMENT>10.63282/3050-9416.IJAIBDCMS-V6I1P102

Das, J. (2024). IoT-enabled smart city governance using AI-based data analytics. *Metaversalize*, *1*(1), 1–15. DOI: 10.22105/metaverse.v1i2.54

"IoT, Big Data, and AI in advancing agriculture: a literature review of smart technology that can ensure sustainability. (2023). Knowledge for Policy.

Martin, D. (2023). Smart Cities: The IoT and Big Data Analytics. Advanced Sciences, 5(2) 45. journal-as.com.DOI: 10.69610/j.as.20231221

Mohammadi, M., Al-Fuqaha, A., Sorour, S., & Guizani, M. (2018). Deep Learning IoT Big Data and Streaming Analytics: A Survey. arXiv preprint arXiv:1712.04301. arXiv.

Naha, R. K., Garg, S., Georgakopoulos, D., Jayaraman, P. P., Gao, L., Xiang, Y., & Ranjan, R. (2018). Survey of Trends, Architectures, Requirements, and Research Directions. arXiv preprint arXiv:1807.00976. arXiv.

Neustein, A., Mahalle, P. N., Joshi, P., & Shinde, G. R. (Eds.). (2023). *AI, IoT, big data and cloud computing for industry 4.0. Springer*. SpringerLink., DOI: 10.1007/978-3-031-29713-7

Samadi, S. (2022). AI, IoT and big data convergence to develop flood analytics. [Frontiers]. *Frontiers in Water, 4*. Advance online publication. DOI: 10.3389/ frwa.2022.786040

Shi, Y., Yang, K., Jiang, T., Zhang, J., & Letaief, K. B. (2020). Efficient Edge AI: Communication Communication-Efficient Edge AI: Algorithms and Systems. arXiv preprint arXiv:2002.09668. arXiv.

Shlezinger, N., & Bajic, I. V. (2022). Collaborative Inference of IoT devices empowered with AI. arXiv preprint ArXiv:2207.11664. arXiv.

KEY TERMS AND DEFINITIONS

AI Inference Actionable Insights: AI inference will process unstructured IoT and Big Data into actionable intelligence, and provide real-time decisions in any industry.

Big Data Analytics Process Optimization: The data analytics determines the bottlenecks and foresees the utilization of resources and enhances the quality of the supply chain and its efficiency.

Edge AI Real-Time Processing: It is possible to make localized decisions using an AI implementation on the IoT devices to minimize latency and bandwidth consumption in the real-time sensitive systems.

Emerging Trends: Edge, 5G: Technologies such as federated learning, explainable AI, 5G, etc make it infinitely bigger, more responsive and transparent.

Energy Management: Smart grids, predictive analytics and demand forecasts are used based on AI to optimize the energy delivery and also to assist in achieving sustainability.

Ethical and Sustainable AI: Future research on adaptive learning, ethical and responsible deployment will guarantee the quality, and also responsible implementation of AI systems.

IoT Implementation Accurate Agriculture: IoT and AI oversee crops and soil condition and irrigation, which enhances resource and crop output.

Predictive Maintenance and Fault Detection: AI will be able to predict equipment failures and minimize the time spent out of the working process, costs on maintenance and work productivity.

Smart Cities and Urban Intelligence: AI inference is used to assist in the operation of the city and environmental management control and management of the traffic which could improve the operations of the city and living standard of people living in the city.

Threats Data Quality and Privacy: Data Quality, model drifting, privacy, and infrastructure constraints also impact on AI performance and reliability.

Chapter 8
From Dataflows to Decisions:
KG-Enhanced AI Inference

Otmane Azeroual
http://orcid.org/0000-0002-5225-389X
University of Hagen, Germany

ABSTRACT

This chapter addresses the challenge of transforming heterogeneous, noisy, and incomplete dataflows into actionable and trustworthy decisions. While machine learning has advanced predictive accuracy, it struggles with interpretability, semantic integration, and generalizability in high-stakes environments. Knowledge Graphs (KGs) provide a structured means of embedding domain semantics and enabling contextualized reasoning, yet existing approaches often focus on isolated techniques such as embeddings, graph neural networks, or symbolic reasoning. The proposed KG-enhanced AI inference framework integrates these methods into an end-to-end pipeline that ingests heterogeneous data, enriches it semantically, applies hybrid inference, and generates interpretable, decision-oriented outputs. Illustrated with applications in healthcare, finance, and industrial monitoring, the framework emphasizes scalability, reliability, and explainability, offering a pathway toward trustworthy AI systems that meet both technical and domain-specific requirements.

1. INTRODUCTION

The rapid proliferation of heterogeneous data sources across domains such as healthcare, finance, environmental science, and manufacturing has intensified the need for methods that can transform raw dataflows into actionable and trustworthy

DOI: 10.4018/979-8-3373-7046-0.ch008

decisions. While advances in machine learning, particularly deep learning, have led to impressive predictive capabilities, they remain constrained by critical limitations. These include the difficulty of handling heterogeneous and incomplete data streams, the lack of transparency and interpretability in decision-making processes, and the limited ability to generalize and transfer knowledge across domains (Doshi-Velez & Kim, 2017; Ribeiro et al., 2016; Azeroual et al., 2025). In high-stakes environments, such as clinical decision support or financial risk management, these shortcomings are especially problematic because decisions must not only be accurate but also accountable, context-aware, and aligned with established domain knowledge.

Knowledge Graphs (KGs) have emerged as a powerful paradigm to address these challenges. By representing entities and their relationships in structured, semantically rich networks, KGs enable the integration of heterogeneous data sources and provide a foundation for contextualized reasoning (Hogan et al., 2021). Unlike purely statistical models, KG-enhanced systems can explicitly embed prior knowledge, constraints, and domain semantics, thereby facilitating more robust inference and supporting transparency and traceability of decision processes. Recent research has shown that integrating KGs with machine learning pipelines can improve both performance and transparency of AI systems. In healthcare, for instance, the use of biomedical KGs has been demonstrated to enhance prediction tasks such as drug recommendation, mortality prediction, and disease progression modeling (Shang et al., 2019; Varshney et al., 2023). Similarly, studies in explainable AI highlight how KG-based reasoning provides user-facing explanations that go beyond feature importance and allow domain experts to understand predictions in terms of causal or relational structures (Samek et al., 2019; Rajabi & Kafaie, 2022).

The community addressed by this chapter spans both technical and applied domains. It is directed toward AI researchers and practitioners working at the intersection of knowledge representation, reasoning, and machine learning, particularly those engaged with graph neural networks, neuro-symbolic systems, and explainable AI. At the same time, it speaks to applied scientists and practitioners in domains where decision-making is sensitive to ethical, legal, or regulatory constraints, including clinicians, financial analysts, and environmental scientists. Finally, policymakers, regulators, and ontology engineers form a crucial audience, as the operationalization of KG-enhanced inference in real-world settings requires not only methodological soundness but also governance and standardization frameworks.

The aim of this chapter is to articulate a coherent perspective on how the integration of KGs with AI inference can transform raw dataflows into trustworthy and explainable decisions. It seeks to provide a synthesis of current research, identify practical challenges in real-world applications, and outline methodological pathways for bridging statistical learning with symbolic reasoning. In particular, the chapter emphasizes hybrid inference architectures that combine data-driven learning with explicit knowledge-based constraints. By doing so, the chapter aspires to foster dialogue between technical AI communities and domain experts, highlighting design patterns, evaluation practices, and governance considerations that can enable reliable KG-enhanced inference in high-stakes environments. Ultimately, the chapter contributes to the broader effort of building AI systems that are not only performant but also interpretable, transferable, and socially responsible.

This chapter is organized to provide both conceptual grounding and practical guidance for implementing KG-enhanced AI inference. Following this introduction, the subsequent sections first review related work and current limitations, providing a critical overview of existing methods and highlighting gaps that motivate the proposed framework. The chapter then presents detailed implementation and architectural considerations, describing how heterogeneous dataflows are integrated, how KG embeddings and hybrid reasoning modules are operationalized, and how practical challenges such as scalability, data quality, and real-time integration are addressed. Next, illustrative use cases and practical application scenarios are discussed, showing how the framework can be applied to domains such as healthcare, finance, and industrial monitoring, along with metrics and scenarios for evaluating effectiveness. Performance considerations and evaluation strategies are subsequently discussed, offering insights into the trade-offs between accuracy, interpretability, and computational complexity. The chapter concludes with a discussion of limitations and avenues for future research, emphasizing ongoing challenges in dynamic, multimodal, and large-scale data environments, and highlighting directions for methodological and technical advancement.

The relevance of this chapter lies in its focus on bridging heterogeneous data integration, knowledge representation, and explainable AI. By systematically connecting statistical and symbolic reasoning through KGs, the chapter addresses urgent needs in high-stakes domains where transparency, traceability, and accountability are as critical as predictive performance. The chapter is intended for a multidisciplinary audience, including AI researchers, data scientists, and engineers, as well as domain experts in healthcare, finance, and environmental monitoring who seek to understand, implement, or evaluate KG-enhanced inference systems. Furthermore, it engages policymakers and ontology engineers by providing insights into best practices for governance, standardization, and methodological rigor.

By presenting both conceptual frameworks and concrete architectural and methodological guidance, this chapter aims to enable the development of AI systems that are not only highly predictive but also interpretable, reliable, and socially responsible, facilitating informed decision-making and fostering trust in AI-assisted workflows.

2. PROBLEM STATEMENT

Despite the rapid progress in machine learning and data-driven decision support, the transformation of complex, heterogeneous dataflows into actionable insights remains a critical challenge. In many practical domains, the data needed for informed decision-making arrives in continuous streams, originates from disparate sources, and spans multiple modalities with varying levels of structure and reliability. For example, in healthcare, structured clinical records, laboratory values, unstructured physician notes, imaging data, and real-time signals from wearable devices contribute to the patient profile. In finance, transactional logs, market data, regulatory reports, and news streams converge into a highly dynamic decision environment. The inherent heterogeneity and velocity of these dataflows render conventional learning-based approaches brittle, often resulting in models that are either too specialized to transfer across domains or too opaque to be trusted by human decision-makers (Yang et al., 2020; Michael et al., 2024).

One of the core problems is that statistical models, even when highly expressive, typically fail to integrate background knowledge and semantic context. A prediction model might detect correlations but lacks the means to encode explicit domain constraints, commonsense reasoning, or causal dependencies. As a result, such models often struggle when deployed outside controlled training conditions. This shortcoming has been repeatedly observed in high-stakes applications. For instance, predictive models for sepsis detection or drug interaction warnings may perform well on retrospective datasets but produce unreliable or even unsafe outputs in live clinical environments because they do not account for knowledge encoded in medical guidelines, ontologies, or pharmacological interaction networks (Shickel et al., 2017; Jensen et al., 2012). Similarly, financial risk models may capture short-term patterns in market behavior yet ignore structural dependencies that domain experts regard as critical, such as regulatory compliance rules or systemic interdependencies between institutions (Butor-Keler & Polasik, 2020).

Another pressing issue lies in the interpretability of decision-making processes. Deep learning approaches often operate as black boxes, offering little insight into the reasoning behind their outputs. This lack of interpretability undermines trust in settings where accountability is indispensable. Clinicians cannot act upon a risk score alone; they require an explanation that relates to patient history, clinical guidelines, and mechanistic pathways. Regulators in finance or policymakers in environmental governance similarly demand transparent reasoning to ensure that algorithmic outputs align with legal and ethical standards (Doshi-Velez & Kim, 2017; Lipton, 2018). Without such contextualized explanations, AI-generated recommendations risk being rejected or underutilized in practice, regardless of their predictive accuracy.

KGs have been proposed as a potential solution to these challenges because they provide a structured means of integrating heterogeneous data with explicit, machine-interpretable semantics. However, the practical integration of KGs into real-world inference systems is itself fraught with obstacles. KGs must be constructed, maintained, and updated in dynamic environments where knowledge is incomplete, noisy, or constantly evolving (Hogan et al., 2021). Moreover, the methods for combining symbolic KG reasoning with sub-symbolic machine learning are still in their infancy. While graph neural networks and embedding techniques offer pathways to bridge the two paradigms, there is a lack of standardized, end-to-end methodologies that simultaneously address scalability, robustness, and explainability in operational systems (Chen et al., 2020).

The central problem this chapter addresses is therefore the gap between the availability of abundant but fragmented dataflows and the need for trustworthy, explainable, and context-sensitive decision support. The challenge is not only technical but also organizational and epistemic: data must be integrated with structured knowledge representations; inference must combine statistical learning with reasoning mechanisms; and outputs must satisfy the expectations of practitioners, regulators, and domain experts. In the absence of such integration, AI systems remain difficult to validate, govern, and reliably deploy in high-stakes contexts.

Building upon this problem statement, it becomes evident that while KGs offer a promising avenue for integrating heterogeneous data and enabling explainable inference, their practical adoption is constrained by both methodological and technical limitations. A systematic review of existing approaches is therefore required to contextualize the proposed framework, identify gaps in current methodologies, and highlight the specific challenges that must be addressed to achieve scalable, interpretable, and robust KG-enhanced AI inference. The following section reviews the state of the art in KG integration, neuro-symbolic reasoning, and hybrid AI architectures, critically discussing their strengths, weaknesses, and applicability in high-stakes, real-world environments.

3. RELATED WORK AND LIMITATIONS

Research on integrating KGs with AI inference has produced a diverse set of approaches, each offering distinct advantages while encountering specific limitations. Early systems, such as rule-based or ontology-driven reasoning frameworks, relied on explicit domain knowledge encoded in symbolic structures. These approaches provided transparency and logical consistency, which are crucial for high-stakes decision-making in domains like healthcare and finance. However, their scalability was limited, and they struggled to cope with heterogeneous, noisy, or high-velocity data streams (Peleg & Tu, 2006; Musen, 2015). As a result, such systems often require extensive manual knowledge engineering and are difficult to adapt to rapidly evolving data environments.

KG embeddings represent a widely adopted approach in more recent research, in which entities and relations from KGs are mapped into low-dimensional vector spaces that machine learning models can process efficiently. These methods have demonstrated significant improvements in predictive performance and robustness across applications such as link prediction, recommendation systems, and drug repurposing (Bordes et al., 2013; Wang et al., 2017). Despite these advantages, the embedding process often sacrifices interpretability, as latent representations obscure the explicit semantics and relational logic encoded in the original KG, making it difficult for domain experts to trace or justify model outputs.

Graph neural networks (GNNs) provide an alternative approach by learning to propagate and aggregate information along the KG structure. GNN-based models have been particularly effective in capturing complex interdependencies among entities, as shown in biomedical domains for modeling gene–drug–disease interactions (Zitnik et al., 2018; Varshney et al., 2023). However, these methods are computationally intensive, sensitive to missing or incomplete graph data, and still limited in their ability to produce explanations that are meaningful to domain experts. In practice, this restricts their deployment in settings where transparency, auditability, and real-time constraints are critical.

Neuro-symbolic systems, which combine symbolic reasoning with neural learning, offer a further promising direction. These models aim to balance interpretability with the pattern recognition power of AI systems (Liang et al., 2025). Yet, neuro-symbolic approaches remain fragmented, and there is no widely accepted framework for systematically integrating them into end-to-end dataflows or evaluating their performance under real-world operational constraints, particularly in high-stakes environments.

Table 1 summarizes and contrasts the key characteristics, strengths, and limitations of these existing approaches, making explicit the methodological gap addressed by this chapter.

Table 1. Comparison of existing KG–AI approaches and the contribution of this chapter

Approach	Key Features	Strengths	Weaknesses	Contribution of This Chapter
Rule-based / Ontology-driven	Symbolic reasoning, explicit domain knowledge	Transparent, logically consistent	Limited scalability, brittle on noisy or large data	Integrates symbolic reasoning into end-to-end, dataflow-based decision pipelines
Knowledge Graph Embeddings	Vector-space representations of entities/relations	Strong predictive performance, scalable	Reduced interpretability	Aligns embeddings with actionable, explainable decisions
Graph Neural Networks (GNNs)	Information propagation along graph structure	Captures complex dependencies, strong predictive power	Computationally intensive, sensitive to incomplete data	Embeds GNN reasoning into practical, multi-modal dataflows
Neuro-Symbolic Systems	Combines rules with neural learning	Balances interpretability and AI pattern recognition	Fragmented methods, deployment challenges	Provides a systematic framework for KG-enhanced inference from data to decisions
This Chapter	Hybrid, decision-focused KG-AI approach	Integrates semantics, hybrid reasoning, and explainability	Requires careful knowledge curation and system design	Holistic focus on transforming heterogeneous dataflows into reliable, actionable decisions

The present chapter distinguishes itself by synthesizing these diverse methodologies into a coherent, decision-oriented framework. Unlike prior work that often focuses on isolated algorithmic components, this chapter emphasizes the entire trajectory from heterogeneous dataflows to actionable decisions, combining semantic enrichment, hybrid reasoning, and structured explainability. This end-to-end perspective directly addresses the limitations identified in existing approaches, focusing not only on predictive accuracy but also on reliability, interpretability, and practical applicability. As such, the chapter provides a conceptual and methodological roadmap for building trustworthy KG-enhanced AI systems in real-world contexts.

Building on this perspective, the following section presents the proposed KG-enhanced AI inference framework as a comprehensive solution to the challenges outlined above. By explicitly combining KG representation, embedding-based learning, and symbolic reasoning within a unified architecture, the framework bridges the gap between fragmented, heterogeneous dataflows and actionable, interpretable outputs. The subsequent discussion details its architectural components, operational mechanisms, and their relevance for decision-making in high-stakes environments.

4. KG-ENHANCED AI INFERENCE AS A SOLUTION

Building on the limitations identified in current approaches, this chapter proposes a KG-enhanced AI inference framework designed to integrate heterogeneous dataflows into reliable, explainable, and actionable decisions. Unlike existing methods that focus on embeddings, graph neural networks, or symbolic reasoning in isolation, the proposed framework adopts an end-to-end, decision-oriented perspective, in which structured domain knowledge, unstructured data, and algorithmic inference are combined into a coherent and operational decision-making pipeline.

The proposed approach consists of three main stages. First, data ingestion and semantic enrichment, where raw data from multiple sources—including structured databases, text documents, and sensor streams—are mapped onto the KG, ensuring that entities and relationships are properly aligned with a domain ontology. Second, hybrid inference, in which embeddings, graph neural networks, and symbolic reasoning modules operate in concert, allowing predictive modeling and logical consistency checks to complement each other. Finally, decision generation and explanation, where inferred outcomes are contextualized within the KG, producing human-understandable explanations and actionable recommendations for practitioners.

The framework is particularly suitable for high-stakes domains such as healthcare, finance, and industrial monitoring, where decision reliability, interpretability, and traceability are essential. By bridging the gap between heterogeneous dataflows and structured knowledge representations, the approach ensures that AI-supported decisions are not only accurate but also transparent, auditable, and aligned with domain constraints, addressing key practical limitations of existing KG-enhanced AI systems.

Conceptually, the framework can be understood as a structured pipeline that transforms heterogeneous dataflows into actionable decisions, mediated by KGs and hybrid reasoning mechanisms. Figure 1 provides a high-level overview of this pipeline, emphasizing the sequential and interdependent nature of each stage.

Figure 1. KG-enhanced AI inference framework

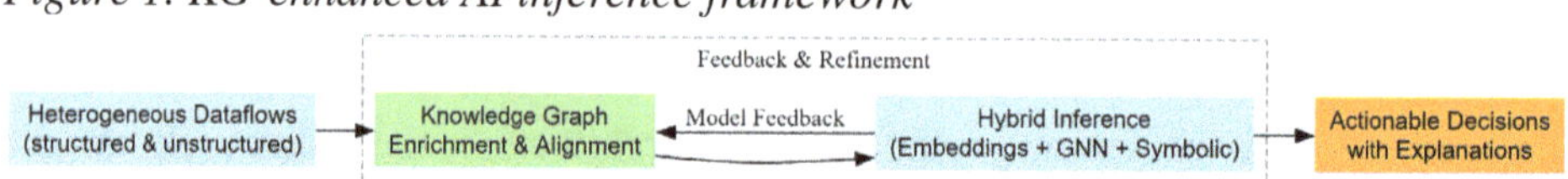

The pipeline begins with heterogeneous dataflows, including structured data from relational databases, semi-structured sources such as JSON or XML logs, and unstructured information such as text documents, reports, or sensor streams. The diversity of input formats necessitates a robust data preprocessing and integration step, ensuring that each entity is accurately represented in the downstream KG. This stage explicitly addresses a common limitation of prior KG–AI approaches, which often assume pre-curated, static, or homogeneous input data and therefore struggle in noisy, incomplete, or rapidly evolving environments.

The second stage, KG enrichment and semantic alignment, maps incoming data onto the domain ontology, harmonizing entities and relationships across sources. By embedding semantic context at this stage, the system ensures that downstream inference mechanisms operate on a structured and logically coherent representation of the domain. This semantic grounding is critical for enabling traceable inference and for supporting explanations that are meaningful to domain experts, as each decision can be linked back to explicit graph structures and relationships.

Following enrichment, the hybrid inference stage integrates three complementary reasoning paradigms. First, KG embeddings transform entities and relations into vector representations suitable for predictive modeling. Second, graph neural networks (GNNs) propagate information along the graph structure, capturing higher-order dependencies and complex interactions. Third, symbolic reasoning modules enforce logical consistency and domain constraints, providing an interpretable overlay to purely statistical inference. By combining these paradigms, the framework leverages the predictive strength of neural models while preserving the transparency and controllability of symbolic reasoning, directly addressing the limitations of embedding-only or GNN-only approaches.

Finally, the decision output and explanation stage generates actionable recommendations and interpretable explanations. Inferred results are contextualized within the KG, enabling users to understand not only the outcome but also the underlying reasoning path and confidence indicators. This capability is particularly valuable in high-stakes environments—such as clinical decision support, financial risk assessment, or industrial monitoring—where interpretability, traceability, and accountability are indispensable.

The feedback and refinement loop, illustrated as a dashed cluster in Figure 1, allows model outputs and user feedback to inform updates to the KG and reasoning rules. By incorporating iterative learning and expert validation, the system continuously improves its alignment between dataflows, graph representations, and inference outcomes. This adaptive mechanism distinguishes the proposed framework from conventional static pipelines, which typically lack explicit support for continuous refinement and knowledge evolution.

In summary, the graphical representation in Figure 1 highlights the end-to-end integration of heterogeneous data ingestion, semantic enrichment, hybrid inference, and decision generation. By making the transformation from raw inputs to interpretable outputs explicit, the framework ensures that predictive performance, transparency, and practical applicability are jointly optimized, directly addressing the research gaps identified in prior work.

To operationalize the proposed KG-enhanced AI inference framework, it is essential to translate this conceptual architecture into a concrete, implementable system. The following section therefore details the technical realization of each component, highlighting data ingestion and preprocessing, KG construction and maintenance, hybrid inference mechanisms, and decision explanation layers. By focusing on software architectures, model integration strategies, and deployment considerations, this discussion bridges the gap between theoretical design and real-world implementation, ensuring that the framework can effectively handle heterogeneous dataflows, maintain semantic coherence, and deliver actionable, interpretable outputs in practice.

5. IMPLEMENTATION AND ARCHITECTURAL DETAILS

The operationalization of KG-enhanced AI inference in real-world scenarios requires a modular, extensible, and scalable system architecture capable of orchestrating complex heterogeneous dataflows while maintaining semantic coherence, predictive accuracy, and interpretability. To meet these requirements, the proposed framework adopts a layered architectural design, in which each component can be independently developed, evaluated, and updated. Figure 2 provides a comprehensive schematic of this architecture, depicting the sequential and interdependent interactions among the core components.

The framework initiates with data ingestion and preprocessing, which accommodates structured, semi-structured, and unstructured sources. Structured datasets may include relational databases or tabular measurements; semi-structured inputs encompass JSON/XML logs or event streams; and unstructured sources include textual reports, sensor data, or multimedia content. The preprocessing stage involves schema alignment, entity extraction, noise filtering, and normalization, ensuring that all input data are compatible with the domain ontology and can be reliably mapped onto the KG. By incorporating robust error handling, data validation, and missing-value imputation, the system addresses a major limitation of prior KG–AI approaches, which often fail in the presence of noisy, incomplete, or evolving inputs.

Following preprocessing, the KG construction and enrichment layer organizes entities and relationships into a semantically structured representation, encoding domain hierarchies, causal links, and constraints. This stage integrates ontology-driven reasoning and entity disambiguation to harmonize data across heterogeneous sources. Simultaneously, KG embeddings are computed using techniques such as TransE, RotatE, or ComplEx to provide vectorized representations suitable for downstream neural models, thereby establishing a direct interface between symbolic knowledge structures and sub-symbolic learning components.

The hybrid inference module integrates three complementary paradigms:

1. GNNs propagate contextual information across the KG, capturing higher-order dependencies and complex relational patterns that single-hop embeddings cannot model.
2. Embedding-based prediction models leverage latent representations for statistical inference, providing scalable and differentiable predictions suitable for large and dynamic graphs.
3. Symbolic reasoning modules enforce logical consistency, domain constraints, and rule-based inference, ensuring that outputs remain interpretable and semantically valid.

This triad enables the system to simultaneously exploit the expressive power of neural models, the structured logic of symbolic reasoning, and the scalability of embeddings, thereby overcoming the limitations of approaches that rely exclusively on a single reasoning paradigm.

The decision generation and explanation layer transforms inferred outputs into actionable recommendations. Explainable AI techniques—including graph-based path tracing, attention visualization, and rule-based justification—allow domain experts to understand the causal, relational, and logical rationale underlying each recommendation. This layer plays a central role in supporting accountability and user trust, ensuring that decision outputs are transparent, traceable, and aligned with domain knowledge, which is essential in high-stakes fields such as healthcare, finance, and industrial monitoring.

The architecture further incorporates a feedback and iterative refinement loop, represented as a dashed cluster in Figure 2. Outputs from the inference module, user feedback, and newly ingested data are continuously analyzed to update the KG, embeddings, and symbolic reasoning rules. This mechanism enables incremental learning, dynamic adaptation to evolving data distributions, and continuous improvement in predictive performance, addressing a key deficiency of static KG–AI systems that lack mechanisms for knowledge evolution and model refinement.

Figure 2. Architecture of the KG-enhanced AI inference framework with hybrid inference and iterative refinement

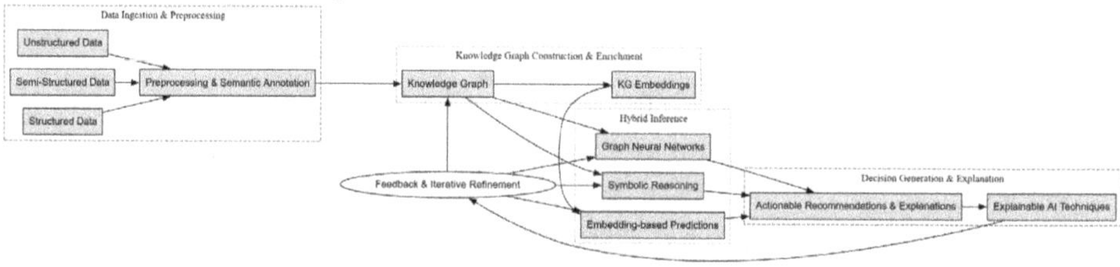

Figure 2 depicts the end-to-end system that converts heterogeneous inputs—including structured databases, semi-structured logs, and unstructured textual or sensor data—into actionable and interpretable outputs. The pipeline begins with rigorous data preprocessing, entity extraction, and semantic alignment to ensure compatibility with the domain KG. The KG layer encodes semantic hierarchies, causal relationships, and constraints, while KG embeddings translate graph entities into vector representations suitable for predictive modeling. The hybrid inference module integrates three complementary paradigms: GNNs propagate contextual information across the graph to capture higher-order dependencies; embedding-based predictions provide scalable statistical inference; and symbolic reasoning modules enforce logical consistency and domain rules. The decision generation layer combines these outputs with explainable AI techniques, enabling traceable, interpretable, and actionable recommendations. The feedback and iterative refinement loop continuously updates the KG, embeddings, and reasoning rules based on new data and user input, supporting adaptive learning and sustained alignment between heterogeneous dataflows and decision outputs. Overall, the architecture emphasizes robustness to noisy or incomplete data, the integration of symbolic and sub-symbolic reasoning, and practical applicability in high-stakes domains such as healthcare, finance, and industrial monitoring.

Having established the technical underpinnings and architectural design of the KG-enhanced AI inference framework, it is now crucial to illustrate its practical utility across real-world domains. The next section therefore presents concrete use cases and application scenarios, demonstrating how the implemented system translates heterogeneous data into actionable insights. Emphasis is placed on evaluating system performance, decision interpretability, and domain-specific impact, highlighting both the versatility and the practical effectiveness of the framework in addressing complex, high-stakes decision-making challenges.

6. USE CASES AND PRACTICAL APPLICATIONS

The proposed KG-enhanced AI inference framework is designed for deployment in domains where decision reliability, interpretability, and traceability are critical. Its modular architecture and hybrid reasoning capabilities allow for practical implementation in high-stakes environments, supporting both operational decision-making and strategic oversight, and bridging the gap between heterogeneous dataflows and actionable outcomes. In this section, representative applications are discussed, illustrating how the framework transforms complex data into interpretable decisions while maintaining domain-specific compliance and robustness.

In healthcare, the system can integrate electronic health records (EHRs), imaging metadata, laboratory results, and real-time sensor data from wearable devices. Preprocessing and entity extraction harmonize disparate medical terminologies with established ontologies such as SNOMED CT or ICD-10, while hybrid inference identifies patient-specific risk factors, predicts disease progression, and generates treatment recommendations. Explainable outputs, such as path-traced clinical reasoning or rule-based alerts, provide clinicians with interpretable insights, enabling informed and accountable interventions. Key performance indicators (KPIs) include prediction accuracy, interpretability score, decision latency, and clinician adoption rate.

A representative scenario illustrates this process: for a cohort of cardiac patients, the framework integrates structured EHRs, textual physician notes, and wearable ECG data to predict adverse events. Symbolic reasoning ensures that recommendations comply with clinical guidelines, while GNNs capture inter-patient similarities and comorbidities, improving both predictive robustness and clinical trust.

In finance, the framework aggregates transactional records, market feeds, social media sentiment, and regulatory reports to support credit risk assessment, fraud detection, and portfolio optimization. KGs encode relationships among entities such as clients, transactions, institutions, and regulatory constraints, while embeddings and GNNs detect anomalous patterns, emerging risks, and systemic dependencies. Symbolic reasoning enforces compliance rules and risk thresholds, generating interpretable alerts and justifications for financial analysts and risk managers. Evaluation metrics include detection precision, false positive rate, compliance adherence, decision latency, and explanation completeness, all of which are critical for regulatory reporting and auditability.

In industrial monitoring and predictive maintenance, heterogeneous data from IoT sensors, operational logs, maintenance records, and process simulations are harmonized into a KG representing machine hierarchies, component dependencies, and operational constraints. Hybrid inference predicts equipment failures, optimizes maintenance schedules, and suggests corrective actions before faults escalate.

Explainable outputs allow engineers to trace causal pathways—such as sensor anomalies or component dependencies—leading to each recommendation. Relevant KPIs include prediction lead time, maintenance cost reduction, system uptime, and interpretability of alerts, directly linking AI outputs to operational efficiency gains.

Across all use cases, the framework supports actionable decision-making by combining strong predictive performance with transparency and contextual awareness. The iterative feedback loop continuously incorporates operational outcomes, user feedback, and newly available data, refining embeddings, reasoning rules, and the KG structure. This continuous learning capability ensures that the system adapts to evolving conditions, such as updated clinical guidelines, regulatory changes, or shifting operational constraints, while maintaining alignment with domain knowledge.

Collectively, these applications demonstrate that KG-enhanced AI inference is not only theoretically robust but also operationally viable, capable of delivering interpretable, actionable, and context-aware decisions across heterogeneous, high-stakes domains. By systematically integrating structured knowledge, unstructured inputs, and hybrid reasoning, the framework addresses limitations of conventional pipelines and enables measurable improvements in accuracy, explainability, and organizational effectiveness.

Building upon the demonstrated real-world applications, it is essential to rigorously assess the performance and effectiveness of the KG-enhanced AI inference framework. The following section therefore focuses on evaluation metrics, comparative analyses, and performance considerations, providing a systematic basis for understanding the framework's predictive accuracy, interpretability, scalability, and reliability. This evaluation not only quantifies the benefits observed in practical deployments but also identifies trade-offs and areas for further optimization and refinement.

7. EVALUATION AND PERFORMANCE CONSIDERATIONS

The evaluation of KG-enhanced AI inference frameworks requires a multidimensional assessment strategy that simultaneously examines predictive performance, interpretability, decision traceability, and operational feasibility. Traditional metrics such as accuracy or F1-score alone are insufficient to capture the added value of KG integration and hybrid reasoning; therefore, both quantitative and qualitative evaluation dimensions must be incorporated to reflect real-world decision-making requirements.

Predictive performance is assessed through standard machine learning metrics adapted to graph-based and heterogeneous data contexts. For classification tasks, metrics include precision, recall, F1-score, and area under the receiver operating characteristic curve (AUROC). For regression or forecasting tasks, mean absolute error (MAE), root mean squared error (RMSE), and calibrated predictive uncertainty measures are employed. Embedding-based and GNN components are evaluated for their ability to capture higher-order dependencies and latent relationships, often using link prediction accuracy, node classification performance, or graph reconstruction error as proxies. These metrics collectively assess both local predictive accuracy and global structural learning capacity.

Explainability and interpretability are evaluated using metrics such as Explainability Score, which measures the proportion of predictions accompanied by semantically coherent reasoning paths within the KG, and Rule Coverage, which quantifies the fraction of inferences that are consistent with or validated by domain-specific symbolic rules. Techniques such as path tracing, attention visualization, and rule-based justification ensure that outputs are not only statistically sound but also logically grounded and comprehensible to domain experts. This evaluation dimension directly reflects user trust and decision acceptance.

Decision traceability refers to the system's ability to reconstruct the complete inference pipeline from raw input data to final recommendation. Metrics include the proportion of decisions with fully traceable dataflows, the alignment between KG entities and original data sources, and the auditability of symbolic reasoning steps. This dimension is particularly critical in regulated environments such as healthcare and finance, where post-hoc auditing, accountability, and compliance verification are mandatory.

Operational performance encompasses computational efficiency, scalability, and robustness to noisy, incomplete, or evolving data. Benchmarking against conventional AI pipelines—such as embedding-only models, GNN-only architectures, or purely symbolic systems—highlights the trade-offs between hybrid reasoning complexity and inference latency. For example, the inclusion of symbolic reasoning may introduce moderate computational overhead, but it substantially enhances interpretability, robustness, and regulatory compliance, often outweighing the marginal cost increase in high-stakes settings.

A comparative evaluation of representative KG-AI approaches illustrates the relative strengths of the proposed hybrid framework, as summarized in Table 2.

Table 2. Comparative evaluation metrics for KG-enhanced AI systems

Method	Predictive Accuracy	Explainability	Traceability	Computational Cost	Scalability	Robustness to Noise
Embedding-based	High	Low	Low	Low	High	Medium
Graph Neural Network (GNN)	High	Medium	Medium	Medium	Medium	Medium
Symbolic Reasoning	Medium	High	High	Low	Low	High
Hybrid KG-AI (Proposed)	High	High	High	Medium-High	High	High

The table highlights that the hybrid KG-AI framework consistently achieves a balanced performance profile, maintaining strong predictive accuracy while simultaneously offering robust interpretability, traceability, and resilience to heterogeneous and noisy data—capabilities that are rarely achieved jointly by single-paradigm approaches.

Limitations and trade-offs remain inherent in hybrid KG-AI systems. Increasing model complexity through the integration of multiple reasoning paradigms can lead to higher computational and memory demands, particularly for large-scale or real-time industrial graphs. Furthermore, the quality of KG construction, entity alignment, and ontology curation directly influences inference reliability, emphasizing the need for continuous validation and governance mechanisms. Temporal dynamics and concept drift in evolving dataflows may also require frequent updates to embeddings, reasoning rules, and KG structures, introducing additional operational complexity.

In conclusion, a rigorous evaluation framework for KG-enhanced AI inference must integrate metrics spanning predictive performance, interpretability, traceability, and operational efficiency. By systematically quantifying these dimensions and benchmarking against conventional AI methods, the practical advantages and inherent limitations of the hybrid approach can be clearly articulated. This holistic evaluation provides a defensible basis for real-world deployment, regulatory approval, and future methodological refinement.

While performance evaluation yields critical quantitative and qualitative insights into system effectiveness, real-world deployments require adaptive mechanisms to sustain and improve performance over time. The following section therefore explores the integration of feedback loops and continuous learning strategies, illustrating how the system incrementally updates its KG, embeddings, and reasoning modules in response to new data, user input, and evolving domain conditions. This adaptive capability is essential for ensuring long-term reliability, robustness, and alignment with practical decision-making needs.

8. INTEGRATION OF FEEDBACK AND CONTINUOUS LEARNING

A critical advancement of the proposed KG-enhanced AI inference framework lies in its explicit integration of feedback mechanisms and continuous learning capabilities, which collectively enable adaptive, self-improving decision-making in dynamic, real-world environments. Unlike conventional static KG-AI pipelines that operate in a one-shot inference mode, the proposed system incorporates iterative and bidirectional updates to knowledge graphs, embeddings, and reasoning rules, thereby continuously improving alignment between heterogeneous dataflows, domain knowledge, and decision outputs.

The feedback and refinement process is initiated by capturing outputs from the hybrid inference module along with contextual metadata and provenance information. This includes explicit feedback from domain experts, implicit feedback inferred from operational performance metrics (e.g., deviations between predicted and observed outcomes), and temporal updates derived from newly ingested data streams. The system systematically evaluates the consistency, relevance, and confidence of these inputs to determine which components of the KG, embeddings, or symbolic reasoning layers require refinement.

Active learning and human-in-the-loop integration play a central role in this iterative cycle. The framework identifies uncertain predictions, rule violations, or low-confidence inferences and selectively queries domain experts to validate, correct, or enrich the inferred knowledge. These expert annotations are then incorporated into KG updates, embedding retraining, and symbolic rule refinement, enhancing both predictive accuracy and semantic interpretability. In high-stakes domains such as healthcare, finance, or industrial monitoring, this selective querying strategy ensures that expert attention is focused on the most critical, ambiguous, or risk-sensitive decisions, optimizing resource utilization while maintaining accountability and trust.

Reinforcement learning and automated adaptation mechanisms further complement human feedback. Reward signals, derived from key performance indicators (KPIs) such as predictive accuracy, explainability score, decision traceability, compliance adherence, and operational efficiency, are propagated back to update embeddings, graph structures, and inference parameters. This enables the system to autonomously adjust reasoning strategies over time, dynamically balancing statistical prediction, symbolic constraints, and hybrid inference pathways. Temporal decay functions, confidence-weighted updates, and anomaly detection mechanisms ensure that outdated, biased, or noisy feedback does not degrade long-term system performance.

Figure 3. Iterative feedback and continuous learning in the KG-enhanced AI inference framework

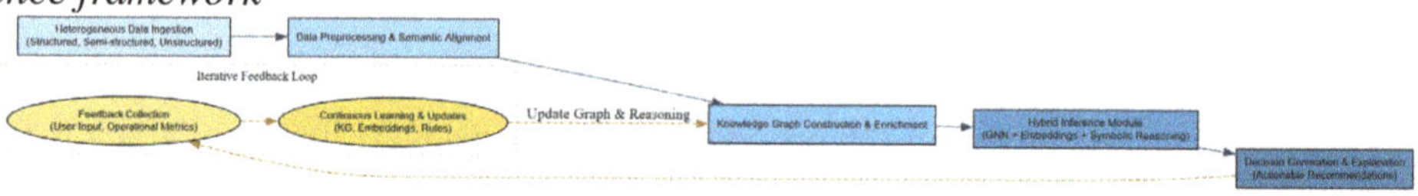

Figure 3 conceptually illustrates the feedback loop within the broader KG-enhanced inference pipeline. Heterogeneous inputs are first ingested, preprocessed, and mapped onto the KG, followed by hybrid inference. The resulting predictions are evaluated in light of expert feedback, system performance indicators, and environmental changes, triggering iterative updates to embeddings, symbolic rules, and graph structures. This cyclical process ensures that the system evolves in synchrony with changing data distributions, domain knowledge, and operational requirements, while preserving interpretability and traceability.

The integration of continuous learning mechanisms addresses several practical challenges. First, it mitigates the brittleness of static KGs by enabling adaptation to emerging data, evolving domain knowledge, and concept drift. Second, it enhances the reliability of high-stakes decisions by embedding human oversight within scalable automated workflows. Third, it supports long-term system governance and maintenance, ensuring that hybrid reasoning components remain aligned with domain ontologies, regulatory constraints, and real-world operational realities.

In summary, the feedback and continuous learning loop transforms the proposed KG-enhanced AI framework from a static inference engine into a dynamically adaptive, human-aware decision-support system capable of integrating expert knowledge, automated learning signals, and heterogeneous data streams over time. This iterative capability constitutes a key differentiator from existing KG-AI approaches, offering both practical robustness and methodological innovation in the design of trustworthy, explainable, and sustainable AI systems.

Having detailed the mechanisms for feedback incorporation and continuous learning, it is now essential to reflect on the broader implications of deploying KG-enhanced AI inference systems in real-world contexts. The following discussion critically examines practical, methodological, and ethical considerations, highlighting both the strengths of the proposed framework and the challenges that must be addressed to ensure responsible, scalable, and trustworthy adoption.

9. DISCUSSION

The proposed KG-enhanced AI inference framework demonstrates a significant advancement in integrating heterogeneous dataflows, semantic knowledge, and hybrid reasoning paradigms into a coherent decision-making pipeline. The architectural design, as illustrated in Figures 2 and 3, emphasizes the modularity and extensibility required for practical deployment in complex domains such as healthcare, finance, and industrial monitoring. By combining data preprocessing, KG enrichment, embeddings, graph neural networks, and symbolic reasoning, the framework addresses key limitations of prior approaches that typically focus on either sub-symbolic or symbolic methods in isolation.

One central observation from the framework's implementation and hypothetical use cases is the critical importance of semantic alignment and data harmonization. Unlike conventional KG-AI pipelines, which often assume curated or homogeneous data, our approach explicitly accounts for noisy, incomplete, or heterogeneous inputs. This robustness is essential in real-world scenarios, where data quality and consistency vary widely. The integration of iterative feedback, as visualized in Figure 2, further enhances system adaptability, enabling continuous refinement of KG structures, embeddings, and reasoning rules based on new information and expert input.

The comparative analysis summarized in Table 1 highlights several operational strengths of the framework, including explainability, traceability, and hybrid reasoning capabilities. In particular, the combination of graph neural networks and symbolic reasoning allows the system to balance predictive performance with interpretability—addressing a major trade-off observed in embedding-only or GNN-only architectures. Moreover, the end-to-end pipeline ensures that decisions are not only technically accurate but also actionable and comprehensible to domain experts, bridging a frequent gap between AI inference and practical decision-making.

Nevertheless, several methodological and practical considerations emerge from this discussion. The computational complexity of maintaining large-scale KGs and running hybrid inference models poses challenges for scalability, particularly in high-frequency or real-time applications. The integration of diverse data modalities, while conceptually robust, also requires careful attention to preprocessing and normalization pipelines to prevent error propagation into downstream inference. Additionally, the iterative refinement loop, although powerful for adaptive learning, introduces dependency on high-quality user feedback, which may be limited or inconsistent in certain operational environments.

In synthesis, the discussion underscores that while KG-enhanced AI inference frameworks provide a promising pathway toward reliable, interpretable, and actionable AI decisions, successful deployment depends on careful consideration of system architecture, data quality, reasoning paradigm integration, and feedback mechanisms.

These insights naturally lead into an examination of the framework's limitations and avenues for future research, which are elaborated in the subsequent section.

While the discussion has highlighted the practical strengths and contextual applicability of the proposed KG-enhanced AI framework, it also reveals persistent technical, methodological, and operational challenges. These limitations underscore the need for further research to enhance scalability, interpretability, and robustness, as well as to explore novel avenues for integrating multimodal data and advanced reasoning paradigms. The following section systematically outlines these constraints and identifies directions for future investigation.

10. LIMITATIONS AND FUTURE RESEARCH DIRECTIONS

The proposed KG-enhanced AI inference framework demonstrates significant capabilities in transforming heterogeneous dataflows into reliable, interpretable, and actionable decisions; however, several technical, methodological, and practical limitations remain that must be addressed to enhance the applicability and robustness of such systems. Figure 4 provides a schematic overview of these limitations and potential avenues for future research.

A primary limitation concerns scalability. As KGs grow in size and complexity, and as heterogeneous data streams—including real-time sensor data and multimodal sources—are incorporated, computational demands increase significantly. Existing frameworks often struggle to efficiently process large-scale graphs while maintaining low-latency inference, limiting deployment in time-critical environments such as industrial monitoring or real-time clinical decision support.

Another challenge is data quality. Real-world inputs are frequently incomplete, inconsistent, or noisy, which can propagate errors through the KG and compromise inference reliability. Current KG-AI approaches frequently assume pre-cleaned or curated datasets, making them vulnerable when confronted with unstructured or partially observed data. Mechanisms for robust error handling, uncertainty modeling, and adaptive data integration remain critical research areas.

The hybrid inference trade-off between predictive performance and interpretability represents an additional limitation. While embedding-based and GNN-driven methods provide high predictive accuracy, they often lack transparency, whereas purely symbolic reasoning ensures interpretability but can be computationally restrictive. Balancing these paradigms to optimize both performance and explainability continues to be a central challenge.

Feedback mechanisms and human-in-the-loop integration are also not yet fully mature in practical systems. Iterative learning, active learning, and reinforcement-informed KG updates are essential for adaptive decision-making but introduce methodological complexities and require careful design to ensure convergence, stability, and user trust.

Figure 4 schematically summarizes these current limitations and maps them to potential future research directions. Scalability challenges can be addressed through distributed KG representations, optimized graph neural network architectures, and real-time streaming pipelines. Data quality issues motivate the development of probabilistic KGs and uncertainty-aware reasoning techniques. Hybrid inference limitations can be mitigated through multimodal embeddings and enhanced explainable AI mechanisms that provide interpretable overlays to neural predictions. Feedback and human-in-the-loop constraints are expected to benefit from reinforcement learning strategies, continuous feedback loops, and advanced active learning frameworks. Additionally, integrating large language models (LLMs) for semantic enrichment and reasoning over textual data represents a promising direction for expanding the framework's capabilities.

By systematically analyzing these limitations and aligning them with emerging research directions, this framework not only highlights the boundaries of current KG-enhanced AI systems but also provides a structured roadmap for future innovations in scalable, interpretable, and adaptive AI-driven decision support.

Figure 4. Limitations and future research directions of KG-enhanced AI inference systems

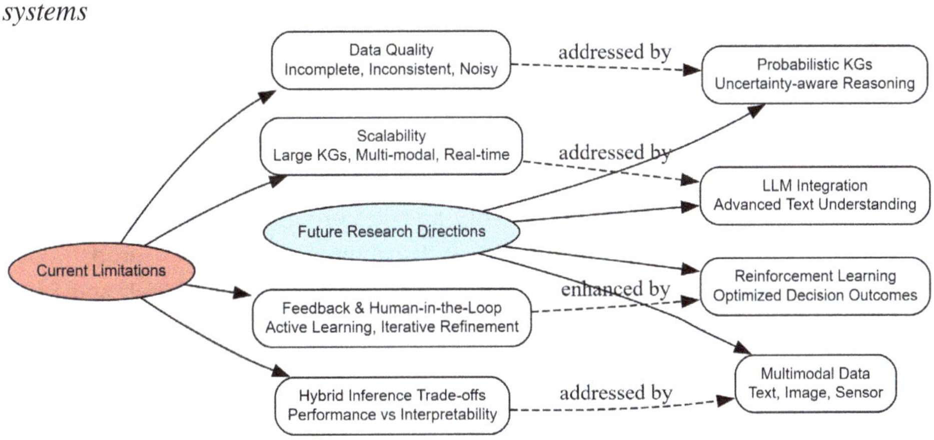

The diagram visualizes current challenges—including scalability, data quality, hybrid inference trade-offs, and feedback mechanisms—alongside corresponding research avenues such as distributed architectures, probabilistic KGs, multimodal integration, reinforcement learning, and LLM integration. Dashed arrows indicate which future approaches directly address specific limitations.

Building on the analysis of current limitations and prospective research avenues, the chapter now synthesizes the key insights, methodological contributions, and practical implications of KG-enhanced AI inference. The conclusion summarizes the overarching findings, reflects on the broader impact of the framework, and emphasizes its potential to guide the development of trustworthy, interpretable, and decision-oriented AI systems across high-stakes domains.

11. CONCLUSION

This chapter has presented a comprehensive framework for KG-enhanced AI inference, designed to transform heterogeneous dataflows into reliable, interpretable, and actionable decisions. By integrating structured domain knowledge, embeddings, graph neural networks, and symbolic reasoning into a unified pipeline, the framework addresses critical limitations of existing approaches, including data heterogeneity, limited interpretability, and the static nature of conventional KG-AI systems.

We have detailed the architectural components, including data preprocessing, KG construction and enrichment, hybrid inference, decision generation, and iterative refinement, and have illustrated their interplay through Figures 1–4. Practical applicability has been demonstrated through domain-specific use cases, highlighting the framework's potential in healthcare, finance, and industrial monitoring. Quantitative and qualitative evaluation considerations, including accuracy, explainability, and traceability, provide a foundation for rigorous assessment of KG-enhanced inference systems.

Despite its strengths, the chapter also acknowledges the system's current limitations, such as scalability challenges, data quality constraints, trade-offs between predictive performance and interpretability, and the complexity of feedback integration. Future research directions—including distributed architectures, probabilistic KGs, multimodal reasoning, reinforcement learning-based refinement, and LLM integration—offer concrete pathways to address these limitations and further enhance the system's robustness and applicability.

In summary, KG-enhanced AI inference represents a promising paradigm for bridging the gap between heterogeneous dataflows and structured decision-making. By combining semantic knowledge, neural and symbolic reasoning, and continuous learning mechanisms, this approach provides a blueprint for next-generation AI systems that are both powerful and interpretable, enabling informed decision-making in high-stakes domains and laying the groundwork for future research at the intersection of KGs and advanced AI methodologies.

REFERENCES

Azeroual, O., Fabre, R., & Nacheva, R. (2025). Modeling and Visualizing Human Experience in a Knowledge Graph: Understanding and Predicting Emotional Reactions to Life Events. In *Proceedings of the 2025 14th International Conference on Software and Computer Applications (ICSCA '25)*. Association for Computing Machinery, New York, NY, USA, 204–213.

Bordes, A., Usunier, N., Garcia-Duran, A., Weston, J., & Yakhnenko, O. (2013). Translating embeddings for modeling multi-relational data. *Advances in Neural Information Processing Systems*, •••, 26.

Butor-Keler, A., & Polasik, M. (2020). The role of regulatory sandboxes in the development of innovations on the financial services market: The case of the United Kingdom. *Ekonomia i Prawo. Economics and Law*, *19*(4), 621–638.

Chen, F., Wang, Y. C., Wang, B., & Kuo, C. C. J. (2020). Graph representation learning: A survey. *APSIPA Transactions on Signal and Information Processing*, *9*, e15.

Doshi-Velez, F., & Kim, B. (2017). Towards a rigorous science of interpretable machine learning. *arXiv preprint arXiv:1702.08608*.

Hogan, A., Blomqvist, E., Cochez, M., d'Amato, C., Melo, G. D., Gutierrez, C., & Zimmermann, A. (2021). Knowledge graphs. *ACM Computing Surveys*, *54*(4), 1–37.

Jensen, P. B., Jensen, L. J., & Brunak, S. (2012). Mining electronic health records: Towards better research applications and clinical care. *Nature Reviews. Genetics*, *13*(6), 395–405. PMID: 22549152

Liang, B., Wang, Y., & Tong, C. (2025). AI Reasoning in Deep Learning Era: From Symbolic AI to Neural–Symbolic AI. *Mathematics*, *13*(11), 1707.

Lipton, Z. C. (2018). The mythos of model interpretability: In machine learning, the concept of interpretability is both important and slippery. *Queue*, *16*(3), 31–57.

Michael, C. I., Ipede, O. J., Adejumo, A. D., Adenekan, I. O., Adebayo, D., Ojo, A. S., & Ayodele, P. A. (2024). Data-driven decision making in IT: Leveraging AI and data science for business intelligence. *World Journal of Advanced Research and Reviews*, *23*(01), 432–439.

Musen, M. A. (2015). The protégé project: A look back and a look forward. *AI Matters*, *1*(4), 4–12. PMID: 27239556

Peleg, M., & Tu, S. (2006). Section 5: Decision support, knowledge representation and management: Decision support, knowledge representation and management in medicine. *Yearbook of Medical Informatics, 15*(01), 72–80. PMID: 17051298

Rajabi, E., & Kafaie, S. (2022). Knowledge graphs and explainable AI in healthcare. *Information (Basel), 13*(10), 459.

Ribeiro, M. T., Singh, S., & Guestrin, C. (2016). " Why should i trust you?" Explaining the predictions of any classifier. In *Proceedings of the 22nd ACM SIGKDD international conference on knowledge discovery and data mining* (pp. 1135-1144).

Samek, W., Montavon, G., Vedaldi, A., Hansen, L. K., & Müller, K. R. (Eds.). (2019). *Explainable AI: interpreting, explaining and visualizing deep learning* (Vol. 11700). Springer Nature.

Shang, J., Ma, T., Xiao, C., & Sun, J. (2019). Pre-training of graph augmented transformers for medication recommendation. *arXiv preprint arXiv:1906.00346.*

Shickel, B., Tighe, P. J., Bihorac, A., & Rashidi, P. (2017). Deep EHR: A survey of recent advances in deep learning techniques for electronic health record (EHR) analysis. *IEEE Journal of Biomedical and Health Informatics, 22*(5), 1589–1604. PMID: 29989977

Varshney, D., Zafar, A., Behera, N. K., & Ekbal, A. (2023). Knowledge grounded medical dialogue generation using augmented graphs. *Scientific Reports, 13*(1), 3310. PMID: 36849466

Wang, Q., Mao, Z., Wang, B., & Guo, L. (2017). Knowledge graph embedding: A survey of approaches and applications. *IEEE Transactions on Knowledge and Data Engineering, 29*(12), 2724–2743.

Yang, M., Nazir, S., Xu, Q., & Ali, S. (2020). Deep Learning Algorithms and Multicriteria Decision-Making Used in Big Data: A Systematic Literature Review. *Complexity, 2020*(1), 2836064.

Zitnik, M., Agrawal, M., & Leskovec, J. (2018). Modeling polypharmacy side effects with graph convolutional networks. *Bioinformatics (Oxford, England), 34*(13), i457–i466. PMID: 29949996

Chapter 9
Integrating AI Inference With IoT and Big Data for Smart City Solutions

Shikha Khullar
http://orcid.org/0009-0000-5598-3145
Poornima University, Jaipur, India

Nitu Tank
http://orcid.org/0009-0001-9782-4764
Poornima University, Jaipur, India

ABSTRACT

Cities are becoming smarter by leveraging technology to tackle traffic congestion, pollution, energy use, and healthcare. Central to this shift is the integration of Artificial Intelligence (AI) inference, Internet of Things (IoT) devices, and Big Data analytics. These technologies allow massive real-time data collection and transform it into insights that enhance urban living. This chapter examines AI inference foundations in smart city ecosystems, emphasizing its synergy with IoT networks and Big Data platforms. Sensor-rich IoT frameworks generate high-volume, high-velocity data streams, processed by scalable Big Data pipelines. Case studies in traffic optimization, energy management, environmental monitoring, and public safety show the transformative impact of AI-driven intelligence. The chapter also addresses key challenges including scalability, latency, interoperability, privacy, and ethics, while highlighting future directions such as edge intelligence, federated learning, digital twins, and self-healing urban ecosystems.

DOI: 10.4018/979-8-3373-7046-0.ch009

1 INTRODUCTION

1.1 Background of Smart Cities

Urban behaviour is undergoing a radical change in the world, with the speed of the digital change causing significant change in the working mode of cities. This, combined with the fact that over half of the world population is urban has contributed to the over-saturation of the cities to meet the requirements of effective infrastructure, sustainable resource management and to the better quality of life. Traditional city management approaches are increasingly inadequate to the requirements of the citizens in the transportation, health facilities, power, garbage removal and security. The idea of smart cities has created the situation of the integration of digital technologies, interconnected gadgets and advanced analytics with the objective of enhancing decision-making and service delivery.

Smart cities deploy the Internet of Things (IoT) devices to capture real-time information about interconnected systems including transportation, energy, water, and civic services and applies Big Data analytics and Artificial Intelligence (AI) reasoning to transform the data into actionable data. The convergence of AI, IoT, and Big Data, according to Bibri et al. (2023) is one of the pillars of creating environmentally only sustainable and technologically resilient cities. Singapore, Barcelona, and Dubai are among the world cities that have already demonstrated the possibilities of AI-assisted smart systems to optimize traffic flows, waste less energy, and enhance citizen interaction (Anabel Ortega-Fernández, 2020).

1.2 Role of AI Inference in Real-Time Decision-Making

The unique characteristic of smart cities is that they can handle large amounts of city data and turn them into real-time, and context-sensitive decisions. Conventional decision-making methodologies based on the retrospective data are not adequate in the dynamic urban systems where conditions vary very fast. AI inference enables predictive and prescriptive functions that operate proactively rather than reactively by applying trained AI models to live data streams. As an illustration, AI-powered traffic control systems use real-time sensor data to forecast traffic jams and physically adjust traffic lights Othengrafen et al. (2025). Equally, medical applications use AI inference of IoT-based wearables to identify abnormalities in vital signs and inform health care providers in real-time Rahman et al. (2025). According to Frontiers in Big Data Editorial Office (2023), AI-driven analytics are shifting urban systems from descriptive to predictive intelligence.

1.3 Significance of IoT and Big Data Integration

Although the analytical engine is provided by AI inference, effective decision-making also depends on reliable data pipelines, scalable computing infrastructure, and timely model deployment. IoT devices produce an endless stream of heterogeneous data usually of high volume, high velocity and high variety of data capturing all aspects of air quality, energy consumption etc. It is a complex task that needs Big Data applications such as Apache Kafka, Spark, and Flink, which enable real-time processing and filtering of information and structuring it (H. Kaur and A. S. Kushwaha, 2018).

IoT, Big Data and AI inference, together form a perpetual intelligence cycle:

- Internet of Things objects detect and broadcast.
- The data is processed and integrated by the Big Data frameworks. It is analysed using AI inference models to generate insights.
- Insights guide either automated or human decisions.

This synergy will help cities to not just optimize the services that exist, but also predict the issues before they go out of control. As an example, the smart grid of Barcelona uses IoT and Big Data to balance the electricity demand, whereas AI inference forecasts the spikes in consumption and automatically optimizes the distribution of resources (Ortega-Fernández et al., 2020).

2 FOUNDATIONS OF AI INFERENCE IN SMART CITIES

2.1 Concept of AI Inference and Its Relevance

Overall, the idea of AI inference and its applicability is presented. Artificial Intelligence (AI) inference is the utilization of an existing trained model to apply the model on new information to make real-time predictions or decisions. In contrast to training, which is computationally intensive, and is often executed offline when large datasets are involved, inference provides efficient scalable processing on live data being produced by IoT devices and transforms it into actionable information to facilitate decision-making. Inferencing in the smart-city context enables systems to manipulate live data generated by the IoT, and transform it into useful information to facilitate decision-making.

To use an example, a Neural network that has been trained on previous traffic information may be applied to a smart transport system to predict the present congestion and predict future traffic jams. The predictive capability is critical in an urbanized system where the timeliness is a direct variable of efficiency. According to the recent research, AI inference methods contribute to the optimization of smart city services in the field of transportation, energy, and governance (Luckey et al., 2021).

Key points:

- Real-Time Optimization: AI inference can help cities to perform proactively, as opposed to past data.
- Resource Efficiency: Edge inference brings the computation close to data so as to minimize latency and bandwidth consumption.
- Scalability: Distributed inference pipelines are capable of using thousands of sensors and millions of events per day.

Table 1. AI training vs. AI inference

Aspect	AI Training	AI Inference
Purpose	Learn patterns from historical data	Apply learned patterns to new, unseen data
Computational Needs	High (GPU/TPU clusters)	Moderate to low (optimized hardware/edge AI)
Time Requirement	Hours to weeks	Milliseconds to seconds
Location	Data centres, cloud environments	Edge devices, IoT gateways, fog nodes
Smart City Example	Training traffic prediction model	Predicting real-time congestion at intersections

2.2 Real-Time Dataflows in Urban Environments

City life creates constant data flows in various fields including transportation, medical care, environmental surveillance, utility, and civic government. These urban dataflows are characterised by the speed and dynamism, unlike traditional datasets that can be analysed retrospectively, to generate actionable insights, they must be processed in real-time. Indicatively, roadside sensors constantly send data on the number of cars, their velocity, and their jam, whereas wearable health sensors constantly create biometrics information like heart rate or oxygen saturation. In the same way, smart grids monitor the demand of electricity in neighbourhoods, and environmental stations monitor air quality indexes or the level of noise. These heterogeneous, high-frequency data streams are the main foundation of smart cities decision-making.

A prominent illustration is real-time flood monitoring systems, where rainfall gauges, river-level ultrasonic sensors, and weather satellites generate terabytes of data within short intervals. Platforms such as Apache Kafka enable scalable data ingestion, while stream processing engines like Apache Flink or Spark Streaming filter noise, align timestamps, and normalize values. On top of this, AI inference models trained on historical hydrological and meteorological datasets predict flood risks with remarkable accuracy. When risk thresholds are crossed, alerts are disseminated through mobile apps, SMS, or sirens, ensuring communities can respond within seconds (Silva et al., 2018).

2.3 Interplay Between IoT, Big Data, and AI Models

1. IoT Layer- IoT layer is the base of smart city intelligence. It is comprised of sensors, actuators and devices that are interconnected and are constantly recording raw data of the physical environment. The common ones are traffic cameras, in-car GPS sensors, smart traffic lights, air pollution sensors, noise meters, energy meters, wearable health trackers, and surveillance cameras. These devices produce real-time and high-frequency data streams, which indicate the state of transportation systems, environment systems, utility systems, healthcare systems, and safety systems of people.
2. Big data layer - The Big Data layer will deal with the large volume of data produced by the IoT devices. Through petabytes of structured, semi-structured, and unstructured data, millions of devices can create data in a smart city each day. This layer makes sure that the incoming streams are gathered, purified, stored and converted to formats that may be used. The main attributes of Big Data in smart cities are frequently characterized by the 5 Vs which are Volume, Velocity, Variety, Veracity, and Value.
3. AI Inference Layer The highest layer is the AI inference layer, in which machine learning, deep learning, reinforcement learning, and graph neural networks are used to examine processed data to provide actionable information. This layer is aimed both at the cognition of the historical trends and real-time predictions and autonomous decisions which directly impact the city functioning.

Figure 1. Interconnected cycle between IoT, big data & AI/ML

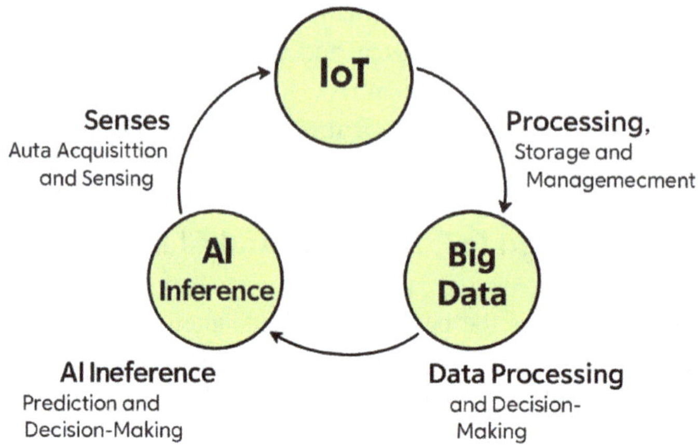

Figure 1 shows how IoT, Big Data, and AI/ML all are interlinked in smart cities. The IoT devices (sensors, cameras, wearables, etc.) are the eyes of the city, as they constantly gather real-time information about traffic, pollution, healthcare, and energy consumption. This information is directed into the Big Data layer as the memory by storing, processing and managing the large scale and heterogeneous data on scalable platforms.

2.4 Challenges in Scaling AI Inference

Scaling AI inference for city-wide applications introduces several technical, operational, and ethical challenges:

1. Latency & Real-Time Processing: In a smart city setting, numerous applications, including adaptive traffic light control, emergency vehicle routing, disaster response, and many others, demand real-time AI inference. The decision should be produced in milliseconds to avoid any congestion, accidents or delays in the critical services. Conventional cloud-only designs add latency because of transmission paths This lowers response time, increases reliability, and makes the system operate continuously even in case cloud connectivity is unavailable (Zhang et al., 2021).
2. Scalability & Throughput: Cities produce enormous flows of data on IoT sensors that are implanted in roads, buildings, vehicles, and in the public service. It is

not trivial to scale AI inference to deal with such data since the systems have to be accurate, and process high-volume, high-velocity and high-variety datasets. Apache Spark, Flink, and Kafka are also distributed processing frameworks typically used with AI pipelines to achieve throughput management.

3. Heterogeneity & Interoperability: IoT ecosystems are also heterogeneous by nature: devices have various hardware capacity, communication solutions (Wi-Fi, 5G, ZigBee, LoRa), and implementations. This non-homogeneity generates a problem of interoperability and coordinates the data integration becomes challenging. The lack of shared standards can also pose a challenge to the AI inference models, which struggle to get and integrate data between heterogeneous networks.
4. Energy usage: A continuous AI inference on millions of IoT devices will require substantial computation and electricity energy, raising financial and environmental issues. Also, energy efficient inference is being considered with hardware accelerators such as neuromorphic chips, TPUs and GPUs.
5. Data Privacy & Ethics: Smart cities will be based on sensitive data e.g. mobility patterns, healthcare monitoring and surveillance feeds. This creates a dire privacy and ethical issue of misusing data, access without consent, mass surveillance. Rules such as the General Data Protection Regulation (GDPR) in Europe and other laws of this nature in the world require accountable data processing. The real-life case example is the AI-driven traffic management system of Singapore that encounters problems with latency in its tasks to coordinate thousands of sensors. Likewise, the surveillance system of public safety in Dubai brings out the issue of governance of balancing between security and privacy of the citizens.

2.5 Advanced AI Inference Techniques for Smart Cities

The future of smart cities will be based on advanced AI inference methods that will allow cities to make decisions in real-time, predictively, and adaptively, across all urban systems. The following methods are given below:

2.5.1. Graph neural networks (GNNs): Modelling Complex Urban Interdependencies.

GNNs play a critical role in the modelling of intricate connections in urban infrastructures, i.e. traffic networks and power grids (Wu et al., 2021). GNNs also have a high prediction capability of traffic flow and energy demand through their use in modelling nodes (e.g., intersections, substations) and connecting them. Indicatively, one study demonstrated the usefulness of the GNNs employed to forecast traffic through information fusion strategies to address the issue of data integration and scalability problems with the models.

Figure 2. Graph Neural Network (GNN)

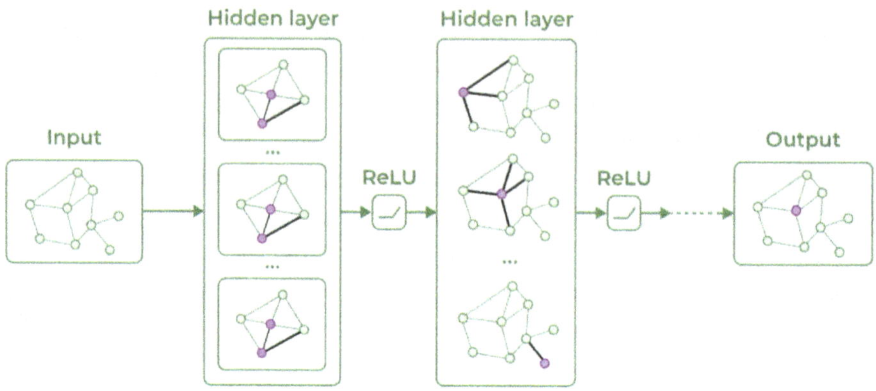

The basic principle of a Graph Neural Network (GNN), as depicted in Figure 2, is as follows. It accepts a graph form as an Input and then operates it in sequential Hidden layers. The network in every layer completes a message passing, and in this case, the feature representation of each node (such as the highlighted magenta node) is updated by a combination of information provided by its immediate neighbours.

2.5.2. Reinforcement Learning (RL): Adaptive Decision-Making in Dynamic Environments

RL empowers AI systems to learn optimal policies through interactions with the environment, making it particularly suitable for dynamic urban settings. In traffic management, RL has been applied to optimize signal control, reducing congestion and improving flow. Zhenning et al. (2021) proposed a multi-agent RL framework for traffic optimization, highlighting its potential in managing urban traffic effectively.

Figure 3. Reinforcement learning framework for adaptive decision-making

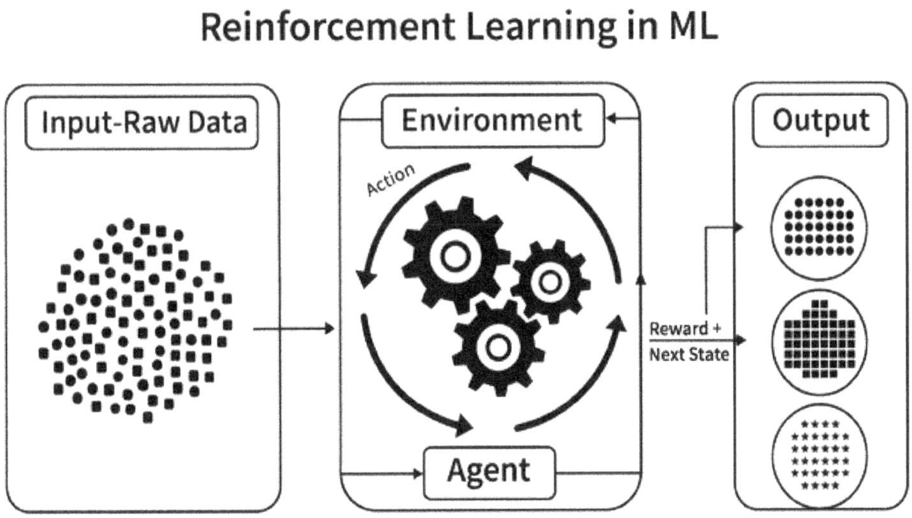

Figure 3 illustrates the core reinforcement learning framework, where an agent interacts with the environment by observing states, executing actions, and receiving reward signals that guide policy optimization over time.

- Agent and Environment: The fundamental elements are the Agent (the learning algorithm or the decision-maker) and the Environment (the world or problem space).
- Input: The process starts with entry of the Raw Data which is the first state or the current observation of the Environment that the Agent is exposed to.
- Action: This information is processed by the Agent and an Action (denoted by the arrows returning to the Environment) is performed by the Agent.
- Feedback Loop: The environment acts by reacting to the action of the agent by moving to a new state and rewarding or punishing the agent. This interaction is a learning loop; what is usually called the exploration exploitation process with which the agent can assess the effects of its actions. The aim of the agent is to acquire an optimal policy: a collection of decision rules, which are most likely to lead to a high expected cumulative reward in the long term.
- Output: The ultimate Output is the acquired, optimal strategy, in which original raw data is satisfactorily structured or classified in accordance with the

effective actions undertaken (as illustrated by the separate and sorted out combinations of shapes).

2.5.3. Multimodal Inference: Integrating Diverse Data Sources for Holistic Analysis

Multimodal inference Multimodal inference refers to the synthesis of data collected through multiple channels like sensors on the Internet of Things, social media, and satellite images to give a complete picture of the urban phenomenon (Han et al., 2025) reviewed multimodal spatio-temporal data visualization tools that can be used to optimize the transport network and reduce congestion in the transport sector.

2.5.4. Federated Learning: AI Privacy-Preservation on Nodes in Distributed Systems

Federated learning can allow model training on decentralized machines without exchanging raw data at all, which is a vital concern in smart cities (Ghadi et al., 2023) mentioned the integration of federated learning with IoT in smart cities, and its contribution to improving security and privacy. Additionally, Tan et al. (2024) introduced a federated learning architecture that preserved privacy to actively coordinate IoT maintenance timetables, as an example of application to the urban infrastructures management. Recent surveys highlight open challenges in federated learning, including communication efficiency, system heterogeneity, and robustness in large-scale deployments (Kairouz et al., 2021).

3. IOT INFRASTRUCTURE FOR SMART CITIES

3.1 Sensors, Devices, and Connectivity Frameworks

Smart cities rely on a heterogeneous ecosystem of sensors and connected devices to continuously monitor urban environments and enable data-driven decision-making. These devices are designed for specialized functions and are often developed using diverse measurement standards, data formats, and communication protocols, making interoperability a fundamental challenge in large-scale deployments (Al-Fuqaha et al., 2015). Connectivity frameworks facilitate data exchange between sensors, edge nodes, and processing platforms through a range of wired and wireless technologies. The major categories of sensors and devices deployed in smart cities, along with their representative connectivity technologies and primary applications, are summarized in Table 2. Connectivity solutions in these systems range from short-range protocols such as Bluetooth Low Energy (BLE), Zigbee, and Wi-Fi to cellular networks (4G/5G) and Low-Power Wide-Area Networks (LPWANs) such as LoRaWAN and NB-IoT, selected based on latency, bandwidth, coverage, and energy-efficiency requirements. To further support real-time analytics and reduce network load, edge and fog computing architectures are increasingly integrated to preprocess data closer to its source before transmission to cloud platforms (Chiang & Zhang, 2016).

Table 2. Sensors, devices, and connectivity frameworks in smart cities

Category	Representative Devices / Technologies	Connectivity Frameworks	Primary Applications
Environmental Sensors	Air quality sensors (PM2.5, PM10, NO_2, CO), temperature, humidity, noise, water-quality sensors	LoRaWAN, NB-IoT, Zigbee, Wi-Fi	Environmental monitoring, pollution detection, climate analysis, and sustainability planning (Mead et al., 2013).
Traffic and Mobility Sensors	GPS trackers, RFID tags, inductive loop detectors, traffic cameras	4G/5G, Wi-Fi, Dedicated short-range links	Real-time traffic monitoring, congestion management, adaptive signal control, traffic forecasting, and emergency response (Bifulco et al., 2016).
Energy and Utility Sensors	Smart electricity, gas, and water meters; grid sensors; renewable energy monitors	NB-IoT, LoRaWAN, Power-line communication	Demand forecasting, grid stability monitoring, outage detection, and energy efficiency in smart grids (Depuru et al., 2011).
Public Safety Devices	CCTV cameras, acoustic sensors, surveillance systems	4G/5G, Wi-Fi, fiber networks	Crime prevention, traffic enforcement, crowd monitoring, abnormal event detection, and emergency response with privacy considerations.
Healthcare IoT Devices	Wearable sensors, smartwatches, remote patient monitoring systems	BLE, Wi-Fi, cellular networks	Continuous health monitoring, chronic disease management, telemedicine, and preventive healthcare services (Gubbi et al., 2013).
Cross-Cutting IoT Infrastructure	Gateways, edge nodes, fog servers	BLE, Zigbee, Wi-Fi, LPWANs, 4G/5G	Data aggregation, preprocessing, latency reduction, and secure data transmission to cloud platforms (Al-Fuqaha et al., 2015; Chiang & Zhang, 2016).

3.2 Data Collection, Transmission, and Preprocessing

The most important and critical pipeline that transforms the raw sensory signals into trusted inputs to the Big Data platforms and AI inference is data collection, transmission, and preprocessing.

- Data collection: Data collection in cities takes a number of forms, including sensor-generated streams, administrative records, and user-generated data from digital platforms. Sampling frequency and reliability is highly dependent on device capabilities (battery life, compute, memory), sensor calibration, and local conditions (temperature, interference). Aspects like sampling rate need to be selected by designers based on a tradeoff between information fidelity and power consumption and bandwidth and storage consumption; low-power environmental sensors might have reduced sampling rates than traffic-counting devices. More broad surveys of IoT sensing and preprocessing are used to explain the impact of these tradeoffs on downstream analytics and model accuracy.
- Data transmission: after this data has been gathered, the data should be sent out of the sensors to processing devices which may be locally based, at the edge devices or cloud systems. The smart cities have communication structures that use a variety of technologies depending on the distance, bandwidth, and power needs. Short-range networks such as BLE, Zigbee, and Wi-Fi are used to provide contact between devices within buildings or local regions. The 4G and 5G networks are cellular with high-speed and low-latency connections suitable in real-time applications like video surveillance or autonomous vehicles. In situations which require distance and low power intensity such as long distance,
- Low-Power Wide- Area Networks (LPWAN) such as LoRaWAN and NB-IoT are useful in enabling the sensors that may be scattered around the city to be able to transmit data efficiently without necessarily having to replace their batteries frequently.
- Data Preprocessing: Data is pre-processed in order to improve its quality and usability before it can be analysed to make a decision. Preprocessing entails the purification of the data so that it can be devoid of noise, inconsistencies or missing values; particularly where heterogeneous sources are used. Edge and fog computing are important in this phase as they can make an initial computation where the data is given, which is less latent and does not require as much data to be sent to central servers.

3.3 Edge, Fog, and Cloud Architectures for IoT Data

All three layers combine to create a hierarchical architecture that can compromise among the latency, storage, and computational needs.

I. **Edge Computing:** Edge computing means processing data at the location where it has been created, at the edge of the network. Preliminary processing

Preliminary processing (e.g., filtering, aggregation, or anomaly detection) can be done by the IoT device (e.g., sensor, camera, or smart meter) before further processing. This has minimized latency, minimized network bandwidth, and made real-time decision-making possible, which is essential to applications like traffic management, autonomous cars, and emergency response. Also, local data processing improves security and privacy because sensitive data is not required to be transported at a long distance (Satyanarayanan, 2017).

II. **Fog Computing:** Fog computing is the overlay between edge devices and the cloud and offers an additional level of computational and storage features nearer to the point of data origin. Fog nodes, commonly implemented on routers, gateways or local servers, are capable of performing tasks that are more complex than those of the edge devices (like video analytics, predictive maintenance or localized data aggregation). By spreading processing to edge and fog layers the system can serve applications that need low latency as well as moderate computation power. Fog computing is also useful in lessening the burden on central cloud servers by handling and sifting heavy volumes of information on the cloud server (Bonomi et al., 2012).

III. **Cloud Computing:** Cloud computing is the centralized large-scale data storage and processing and analytics infrastructure. The cloud is capable of processing large datasets and high-level analytics, training machine learning models, and storing data over extensive periods of time, unlike edge and fog layers. Cities have city-wide applications like urban planning, energy optimization and policy decision-making, which are best suited on cloud platforms, as these all involve aggregated historical data between several sources. Although cloud computing implies increased latency over edge and fog computing, its scalability and computing capabilities render it a necessity in full-scale data analysis.

4. BIG DATA ANALYTICS IN URBAN SYSTEMS

Smart cities will produce large amounts of data as they advance and this data could be in the form of IoT sensors, traffic cameras, utility meters, social media and mobile applications (Gubbi et al., 2013). This urban data can be described in terms of the 5Vs of volume, velocity, variety, veracity and value. This causes cities to generate terabytes of information every day that come in real-time streams that need instant processing (Bonomi et al., 2012).

4.1 Characteristics of Big Data in Smart Cities (5Vs)

Big Data generated in smart cities is commonly characterized by five key dimensions—Volume, Velocity, Variety, Veracity, and Value which collectively define the scale, complexity, quality, and usefulness of urban data. These characteristics influence the design of data storage architectures, real-time processing frameworks, and AI-driven analytics pipelines required for effective urban decision-making. A summary of the 5Vs and their implications for smart city applications is provided in Table 3.

Table 3. Characteristics of big data in smart cities (5Vs)

Dimension	Description	Smart City Implications / Examples
Volume	Refers to the massive amount of data generated daily from traffic sensors, CCTV systems, utility meters, transportation networks, and social media platforms, often reaching terabytes or petabytes in large cities.	Enables large-scale analysis of mobility, energy usage, public safety, and citizen behavior but requires scalable storage and distributed computing infrastructures.
Velocity	Describes the speed at which urban data is generated, transmitted, and processed, with a significant portion produced in real time.	Supports time-critical applications such as adaptive traffic signal control, emergency response systems, and real-time energy monitoring using platforms like Kafka, Spark, and Flink (Dastjerdi & Buyya, 2016).
Variety	Represents the heterogeneity of urban data, including structured (databases), semi-structured (IoT logs), and unstructured data (video, images, audio, social media).	Requires advanced data integration and fusion techniques to combine multiple sources for applications such as pollution detection and congestion analysis.
Veracity	Concerns the accuracy, reliability, and trustworthiness of data, which may be affected by sensor faults, communication errors, or noise.	Necessitates data cleaning, validation, and preprocessing to ensure reliable analytics in critical domains like healthcare, public safety, and energy systems.
Value	Focuses on transforming raw data into actionable insights that improve city operations and citizen well-being.	Enables predictive maintenance, optimized resource allocation, improved service delivery, and enhanced quality of life for urban residents.

4.2 Real-Time Stream Processing Frameworks

It is imperative in smart cities, where IoT devices, traffic sensors, CCTV cameras, and public utilities are creating large continuous streams of data.

1. **Apache Kafka:** Apache Kafka is a high-throughput, fault-tolerant, and low-latency streaming platform, which is designed to support data ingestion. It serves as a message mediator, receiving information at the end of various producers

(sensors, IoT appliances, social media feeds) and transmitting it to the consumers (analytics engines, databases, dashboards). Kafka is very popular in smart cities and is used to feed traffic sensors, energy meters, or live social media notifications. Its distributed structure can be horizontally scaled, whereas its persistence makes it reliable (T. P. Raptis and A. Passarella, 2023).

2. **Apache Spark:** Apache Spark Structured streaming is a large-scale data processing framework (batch and real-time) (Zaharia, 2012). It is compatible with the micro-batch processing (where incoming streams are only processed at small intervals), and it can be combined with ML libraries to run predictive analytics. Spark is utilized in smart cities to predict traffic congestion, predict energy demand, or analyze the data of environmental sensors. Its advanced API enables users to program queries on streaming data as they would with static data.
3. **Apache Flink:** Apache Flink is a legitimate real-time stream processing engine with the capability of performing low-latency, event-based computations. In contrast to micro-batching of Spark, Flink does not store data but processes it in real-time, which is essential in applications that need immediate responses, e.g., dynamic traffic lights, tracking an on-the-fly bus, and assigning emergency responses. Flink also offers stateful, fault tolerant and complex event processing (CEP), pattern detection on streaming data (Carbone, 2015).

Table 4. Comparison and use in smart cities

Framework	Processing Type	Use Cases in Smart Cities	Strengths
Kafka	Messaging / Data Broker	Traffic sensor feeds, utility meters	High-throughput, fault-tolerant
Spark	Micro-batch Streaming	Predictive analytics, energy demand, pollution monitoring	Scalable, ML integration
Flink	True real-time Streaming	Dynamic traffic signals, emergency alerts	Low latency, stateful event processing

Table 4 shows, these frameworks allow smart cities to ingest, process, analyze, and act on real-time data efficiently, enabling adaptive decision-making, reduced response times, and enhanced urban management.

4.3 Predictive and Prescriptive Analytics for City Operations: Big Data Analytics in smart cities goes beyond reporting to predictive and prescriptive insights:

Predictive Analytics: Predictive analytics is the predictive process where past and real-time information is used to predict the future occurrences or trends to ensure that cities can predict upcoming issues and respond upstream. Predictive analytics in smart cities attracts data which is provided by IoT sensors, traffic sensors, transportation logs, energy meters, weather sensors, and social media feeds. Regression models, time series forecasting, decision trees, and neural networks are some of the machine learning methods that have been utilized in discovering patterns and correlations that can be used to make a prediction. Predictive analytics may resolve such issues by forecasting any water shortage, air pollution increase, or emergency cases before they happen and ensure that the city authorities prepare resources and reduce risks. The first one is that predictive insights allow making decisions proactively instead of reactively that enhances the performance of the operations and citizen satisfaction. Prescriptive Analytics: Prescriptive analytics is an extension of the predictive analytics, with specific recommendations as to the best course of action to desirable outcomes given the predictions. Whereas predictive analytics provides answers to the question, what is likely to happen.

Prescriptive analytics: It provides answers to the question, what should we do about it. Prescriptive analytics entails the use of optimization algorithms, simulation models and decision support systems to compare the various courses of action and choose the most effective action. As an example, given that predictive analytics predicts a traffic jam at a specific intersection during rush hour, the prescriptive one can recommend that some of the traffic streams should be diverted, adjust the signal timings or send more transport vehicles. Equally, it will be able to streamline waste pick-ups or street lighting according to anticipated use and demand.

4.4 Data Governance, Privacy, and Security Issues

Data governance is the development of policies, standards, and procedures to help assure that the data is correct, reliable, and consistent across different systems in the city, such as transportation, healthcare, and energy, and those in the public safety field. It sets data ownership, access controls and lifecycle management, which facilitates the integration process effortlessly and enhances accountability besides aiding in meeting regulatory standards. The issue of privacy is also very vital because city data records usually contain sensitive data about citizens like their whereabouts, health data, social patterns, and economic dealings (Conti et al., 2018).

Identity theft, profiling or intrusive surveillance may occur as a result of misuse or unauthorized access. Anonymization, pseudonymization and data aggregation are techniques that preserve individual identities and enable meaningful analysis. Ethical data collection and use are associated with compliance with the regulations like GDPR, HIPAA, and local data protection laws (Van Zoonen, 2016). Security is a reply to cyberattacks, malware, unauthorized access, and vulnerabilities of the network (Sicari et al., 2015).

Smart city infrastructures are especially prone as they are quite interconnected. Multi-layered solutions that involve end-to-end encryption, secure authentication, intrusion detection systems and regular patching are required. The use of edge and fog coding can also assist in improving the level of security by performing sensitive data processing on the device to minimize exposure to the network (Perera et al., 2015).

5. AI INFERENCE MODELS FOR SMART CITY APPLICATIONS

5.1 Machine Learning and Deep Learning Models for Inference

Inferencing, in this context, can be described as real-time or near-real-time prediction and decision-making based on trained models being applied to live sensor, Internet of Things, urban, environmental, and social streams of data. They are normally trained offline by one of the three learning paradigms supervised, unsupervised or hybrid and then deployed to make rapid, scalable inferences in operational smart cities. ML models allow cities to find trends in high-volume, non-homogeneous data created by IoT sensors, surveillance networks, GPSs, and other citizen-focused applications and find applications in traffic flow prediction, route optimization, and energy demand forecasting. Nevertheless, conventional ML methods can hardly be used to represent the intricate spatio-temporal correlations in urban systems, especially in large-scale transportation networks. Deep learning has the potential to expand ML functions by exploiting neural structures like Convolutional Neural Networks (CNNs) and Recurrent Neural Networks (RNNs) to work with data of high dimensions and time resolution. It is possible to infer CCTV feeds in real-time and detect traffic accidents and pedestrians using CNN-based inference (Pustokhina et al., 2021).

In the same way, RNN and Long Short-term memory (LSTM) networks are popular in time-series inference, such as urban mobility prediction, as well as predicting energy usage. Graph Neural Networks (GNNs) are a promising paradigm of inference to overcome the limitations of traditional models to model networked urban infrastructures. GNNs can better represent interconnections between road segments and the entire network as well as, therefore, improve the accuracy of predictions and scalability of smart city tasks because they are more inclined to reflect the spatial relationships of road infrastructure and the dynamics of traffic systems (Fan et al., 2025).

Deep Learning Models for Smart Cities

Machine Learning and its sub-category, Deep Learning (DL), is now one of the most powerful paradigms to address issues in smart city ecosystems. Unlike other features used by traditional ML models, deep learning algorithms do not require human-engineered features, and instead learn hierarchical representations on raw data. This ability makes them particularly befitting to handle the high data volumes that are very dimensional and very diverse in an urban environment. The smart cities rely on the different sources of information such CCTV video recordings, satellite images, sensor data, GPS positions, and social media posts. Deep learning can be used to process this multimodal information to produce valid inferences to challenges including traffic control, observation of civic safety, energy savings, as well as environmental prediction. One of the best applications of deep learning in smart cities is computer vision. Convolutional Neural Networks (CNNs) can also be used extensively in the analysis of real-time video feeds of surveillance cameras in order to identify traffic crime, track human behavior and identify accidents.

Using an example of car, bike and pedestrian recognition by CNN-based models, the authorities can impose safety laws and design more pedestrian-friendly systems. Similarly, the road conditions and obstacle locations can be classified through models of semantic segmentation and is necessary to introduce autonomous vehicles and intelligent transport systems.

5.2 Reinforcement Learning (RL) for Adaptive Urban Systems

The models based on Reinforcement Learning (RL) allow making adaptive choices in cities of the future since they can learn about the optimal course of action through exposure to the dynamic systems. Contrary to the typical rule-based RL models, they evolve policies according to emerging conditions and, therefore, may be applied in real-time urban settings such as traffic lights, energy optimization, and resource allocation (Sutton and Barto, 2018). The smart transportation systems have RL agents that adjust dynamical schedules every traffic light to minimize traffic jam and travel time waste depending on the existing traffic density and flow conditions (Van der Pol & Oliehoek, 2016). Similarly, smart grids employ RL techniques to support the adaptive allocation of energy by balancing dynamic demands and renewable energy generation. The most recent trends of deep reinforcement learning integrate neural networks and RL algorithms to enable the agent to act on large cities by accepting high-dimensional sensor information and spatio-temporal inputs (Moerland et al., 2023).

Types of Reinforcement Learning in Smart Cities:

1. Value-Based Reinforcement Learning: Value-based RL focuses on estimating the value of each state or state-action pair and choosing actions that maximize expected returns. The most common example is Q-Learning, where the agent learns a Q-function that represents the expected utility of taking an action in a given state. In smart cities, Q-learning has been widely applied to traffic signal optimization. Each intersection acts as an RL agent that decides whether to switch lights based on current traffic density. Over time, the agent learns strategies that minimize congestion and waiting times. For instance, when traffic flow increases in one direction, the RL agent learns to extend the green signal, while keeping delays low for cross-traffic (Van der Pol & Oliehoek, 2016).
2. Policy-Based Reinforcement Learning: Policy-based methods directly learn a mapping from states to actions without relying on a value function. Instead of predicting long-term values, they optimize the policy itself, often using gradient-based methods. An example in smart cities is energy management in smart grids. Here, RL agents continuously adjust energy distribution between renewable sources, storage units, and consumers. A policy-gradient method learns to balance supply and demand while reducing energy costs and ensuring stability. Policy-based RL is especially useful in continuous action spaces, such as adjusting the power output of solar panels or smart charging schedules for electric vehicles Yu and Sun (2020) proposed a policy-based reinforcement learning approach for time series anomaly detection.
3. Model-Based Reinforcement Learning: Model-based RL takes the next step and constructs a predictive model of the environment. The agent does not just learn based on the past experiences but tries to simulate the various futures and the most appropriate actions are chosen based on the model. Model-based RL may be used in urban water management to simulate rainfall, drainage flows, and demand by the citizens. Through prediction of these dynamics, the RL system can manage to optimize on the water being released out of the reservoirs or to manipulate the pumping systems in order to avoid floods. On the same note, in mass transit, model-based RL is able to model passenger flows to determine how buses or trains can run to minimize overcrowding by adjusting their timetable based on passenger volume (Thomas M. Moerland, 2023).

4. Deep Reinforcement Learning (DRL): Deep RL is a type of reinforcement learning that can address high-dimensional data such as images, videos, sensor streams, and more. Cars are examples of RL agents which sense the road situation through cameras and sensors and then make decisions based on these inputs like braking, accelerating or changing lanes. The second use case is smart mobility services, in which DRL aids in the distribution of shared bikes or ride-hailing cars depending on the predicted demand trends, enhancing the availability of services and minimizing the waiting time (Kiran, 2021).
5. Multi-Agent Reinforcement Learning (MARL): In cities, problems rarely involve a single decision-maker. Instead, multiple RL agents often operate simultaneously, interacting with one another. Multi-Agent Reinforcement Learning (MARL) addresses this by enabling agents to collaborate or compete within shared environments. A prime example is city-wide traffic control. Each intersection is managed by an RL agent, but all agents must coordinate to prevent network-wide congestion. MARL has also been explored in smart energy trading, where households, electric vehicles, and utilities act as agents, negotiating energy consumption and pricing. By fostering cooperation, MARL creates a balance between individual goals and collective urban efficiency. **Adaptive urban systems** use RL to adjust to changing conditions (rush hours, weather, events) to optimally control resources, reduce congestion, energy consumption etc.

5.3 Urban System Modeling with Graph Neural Networks

Graph Neural Networks (GNNs) are also efficient to use with complex urban systems where the entities are interconnected and the data is not in a Euclidean format. The infrastructure elements in the smart cities (road segments, intersections, power grids and communication networks) can be naturally modeled as graphs such that all entities are represented as nodes and the relationships between the entities as edges. GNN-based inference is useful to model the spatial relationships and the temporal dynamics, which facilitates correct prediction of traffic movement, congestion spread, and infrastructure use. GNNs are able to outperform traditional machine learning models, which are unable to operate effectively on relational data, especially when working with large-scale transportation networks and mobility prediction tasks using message-passing mechanisms (Fan et al., 2025). Consequently, GNN has emerged as a fundamental modeling unit of real-time urban analytics and intelligent transportation systems.

Case Study: Traffic Flow Prediction in Urban Areas Using Graph Neural Networks (GNNs)

Transport systems in any given urban area represent a complex network in nature, with the flow of traffic being determined by the topology of road network, interactions between vehicles, and other external influence factors like weather, accidents, and other events of the people. The conventional traffic prediction techniques such as the use of statistical models or the use of traditional machine learning techniques tend to have difficulties with the spatial relation of the various road segments and time dynamics of traffic patterns. Graph Neural Networks (GNNs) have become one of the most potent methods of addressing these restrictions, as traffic is modeled as a graph-structured problem (Fan et al., 2025).

Problem Definition-This case study aims at predicting traffic on urban road network in real-time, to allow easier management of traffic, alleviation of congestions and sound urban planning. The graph has each road segment as a node and the connections between the roads (e.g. intersection or adjacent roads) as edges. The features of the node may be historic traffic volume, average speed, occupancy or even context details like weather conditions or local events. GNNs also can capture the spatial relations among road segments in the urban traffic network, as well as capture temporal dynamics of traffic patterns, by considering the urban traffic network as a graph.

Data Collection and Preprocessing-Various sources of data, such as loop detectors placed in the road, GPS traces of vehicles, traffic cameras, and IoT sensors are used to gather data. Traffic flow history data gives time series of the road segments and the network topology is a graph representation. Normalization of traffic metrics, dealing with missing values, and the creation of adjacency matrices that are used to indicate the connectivity between road segments are some of the preprocessing steps. Spatial distance weighting or correlation of the traffic flow between adjacent nodes may also be advanced as part of the preprocessing to enhance the graph representation. The GNN Architecture of Traffic Forecasting Graph Neural Networks, especially Graph Convolutional Networks (GCNs) and Spatio-Temporal Graph Neural Networks (ST-GNNs) are applied in the task of predicting urban traffic. In a typical ST-GNN model:

1. Spatial Module: GCN layers combine traffic data of the adjacent nodes, which encode spatial correlations across the road network. In the given example, traffic flow may be affected by the congestion of other roads; the GNN discovers such relationships on its own (Ul Abideen, 2024).
2. Temporal Module: Recurrent layers (e.g. LSTMs or Temporal Convolutional Networks (TCNs)) capture the temporal dynamics of traffic at every node. This

enables the system to forecast the future traffic movement using past sequences.
3. Output Layer: Final predictions give the estimates of traffic flow or speed of each road segment in a given future horizon (ex: 5, 15, or 30 minutes ahead).

Results and Observations-In more urban case studies, like New York City or Los Angeles, GNN-based models are better than traditional statistical and machine learning approaches in both accuracy and robustness. They are also good at capturing the non-linear dependencies of traffic and responding to unexpected disturbances like an accident or roadblock. It has been shown that GNNs are capable of minimizing the mean absolute error (MAE) and root mean square error (RMSE) by 15-30 percent relative to the baseline models. In addition, the graph-based model scales to large metropolitan networks where traditional techniques cannot capture the advanced spatial relationships.

5.4 Multimodal Inference: Combining IoT, Social, and Environmental Data

One of the main elements of multimodal inference is the IoT data. The sensors installed in the urban infrastructure record an extensive range of real-time data, namely: traffic flow, loop detectors, GPS trackers, smart cameras; utility use, smart meters measuring electricity, water, and gas consumption; and city safety signals, surveillance cameras or acoustic sensors. Such data can give high-resolution and continuous measurements of the urban phenomena, enabling predictive models to keep close track of the system and act on the system in real-time. Social data supplements IoT signals because it offers perspectives about humans. Social media networks, mobile apps and other digital services create information streams that indicate the mood of the population, the trend of crowds, and activity patterns.

As an example, one can notice Twitter posts or event check-ins that can tell the name of the places with sudden people inflows, and the use of mobile apps patterns that may tell about traffic hot spots or migration trends. By adding this layer of social aspects, predictive systems can capture the human behavior, real-time events that cannot be immediately sensed by the physical sensors. Another important dimension is environmental data which records the values of air quality, temperature, humidity, pollution values, and noise. Such measurements can be of great importance in knowing about risks to urban health, energy demand, and sustainability. Predictive models have the potential to identify the relationships between environmental data and IoT and social signals, including the influence of traffic congestion on air quality or the effect of weather on urban mobility.

6. INTEGRATION FRAMEWORK

6.1 AI Inference with IoT and Big Data

The integration of AI inference with IoT and Big Data forms the core operational framework of smart city ecosystems. This framework connects distributed IoT devices, scalable big data platforms, and AI inference engines to enable real-time analytics and informed urban decision-making. IoT devices—including sensors, cameras, GPS trackers, and smart meters—continuously generate large volumes of heterogeneous data that must be efficiently collected, filtered, and preprocessed to ensure reliability and consistency. Preprocessing plays a critical role in transforming raw data into usable inputs by addressing noise, missing values, and inconsistencies before inference is performed. Once prepared, the data is ingested into big data platforms such as Hadoop, Apache Spark, or cloud-native data lakes, which support distributed storage and large-scale processing of both historical and streaming data. These platforms provide the computational backbone required for deploying AI inference models that operate at city scale, enabling timely and data-driven responses across urban systems (Hashem et al., 2015).

6.2 Pipelines of Real Time Decision-Making

At the core of AI-based smart city systems, real-time decision-making pipelines allow a city to consume a steady flow of IoT data and make immediate decisions. These pipelines consist of sequential steps of data ingestion, preprocessing, inference and action execution. As an example, a traffic sensor, surveillance cameras, and GPS trackers provide ongoing real-time information into the pipeline. Apache Kafka or MQTT message brokers are commonly employed to utilize high-throughput streaming data by the ingestion layer (Boddu, 2025). After being obtained, the preprocessing methods (cleaning of data, normalization, and feature extraction) make the raw inputs prepared to use AI models.

6.3 Model Implementation and Serving of AI in Smart City Pools

The implementation of AI models in smart cities is not as straightforward as in conventional IT infrastructure since it involves the implementation of multi-layered integration of cloud, fog, and edge infrastructure. After the training, models are to be launched into the production environments, where they can handle live data at all times. Model serving: It packages trained models and provides them in an API or runtime service like TensorFlow Serving, ONNX Runtime, or PyTorch Serve (Yang, 2022). These tools are used to make sure that the model can be queried by several applications: within the scope of traffic forecasting, as well as in healthcare monitoring. One of the most important factors is location of models. Cloud and fog nodes support large-scale, resource-intensive calculations like simulations of urban planning although regional analysis is performed on the fog nodes, and low-latency inference is done through edge devices to make a decision promptly (Shi & Dustdar, 2016). As an example, an AI model, which views videos and identifies accidents, can be executed on edge devices near cameras to provide immediate notifications, and processed on the cloud (in the long-term) to provide long-term analysis of safety. To realize machine learning product ionization (as (Sculley et al., 2015) suggest), machine learning pipelines must incorporate powerful monitoring, versioning, and continuous retraining to fit new data landscapes.

7. CHALLENGES AND LIMITATIONS

Although it is a promising concept, the incorporation of AI inference with IoT and big data in smart cities has several challenges. Data heterogeneity and quality is the first challenge. IoT devices produce continuous large and heterogeneous flows of data, such as the numerical sensor measurements, video streams, and geospatial data. Sophisticated preprocessing structures are needed to process this heterogeneous data, and the quality of the data may negatively affect the accuracy of the AI models. As reiterated, discrepancies and noise in IoT data have been a core impediment to sound real-time decision making. Scalability and infrastructure is another limitation. Implementing AI pipelines with edge, fog, and cloud layers require heavy investments in hardware, connectivity, and maintenance.

Cities that have small resources might fail to provide such extensive deployments. In addition, the introduction of the distributed computing architecture like Spark or Flink presents some complexity in its operation, and thus they need competent skills to tune and scale. Security and privacy are also an urgent problem. The IoT devices usually gather personal and environmental sensitive information which poses ethical and regulatory concerns. Indeed, AI-driven surveillance cameras may make citizens safer, yet they might also threaten the privacy of citizens. As Roman et al. (2013) point out, cyber-attacks, data breaches, and unauthorized access are especially dangerous to the IoT ecosystems, and that is why effective governance is necessary. Lastly, there is the issue of latency limitations.

8. FUTURE DIRECTIONS

It can be expected that future research and development efforts in the area of AI inference of smart cities will be centered on federated and decentralized learning models. Federated learning can be utilized in particular by medical devices and smart devices to train AI models locally, ensuring privacy and lessening the burden of communication overhead. federated learning is potentially especially effective in privacy-aware settings like medical and mobility tracking in cities. Explainable AI (XAI) on smart city platforms is also another direction that is going to be adopted in the future. The existing AI systems tend to be black-box systems, and thus, the stakeholders find it hard to comprehend how decisions are made. Combining interpretability techniques, urban designers and locals will develop more trust in artificial intelligence-based services. Sustainable computing and green AI are also new directions. Large-scale AI and IoT implementations are high energy consumers that need to be optimized to minimize computing costs and carbon footprints in the future. Until more efficient approaches to energy conservation are implemented, training and implementing large AI models may lead to environmental issues, as Strubell et al. (2019) mention.

CONCLUSION

Artificial intelligence and IoT and big data have some potential transformative opportunities in the framework of smart cities, enabling the decision-making process to be conducted in real-time, predictive analytics to be carried out, and adaptive governance to be undertaken. Cities can be better empowered through distributed computing to provide scalable infrastructures and advanced machine learning to overcome their issues such as traffic congestion, energy demand and safety of their citizens. However, these opportunities are associated with difficulties and some of these difficulties are the difficulty in scalability, and latency, privacy and cost of infrastructure. The remedies to these must be in form of regular innovation, good governance and proper collaboration with stakeholders. The future of AI-based smart cities lies in the realization of privacy protecting technologies, introduction of explainable and energy saving AI systems and cross-domain data streaming. Hence, the only solution is to strike a balance between technology and humanistic leadership. As long as these challenges are effectively met, AI inference with IoT and big data will be one of the keys to creating urban settings based on sustainability, resilience, and humanity.

REFERENCES

Al-Fuqaha, A., Guizani, M., Mohammadi, M., Aledhari, M., & Ayyash, M. (2015). Internet of Things: A survey on enabling technologies, protocols, and applications. *IEEE Communications Surveys and Tutorials, 17*(4), 2347–2376. DOI: 10.1109/COMST.2015.2444095

Bibri, S. E., Alexandre, A., Sharifi, A., & Krogstie, J. (2023). Environmentally sustainable smart cities and their converging AI, IoT, and big data technologies and solutions: An integrated approach to an extensive literature review. *Energy Informatics, 6*, 9. PMID: 37032812

Bifulco, G. N., Pariota, L., Brancati, R., & Fusco, G. (2016). Collecting traffic data through floating car data: Potentials, issues and applications. *Procedia Engineering, 134*, 36–45.

Boddu, Y. (2025). AI agents for real-time operational decision making: Embedding intelligence in data pipelines. *Journal of Computer Science and Technology Studies, 7*(5), 867–872. DOI: 10.32996/jcsts.2025.7.5.99

Bonomi, F., Milito, R., Zhu, J., & Addepalli, S. (2012). Fog computing and its role in the Internet of Things. In *Proceedings of the 1st ACM Workshop on Mobile Cloud Computing (MCC '12)*.

Carbone, A.. (2015). Apache Flink: Stream and batch processing in a single engine. *A Quarterly Bulletin of the Computer Society of the IEEE Technical Committee on Data Engineering.*

Chiang, M., & Zhang, T. (2016). Fog and IoT: An overview of research opportunities. *IEEE Internet of Things Journal, 3*(6), 854–864.

Conti, M., Dehghantanha, A., Franke, K., & Watson, S. (2018). Internet of Things security and forensics: Challenges and opportunities. *Future Generation Computer Systems, 78*, 544–546.

Dastjerdi, A. V., & Buyya, R. (2016). Fog computing: Principles, architectures, and applications. In Buyya, R., & Dastjerdi, A. V. (Eds.), *Internet of Things: Principles and paradigms.*

Depuru, S. S. S. R., Wang, L., & Devabhaktuni, V. (2011). Smart meters for power grid: Challenges, issues, advantages and status. *Renewable & Sustainable Energy Reviews, 15*(6), 2736–2742. DOI: 10.1016/j.rser.2011.02.039

Fan, G., Sabri, A. Q. M., & Rahman, S. S. A. (2025). Emerging trends in graph neural networks for traffic flow prediction: A survey. *Archives of Computational Methods in Engineering*. Advance online publication. DOI: 10.1007/s11831-025-10286-9

Frontiers in Big Data Editorial Office. (2023). From descriptive analytics to predictive and prescriptive intelligence: The role of AI in real-time decision-making. *Frontiers in Big Data, 6*, 1178432. Advance online publication. DOI: 10.3389/fdata.2023.1178432

Ghadi, Y. Y., Mazhar, T., & Faisal, S. (2023). Integration of federated learning with IoT for smart cities: Applications, challenges and solutions. *PeerJ. Computer Science*. PMID: 38192447

Gubbi, J., Buyya, R., Marusic, S., & Palaniswami, M. (2013). Internet of Things (IoT): A vision, architectural elements, and future directions. *Future Generation Computer Systems, 29*(7), 1645–1660.

Han, X., Li, Z., Cao, H., & Hou, B. (2025). Multimodal spatio-temporal data visualization technologies for contemporary urban landscape architecture: A review and prospect in the context of smart cities. *Land (Basel), 14*(5), 1069. DOI: 10.3390/land14051069

Hashem, I. A. T., Yaqoob, I., Anuar, N. B., Mokhtar, S., Gani, A., & Khan, S. U. (2015). The rise of "big data" on cloud computing: Review and open research issues. *Information Systems, 47*, 98–115.

Kairouz, P., McMahan, H. B., Avent, B., Bellet, A., Bennis, M., Bhagoji, A. N., … Yu, F. X. (2021). Advances and open problems in federated learning. *Foundations and Trends® in Machine Learning, 14*(1–2), 1–210. DOI: 10.1561/2200000083

Kiran, B. R. (2021). Deep reinforcement learning for autonomous driving: A survey. *IEEE Transactions on Neural Networks and Learning Systems*.

Luckey, D., Fritz, H., Legatiuk, D., Dragos, K., & Smarsly, K. (2021). Artificial intelligence techniques for smart city applications. In E. Toledo Santos & S. Scheer (Eds.), *Proceedings of the 18th International Conference on Computing in Civil and Building Engineering (ICCCBE 2020)* (Lecture Notes in Civil Engineering, Vol. 98). Springer. DOI: 10.1007/978-3-030-51295-8_1

Mead, M. I., Popoola, O. A. M., & Stewart, G. B.. (2013). The use of electrochemical sensors for monitoring urban air quality in low-cost, high-density networks. *Atmospheric Environment, 70*, 186–203. DOI: 10.1016/j.atmosenv.2012.11.060

Moerland, T. M., Broekens, J., Plaat, A., & Jonker, C. M. (2023). Model-based reinforcement learning: A survey. *Foundations and Trends® in Machine Learning, 16*(1), 1–118. DOI: 10.1561/2200000086

Othengrafen, F., Sievers, L., & Reinecke, E. (2025). From vision to reality: The use of artificial intelligence in different urban planning phases. *Urban Planning, 10*. Advance online publication. DOI: 10.17645/up.8576

Perera, C., Ranjan, R., Wang, L., Khan, S., & Vasilakos, A. V. (2015). Big data privacy in the Internet of Things era. *IEEE Cloud Computing, 3*(2), 36–45. DOI: 10.1109/MCC.2016.31

Pustokhina, I. V., Pustokhin, D. A., Vaiyapuri, T., Gupta, D., Kumar, S., & Shankar, K. (2021). An automated deep learning based anomaly detection in pedestrian walkways for vulnerable road users safety. *Safety Science, 142*, 105356. DOI: 10.1016/j.ssci.2021.105356

Rahman, A., Kundu, D., Debnath, T., Rahman, M., Das, U. K., Miah, A. S. M., & Muhammad, G. (2025). From AI to the era of explainable AI in Healthcare 5.0: Current state and future outlook. *Expert Systems: International Journal of Knowledge Engineering and Neural Networks*. Advance online publication. DOI: 10.1111/exsy.70060

Roman, R., Zhou, J., & Lopez, J. (2013). On the features and challenges of security and privacy in distributed Internet of Things. *Computer Networks, 57*(10), 2266–2279.

Satyanarayanan, M. (2017). The emergence of edge computing. *Computer, 50*(1), 30–39.

Sculley, D., Holt, G., Golovin, D., Davydov, E., Phillips, T., Ebner, D., & Dennison, D. (2015). Hidden technical debt in machine learning systems. *Advances in Neural Information Processing Systems*, •••, 28.

Shi, W., & Dustdar, S. (2016). The promise of edge computing. *Computer, 49*(5), 78–81.

Sicari, S., Rizzardi, A., Grieco, L. A., & Coen-Porisini, A. (2015). Security, privacy and trust in Internet of Things: The road ahead. *Computer Networks, 76*, 146–164.

Silva, B. N., Khan, M., & Jung, C. (2018). Urban planning and smart city decision management empowered by real-time data processing using big data analytics. *Sensors (Basel), 18*(9), 2994. DOI: 10.3390/s18092994 PMID: 30205499

Strubell, E., Ganesh, A., & McCallum, A. (2019). Energy and policy considerations for deep learning in NLP. In *Proceedings of the 57th Annual Meeting of the Association for Computational Linguistics* (pp. 3645–3650). DOI: 10.18653/v1/P19-1355

Sutton, R. S., & Barto, A. G. (2018). *Reinforcement learning: An introduction* (2nd ed.). MIT Press.

Van der Pol, E., & Oliehoek, F. A. (2016). Coordinated deep reinforcement learners for traffic light control. *Proceedings of the NIPS Workshop.*

Van Zoonen, L. (2016). Privacy concerns in smart cities. *Government Information Quarterly*, *33*(3), 472–480.

Wu, Z., Pan, S., Chen, F., Long, G., Zhang, C., & Yu, P. S. (2021). A comprehensive survey on graph neural networks. *IEEE Transactions on Neural Networks and Learning Systems*, *32*(1), 4–24. DOI: 10.1109/TNNLS.2020.2978386 PMID: 32217482

Yu, M. & Sun, S. (2020). Policy-based reinforcement learning for time series anomaly detection. *Engineering Applications of Artificial Intelligence, 95*. 103919. 10.1016/j.engappai.2020.103919.

Zaharia, P. (2012). Introduction of the New Public Management in the Romanian and Swiss Local Public Administration. *Economic Insights - Trends and Challenges*, *64*(4).

Zhang, C., Lin, J., & Wang, Y. (2021). Towards efficient deep learning inference in edge computing: A review. *IEEE Communications Surveys and Tutorials*, *23*(3), 2107–2135.

Zhenning, L., Hao, Y., Guohui, Z., Shangjia, D., & Xu, C.-Z. (2021). Network-wide traffic signal control optimization using a multi-agent deep reinforcement learning. *Transportation Research Part C, Emerging Technologies*, *125*, 103059. DOI: 10.1016/j.trc.2021.103059

Chapter 10
Implementing AI, Big Data, and the IoT:
Ethical and Regulatory Considerations

Irfan Ahmad Khan
http://orcid.org/0000-0003-3357-9429
Rai University, Ahmedabad, India

Ausaf Ahmad Malik
http://orcid.org/0009-0002-4112-8476
Chandigarh University, Mohali, India

Abhilash Agarwal
http://orcid.org/0009-0000-2146-1170
Rai University, Ahmedabad, India

ABSTRACT

The integration of Artificial Intelligence, Big Data analytics and the Internet of Things is reshaping real-time decision-making, creating the need for strong ethical and regulatory safeguards. This chapter explores equitable AI deployment, privacy protection in continuous data flows, and bias reduction through auditing and diverse datasets, aligned with IEEE guidelines and the EU AI Act. It examines privacy issues arising from IoT-driven sensitive data and highlights anonymization, consent protocols and edge computing to support compliance with frameworks such as the GDPR and CCPA. The discussion extends to global regulatory trends, including FTC transparency guidance and ITU IoT security standards, emphasizing the balance

DOI: 10.4018/979-8-3373-7046-0.ch010

between innovation and accountability. Case insights from healthcare and social media reflect practical challenges and demonstrate how thoughtful governance supports trustworthy digital ecosystems.

1. INTRODUCTION

The rapid intersection of Artificial Intelligence (AI), Big Data, and the Internet of Things (IoT) has altered the digital environment in ways that were difficult to imagine even a decade ago. Their integration has enabled systems that respond in real time, support automated processes, and generate insights that are sensitive to context. Collectively, these technologies serve as the operational foundation for modern industries and the broader data-driven economy. Their impact is evident across sectors such as healthcare, education, manufacturing, transportation, and social media, where they contribute to improved efficiency and more informed decision-making. At the same time, the growing dependency on interconnected data ecosystems raises difficult questions related to privacy, ethical responsibility, and regulatory oversight (Batool et al., 2025).

From a technical standpoint, the collaboration among these three domains is anchored in a layered architecture. IoT devices act as the primary data-generating elements, continuously producing sensor readings that travel across cloud and, increasingly, edge-computing infrastructures. Big Data frameworks commonly supported by distributed platforms such as Hadoop and Spark store, filter, and process these large and often unstructured datasets (Khan et al., 2021). AI models, including machine learning and deep learning techniques, subsequently convert this information into patterns and predictions that can guide decisions in real time. Industries have adopted these combined capabilities for purposes such as predicting equipment failures, optimizing urban mobility, and supporting continuous patient monitoring in clinical environments. However, the complex flow of data across devices, networks, and analytical layers introduces a wide surface for cyber threats, data tampering, and unauthorized access.

What makes this ecosystem particularly sensitive is its dependence on extensive datasets collected through IoT networks and refined using Big Data pipelines before becoming inputs for AI models. This dependence increases both the volume and vulnerability of personal and organizational information. Although these technologies substantially enhance accuracy and operational intelligence, they also create ethical tensions involving bias, surveillance, and opaque algorithmic behavior. Recognizing these risks, governments and institutions around the world have begun developing frameworks that align technological innovation with principles of responsible governance. Initiatives such as the European Union's General Data Protection Regulation (GDPR) (European Union, 2018) and UNESCO's Recommendation on the Ethics of Artificial Intelligence (UNESCO, 2021) reflect a growing commitment to protecting human dignity, promoting transparency, and ensuring accountability.

Despite these efforts, regulatory systems often struggle to keep pace with rapid technological change. As a result, a persistent gap exists between technological possibilities and the legal or ethical boundaries intended to guide them. Scholars increasingly argue that responsible governance must involve ongoing assessment of accountability, transparency, and explainability across all layers of the technological stack (Pizzi et al., 2023). Ethical decision-making in this context cannot rely solely on technical optimization; it must be grounded in human-centered values such as fairness, inclusion, and trustworthiness.

This chapter examines how the convergence of AI, Big Data, and IoT challenges existing ethical frameworks and regulatory structures. The following sections outline their technical foundations, highlight major privacy and security concerns, and discuss emerging policy considerations. To situate these issues in practice, the chapter also presents case studies drawn from healthcare and social media environments.

2. TECHNOLOGICAL OVERVIEW

The integration of AI, Big Data, and IoT operates through a layered and interdependent technological structure that transforms dispersed, unprocessed information into meaningful insights. At the base of this ecosystem are IoT devices ranging from environmental sensors and wearable health monitors to smart meters and embedded industrial controllers. These devices function as primary data acquisition points, capturing continuous streams of information related to physiological changes, environmental variations, or everyday user activity. Using communication technologies such as Wi-Fi, 5G, Bluetooth, and Low-Power Wide-Area Networks (LPWAN), these data streams are securely transmitted to cloud platforms or data centres where further processing can occur (Zamani, 2022).

The Big Data layer serves as the analytical backbone of the entire system. It is responsible for managing the high volume, velocity, and variety of data generated by IoT devices. Frameworks such as Hadoop and Apache Spark support distributed storage, high-performance computation, and fault-tolerant processing, making them suitable for large-scale analytics in diverse application areas (Zamani et al., 2024). Before data can be used effectively by AI models, it must undergo several preparatory steps including cleaning, normalization, transformation, and feature selection. These processes are essential not only for analytical accuracy but also for minimizing potential bias that may influence downstream machine-learning outputs.

Building upon these foundational components, the AI layer provides the system with its intelligent capabilities. Machine learning, deep learning, and natural language processing algorithms help identify patterns and correlations that would be nearly impossible to detect manually. The impact of these techniques is already visible across multiple sectors. In healthcare, for instance, AI can evaluate real-time patient data collected from IoT sensors to flag anomalies or predict early signs of illness (Obayya et al., 2022). In contrast, social media platforms rely on AI to interpret user behaviour and tailor content an approach that increases engagement but also raises critical concerns about manipulation, misinformation, and embedded bias (Lyons & Ward, 2024).

This integrated system can be visualized through six interconnected layers:

- Sensing and Data Acquisition – IoT sensors collect raw environmental or user-generated data.
- Transmission and Networking – Secure communication protocols transfer data across networks.
- Storage and Processing – Big Data tools enable distributed storage and large-scale analytics.
- Intelligent Analysis – AI models derive insights, classifications, or predictions from processed data.
- Decision and Action – Automated or semi-automated decisions are executed based on analytical results.
- Feedback and Governance – Continuous oversight ensures compliance with ethical, security, and regulatory requirements.

Despite its efficiency and scalability, this architecture exposes a wide range of vulnerabilities. The rapid increase in connected devices expands the attack surface, making IoT infrastructures highly susceptible to breaches, spoofing, and unauthorized data extraction (Kaur, 2025). Another concern involves the re-identification of supposedly anonymized datasets, which can compromise user privacy when combined with AI-driven inference techniques. Algorithmic bias, often embedded unintentionally during data collection or model training, further threatens fairness and inclusivity.

To address these vulnerabilities, researchers and practitioners advocate incorporating privacy-preserving methods throughout the data lifecycle. Approaches such as differential privacy, federated learning, and homomorphic encryption are gaining attention for their potential to strengthen protections without hindering analytic value (Kaur, 2025). Alongside these, mechanisms such as algorithmic auditing, transparency reports, and explainable AI tools provide structured ways to assess accountability and clarify decision-making pathways within complex AI systems (Ali, 2023).

A comprehensive understanding of these technological layers is vital for policy-makers, system architects, and industry leaders who aim to develop ethical guidelines that evolve alongside ongoing advances. Responsible innovation must be embedded from the earliest stages of design, ensuring that decisions regarding data collection, model development, and automated action consistently align with ethical and legal expectations. Such a balanced approach is essential for cultivating technological ecosystems that are sustainable, trustworthy, and resilient in the expanding AI era (van de Poel, 2025).

3. CHALLENGES TO DATA PRIVACY & SECURITY

As AI, Big Data, and IoT systems become increasingly intertwined, concerns regarding data privacy and security have moved to the forefront for citizens, institutions, and regulatory bodies. Each stage of the digital ecosystem, from the point at which data are collected to their storage, analysis, and eventual use in automated decisions, carries its own vulnerabilities. When these vulnerabilities are not adequately addressed, the reliability and credibility of the entire system come into question (Amin et al., 2024). This section outlines the major categories of challenges, compares their implications, and emphasizes their importance in maintaining public trust.

3.1 Data Privacy Challenges

One of the most pressing privacy issues stems from the unauthorized collection, processing, or sharing of personal information. IoT devices, by design, collect continual data streams that can reveal intimate details about individuals, including daily routines, physical locations, health indicators, and social patterns (Jethava & Rao, 2025). In many cases, users either do not fully understand the extent of data being gathered or are not informed about how these data may be used downstream, leading to persistent concerns about consent and transparency (Taha, 2025).

A second challenge relates to the limitations of traditional anonymization techniques. Although personal identifiers may be removed, seemingly anonymous datasets can often be re-identified by correlating them with external information sources (Zhang et al., 2026). Studies have shown that a remarkably small number of data points, such as ZIP code, gender, and date of birth are sufficient to re-identify a large majority of individuals, sometimes as high as 87% (Kaabachi et al., 2025). This raises critical questions about the effectiveness of current privacy-preservation strategies.

The global movement of data adds another layer of complexity. Regulations vary substantially across jurisdictions for instance, the European Union's GDPR places strict controls on data processing and transfer, while India's Digital Personal Data Protection Act (DPDPA) outlines a different set of compliance requirements (European Parliament, 2016). Organizations operating across borders must navigate this regulatory heterogeneity, making compliance a challenging and resource-intensive process.

3.2 Data Security Challenges

Alongside privacy issues, the security landscape becomes increasingly complex as the number of connected devices expands. Many IoT devices operate with minimal built-in protection, relying on weak encryption, outdated firmware, or proprietary communication protocols that lack uniform security standards (Hilal et al., 2022). Such weaknesses create significant opportunities for cybercriminals. The Mirai botnet attack, for example, demonstrated how thousands of unsecured devices could be compromised simultaneously and used to launch large-scale distributed denial-of-service attacks (Antonakakis, 2017).

Another persistent threat arises from insiders. Employees, contractors, or third-party vendors with legitimate access to sensitive information may intentionally exploit it or inadvertently expose it through careless practices (Paracha et al., 2024). Striking an appropriate balance between operational accessibility and robust authentication, authorization, and monitoring mechanisms remains a difficult but essential task for organizations.

AI-driven systems introduce additional risks through adversarial attacks, in which subtle manipulations in input data often imperceptible to humans cause algorithms to produce incorrect or harmful outputs (Alabdulkreem et al., 2023). These attacks bypass many traditional security controls, revealing a need for new forms of algorithmic resilience and model-level defence strategies.

3.3 Comparative View: Privacy vs Security Challenges:

Table 1. Presents a comparative view of privacy vs security challenges

Aspect	Privacy Challenges	Security Challenges	Impact Level
Nature	Misuse or unauthorized access to personal data	Breaches and attacks compromising data integrity	High
Common Causes	Lack of transparency, weak consent mechanisms, inadequate regulations	Poor encryption, outdated systems, insider threats	Medium to High
Example	Re-identification of anonymized data (Kaabachi et al., 2025)	Mirai botnet attack (Antonakakis, 2017)	High
Preventive Measures	Strong data governance, consent-based collection	End-to-end encryption, intrusion detection	High
Regulatory Frameworks	GDPR, DPDPA (European Parliament, 2016)	ISO/IEC 27001, NIST Cybersecurity Framework (Alabdulkreem et al., 2023)	Medium

3.4 Why Addressing These Challenges Matters:

Neglecting privacy and security concerns can undermine public confidence, reduce user participation, and ultimately destabilize digital services. Privacy violations often result in reputational harm, financial liability, and legal sanctions, while security breaches can disrupt essential operations in critical sectors such as healthcare, banking, transportation, and public administration (Al Duhayyim et al., 2022). Beyond technical consequences, these challenges carry moral implications, as individuals have the right to autonomy, dignity, and protection from misuse of their data.

Therefore, reinforcing data privacy and security is not merely a technological requirement but a governance responsibility. It plays a central role in enabling sustainable innovation, encouraging ethical deployment of emerging technologies, and fostering a digital environment in which individuals and institutions can interact with confidence (Floridi, 2016).

3.5 Comparative Table of Threats, Impacts and Mitigations:

Table 2. Summarizing key challenges

Challenge Category	Potential Impact	Mitigation Approaches
Device / sensor vulnerability	Unauthorized data capture, spoofing, false sensor injection	Secure boot, firmware updates, device authentication, tamper detection
Network/Transmission risk	Data interception, manipulation, service disruption	End-to-end encryption (TLS/DTLS), network segmentation, intrusion detection systems
Storage/Analytics risk	Large-scale data breach, re-identification, analytics bias	Encryption at rest, role-based access, anonymization, differential privacy, audit logs
Data governance & lifecycle	Data retained too long, unknown data flows, misuse of secondary use	Data-minimization, purpose limitation, metadata tracking, transparent data governance
Regulation & cross-border risk	Legal non-compliance fines, loss of trust, jurisdictional conflicts	Privacy-by-design, data localization where needed, privacy impact assessments
Human/Organizational risk	Insider threat, social engineering, poor configuration	Security training, least-privilege policies, continuous monitoring, vendor risk management

Sources: Adapted and summarized based on multiple reviews of Big Data and IoT security and privacy challenges (Khalil et al., 2023).

3.6 Key Dimensions of the Challenge

The privacy and security difficulties associated with AI, Big Data and the IoT stem from several interconnected dimensions. Each of these dimensions' influences how data is collected, processed and ultimately used in decision-making systems.

- **The 4Vs of Big Data: Volume, Variety, Velocity and Veracity:** The traditional characteristics of Big Data Volume, Variety, Velocity and Veracity continue to shape the complexity of securing digital ecosystems as shown in Figure1, Massive volumes of data are generated from IoT devices round the clock, often in unstructured or semi-structured formats. Their rapid movement across networks makes continuous monitoring difficult. Equally important is the issue of veracity, which concerns the reliability and accuracy of data. If the underlying data is incomplete, tampered with, or misleading, even well-designed AI models can fail or give biased outputs. These combined factors significantly amplify privacy and security demands in modern systems (Marr, 2021).

Figure 1. The 4Vs of big data

Conceptual representation of the core Big Data characteristics (4Vs) illustrated security challenges within digital ecosystem shown in Figure 1.

- **Complex value-chains & multiple stakeholders**: In an AI-IoT environment, data typically travels through a long pipeline beginning at sensors, passing through gateways, storage layers, analytics engines, and finally into automated or human-assisted decision modules. As shown in Figure 2. At each point, a different technical or organizational entity may be responsible for the data. This fragmentation often leads to unclear accountability and increases the chances of data exposure, configuration errors, or undocumented data sharing. As the number of actors involved increases, so does the difficulty of ensuring consistent security and privacy practices across the entire chain (Biswas et al., 2022).

Figure 2. End to end data transformation system

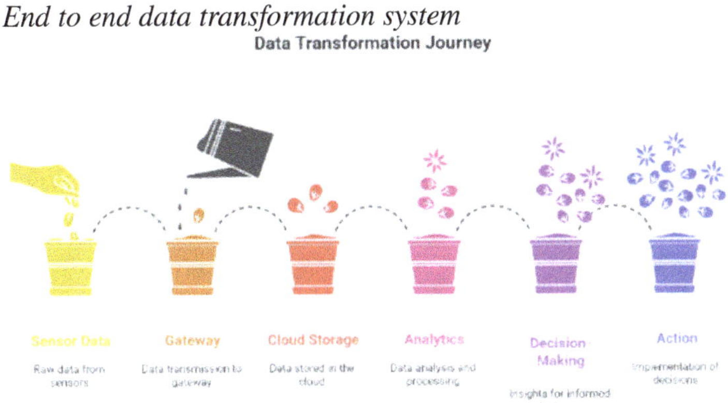

Data Flow pipeline in AI-IoT environment from sensor through gateways, storage and analytics layers to automated shown in Figure 2.

- **Emerging technical and regulatory gaps**: While technologies such as federated learning, secure edge computing, differential privacy, and Blockchain-enabled trust mechanisms show great promise, their adoption remains uneven. Many industries continue to rely on older architectures that were never designed for large-scale, data-intensive AI systems. At the same time, regulatory frameworks struggle to keep pace with rapidly evolving data practices, as shown in the SWOT analysis of technical and regulatory gaps shown in Figure 3. Questions around cross-border data flows, data monetization patterns, and long-term accountability in AI-driven decisions remain largely unresolved in many jurisdictions (Ali et al., 2021).

Figure 3. SWOT analysis of technical and regulatory gaps

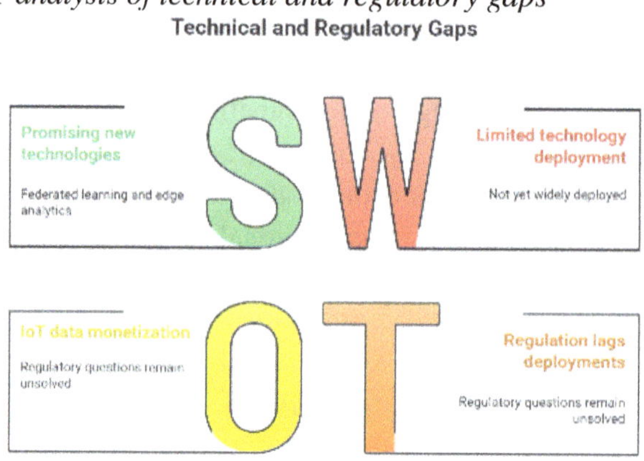

SWOT analysis illustrating technical and regulatory gaps highlighting challenges in aligning regulatory framework shown in Figure 3.

Emerging and Future Risks:

As digital ecosystems expand, several new categories of risks are beginning to surface. These emerging risks do not replace existing challenges; instead, they add further complexity to the governance landscape.

- **Edge/Cloud hybrid attacks**: With processing shifting closer to the edge, attackers often target less-protected edge devices as entry points to compromise the larger cloud infrastructure (Pathak et al., 2024).

- **Re-identification via AI**: Even datasets believed to be anonymized can be cross-referenced with external information. AI's pattern-matching capabilities make it easier to infer identities, raising serious privacy concerns (Sondeck & Laurent, 2025).
- **Data monetization & secondary use**: Organizations increasingly treat data as an economic asset. However, once data is repurposed without clear user consent, individuals lose visibility and control over how their information is exploited (Cheng & Bilal, 2025).
- **Regulatory lag & fragmentation**: IoT ecosystems frequently operate across national borders. Variations in privacy laws, security requirements, and reporting obligations create uncertainty and heighten compliance risks for global deployments (Israel, 2023).
- **Quantum/cryptographic vulnerabilities**: Although quantum computing is still emerging, it poses a potential threat to current encryption standards. IoT deployments with long lifespans such as industrial sensors may remain in use long after quantum-resistant cryptography becomes necessary (Gitonga, 2025).

4. CASE STUDIES FROM THE MODERN HEALTHCARE

The extensive influence of the AI, Big Data, and the IoT on the healthcare industry has brought about the age of new opportunities to make the diagnostics, personalised therapy, effective treatment and management of the patients. Nonetheless, there are always two sides to the technological revolution and a host of ethical problems and regulatory issues are emerging, which require stringent scrutiny.

4.1 Artificial Intelligence in Medical Diagnostics and Treatment

The future of AI in healthcare is enormous, with numerous benefits brought to the quality of care by means of more effective and accurate medical evaluation and treatment prescriptions (Gitonga, 2025). The applications of AI are not limited to medical diagnostic purposes like text and image recognition, clinician decision support, and even direct treatment applications including 'robotic surgery', 'state of the art exoskeletons', 'virtual psychotherapy' and 'therapeutic care robots'. Such applications have the potential to bring significant progress (Borkar & De, 2025), but the trend towards further implementation of these applications in healthcare systems also creates a range of problematic ethical issues related to patient safety, personal freedom and the primary trust between patients and healthcare professionals.

One of the main ethical issues is the possibility of AI systems being non-empathetic or dehumanising healthcare. Although AI is able to examine a lot of data in a shorter time and with more precision than human workers do, the humanness aspect of loving care is hard to imitate. Moreover, data security is also a crucial issue because AI systems can often be sensitive to highly confidential patient data. Another pressing issue is the potential for algorithmic bias in clinical decision-making. The models of AI trained on biased or unrepresentative data may further or even increase the current health inequities, causing unfair treatment or diagnoses, particularly in cases of marginalised groups. For example, a South Korean study on breast cancer detection (Fahim et al., 2025) reported that AI performed well in terms of sensitivity (90%), but it raised concerns about bias because it omitted heterogeneous populations, which may have adversely impacted underrepresented groups. Similarly, partnerships like those between Massachusetts General Hospital and 'Radiology AI' at MIT (Caldas et al., 2025), which achieved an accuracy of 94% in identifying nodules in the lungs, underscore the importance of transparency in preventing over-dependence and ethics violations. The researchers recommend a cautious approach to these ethical issues to ensure that AI usage can truly benefit patients without compromising basic ethical principles. Continued research on case studies from various healthcare settings is vital for demonstrating the practical consequences of these ethical dilemmas and identifying areas where existing studies on AI ethics have not been adequately explored. To illustrate, the application of GPT-4 in complex diagnosis in 2025 demonstrated the potential of this tool. However, it is essential to note that its use should be supported by validation and ethical controls to prevent false diagnoses (Houssein et al., 2025).

4.2 The Use of Big Data Analytics in Surveillance of Public Health

Big Data analytics has revolutionised the way we conduct public health, offering effective means to monitor diseases, predict outbreaks and administer specific aspects of population health by enabling people to merge and combine different types of data into one and subsequently analyse it (Zhan et al., 2025). Timely detection of disease outbreaks and project models is also a vital advantage. Nevertheless, the pervasiveness of digital technologies and new sources of information regarding public health, especially during times of increased global health emergencies like the pandemic, raises concerns about deep privacy issues (Idahor et al., 2025).

The inherent conflict between public health requirements and individual privacy rights is one of the main challenges. Surveillance in the field of health care frequently presupposes the utilisation of a large amount of personal information, and in the absence of appropriate control, it can be misused or result in the invasion of privacy. This conflict is further complicated by the era of the IoT, where constant data flows from multiple devices can be integrated into a surveillance system (Donelle et al., 2023). There is an implicit dichotomy that usually exists where the decision-makers give more weight to the legal requirements than to the moral aspect of taking measures of public health surveillance. This method can be hypothetically justified legally, but the ethical concern on a wider scale can be neglected. Studies show that it is crucial to know the general perceptions and readiness of the population to provide digital data to the purposes of the national health due to the undermining of people's confidence in science and research. A systematic review of digital detection surveillance systems for infectious diseases revealed six cardinal themes, grouped by individual, organisational, and societal levels, as well as awareness of implementation, digital integrity, trust, privacy and confidentiality, civil rights and governance (Lopez, 2025). These topics highlight the complexity of the privacy issue and the need for extensive ethical and regulatory policies to strike a balance between the demands of population well-being and individual rights.

The examples of these problems in 2025 would be the hack of the *Yale* new haven health system to reveal 5.5 million patients with Social Security numbers and other patient data (Zhao et al., 2021), and the ransomware attack at “Eisource”, where 5.4 million medical records were stolen (Viswanathan, 2025). The wrong setting of the *Blue Shield* of California caused the sharing of 4.7 million members with *Google* which escalated the risk of targeted advertising (Olsen, 2025). The health related collaboration between the *White House* and *Big Tech* was criticised as a privacy risk due to the possibility of creating digital ecosystems (Knutsson, 2025).

4.3 Remote Patient Monitoring IoT Devices

Devices of *Internet of Medical Things* (IoMT) such as advanced life-support devices or even a simple wearable that recovers the most basic vital statistics, are rapidly becoming a common tool and potentially provide a way out when it comes to remote patient monitoring. With these devices, tracking of health parameters is possible at any time, providing proactive care and enhancing outcomes, especially when managing chronic health conditions (Katiyar, 2025). However, with this increased popularity, major concerns about user safety, the protection of sensitive health information, and the overall cybersecurity threats posed by interconnected medical devices begin to emerge.

One of the biggest challenges is the unstable regulatory environment of these technologies. Most consumer-based wellness monitoring devices demonstrate differences in their levels of regulation, and some have little to no quality data on their effectiveness or safety. This lacks strict supervision, which may lead to the deployment of devices without proper validation, potentially undermining patient safety and data integrity (Alanazi, 2025). *Remote Patient Monitoring* (RPM) in practice within large healthcare systems, particularly for chronic disease management, has not been studied extensively, and a knowledge gap has been identified regarding how RPM technologies can be utilised to impact clinical practice and patient experiences. Moreover, there are also complex technical and operational aspects of RPM integration, including significant challenges related to data privacy, data security, and compatibility with various systems and devices (Mennella et al., 2024). An example is the EU, which has expressed significant concern over the communication of devices with cloud platforms in remote health monitoring, which necessitates robust mechanisms for collecting and interpreting biometric and physiological data. These regulatory loopholes and technical challenges are among the issues that must be addressed to fully realise the potential of the IoMT in patient care and mitigate the inherent risks (Stevens et al., 2025).

FDA approvals of devices like glucose monitors by "Dexcom" and "Portrait Mobile" by *GE Healthcare* exemplify the compliance requirements of the landscape of the U.S. in 2025 (Ahmed et al., 2025). However, there remain challenges in the areas of data transmission as secure under HIPAA and interoperability of EHR systems through such standards as HL7/FHIR (Angelucci et al., 2025). The AI analytics of a heart failure predictor developed by *Biofourmis* were also questioned on how it evolves after deployment with an emphasis on auditability. The issue of accessibility was also raised in surveys where 74 OF physicians said RPM may increase disparities (Ademola et al., 2024).

5. GLOBAL STUDY OF SOCIAL MEDIA IN DIGITAL ERA

The ubiquitous presence of AI, Big Data, and the IoT has defined the future of social media as a sophisticated set of opportunities and enormous ethical and regulatory issues. The amount of content that is produced on the social media platforms necessitates the application of the AI systems in the moderation of the social media, particularly addressing the challenges of hate speech. Although AI has unmatched possibilities to filter and censor enormous quantities of online data, the issue of its possible censorship and the silencing of crucial voices is becoming increasingly important, which will affect free speech.

5.1 Freedom of Speech and Human Reduced Censorship

The major ethical crisis in the sphere of freedom of speech and the necessity to cut down harmful material appears. AI algorithms, especially those conditioned on Western-centric models, can limit free speech in culturally and linguistically diverse areas, like the *Global South*, in a disproportionate way. It can result in either the over-removal of legal content or removal of harmful content at a slow rate, which only propagates inequality and restricts free speech (Thompson et al., 2024). As an example, the moderation tools of low-resource languages are difficult to construct, because the monopoly of user information by tech companies and their lack of investments only worsens existing inequities in history (Balendra, 2025).

Moreover, the usage of AI to control the content has some questions about human control and responsibility. Researchers state that overall monitoring of AI systems is the most possible way of its human control, despite the inability to ensure complete protection of personal freedom of expression. The AI Act of the EU is a worthy effort at regulating the uses of AI that are deemed high-risk, and this case includes AI-based content moderation. The effect of AI on the popular space can be seen as well in the ability to promote deliberative discussion or polarisation of society, which indicates that AI implementation in community management should be approached with caution (Gomes & Sultan, 2024). The importance of ethical scaling on content moderation is that it underlines the necessity of engaging community intermediaries who have a social justice agenda to enhance the annotation of extreme speech and include them in the AI model-building lifecycle.

In *Myanmar* in 2025, algorithms that amplified hate speech targeted 'Rohingya' were used by Meta (Shetty et al., 2025), which helped spread violence and in *Palestine* pro-Palestine posts were banned, shadow-banning journalists (Schissler, 2025). In 2024, the elections of India were not assessed, thus permitting disinformation to thrive (Hamza, 2025) and *Kenya* had its moderator cuts stimulating hate speech in low-resource languages (Bureau, 2024).

5.2 User Profiling and Targeted Advertising on Big Data

The concept of big data analytics has transformed social media to allow businesses and organisations to be aware of user behaviour, preferences and trends to improve marketing strategies by using innovative personalised advertising. Nonetheless, the fact that it is possible to create psychological profiles based on digital footprints and manipulate attitudes or behaviour with specific interventions casts dubious concerns on privacy and is ethically questionable. The case of *Cambridge Analytica* (Mossie & Wang, 2020) can be regarded as one of the most notable examples, as it demonstrates how influence on voter behaviour can be exercised through psychographic advertising, a type of advertising based on profiling social media users. Privacy of data is not properly informed to users, and they end up taking up policies without even understanding their contents. The practice of selling personal data to personalise advertisements and engage in political micro-targeting is viewed as a chilling concept that has compromised privacy and is capable of influencing the electorate (Schneble et al., 2018).

Targeted advertising utilises massive volumes of individual data to categorise users according to their interests, location, age, gender, and various characteristics. Although this presents new opportunities for advertisers, it has raised serious privacy concerns among individuals and organisations. Ethical concerns regarding the use of algorithmic targeting systems are also associated with web users' perceptions of targeted advertising in terms of data knowledge, cookie consent, and the phenomenon known as algorithmic disillusionment (Simchon et al., 2024). Moreover, psychological targeting deters the boundaries between the private and the public information, as it presents a threat to the classical conceptualizations of the privacy because of the outdated tradition of the notice and consent. The efficacy of political advertisements that are specifically targeted is also under question, and research conducted is examining the question of user privacy in relation to targeted political advertisements in reply to the traditional advertisement of products (Themistocleous et al., 2022).

In 2025, the proxy profiling of sensitive features by Meta results in job advertisements being discriminatory based on gender, houses being discriminatory based on race, and gambling being predatory based on their targets (Baum et al., 2023). The use of generative AI in advertisements increased opaqueness and its detriments include sharing NHS health data and fraud on vulnerable individuals.

5.3 IoT Integration Toward Social Platforms

The prospective nature of the IoT devices to be coupled with social media platforms raises other levels of ethical and societal issues, especially the ownership, privacy and security of data. Although IoT applications have the prospects of enhancing different spheres of life, its combination with social platforms may amplify concerns regarding security threats, biases, deprivations of agency, and human control and provoke other concerns including ethical content generation (Dotto, 2025).

The spread of IoT devices leaves an ethical grey zone especially as the idea of the "Internet of Bodies" gains traction, where the human body and brain create a network. This has disrupted established ideas of ownership where users may not have control over their IoT devices and their data. The list of the most urgent problems with the IoT setting usually includes the problems of ethical and data privacy. When IoT information is injected into social platforms, the amount and sensitivity of personal information shared may increase exponentially (Sadhu et al., 2022). To secure IoT digital health ethical approaches like focusing on data privacy, informed consent, user autonomy and regulatory compliance are important. Likewise, an overall assessment framework of IoT technologies in digital health identifies such major axes as data privacy and security, informed consent, user autonomy, and ethical design. These issues are magnified by the possibility that social media platforms may use this stream of unremitting personal information to do additional profiling and targeting and casting the very question of explicit consent and the degree to which individuals own the information (Celik & Eltawil, 2022).

The IoT users are guaranteed the rights to access and share data under the EU Data Act, 2025 but issues such as consent in ubiquitous processing and ownership in smart cities, where wearable data may merge with social feeds with no explicit policies, arise. The data gathered by voice assistants is dangerous unless the consent is explicitly sought (De Barros, 2024).

5.4 International Approach to Social Media Regulations and Ethics

The international character of social media has prompted different and even conflicting rules on a governmental level across the globe. Various nations have been formulating policies to respond to the effects of social media on society and have different methods of holding the platforms accountable for spreading disinformation and other distasteful content. European nations are defining the scope of accountability for social platforms through diverse policies, leading to the emergence of different models of accountability, including law-regulated self-regulation and pure self-regulation (Savin & Nielsen, 2025). UNESCO has also designed international principles of governing digital platforms reflecting decades of effort on freedom of expression, to guide governance, regulation, companies and civil society in the direction of an "Internet of Trust" (De Blasio & Selva, 2021).

The existence of cross-national comparisons of content moderation laws, including the "NetzDG" in Germany and "POFMA" in Singapore, as their domestic policies are raising the stakes of platform liability in regard to content moderation in the 'war on misinformation' (Prastacos et al., 2024). These discussions consider various aspects, including definitions of content and misinformation, moderation, transparency, fines, and external oversight, often informed by human rights-based recommendations from entities such as the UN and UNESCO. The plan here is to create global dialogue and promote harmonisation of rules governing social media internationally so that there is a balance between technology and responsible usage. The social media impact on human relationships, consumption habits, and privacy are some of the issues and ethical concerns of using social media that are rampant. Scholars are also mapping the space of social media regulation to learn the various government interventions on such layered problems (Santos et al., 2025).

UNESCO assisted self-regulation on disinformation in South East Europe and Turkey in 2025 and a South Asia code on conflict-sensitive reporting. Age verification was required by the U.S. state laws and the content liability was imposed by EU rulings against the provider of such information, Meta. The perspective of OECD encouraged the future-oriented regulations.

6. RECOMMENDATIONS

The fast development Digi-tech in the spheres of healthcare and social media requires proactive and multidimensional responses to reduce the ethical risks and regulatory loopholes. Based on the modern trends in 2025 including the stronger emphasis on bias reduction when using AI diagnostics and the adoption of updated privacy laws that would include IoT vulnerabilities, this section outlines the recommendations under different headings. These suggestions are based on the existing frameworks and include the UNESCO ethics recommendations as well as OECD AI principles and integrate practical illustrations to determine the viability. The overall goal is to balance innovation in technology and protection of society to promote trust and fairness in industries.

i. Formulating Strong Ethical Principles

It is necessary to develop dynamic moral standards that will help avoid the pitfalls of AI, Big Data, and IoT. Information control, privacy improvement, and fairness of algorithms should be the initial priority of such guidelines, which should follow the development of technologies to avoid dehumanisation and inequalities. As it is important to strike the right balance between the innovation and ethics by continuing to engage with the stakeholders. This is exemplified by the 2024 guidance issued by the WHO on large multi-model models, which is extended into 2025 practises, which contains more than 40 guidelines that governments and providers should follow to guarantee that AI does not violate privacy and equity in health applications (McCarthy et al., 2023). In the case of IoT in remote patient monitoring, ethical principles, focus on user autonomy and fairness, a feature also present in the study by *Mount Sin Ai Hospital* in 2025, which demonstrated the system's biased nature in its treatment recommendations on the same condition based on the demographic, hence the necessity of diverse datasets. To encourage algorithmic transparency, it is recommended to incorporate ethics throughout the designing phase, as proposed in the March 2025 of *Nature* review on minimising bias in algorithms, which outlines the idea of data auditing to prevent enhancing health disparities in the marginalised population. This is further demonstrated in the May 2025 survey by *PLOS Digital Health*, which examines methods of AI fairness in healthcare, including periodic bias evaluation of medical imaging (Sonicki, 2024).

Guidelines in the healthcare setting should include clear consent, transparency, and bias auditing as the case of the *American Nurses Association* (ANA) May 2025 (Rodriguez et al., 2021) position statement regarding the use of AI in ethical nursing practise. This paper highlights empathetic adoption of AI to optimise patient outcomes without undermining trust, covering the cases of AI-based diagnostics where empathy cannot be substituted. A modern example can be found in the November 2025 framework of Harvard, “From Code to Conscience” (Stokes, 2025), which offers a systematic way of achieving equitable AI in healthcare by setting the limits of tolerance to risks like invasion of privacy and encouraging human intervention in decision-making. Within the social media context, the March 2025 Guidelines by UNESCO on the “Governance of Digital Platforms” emphasise multi-stakeholder cooperation in addressing the issue of Big Data-guided profiling and propose ethical design as a solution to address the problem of manipulative targeting (Bimalendu Patra et al., 2025).

ii. Offering Adaptive Regulatory Frameworks

The regulatory frameworks should be adaptable enough to keep abreast of the technological transformation with risk-based regulation. In the case of social media, sensitive content moderation laws are essential. The *EU Digital Services Act* (DSA) which came into effect in 2025 prohibits targeting based on sensitive characteristics, revising their GDPR-AI intersections, stating that the decisions of algorithms are to be transparent (Shaffique, 2024). According to the report on 41 major regulations issued by *IoT Analytics* in August 2025, the use of IoT is quickly becoming established, such as IoT labelling initiatives in the US to boost consumer confidence in connected devices. The concepts of informed consent form part of the mechanisms used to regulate targeted advertising, according to the predictions of an agile frameworks to adapt to the risks of AI-driven personalization (Usman et al., 2025). The September 2025 IoT cybersecurity compliance plan of the company provides practical solutions, including independent monitoring agencies to maintain democracy in internet targeting.

Within the health domain, the 2025 updates to the HIPAA (Omar et al., 2025) offer greater encryption of *electronic protected health information* (ePHI) and increased security around AI and IoT, which relates to breaches involving more than one million devices, reported in one of the largest 2025 healthcare IoT breaches, also identifing telehealth-related and AI-related changes, prioritising the enforcement areas to avoid the misuse of remote monitoring. Similarly, the *Cyber Resilience Act, 2022* that is already enacted in the EU and whose full implementation is due in 2025 establishes security standards to IoT devices, including those that are connected to social platforms, to guarantee the integrity of data and its interoperability (Lakshamanan, 2025).

iii. Enculturation of International Cooperation

The collaboration between countries is essential to the standardisation of standards and fair AI implementation. The principles of AI employed by OECD direct intergovernmental standards, focusing on reliable AI that upholds human rights. The 2025 report by UNCTAD proposes an AI-for-all framework, which will resolve the infrastructural and skills disparities in the Global South. The Annual AI Governance Report 2025 by ITU emphasises adaptive governance of the global effect of AI. In the case of social media, the release of an October 2025 report on guidelines on generative AI and platforms by UNESCO enables the creation of an Internet of Trust by spreading responsibilities. The 2025 analysis of draught ethics rules in China by Mayer Brown contains an example of harmonisation, which is in line with the WHO principles of healthcare AI. According to *Stanford*, 2025 AI Index, there was a 21.3% increase in the number of mentions of AI in laws around the world, which means that cooperation is necessary because it has increased nine fold since 2016 (Jio, 2025).

The recommending AI ethics that, up to now, is still in place at UNESCO encourages principles of proportionality and privacy protection, and these are promoted internationally. This is the case with the 2025 Global Conference on AI, Security, and Ethics organised by UNIDIR, which brought together diplomats to discuss cross-border concerns. A 13-point roadmap is proposed by China in August 2025 it "Action Plan on Global AI Governance" that is centred on ethical data sharing and capacity building (Cheng & Bilal, 2025).

7. CONCLUSION

The integration of Big Data, AI, and IoT is transforming modern systems by strengthening efficiency, accuracy, and intelligent decision-making. These technologies now support critical domains such as healthcare, governance, and social platforms, offering new possibilities for monitoring, prediction, and personalized services. However, their rapid growth also brings essential concerns related to privacy, security, fairness, and accountability. Issues such as biased decisions, unregulated data use, and opaque system behaviour highlight the need for responsible governance. To ensure sustainable and trustworthy adoption, ethical principles and transparent processes must guide every stage of technological design and deployment. A balanced approach one that protects individual rights while encouraging innovation will allow institutions to fully benefit from these advancements. By promoting integrity, clarity, and human-centred values, society can embrace these emerging technologies with confidence and long-term trust.

8. FUTURE SCOPE

Future research can explore stronger regulatory models, clearer data-protection frameworks, and practical guidelines for responsible use of emerging technologies. There is also scope to study how organizations can balance innovation with ethical obligations while improving transparency and accountability. Further work on interoperable systems, secure data-sharing, and community-centric policies will help institutions adopt Big Data, AI, and IoT solutions with greater trust and long-term reliability.

REFERENCES

Ademola, A., George, C., & Mapp, G. (2024). Addressing the interoperability of electronic health records: The technical and semantic interoperability, preserving privacy and security framework. *Applied System Innovation*, *7*(6), 116. DOI: 10.3390/asi7060116

Ahmed, S. F., Sharmin, S., Kuldeep, S. A., Lameesa, A., & Alam, Md. S. B., Liu, G., & Gandomi, A. H. (2025). Transformative impacts of the internet of medical things on modern healthcare. *Results in Engineering*, *25*, 103787. DOI: 10.1016/j.rineng.2024.103787

Al Duhayyim, M., Alshahrani, H. M., Al-Wesabi, F. N., Al-Hagery, M. A., Hilal, A. M., & Zaman, A. S. (2022). Intelligent machine learning based EEG signal classification model. *Computers, Materials & Continua*, *71*(1), 1821.

Alabdulkreem, E., Alotaibi, S. S., Alamgeer, M., Marzouk, R., Hilal, A. M., Motwakel, A., & Rizwanullah, M. (2023). Intelligent Cybersecurity Classification Using Chaos Game Optimization with Deep Learning Model. *Computer Systems Science and Engineering*, *45*(1), 971–983.

Alanazi, A. (2025). The potential, applications, and challenges of internet of things (Iot) technologies from the perspectives of clinicians. *Cureus*. Advance online publication. DOI: 10.7759/cureus.85847

Ali, M. S., Vecchio, M., & Antonelli, F. (2021). A blockchain-based framework for IoT data monetization services. *The Computer Journal*, *64*(2), 195–210. DOI: 10.1093/comjnl/bxaa119

Ali, S., et al. (2023). Explainable Artificial Intelligence (XAI): What we know and what we need to know. (survey)

Amin, M. A. S., Kim, S., Amin Rishat, M. A., Tang, Z., & Ahn, H. (2024). A Systematic Literature Review of Privacy Information Disclosure in AI-Integrated Internet of Things (IoT) Technologies. *Sustainability*, *17*(1), 8.

Angelucci, A., Greco, M., Cecconi, M., & Aliverti, A. (2025). Wearable devices for patient monitoring in the intensive care unit. *Intensive Care Medicine Experimental*, *13*(1), 26. DOI: 10.1186/s40635-025-00738-8

Antonakakis, M.. (2017). Understanding the Mirai botnet. *USENIX Security Symposium*, 1093–1110.

Balendra, S. (2025). Meta's AI moderation and free speech: Ongoing challenges in the Global South. Cambridge Forum on AI: Law and Governance, 1, e21. doi:DOI: 10.1017/cfl.2025.5

Batool, A., Zowghi, D., & Bano, M. (2025). *AI governance: A systematic literature review. AI and Ethics.* Springer., DOI: 10.1007/s43681-024-00653-w

Baum, K., Abramova, O., Meißner, S., & Krasnova, H. (2023). The effects of targeted political advertising on user privacy concerns and digital product acceptance: A preference-based approach. *Electronic Markets*, *33*(1), 46. DOI: 10.1007/s12525-023-00656-1

Bimalendu Patra, B., Saha, S., Bhattacharyya, P., & Adhikary, S. (2025). Sdgs and the future of governance: Legal, managerial and technological approaches. In Integrated Publications (pp. 01–350). Integrated Publications. DOI: 10.62778/int.book.602

Biswas, A. R., Dupont, C., & Pham, C. (2022). IoT, Cloud and BigData Integration for IoT Analytics. In Building Blocks for IoT Analytics (pp. 11-37). Routledge. DOI: 10.1201/9781003337423-3

Borkar, S. R., & De, A. (2025). Artificial intelligence in internal medicine: A study on reducing diagnostic errors and enhancing efficiency. *The European Journal of Cardiovascular Medicine*, *15*, 105–111. DOI: 10.61336/ejcm/25-09-19

Bureau, T. H. (2024, March 25). Misinformation during Indian elections: The saga from 2019 to 2024. The Hindu. https://www.thehindu.com/news/national/misinformation-during-indian-elections-the-saga-from-2019-to-2024/article67989996.ece

Caldas, F. A. A., Caldas, H. C., Henrique, T., Jordão, P. H. F., Fernandes-Ferreira, R., Souza, D. R. S., & Bauab, S. D. P. (2025). Evaluating the performance of artificial intelligence and radiologists accuracy in breast cancer detection in screening mammography across breast densities. *European Journal of Radiology Artificial Intelligence*, *2*, 100013. DOI: 10.1016/j.ejrai.2025.100013

Celik, A., & Eltawil, A. M. (2022). The internet of bodies: The human body as an efficient and secure wireless channel. *IEEE Internet of Things Magazine*, *5*(3), 114–120. DOI: 10.1109/IOTM.001.2100209

Cheng, Y. W., & Bilal, A. (2025). Regulatory data privacy concerns in proliferating IoT era of telecommunication data monetisation: A systematic literature review. *Computing*, *107*(9), 190. DOI: 10.1007/s00607-025-01542-8

Cheng, Y. W., & Bilal, A. (2025). Regulatory data privacy concerns in proliferating IoT era of telecommunication data monetisation: A systematic literature review. *Computing*, *107*(9), 190. DOI: 10.1007/s00607-025-01542-8

De Barros, E. C. (2024). Understanding the influence of digital technology on human cognitive functions: A narrative review. *IBRO Neuroscience Reports, 17*, 415–422. DOI: 10.1016/j.ibneur.2024.11.006

De Blasio, E., & Selva, D. (2021). Who is responsible for disinformation? European approaches to social platforms' accountability in the post-truth era. *The American Behavioral Scientist, 65*(6), 825–846. DOI: 10.1177/0002764221989784

Donelle, L., Comer, L., Hiebert, B., Hall, J., Shelley, J. J., Smith, M. J., Kothari, A., Burkell, J., Stranges, S., Cooke, T., Shelley, J. M., Gilliland, J., Ngole, M., & Facca, D. (2023). Use of digital technologies for public health surveillance during the COVID-19 pandemic: A scoping review. *Digital Health, 9*. Advance online publication. DOI: 10.1177/20552076231173220

Dotto, C. (2025, February 28). Facebook enables gender discrimination in job ads, European human rights body rules | CNN Business. CNN. https://www.cnn.com/2025/02/28/tech/facebook-gender-discrimination-europe-ruling-asequals-intl

European Parliament. (2016). *General Data Protection Regulation (GDPR)*. Official Journal of the European Union.

European Union. (2018). General Data Protection Regulation (GDPR). https://gdpr-info.eu/

Fahim, Y. A., Hasani, I. W., Kabba, S., & Ragab, W. M. (2025). Artificial intelligence in healthcare and medicine: Clinical applications, therapeutic advances, and future perspectives. *European Journal of Medical Research, 30*(1), 848. DOI: 10.1186/s40001-025-03196-w

Floridi, L. (2016). *Information quality and the philosophy of information*. Springer.

Gitonga, C. K. (2025). Urgency of quantum-resistant algorithms and practical considerations for IoT. Compute: Journal of Advanced Computing Technologies?? 10.xxx/compute.146

Gomes, A. B., & Sultan, A. (2024). Problematizing content moderation by social media platforms and its impact on digital harm reduction. *Harm Reduction Journal, 21*(1), 194. DOI: 10.1186/s12954-024-01104-9

Hamza, A. T. (2025). Analysis of social media suppression of war crimes against palestine. DOI: 10.13140/RG.2.2.23401.81764

Hilal, A. M., Alzahrani, J. S., Abunadi, I., Nemri, N., Al-Wesabi, F. N., Motwakel, A., & Zamani, A. S. (2022). Intelligent deep learning model for privacy preserving IIoT on 6G environment. *Computers, Materials & Continua, 72*(1), 333.

Houssein, E. H., Gamal, A. M., Younis, E. M., & Mohamed, E. (2025). Explainable artificial intelligence for medical imaging systems using deep learning: A comprehensive review. *Cluster Computing*, *28*(7), 469.

Idahor, C. O., Esomu, E.-J. O., Ogbonna, N., Momoh, Z., Ogbeide, O. A., Ikhu-Omoregbe, O., Adigwe, A., Erhabor, O. M., Osaghae, O., & Orons, N. (2025). Infectious disease surveillance in the era of big data and ai: Opportunities and pitfalls. *Cureus*. Advance online publication. DOI: 10.7759/cureus.93929

Israel, D. (2023, April 18). Assessing the effectiveness of cross-border data flow regulations in the age of artificial intelligence (AI). *SSRN*. DOI: 10.2139/ssrn.4448648

Jelassi, T. (2024). Towards an internet of trust Unesco's guidelines for the governance of digital platforms. In Prastacos, G., & Pouloudi, N. (Eds.), *Leading and Managing in the Digital Era* (Vol. 69, pp. 3–12). Springer Nature Switzerland., DOI: 10.1007/978-3-031-65782-5_1

Jethava, G., & Rao, U. P. (2025). A Comprehensive Review of Privacy Challenges and Anonymization Strategies in Online Social Networks. *Discover Computing*, *28*, 336.

Jio, A. (2025) China ai strategy: Policy, regulation & global impact in 2025. Ashley Dudarenok. https://ashleydudarenok.com/china-ai-strategy/

Kaabachi, B., Despraz, J., Meurers, T., Otte, K., Halilovic, M., Kulynych, B., Prasser, F., & Raisaro, J. L. (2025). A Scoping Review of Privacy and Utility Metrics in Medical Synthetic Data. npj. *Digital Medicine*, *8*, 60.

Katiyar, P. (2025, September 23). Big tech is coming for your health data. Here's how to protect your information. Rewire News Group. https://rewirenewsgroup.com/2025/09/23/white-house-health-data-big-tech/

Kaur, R.. (2025). A survey on privacy preservation techniques in IoT systems. *Preprints*.org. DOI: 10.20944/preprints202503.0979.v1

Khalil, M. K., Al Amri, A. A. S., Al Balushi, M. K., Al Qassabi, S., & Rao, N. V. (2023, May 31). Data Privacy and Security Challenges in Big Data Analytics: A Review of Current Solutions and Future Directions. Journal for Student Research. https://www.jsr.org/index.php/path/article/view/2260/1372

Khan, R., Rehman, M. H., Zangoti, H. M., & Afzal, M. K. (2021). Digital twin: Recent advances, security challenges, and industrial applications. *IEEE Access : Practical Innovations, Open Solutions*, *9*, 157080–157112.

Knutsson, K. (2025, April 26). Blue Shield exposed 4.7M patients' health data to Google. Fox News. https://www.foxnews.com/tech/blue-shield-exposed-4-7m-patients-health-data-google-2

Lakshamanan, R. (2025). New hipaa rules mandate 72-hour data restoration and annual compliance audits. The Hacker News. Retrieved November 29, 2025, from https://thehackernews.com/2024/12/new-hipaa-rules-mandate-72-hour-data.html

Lopez, I. (2025). Assessing privacy risks in the White House's private health tracking system. Brookings. Retrieved November 28, 2025, from https://www.brookings.edu/articles/assessing-privacy-risks-in-the-white-houses-private-health-tracking-system/

Lyons, T., & Ward, P. (2024). Algorithmic transparency and accountability in social media platforms. *Social Media + Society*, *10*(1). Advance online publication. DOI: 10.1177/20563051241234567

Marr, B. (2021, July 2). What are the 4 Vs of Big Data? BernardMarr.com. https://bernardmarr.com/what-are-the-4-vs-of-big-data/

Maslej, N., Fattorini, L., Perrault, R., Gil, Y., Parli, V., Kariuki, N., Capstick, E., Reuel, A., Brynjolfsson, E., Etchemendy, J., Ligett, K., Lyons, T., Manyika, J., Niebles, J. C., Shoham, Y., Wald, R., Walsh, T., Hamrah, A., Santarlasci, L., . . . Oak, S. (2025). Artificial intelligence index report 2025 (No. arXiv:2504.07139). arXiv. /arXiv.2504.07139DOI: 10.48550

McCarthy, S., Rowan, W., Mahony, C., & Vergne, A. (2023). The dark side of digitalization and social media platform governance: A citizen engagement study. *Internet Research*, *33*(6), 2172–2204. DOI: 10.1108/INTR-03-2022-0142

Mennella, C., Maniscalco, U., De Pietro, G., & Esposito, M. (2024). Ethical and regulatory challenges of AI technologies in healthcare: A narrative review. *Heliyon*, *10*(4), e26297. DOI: 10.1016/j.heliyon.2024.e26297

Mossie, Z., & Wang, J.-H. (2020). Vulnerable community identification using hate speech detection on social media. *Information Processing & Management*, *57*(3), 102087. DOI: 10.1016/j.ipm.2019.102087

Obayya, M., Nemri, N., Nour, M. K., Al Duhayyim, M., Mohsen, H., Rizwanullah, M., & Motwakel, A. (2022). Explainable artificial intelligence enabled TeleOphthalmology for diabetic retinopathy grading and classification. *Applied Sciences (Basel, Switzerland)*, *12*(17), 8749.

Olsen, E. (2025). Data breach at healthcare services firm Episource affects 5.4M. Cybersecurity Dive. Retrieved November 28, 2025, from https://www.healthcaredive.com/news/episource-healthcare-data-breach-impacts-5-4-million/751103/

Omar, M., Soffer, S., Agbareia, R., Bragazzi, N. L., Apakama, D. U., Horowitz, C. R., Charney, A. W., Freeman, R., Kummer, B., Glicksberg, B. S., Nadkarni, G. N., & Klang, E. (2025). Sociodemographic biases in medical decision making by large language models. *Nature Medicine*, *31*(6), 1873–1881. DOI: 10.1038/s41591-025-03626-6

Paracha, A., Arshad, J., & Farah, M.. (2024). Machine Learning Security and Privacy: A Review of Threats and Countermeasures. *EURASIP Journal on Information Security*, *2024*, 10.

Pathak, M., Mishra, K. N., & Singh, S. P. (2024). Securing data and preserving privacy in cloud IoT-based technologies an analysis of assessing threats and developing effective safeguard. *Artificial Intelligence Review*, *57*, 269. DOI: 10.1007/s10462-024-10908-x

Pavlidou, V., Otterbacher, J., & Kleanthous, S. (2022). User perception of algorithmic digital marketing in conditions of scarcity. In Themistocleous, M., & Papadaki, M. (Eds.), *Information Systems* (Vol. 437, pp. 319–332). Springer International Publishing., DOI: 10.1007/978-3-030-95947-0_22

Pizzi, G., Caputo, A., & Corvino, A. (2023). Responsible artificial intelligence governance: A review and research framework. *The Journal of Strategic Information Systems*, *34*(2), 101779. DOI: 10.1016/j.jsis.2024.101779

Rodriguez, C. A., Gopalakrishnan, L., Del Cid, M., Folk, J. B., Yonek, J., & Tolou-Shams, M. (2021). The ethical implications of using social media to engage and retain justice-involved youth in behavioral health research. *Journal of Empirical Research on Human Research Ethics; JERHRE*, *16*(4), 356–363. DOI: 10.1177/15562646211039701

Sadhu, P. K., Yanambaka, V. P., & Abdelgawad, A. (2022). Internet of things: Security and solutions survey. *Sensors (Basel)*, *22*(19), 7433. DOI: 10.3390/s22197433

Santos, A., Cazzamatta, R., & Napolitano, C. J. (2025). Holding platforms accountable in the fight against misinformation: A cross-national analysis of state-established content moderation regulations. *The International Communication Gazette*, *87*(8), 729–750. DOI: 10.1177/17480485251348550

Savin, A., & Nielsen, M. F. (2025). The data-driven home: Towards a more coherent regulatory framework for smart homes in the European Union. *Information & Communications Technology Law*, •••, 1–21. DOI: 10.1080/13600834.2025.2572918

Schissler, M. (2025). Beyond hate speech and misinformation: Facebook and the rohingya genocide in myanmar. *Journal of Genocide Research, 27*(3), 445–470. DOI: 10.1080/14623528.2024.2375122

Schneble, C. O., Elger, B. S., & Shaw, D. (2018). The Cambridge Analytica affair and Internet-mediated research. *EMBO Reports, 19*(8), e46579. DOI: 10.15252/embr.201846579

Shaffique, M. R. (2024). Cyber Resilience Act 2022: A silver bullet for cybersecurity of IoT devices or a shot in the dark? *Computer Law & Security Review, 54*, 106009. DOI: 10.1016/j.clsr.2024.106009

Shetty, D. K., Vijaya Arjunan, R., Cenitta, D., Makkithaya, K., Hegde, N. V., & Bhatta, B, S. R., Salu, S., Aishwarya, T. R., Bhat, P., & Pullela, P. K. (2025). Analyzing AI regulation through literature and current trends. *Journal of Open Innovation, 11*(1), 100508. DOI: 10.1016/j.joitmc.2025.100508

Simchon, A., Edwards, M., & Lewandowsky, S. (2024). The persuasive effects of political microtargeting in the age of generative artificial intelligence. *PNAS Nexus, 3*(2), pgae035. Advance online publication. DOI: 10.1093/pnasnexus/pgae035

Sondeck, L. P., & Laurent, M. (2025). Practical and ready-to-use methodology to assess the re-identification risk in anonymized datasets. *Scientific Reports, 15*, 23223. Advance online publication. DOI: 10.1038/s41598-025-04907-3

Sonicki, Z. (2024). Large multi-modal models – the present or future of artificial intelligence in medicine? *Croatian Medical Journal, 65*(1), 1–2. DOI: 10.3325/cmj.2024.65.1

Stevens, J., Ghapanchi, A. H., Purarjomandlangrudi, A., & Bruce, S. (2025). Patient experiences of remote patient monitoring: Implications for health literacy and therapeutic relationships. *Technologies, 13*(10), 464. DOI: 10.3390/technologies13100464

Stokes, L. (2025). Ana position statement: The ethical use of artificial intelligence in nursing practice. *OJIN: The Online Journal of Issues in Nursing, 30*(2). Advance online publication. DOI: 10.3912/OJIN.Vol30No02PoSCol03

Taha, K. (2025). Big Data Analytics in IoT, Social Media, NLP, and Information Security: Trends, Challenges, and Applications. *Journal of Big Data, 12*, 150.

Thompson, J. A., Hersch, D., Kasozi, R. N., Miner, M. H., & Adam, P. (2024). Disparities in offering enrollment in remote patient monitoring for covid-19. *Telemedicine Journal and e-Health, 30*(3), 715–721. DOI: 10.1089/tmj.2023.0150

UNESCO. (2021). Recommendation on the Ethics of Artificial Intelligence. https://unesdoc.unesco.org/ark:/48223/pf0000380455

Usman, Y., Ihejirika, C. J., Offor, S. N., Akl, R., & Chataut, R. (2025). Green cybersecurity: Leveraging ai, ml, and llms to optimize energy, threat detection, and sustainability frameworks. *IEEE Access : Practical Innovations, Open Solutions, 13*, 159345–159379. DOI: 10.1109/ACCESS.2025.3602451

van de Poel, I. (2025). *Responsible AI, ethics, and the AI lifecycle: How to consider the human influence? AI and Ethics*. Springer., DOI: 10.1007/s43681-025-00666-z

Viswanathan, H. (2025, October 31). YNHHS reaches preliminary $18 million settlement over data breach. Yale Daily News. https://yaledailynews.com/blog/2025/10/31/ynhhs-reaches-preliminary-18-million-settlement-over-data-breach/

Zamani, A. (2022). Artificial Intelligence - The New. *Machine Learning*.

Zamani, A. S., Hashim, A. H. A., Shatat, A. S. A., Akhtar, M. M., Rizwanullah, M., & Mohamed, S. S. I. (2024). Implementation of machine learning techniques with big data and IoT to create effective prediction models for health informatics. *Biomedical Signal Processing and Control, 94*, 106247.

Zhan, L., Dang, X., Xie, Z., Zeng, C., Wu, W., Zhang, X., Zhang, L., & Cai, X. (2025). Evaluating GPT-4o in infectious disease diagnostics and management: A comparative study with residents and specialists on accuracy, completeness, and clinical support potential. *Digital Health, 11*. Advance online publication. DOI: 10.1177/20552076251355797

Zhang, Y., Gong, Y., Shi, M., & Yang, X. (2026). Privacy risk of transportation location-Based data: Re-identification and de-anonymization. *Transportation Research Part C, Emerging Technologies, 183*, 105495.

Zhao, I. Y., Ma, Y. X., Yu, M. W. C., Liu, J., Dong, W. N., Pang, Q., Lu, X. Q., Molassiotis, A., Holroyd, E., & Wong, C. W. W. (2021). Ethics, integrity, and retributions of digital detection surveillance systems for infectious diseases: Systematic literature review. *Journal of Medical Internet Research, 23*(10), e32328. DOI: 10.2196/32328

Compilation of References

Abbas, N., Zhang, Y., Taherkordi, A., & Skeie, T. (2018). Mobile edge computing: A survey. *IEEE Internet of Things Journal*, *5*(1), 450–465. DOI: 10.1109/JIOT.2017.2750180

Abbood, M. M. (2025). Investigation of IoT and deep learning techniques integration for smart city applications. *American Journal of Computing and Engineering*, *8*(1), 57–68.

Abdel-Basset, M., Hawash, H., Elhoseny, M., & Chakrabortty, R. K. (2020). Federated learning for cybersecurity in IoT: Concepts, challenges, and future directions. IEEE Internet of Things Journal, 8(12), 9878–9895. .DOI: 10.1109/JIOT.2020.3039999

Abdul, A., Vermeulen, J., Wang, D., Lim, B. Y., & Kankanhalli, M. (2020). Trends and trajectories for explainable, accountable and intelligible systems: An HCI research agenda. *Proceedings of the 2020 CHI Conference on Human Factors in Computing Systems*, 1–14. .DOI: 10.1145/3313831.3376329

Abreha, H. G., Hayajneh, M., & Serhani, M. A. (2022). Federated learning in edge computing: A systematic survey. *Sensors (Basel)*, *22*(2), 450. DOI: 10.3390/s22020450 PMID: 35062410

Ademola, A., George, C., & Mapp, G. (2024). Addressing the interoperability of electronic health records: The technical and semantic interoperability, preserving privacy and security framework. *Applied System Innovation*, *7*(6), 116. DOI: 10.3390/asi7060116

Ahmed, S. F., Sharmin, S., Kuldeep, S. A., Lameesa, A., & Alam, Md. S. B., Liu, G., & Gandomi, A. H. (2025). Transformative impacts of the internet of medical things on modern healthcare. *Results in Engineering*, *25*, 103787. DOI: 10.1016/j.rineng.2024.103787

Al Duhayyim, M., Alshahrani, H. M., Al-Wesabi, F. N., Al-Hagery, M. A., Hilal, A. M., & Zaman, A. S. (2022). Intelligent machine learning based EEG signal classification model. *Computers, Materials & Continua*, *71*(1), 1821.

Alabdulkreem, E., Alotaibi, S. S., Alamgeer, M., Marzouk, R., Hilal, A. M., Motwakel, A., & Rizwanullah, M. (2023). Intelligent Cybersecurity Classification Using Chaos Game Optimization with Deep Learning Model. *Computer Systems Science and Engineering*, *45*(1), 971–983.

Alajlan, N. N., & Ibrahim, D. M. (2025). Deep smart cities: A review of smart cities applications-based an inference of deep learning upon iot devices. *population, 5*, 6.

Alajlan, N. N., & Ibrahim, D. M. (2025). Deep smart cities: A review of smart cities applications-based an inference of deep learning upon IoT devices. *Journal of Advanced Research in Applied Sciences and Engineering Technology*, *47*(2), 94–120.

Alanazi, A. (2025). The potential, applications, and challenges of internet of things (Iot) technologies from the perspectives of clinicians. *Cureus*. Advance online publication. DOI: 10.7759/cureus.85847

Aledhari, M., Razzak, R., Parizi, R. M., & Zhang, Q. (2020). Federated learning: A survey on enabling technologies, protocols, and applications. IEEE Access, 8, 140699–140725. .DOI: 10.1109/ACCESS.2020.3013541

Al-Fuqaha, A., Guizani, M., Mohammadi, M., Aledhari, M., & Ayyash, M. (2015). Internet of things: A survey on enabling technologies, protocols, and applications. *IEEE Communications Surveys and Tutorials*, *17*(4), 2347–2376.

Al-Fuqaha, A., Guizani, M., Mohammadi, M., Aledhari, M., & Ayyash, M. (2015). Internet of Things: A survey on enabling technologies, protocols, and applications. *IEEE Communications Surveys and Tutorials*, *17*(4), 2347–2376. DOI: 10.1109/COMST.2015.2444095

Al-Garadi, M. A., Mohamed, A., Al-Ali, A. K., Du, X., Ali, I., & Guizani, M. (2020). A survey of machine and deep learning methods for internet of things (IoT) security. *IEEE Communications Surveys and Tutorials*, *22*(3), 1646–1685.

Ali, S., et al. (2023). Explainable Artificial Intelligence (XAI): What we know and what we need to know. (survey)

Ali, M. S., Vecchio, M., & Antonelli, F. (2021). A blockchain-based framework for IoT data monetization services. *The Computer Journal*, *64*(2), 195–210. DOI: 10.1093/comjnl/bxaa119

Ali, S. I., Jadhav, J., Arunkumar, R., & Kanagavalli, N. (2022). A smart resource utilization algorithm for high speed 5G communication networks based on cloud servers. *ICTACT Journal on Communication Technology*, *13*(4), 2800–2804.

Ali, S. I., Ravuri, H. K., Lakshmi, V. T., Ramya, A., Lavanya, K., & Bahade, S. (2024). The role of nanomaterials in the development of high-performance batteries. *Nanotechnology Perceptions*, *20*(S11), 1125–1140. https://www.nano-ntp.com

AlNusif, M. (2025). Explainable AI in edge devices: A lightweight framework for real-time decision transparency. *International Journal of Engineering and Computer Science*, *14*(07), 27447–27472. DOI: 10.18535/ijecs.v14i07.5181

Alwakeel, A. M. (2021). An overview of fog computing and edge computing security and privacy issues. *Sensors (Basel)*, *21*(24), 8226. PMID: 34960320

Alwarafy, A., Al-Thelaya, K. A., Abdallah, M., Schneider, J., & Hamdi, M. (2020). A survey on security and privacy issues in edge-computing-assisted internet of things. *IEEE Internet of Things Journal*, *8*(6), 4004–4022.

Amin, M. A. S., Kim, S., Amin Rishat, M. A., Tang, Z., & Ahn, H. (2024). A Systematic Literature Review of Privacy Information Disclosure in AI-Integrated Internet of Things (IoT) Technologies. *Sustainability*, *17*(1), 8.

Angelucci, A., Greco, M., Cecconi, M., & Aliverti, A. (2025). Wearable devices for patient monitoring in the intensive care unit. *Intensive Care Medicine Experimental*, *13*(1), 26. DOI: 10.1186/s40635-025-00738-8

Antonakakis, M.. (2017). Understanding the Mirai botnet. *USENIX Security Symposium*, 1093–1110.

Aouedi, O., Vu, T. H., Sacco, A., Nguyen, D. C., Piamrat, K., Marchetto, G., & Pham, Q. V. (2024). A survey on intelligent Internet of Things: Applications, security, privacy, and future directions. *IEEE Communications Surveys and Tutorials*.

Atzori, L., Iera, A., & Morabito, G. (2017). Understanding the Internet of Things: Definition, potentials, and societal role of a fast-evolving paradigm. *Ad Hoc Networks*, *56*, 122–140.

Awaisi, K. S., Ye, Q., & Sampalli, S. (2024). A survey of industrial AIoT: Opportunities, challenges, and directions. *IEEE Access : Practical Innovations, Open Solutions*.

Azeroual, O., Fabre, R., & Nacheva, R. (2025). Modeling and Visualizing Human Experience in a Knowledge Graph: Understanding and Predicting Emotional Reactions to Life Events. In *Proceedings of the 2025 14th International Conference on Software and Computer Applications (ICSCA '25)*. Association for Computing Machinery, New York, NY, USA, 204–213.

Bagdasaryan, E., Veit, A., Hua, Y., Estrin, D., & Shmatikov, V. (2020, June). How to backdoor federated learning. In *International conference on artificial intelligence and statistics* (pp. 2938-2948). PMLR.

Bakhtiarnia, A., Milošević, N., Zhang, Q., Bajović, D., & Iosifidis, A. (2022). Dynamic split computing for efficient deep edge intelligence [Preprint]. arXiv. https://arxiv.org/abs/2205.11269

Balendra, S. (2025). Meta's AI moderation and free speech: Ongoing challenges in the Global South. Cambridge Forum on AI: Law and Governance, 1, e21. doi:DOI: 10.1017/cfl.2025.5

Banitalebi-Dehkordi, A., Vedula, A., Pei, J., Xia, L., Wang, J., & Zhang, H. (2021). *Auto-Split: A general framework of collaborative edge-cloud AI.* In *Proceedings of the 27th ACM SIGKDD Conference on Knowledge Discovery & Data Mining (KDD '21).* https://doi.org/DOI: 10.1145/3447548.3467078

Bansal, M., Chana, I., & Clarke, S. (2020). A survey on iot big data: Current status, 13 v's challenges, and future directions. *ACM Computing Surveys, 53*(6), 1–59.

Batool, A., Zowghi, D., & Bano, M. (2025). *AI governance: A systematic literature review. AI and Ethics.* Springer., DOI: 10.1007/s43681-024-00653-w

Baum, K., Abramova, O., Meißner, S., & Krasnova, H. (2023). The effects of targeted political advertising on user privacy concerns and digital product acceptance: A preference-based approach. *Electronic Markets, 33*(1), 46. DOI: 10.1007/s12525-023-00656-1

Bibri, S. E., Alexandre, A., & Sharifi, A.. (2023). Environmentally sustainable smart cities and their converging AI, IoT, and big data technologies and solutions: An integrated approach to an extensive literature review. *Energy Informatics.* PMID: 37032812

Bifulco, G. N., Pariota, L., Brancati, R., & Fusco, G. (2016). Collecting traffic data through floating car data: Potentials, issues and applications. *Procedia Engineering, 134*, 36–45.

Bimalendu Patra, B., Saha, S., Bhattacharyya, P., & Adhikary, S. (2025). Sdgs and the future of governance: Legal, managerial and technological approaches. In Integrated Publications (pp. 01–350). Integrated Publications. DOI: 10.62778/int.book.602

Biswas, A. R., Dupont, C., & Pham, C. (2022). IoT, Cloud and BigData Integration for IoT Analytics. In Building Blocks for IoT Analytics (pp. 11-37). Routledge. DOI: 10.1201/9781003337423-3

Boddu, Y. (2025). AI agents for real-time operational decision making: Embedding intelligence in data pipelines. *Journal of Computer Science and Technology Studies*, *7*(5), 867–872. DOI: 10.32996/jcsts.2025.7.5.99

Bonawitz, K., Eichner, H., Grieskamp, W., Huba, D., Ingerman, A., Ivanov, V., Kiddon, C., Konečný, J., Mazzocchi, S., McMahan, H. B., Overveldt, T. V., Petrou, D., Rambhatla, S., & Zhu, M. (2019). Towards federated learning at scale: System design. Proceedings of Machine Learning and Systems, 1, 374–388.

Bonawitz, K., Ivanov, V., Kreuter, B., Marcedone, A., McMahan, H. B., Patel, S., & Seth, K. (2017). Practical secure aggregation for privacy-preserving machine learning. In *Proceedings of the 2017 ACM SIGSAC Conference on Computer and Communications Security* (pp. 1175–1191). https://doi.org/DOI: 10.1145/3133956.3133982

Bonomi, F., Milito, R., Zhu, J., & Addepalli, S. (2012). Fog computing and its role in the Internet of Things. In *Proceedings of the 1st ACM Workshop on Mobile Cloud Computing (MCC '12).*

Bonomi, F., Milito, R., Zhu, J., & Addepalli, S. (2012). Fog computing and its role in the internet of things. *Proceedings of the First Edition of the MCC Workshop on Mobile Cloud Computing*, 13–16. .DOI: 10.1145/2342509.2342513

Bordes, A., Usunier, N., Garcia-Duran, A., Weston, J., & Yakhnenko, O. (2013). Translating embeddings for modeling multi-relational data. *Advances in Neural Information Processing Systems*, •••, 26.

Borkar, S. R., & De, A. (2025). Artificial intelligence in internal medicine: A study on reducing diagnostic errors and enhancing efficiency. *The European Journal of Cardiovascular Medicine*, *15*, 105–111. DOI: 10.61336/ejcm/25-09-19

Bureau, T. H. (2024, March 25). Misinformation during Indian elections: The saga from 2019 to 2024. The Hindu. https://www.thehindu.com/news/national/misinformation-during-indian-elections-the-saga-from-2019-to-2024/article67989996.ece

Butor-Keler, A., & Polasik, M. (2020). The role of regulatory sandboxes in the development of innovations on the financial services market: The case of the United Kingdom. *Ekonomia i Prawo. Economics and Law*, *19*(4), 621–638.

Caldas, F. A. A., Caldas, H. C., Henrique, T., Jordão, P. H. F., Fernandes-Ferreira, R., Souza, D. R. S., & Bauab, S. D. P. (2025). Evaluating the performance of artificial intelligence and radiologists accuracy in breast cancer detection in screening mammography across breast densities. *European Journal of Radiology Artificial Intelligence*, *2*, 100013. DOI: 10.1016/j.ejrai.2025.100013

Carbone, A.. (2015). Apache Flink: Stream and batch processing in a single engine. *A Quarterly Bulletin of the Computer Society of the IEEE Technical Committee on Data Engineering*.

Celik, A., & Eltawil, A. M. (2022). The internet of bodies: The human body as an efficient and secure wireless channel. *IEEE Internet of Things Magazine*, *5*(3), 114–120. DOI: 10.1109/IOTM.001.2100209

Chaganti, K. (2024). Adversarial Attacks on AI-driven Cybersecurity Systems: A Taxonomy and Defense Strategies. *Authorea Preprints*.

Chen, F., Wang, Y. C., Wang, B., & Kuo, C. C. J. (2020). Graph representation learning: A survey. *APSIPA Transactions on Signal and Information Processing*, *9*, e15.

Cheng, L., Gu, Y., Liu, Q., Yang, L., Liu, C., & Wang, Y. (2024). Advancements in accelerating deep neural network inference on AIoT devices: A survey. *IEEE Transactions on Sustainable Computing*, *9*(6), 830–847.

Cheng, Y. W., & Bilal, A. (2025). Regulatory data privacy concerns in proliferating IoT era of telecommunication data monetisation: A systematic literature review. *Computing*, *107*(9), 190. DOI: 10.1007/s00607-025-01542-8

Chen, M., Challita, U., Saad, W., Yin, C., & Debbah, M. (2019). Artificial neural networks-based machine learning for wireless networks: A tutorial. *IEEE Communications Surveys and Tutorials*, *21*(4), 3039–3071.

Chen, M., Hao, Y., Cai, Y., & Li, Y. (2018). Edge computing based smart healthcare system: Trends, challenges and opportunities. *IEEE Access : Practical Innovations, Open Solutions*, *6*, 36636–36645. DOI: 10.1109/ACCESS.2018.2853140

Chiang, M., & Zhang, T. (2016). Fog and IoT: An overview of research opportunities. *IEEE Internet of Things Journal*, *3*(6), 854–864. DOI: 10.1109/JIOT.2016.2584538

Chougule, S. B., Chaudhari, B. S., Ghorpade, S. N., & Zennaro, M. (2024). Exploring computing paradigms for electric vehicles: From cloud to edge intelligence, challenges and future directions. *World Electric Vehicle Journal*, *15*(2), 39.

Conti, M., Dehghantanha, A., Franke, K., & Watson, S. (2018). Internet of Things security and forensics: Challenges and opportunities. *Future Generation Computer Systems*, *78*, 544–546.

Dakhia, Z., Russo, M., & Merenda, M. (2025). AI-Enabled IoT for Food Computing: Challenges, Opportunities, and Future Directions. *Sensors (Basel)*, *25*(7), 2147. PMID: 40218659

Dakshinamurthi, V., Ali, S. I., Karthikeyan, T., & Kulkarni, N. S. (2023). *Causal convolution employing Almeida–Pineda recurrent backpropagation for mobile network design*. ICTACT Journal on Communication Technology, 14(4).

Das, J. (2024). IoT-enabled smart city governance using AI-based data analytics. *Metaversalize*, *1*(1), 1–15. DOI: 10.22105/metaverse.v1i2.54

Dastjerdi, A. V., & Buyya, R. (2016). Fog computing: Principles, architectures, and applications. In Buyya, R., & Dastjerdi, A. V. (Eds.), *Internet of Things: Principles and paradigms*.

De Barros, E. C. (2024). Understanding the influence of digital technology on human cognitive functions: A narrative review. *IBRO Neuroscience Reports*, *17*, 415–422. DOI: 10.1016/j.ibneur.2024.11.006

De Blasio, E., & Selva, D. (2021). Who is responsible for disinformation? European approaches to social platforms' accountability in the post-truth era. *The American Behavioral Scientist*, *65*(6), 825–846. DOI: 10.1177/0002764221989784

Deng, S., Zhao, H., Fang, W., Yin, J., Dustdar, S., & Zomaya, A. Y. (2020). Edge intelligence: The confluence of edge computing and artificial intelligence. *IEEE Internet of Things Journal*, *7*(8), 7457–7469.

Depuru, S. S. S. R., Wang, L., & Devabhaktuni, V. (2011). Smart meters for power grid: Challenges, issues, advantages and status. *Renewable & Sustainable Energy Reviews*, *15*(6), 2736–2742. DOI: 10.1016/j.rser.2011.02.039

Dhanda, S. S., Singh, B., & Jindal, P. (2020). Lightweight cryptography: A solution to secure IoT. *Wireless Personal Communications*, *112*(3), 1947–1980.

Dhirani, L. L., Armstrong, E., & Newe, T. (2021). Industrial IoT, cyber threats, and standards landscape: Evaluation and roadmap. *Sensors (Basel)*, *21*(11), 3901. PMID: 34198727

Donelle, L., Comer, L., Hiebert, B., Hall, J., Shelley, J. J., Smith, M. J., Kothari, A., Burkell, J., Stranges, S., Cooke, T., Shelley, J. M., Gilliland, J., Ngole, M., & Facca, D. (2023). Use of digital technologies for public health surveillance during the COVID-19 pandemic: A scoping review. *Digital Health, 9*. Advance online publication. DOI: 10.1177/20552076231173220

Doshi-Velez, F., & Kim, B. (2017). Towards a rigorous science of interpretable machine learning. *arXiv preprint arXiv:1702.08608.*

Dotto, C. (2025, February 28). Facebook enables gender discrimination in job ads, European human rights body rules | CNN Business. CNN. https://www.cnn.com/2025/02/28/tech/facebook-gender-discrimination-europe-ruling-asequals-intl

Duhayyim, M. A., Elfadil Eisa, T. A., Al-Wesabi, F. N., Abdelmaboud, A., Hamza, M. A., Zamani, A. S., & Marzouk, R. (2022). Deep reinforcement learning enabled smart city recycling waste object classification. *Computers, Materials & Continua, 71*(3).

El Ghati, O., Alaoui-Fdili, O., Chahbouni, O., Alioua, N., & Bouarifi, W. (2024). Artificial intelligence-powered visual internet of things in smart cities: A comprehensive review. *Sustainable Computing : Informatics and Systems, 43*, 101004.

Elmobark, N., & Elhishi, S. (2025a). BlueEdge: Application design for big data cleaning processing using mobile edge computing environments. *Journal of Big Data, 12*(1), 1–39. DOI: 10.1186/s40537-025-01262-y

Elmobark, N., & Elhishi, S. (2025b). BlueEdge neural network approach and its application to automated data type classification in mobile edge computing. *Scientific Reports, 15*(1), 43823. Advance online publication. DOI: 10.1038/s41598-025-30445-z PMID: 41387763

European Parliament. (2016). *General Data Protection Regulation (GDPR).* Official Journal of the European Union.

European Union. (2018). General Data Protection Regulation (GDPR). https://gdpr-info.eu/

Fahim, Y. A., Hasani, I. W., Kabba, S., & Ragab, W. M. (2025). Artificial intelligence in healthcare and medicine: Clinical applications, therapeutic advances, and future perspectives. *European Journal of Medical Research, 30*(1), 848. DOI: 10.1186/s40001-025-03196-w

Fan, G., Sabri, A. Q. M., & Rahman, S. S. A. (2025). Emerging trends in graph neural networks for traffic flow prediction: A survey. *Archives of Computational Methods in Engineering*. Advance online publication. DOI: 10.1007/s11831-025-10286-9

Fathima, S. A. (2025). IoT and Big Data Ecosystems: A Review of Technologies, Use Cases, and Research Trends. International Journal of AI, Big Data, Computational and Management Studies, 6(1), 10-21. ijaibdcms.orgDOI: <ALIGNMENT.qj></ALIGNMENT>10.63282/3050-9416.IJAIBDCMS-V6I1P102

Ficili, I., Giacobbe, M., Tricomi, G., & Puliafito, A. (2025). From sensors to data intelligence: Leveraging IoT, cloud, and edge computing with AI. *Sensors*, *25*(6), Article 1763.

Ficili, I., Giacobbe, M., Tricomi, G., & Puliafito, A. (2025). From sensors to data intelligence: Leveraging IoT, cloud, and edge computing with AI. *Sensors (Basel)*, *25*(6), 1763. DOI: 10.3390/s25061763 PMID: 40292910

Floridi, L. (2016). *Information quality and the philosophy of information*. Springer.

Fouda, M. M., Fadlullah, Z. M., Ibrahem, M. I., & Kato, N. (2024). Privacy-preserving data-driven learning models for emerging communication networks: A comprehensive survey. *IEEE Communications Surveys and Tutorials*.

Frankle, J., & Carbin, M. (2019). The lottery ticket hypothesis: Finding sparse, trainable neural networks. *arXiv preprint arXiv:1803.03635*.

Frontiers in Big Data Editorial Office. (2023). From descriptive analytics to predictive and prescriptive intelligence: The role of AI in real-time decision-making. *Frontiers in Big Data*, *6*, 1178432. Advance online publication. DOI: 10.3389/fdata.2023.1178432

Gao, Y., Zhang, C., & Han, G. (2021). Federated edge learning for intelligent IoT: Recent advances and future challenges. *IEEE Network*, *35*(5), 188–195. DOI: 10.1109/MNET.011.2000637

Ghadi, Y. Y., Mazhar, T., & Faisal, S. (2023). Integration of federated learning with IoT for smart cities: Applications, challenges and solutions. *PeerJ. Computer Science*. PMID: 38192447

Gharavi, H., Granjal, J., & Monteiro, E. (2024). Post-quantum blockchain security for the Internet of Things: Survey and research directions. *IEEE Communications Surveys and Tutorials*, *26*(3), 1748–1774.

Gill, S. S., Golec, M., Hu, J., Xu, M., Du, J., Wu, H., & Uhlig, S. (2025). Edge AI: A taxonomy, systematic review and future directions. *Cluster Computing*, *28*(1), 18.

Gitonga, C. K. (2025). Urgency of quantum-resistant algorithms and practical considerations for IoT. Compute: Journal of Advanced Computing Technologies?? 10.xxx/compute.146

Godase, V. (2025). Edge AI for Smart Surveillance: Real-time Human Activity Recognition on Low-power Devices. *International Journal of AI and Machine Learning Innovations in Electronics and Communication Technology*, *1*(1), 29–46.

Gökbakan, Ü. B., Dümbgen, F., & Caron, S. (2025, May). A data-driven contact estimation method for wheeled-biped robots. In *2025 IEEE International Conference on Robotics and Automation (ICRA)* (pp. 7073-7079). IEEE.

Gomes, A. B., & Sultan, A. (2024). Problematizing content moderation by social media platforms and its impact on digital harm reduction. *Harm Reduction Journal*, *21*(1), 194. DOI: 10.1186/s12954-024-01104-9

Gouiza, N., Jebari, H., & Reklaoui, K. (2024). Integration of iot-enabled technologies and artificial intelligence in diverse domains: Recent advancements and future trends. *Journal of Theoretical and Applied Information Technology*, *102*(5), 1975–2029.

Gubbi, J., Buyya, R., Marusic, S., & Palaniswami, M. (2013). Internet of Things (IoT): A vision, architectural elements, and future directions. Future Generation Computer Systems, 29(7), 1645–1660. .DOI: 10.1016/j.future.2013.01.010

Gubbi, J., Buyya, R., Marusic, S., & Palaniswami, M. (2013). Internet of Things (IoT): A vision, architectural elements, and future directions. *Future Generation Computer Systems*, *29*(7), 1645–1660.

Habib, A. A., Hasan, M. K., Alkhayyat, A., Islam, S., Sharma, R., & Alkwai, L. M. (2023). False data injection attack in smart grid cyber physical system: Issues, challenges, and future direction. *Computers & Electrical Engineering*, *107*, 108638.

Hafeth, D. A., Al-Khafajiy, M., & Kollias, S. (2024). EdgeScan for IoT Contextual Understanding With Edge Computing and Image Captioning. *IEEE Internet of Things Journal*.

Hamza, A. T. (2025). Analysis of social media suppression of war crimes against palestine. DOI: 10.13140/RG.2.2.23401.81764

Han, S., Pool, J., Tran, J., & Dally, W. J. (2015). Learning both weights and connections for efficient neural networks. In Lee, D. D. (Eds.), Vol. 28, pp. 1135–1143). Advances in Neural Information Processing Systems. Curran Associates, Inc.

Han, X., Li, Z., Cao, H., & Hou, B. (2025). Multimodal spatio-temporal data visualization technologies for contemporary urban landscape architecture: A review and prospect in the context of smart cities. *Land (Basel)*, *14*(5), 1069. DOI: 10.3390/land14051069

Hao, Z., Jiang, H., Jiang, S., Ren, J., & Cao, T. (2024). Hybrid SLM and LLM for edge-cloud collaborative inference. In *Proceedings of the Workshop on Edge and Mobile Foundation Models & Workshop on Mobile Computing with Large Language Models (EdgeFM '24)* (pp. 36–41). ACM. https://doi.org/DOI: 10.1145/3662006.3662067

Hashem, I. A. T., Yaqoob, I., Anuar, N. B., Mokhtar, S., Gani, A., & Khan, S. U. (2015). The rise of "big data" on cloud computing: Review and open research issues. *Information Systems, 47*, 98–115. DOI: 10.1016/j.is.2014.07.006

Hemmati, A., Raoufi, P., & Rahmani, A. M. (2024). Edge artificial intelligence for big data: A systematic review. *Neural Computing & Applications*. Advance online publication. DOI: 10.1007/s00521-024-09723-w

He, Q., Lin, J., Fang, H., Wang, X., Huang, M., Yi, X., & Yu, K. (2025). Integrating [G: Applications of Edge Intelligence, Challenges, and Future Directions. *IEEE Transactions on Services Computing*.]. *IoT*, •••, 6.

Heydari, S., & Mahmoud, Q. H. (2025). Tiny machine learning and on-device inference: A survey of applications, challenges, and future directions. *Sensors (Basel), 25*(10), 3191. PMID: 40431982

Hilal, A. M., Alzahrani, J. S., Abunadi, I., Nemri, N., Al-Wesabi, F. N., Motwakel, A., & Zamani, A. S. (2022). Intelligent deep learning model for privacy preserving IIoT on 6G environment. *Computers, Materials & Continua, 72*(1), 333.

Hoenig, A., Roy, K., Acquaah, Y. T., Yi, S., & Desai, S. S. (2024). Explainable AI for cyber-physical systems: Issues and challenges. *IEEE Access : Practical Innovations, Open Solutions, 12*, 73113–73140.

Hogan, A., Blomqvist, E., Cochez, M., d'Amato, C., Melo, G. D., Gutierrez, C., & Zimmermann, A. (2021). Knowledge graphs. *ACM Computing Surveys, 54*(4), 1–37.

Houssein, E. H., Gamal, A. M., Younis, E. M., & Mohamed, E. (2025). Explainable artificial intelligence for medical imaging systems using deep learning: A comprehensive review. *Cluster Computing, 28*(7), 469.

Howard, A. G., Zhu, M., Chen, B., Kalenichenko, D., Wang, W., Weyand, T., . . . Adam, H. (2017). MobileNets: Efficient convolutional neural networks for mobile vision applications. *arXiv preprint arXiv:1704.04861.*

Howard, A., Sandler, M., Chu, G., Chen, L. C., Chen, B., Tan, M., & Le, Q. V. (2019). Searching for MobileNetV3. In *Proceedings of the IEEE/CVF International Conference on Computer Vision* (pp. 1314–1324). https://doi.org/DOI: 10.1109/ICCV.2019.00140

Hu, C., Bao, W., Wang, D., & Liu, F. (2019). Dynamic adaptive DNN surgery for inference acceleration on the edge. *Proceedings - IEEE INFOCOM, 2019*, 1423–1431. DOI: 10.1109/INFOCOM.2019.8737614

Hu, J., & Li, Y. (2021). Secure federated learning for privacy-preserving industrial IoT. *IEEE Transactions on Industrial Informatics, 17*(8), 5612–5621. DOI: 10.1109/TII.2020.3034224

Idahor, C. O., Esomu, E.-J. O., Ogbonna, N., Momoh, Z., Ogbeide, O. A., Ikhu-Omoregbe, O., Adigwe, A., Erhabor, O. M., Osaghae, O., & Orons, N. (2025). Infectious disease surveillance in the era of big data and ai: Opportunities and pitfalls. *Cureus*. Advance online publication. DOI: 10.7759/cureus.93929

International Data Corporation. (2024). *Worldwide edge computing and AI inference market forecast*. IDC.

Iqbal, R., Doctor, F., More, B., Mahmud, S., & Yousuf, U. (2020). Big Data analytics and Computational Intelligence for Cyber–Physical Systems: Recent trends and state of the art applications. *Future Generation Computer Systems, 105*, 766–778.

Israel, D. (2023, April 18). Assessing the effectiveness of cross-border data flow regulations in the age of artificial intelligence (AI). *SSRN*. DOI: 10.2139/ssrn.4448648

Jacob, B., Kligys, S., Chen, B., Zhu, M., Tang, M., Howard, A., & Kalenichenko, D. (2018). Quantization and training of neural networks for efficient integer-arithmetic-only inference. In *Proceedings of the IEEE Conference on Computer Vision and Pattern Recognition* (pp. 2704–2713). https://doi.org/DOI: 10.1109/CVPR.2018.00286

Jelassi, T. (2024). Towards an internet of trust Unesco's guidelines for the governance of digital platforms. In Prastacos, G., & Pouloudi, N. (Eds.), *Leading and Managing in the Digital Era* (Vol. 69, pp. 3–12). Springer Nature Switzerland., DOI: 10.1007/978-3-031-65782-5_1

Jensen, P. B., Jensen, L. J., & Brunak, S. (2012). Mining electronic health records: Towards better research applications and clinical care. *Nature Reviews. Genetics, 13*(6), 395–405. PMID: 22549152

Jethava, G., & Rao, U. P. (2025). A Comprehensive Review of Privacy Challenges and Anonymization Strategies in Online Social Networks. *Discover Computing, 28*, 336.

Jiang, Y., Konečný, J., & Zhang, T. (2020). Federated learning for edge devices: Concepts, challenges, and trends. *ACM Computing Surveys, 53*(3), 1–37. DOI: 10.1145/3394522

Jio, A. (2025) China ai strategy: Policy, regulation & global impact in 2025. Ashley Dudarenok. https://ashleydudarenok.com/china-ai-strategy/

Jouini, O., Sethom, K., Namoun, A., Aljohani, N., Alanazi, M. H., & Alanazi, M. N. (2024). A survey of machine learning in edge computing: Techniques, frameworks, applications, issues, and research directions. *Technologies*, *12*(6), 81.

Kaabachi, B., Despraz, J., Meurers, T., Otte, K., Halilovic, M., Kulynych, B., Prasser, F., & Raisaro, J. L. (2025). A Scoping Review of Privacy and Utility Metrics in Medical Synthetic Data. npj. *Digital Medicine*, *8*, 60.

Kairouz, P., McMahan, H. B., Avent, B., Bellet, A., Bennis, M., Bhagoji, A. N., ... & Zhao, S. (2021). Advances and open problems in federated learning. *Foundations and trends® in machine learning, 14*(1–2), 1-210.

Kairouz, P., McMahan, H. B., Avent, B., Bellet, A., Bennis, M., Bhagoji, A. N., & Zhao, S. (2021). Advances and open problems in federated learning. *Foundations and Trends in Machine Learning*, *14*(1–2), 1–210. https://arxiv.org/abs/1912.04977

Kapoor, D., Gupta, D., & Uppal, M. (2025). Analyzing the impact of edge, fog and cloud computing on predictive maintenance in the Industrial Internet of Things. *Discover Computing*, *28*(1), 207. Advance online publication. DOI: 10.1007/s10791-025-09653-8

Karunambiga, K., Ali, S., Esteban, A., & Pascual, M. (2023). Marketing policy in service enterprises using deep learning model. *International Journal of Intelligent Systems and Applications in Engineering*, *12*(7s), 239–243.

Katiyar, P. (2025, September 23). Big tech is coming for your health data. Here's how to protect your information. Rewire News Group. https://rewirenewsgroup.com/2025/09/23/white-house-health-data-big-tech/

Kaur, R.. (2025). A survey on privacy preservation techniques in IoT systems. *Preprints*.org. DOI: 10.20944/preprints202503.0979.v1

Khalil, M. K., Al Amri, A. A. S., Al Balushi, M. K., Al Qassabi, S., & Rao, N. V. (2023, May 31). Data Privacy and Security Challenges in Big Data Analytics: A Review of Current Solutions and Future Directions. Journal for Student Research. https://www.jsr.org/index.php/path/article/view/2260/1372

Khan, R., Rehman, M. H., Zangoti, H. M., & Afzal, M. K. (2021). Digital twin: Recent advances, security challenges, and industrial applications. *IEEE Access : Practical Innovations, Open Solutions*, *9*, 157080–157112.

Kiran, B. R. (2021). Deep reinforcement learning for autonomous driving: A survey. *IEEE Transactions on Neural Networks and Learning Systems*.

Knutsson, K. (2025, April 26). Blue Shield exposed 4.7M patients' health data to Google. Fox News. https://www.foxnews.com/tech/blue-shield-exposed-4-7m-patients-health-data-google-2

Konečný, J., McMahan, H. B., Yu, F. X., Richtárik, P., Suresh, A. T., & Bacon, D. (2016). Federated learning: Strategies for improving communication efficiency. arXiv preprint arXiv:1610.05492.

Lakshamanan, R. (2025). New hipaa rules mandate 72-hour data restoration and annual compliance audits. The Hacker News. Retrieved November 29, 2025, from https://thehackernews.com/2024/12/new-hipaa-rules-mandate-72-hour-data.html

Leme, R. D. S., de Souza Pinto, J., Zanon, L. G., Sigahi, T. F., Moraes, G. H. S. M. D., Moro, S. R., & Anholon, R. (2025). Information security management: a fuzzy DEMATEL analysis of the new ISO/IEC 27001: 2022 controls. *Information and Computer Security*.

Liang, F., Yu, W., An, D., Yang, Q., Fu, X., & Zhao, W. (2018). A survey on big data-driven security analytics for cyber-physical systems. IEEE Access, 6, 16297–16309. .DOI: 10.1109/ACCESS.2018.2819193

Liang, B., Wang, Y., & Tong, C. (2025). AI Reasoning in Deep Learning Era: From Symbolic AI to Neural–Symbolic AI. *Mathematics*, *13*(11), 1707.

Li, E., Zeng, L., Zhou, Z., & Chen, X. (2020). Edge AI: On-demand accelerating deep neural network inference via edge computing. *IEEE Transactions on Wireless Communications*, *19*(1), 447–457. DOI: 10.1109/TWC.2019.2946140

Lifelo, Z., Ding, J., Ning, H., & Dhelim, S. (2024). Artificial intelligence-enabled metaverse for sustainable smart cities: Technologies, applications, challenges, and future directions. *Electronics (Basel)*, *13*(24), 4874.

Lipton, Z. C. (2018). The mythos of model interpretability: In machine learning, the concept of interpretability is both important and slippery. *Queue*, *16*(3), 31–57.

Li, Q., Wen, Z., Wu, Z., Hu, S., Wang, N., Li, Y., & He, B. (2021). A survey on federated learning systems: Vision, hype and reality for data privacy and protection. *IEEE Transactions on Knowledge and Data Engineering*, *35*(4), 3347–3366.

Li, T., Sahu, A. K., Talwalkar, A., & Smith, V. (2020). Federated learning: Challenges, methods, and future directions. *IEEE Signal Processing Magazine*, *37*(3), 50–60. DOI: 10.1109/MSP.2020.2975749

Liu, Y., Wang, J., Yan, Z., Wan, Z., & Jäntti, R. (2023). A survey on blockchain-based trust management for Internet of Things. *IEEE Internet of Things Journal, 10*(7), 5898–5922.

Lopez, I. (2025). Assessing privacy risks in the White House's private health tracking system. Brookings. Retrieved November 28, 2025, from https://www.brookings.edu/articles/assessing-privacy-risks-in-the-white-houses-private-health-tracking-system/

Luckey, D., Fritz, H., Legatiuk, D., Dragos, K., & Smarsly, K. (2021). Artificial intelligence techniques for smart city applications. In E. Toledo Santos & S. Scheer (Eds.), *Proceedings of the 18th International Conference on Computing in Civil and Building Engineering (ICCCBE 2020)* (Lecture Notes in Civil Engineering, Vol. 98). Springer. DOI: 10.1007/978-3-030-51295-8_1

Lyons, T., & Ward, P. (2024). Algorithmic transparency and accountability in social media platforms. *Social Media + Society, 10*(1). Advance online publication. DOI: 10.1177/20563051241234567

Lyu, L., Yu, H., Yang, Q., & Li, B. (2020). Privacy-preserving collaborative learning for healthcare: Challenges and opportunities. *IEEE Intelligent Systems, 35*(4), 40–49. DOI: 10.1109/MIS.2020.2994093

Maduranga, M. W. P., Tilwari, V., Rathnayake, R. M. M. R., & Sandamini, C. (2024, August). AI-enabled 6G internet of things: Opportunities, key technologies, challenges, and future directions. In *Telecom* (Vol. 5, No. 3, pp. 804-822). MDPI.

Mahmood, M. R., Matin, M. A., Sarigiannidis, P., & Goudos, S. K. (2022). A comprehensive review on artificial intelligence/machine learning algorithms for empowering the future IoT toward 6G era. *IEEE Access : Practical Innovations, Open Solutions, 10*, 87535–87562.

Marr, B. (2021, July 2). What are the 4 Vs of Big Data? BernardMarr.com. https://bernardmarr.com/what-are-the-4-vs-of-big-data/

Martin, D. (2023). Smart Cities: The IoT and Big Data Analytics. Advanced Sciences, 5(2) 45. journal-as.com.DOI: 10.69610/j.as.20231221

McCarthy, S., Rowan, W., Mahony, C., & Vergne, A. (2023). The dark side of digitalization and social media platform governance: A citizen engagement study. *Internet Research, 33*(6), 2172–2204. DOI: 10.1108/INTR-03-2022-0142

McMahan, H. B., Moore, E., Ramage, D., Hampson, S., & Arcas, B. A. Y. (2017). Communication-efficient learning of deep networks from decentralized data. Proceedings of the 20th International Conference on Artificial Intelligence and Statistics (AISTATS), 1273–1282.

McMahan, B., Moore, E., Ramage, D., Hampson, S., & Arcas, B. A. (2017). Communication-efficient learning of deep networks from decentralized data. In *Proceedings of Artificial Intelligence and Statistics* (pp. 1273–1282). https://arxiv.org/abs/1602.05629

Mead, M. I., Popoola, O. A. M., & Stewart, G. B.. (2013). The use of electrochemical sensors for monitoring urban air quality in low-cost, high-density networks. *Atmospheric Environment*, *70*, 186–203. DOI: 10.1016/j.atmosenv.2012.11.060

Meng, W., Li, W., Wang, Y., & Au, M. H. (2020). Detecting insider attacks in medical cyber–physical networks based on behavioral profiling. *Future Generation Computer Systems*, *108*, 1258–1266.

Mennella, C., Maniscalco, U., De Pietro, G., & Esposito, M. (2024). Ethical and regulatory challenges of AI technologies in healthcare: A narrative review. *Heliyon*, *10*(4), e26297. DOI: 10.1016/j.heliyon.2024.e26297

Menon, U. V., Kumaravelu, V. B., Kumar, C. V., Rammohan, A., Chinnadurai, S., Venkatesan, R., & Selvaprabhu, P. (2025). AI-powered IoT: A survey on integrating artificial intelligence with IoT for enhanced security, efficiency, and smart applications. *IEEE Access : Practical Innovations, Open Solutions*.

Meuser, T., Lovén, L., Bhuyan, M., Patil, S. G., Dustdar, S., Aral, A., & Welzl, M. (2024). Revisiting edge ai: Opportunities and challenges. *IEEE Internet Computing*, *28*(4), 49–59.

Michael, C. I., Ipede, O. J., Adejumo, A. D., Adenekan, I. O., Adebayo, D., Ojo, A. S., & Ayodele, P. A. (2024). Data-driven decision making in IT: Leveraging AI and data science for business intelligence. *World Journal of Advanced Research and Reviews*, *23*(01), 432–439.

Moerland, T. M., Broekens, J., Plaat, A., & Jonker, C. M. (2023). Model-based reinforcement learning: A survey. *Foundations and Trends® in Machine Learning*, *16*(1), 1–118. DOI: 10.1561/2200000086

Mohammadi, M., & Al-Fuqaha, A. (2018). Enabling cognitive smart cities using big data and machine learning: Approaches and challenges.

Mohammadi, M., Al-Fuqaha, A., Sorour, S., & Guizani, M. (2018). Deep Learning IoT Big Data and Streaming Analytics: A Survey. arXiv preprint arXiv:1712.04301. arXiv.

Mossie, Z., & Wang, J.-H. (2020). Vulnerable community identification using hate speech detection on social media. *Information Processing & Management*, *57*(3), 102087. DOI: 10.1016/j.ipm.2019.102087

Moss, J., Gordon, J., Duclos, W., Liu, Y., Wang, Q., & Wang, J. (2025). Explainable AI in IoT: A survey of challenges, advancements, and pathways to trustworthy automation. *Electronics (Basel)*, *14*(23), 4622. DOI: 10.3390/electronics14234622

Mudgerikar, A., Sharma, P., & Bertino, E. (2020). Edge-based intrusion detection for IoT devices. [TMIS]. *ACM Transactions on Management Information Systems*, *11*(4), 1–21.

Musen, M. A. (2015). The protégé project: A look back and a look forward. *AI Matters*, *1*(4), 4–12. PMID: 27239556

Naha, R. K., Garg, S., Georgakopoulos, D., Jayaraman, P. P., Gao, L., Xiang, Y., & Ranjan, R. (2018). Survey of Trends, Architectures, Requirements, and Research Directions. arXiv preprint arXiv:1807.00976. arXiv.

Neustein, A., Mahalle, P. N., Joshi, P., & Shinde, G. R. (Eds.). (2023). *AI, IoT, big data and cloud computing for industry 4.0. Springer*. SpringerLink., DOI: 10.1007/978-3-031-29713-7

Nguyen, D. C., Ding, M., Pathirana, P. N., & Seneviratne, A. (2021). Federated learning for industrial Internet of Things: Recent advances and open issues. IEEE Transactions on Industrial Informatics, 17(10), 7225–7237. .DOI: 10.1109/TII.2021.3059095

Nguyen, D. C., Ding, M., Pathirana, P. N., Seneviratne, A., Li, J., & Poor, H. V. (2021). Federated learning for internet of things: A comprehensive survey. *IEEE Communications Surveys and Tutorials*, *23*(3), 1622–1658.

NVIDIA Corporation. (2018). *NVIDIA Jetson AGX Xavier: New era for autonomous machines*. NVIDIA Developer Documentation. https://developer.nvidia.com

Obayya, M., Nemri, N., Nour, M. K., Al Duhayyim, M., Mohsen, H., Rizwanullah, M., & Motwakel, A. (2022). Explainable artificial intelligence enabled TeleOphthalmology for diabetic retinopathy grading and classification. *Applied Sciences (Basel, Switzerland)*, *12*(17), 8749.

Okoli, N. J., & Kabaso, B. (2024). Building a smart water city: Iot smart water technologies, applications, and future directions. *Water (Basel)*, *16*(4), 557.

Olsen, E. (2025). Data breach at healthcare services firm Episource affects 5.4M. Cybersecurity Dive. Retrieved November 28, 2025, from https://www.healthcaredive.com/news/episource-healthcare-data-breach-impacts-5-4-million/751103/

Omar, M., Soffer, S., Agbareia, R., Bragazzi, N. L., Apakama, D. U., Horowitz, C. R., Charney, A. W., Freeman, R., Kummer, B., Glicksberg, B. S., Nadkarni, G. N., & Klang, E. (2025). Sociodemographic biases in medical decision making by large language models. *Nature Medicine*, *31*(6), 1873–1881. DOI: 10.1038/s41591-025-03626-6

Othengrafen, F., Sievers, L., & Reinecke, E. (2025). From vision to reality: The use of artificial intelligence in different urban planning phases. *Urban Planning*, *10*. Advance online publication. DOI: 10.17645/up.8576

Pan, X., Zhang, J., & Li, J. (2020). Blockchain-based federated learning for secure data sharing in industrial IoT. IEEE Transactions on Industrial Informatics, 16(6), 4156–4166. .DOI: 10.1109/TII.2019.2944848

Pan, X., Jiang, A., & Wang, H. (2020). Edge-cloud computing application, architecture, and challenges in ubiquitous power Internet of Things demand response. *Journal of Renewable and Sustainable Energy*, *12*(6), 062702. DOI: 10.1063/5.0014059

Paracha, A., Arshad, J., & Farah, M.. (2024). Machine Learning Security and Privacy: A Review of Threats and Countermeasures. *EURASIP Journal on Information Security*, *2024*, 10.

Pathak, M., Mishra, K. N., & Singh, S. P. (2024). Securing data and preserving privacy in cloud IoT-based technologies an analysis of assessing threats and developing effective safeguard. *Artificial Intelligence Review*, *57*, 269. DOI: 10.1007/s10462-024-10908-x

Pattanaik, B., Kumari, S. S., Kumar, C. K., Pattnaik, M., Ali, S. I., & Kumarasamy, M. (2023). *An innovation of algebraic mathematical-based statistical analysis model for complex number theory*. In *Proceedings of the 2023 International Conference on Disruptive Technologies (ICDT)* (pp. 94–99). IEEE. https://doi.org/DOI: 10.1109/ICDT57929.2023.10151169

Pavlidou, V., Otterbacher, J., & Kleanthous, S. (2022). User perception of algorithmic digital marketing in conditions of scarcity. In Themistocleous, M., & Papadaki, M. (Eds.), *Information Systems* (Vol. 437, pp. 319–332). Springer International Publishing., DOI: 10.1007/978-3-030-95947-0_22

Peleg, M., & Tu, S. (2006). Section 5: Decision support, knowledge representation and management: Decision support, knowledge representation and management in medicine. *Yearbook of Medical Informatics*, *15*(01), 72–80. PMID: 17051298

Perera, C., Ranjan, R., Wang, L., Khan, S., & Vasilakos, A. V. (2015). Big data privacy in the Internet of Things era. *IEEE Cloud Computing*, *3*(2), 36–45. DOI: 10.1109/MCC.2016.31

Pizzi, G., Caputo, A., & Corvino, A. (2023). Responsible artificial intelligence governance: A review and research framework. *The Journal of Strategic Information Systems*, *34*(2), 101779. DOI: 10.1016/j.jsis.2024.101779

Pustokhina, I. V., Pustokhin, D. A., Vaiyapuri, T., Gupta, D., Kumar, S., & Shankar, K. (2021). An automated deep learning based anomaly detection in pedestrian walkways for vulnerable road users safety. *Safety Science*, *142*, 105356. DOI: 10.1016/j.ssci.2021.105356

Rahman, A., Kundu, D., Debnath, T., Rahman, M., Das, U. K., Miah, A. S. M., & Muhammad, G. (2025). From AI to the era of explainable AI in Healthcare 5.0: Current state and future outlook. *Expert Systems: International Journal of Knowledge Engineering and Neural Networks*. Advance online publication. DOI: 10.1111/exsy.70060

Rahman, M. A., Hossain, M. S., Islam, M. S., Alrajeh, N. A., & Muhammad, G. (2020). Secure and provenance enhanced internet of health things framework: A blockchain managed federated learning approach. *IEEE Access : Practical Innovations, Open Solutions*, *8*, 205071–205087. PMID: 34192116

Rahman, M. S., Khalil, I., Moustafa, N., Kalapaaking, A. P., & Bouras, A. (2021). A blockchain-enabled privacy-preserving verifiable query framework for securing cloud-assisted industrial internet of things systems. *IEEE Transactions on Industrial Informatics*, *18*(7), 5007–5017.

Rajabi, E., & Kafaie, S. (2022). Knowledge graphs and explainable AI in healthcare. *Information (Basel)*, *13*(10), 459.

Raoufi, P., Hemmati, A., & Rahmani, A. M. (2024). Deep learning applications in the Internet of Things: A review, tools, and future directions. *Evolutionary Intelligence*, *17*(5), 3621–3654.

Ren, J., Yu, G., He, Y., & Li, G. Y. (2019). Collaborative cloud and edge computing for latency minimization. IEEE Transactions on Vehicular Technology, 68(5), 5031–5044. .DOI: 10.1109/TVT.2019.2906204

Ribeiro, M. T., Singh, S., & Guestrin, C. (2016). " Why should i trust you?" Explaining the predictions of any classifier. In *Proceedings of the 22nd ACM SIGKDD international conference on knowledge discovery and data mining* (pp. 1135-1144).

Rodriguez, C. A., Gopalakrishnan, L., Del Cid, M., Folk, J. B., Yonek, J., & Tolou-Shams, M. (2021). The ethical implications of using social media to engage and retain justice-involved youth in behavioral health research. *Journal of Empirical Research on Human Research Ethics; JERHRE, 16*(4), 356–363. DOI: 10.1177/15562646211039701

Roman, R., Lopez, J., & Mambo, M. (2018). Mobile edge computing, fog et al.: A survey and analysis of security threats and challenges. *Future Generation Computer Systems, 78*, 680–698. https://doi.org//arXiv.1602.00484DOI: 10.48550

Roman, R., Zhou, J., & Lopez, J. (2013). On the features and challenges of security and privacy in distributed Internet of Things. *Computer Networks, 57*(10), 2266–2279.

Sadhu, P. K., Yanambaka, V. P., & Abdelgawad, A. (2022). Internet of things: Security and solutions survey. *Sensors (Basel), 22*(19), 7433. DOI: 10.3390/s22197433

Samadi, S. (2022). AI, IoT and big data convergence to develop flood analytics. [Frontiers]. *Frontiers in Water, 4*. Advance online publication. DOI: 10.3389/frwa.2022.786040

Samek, W., Montavon, G., Vedaldi, A., Hansen, L. K., & Müller, K. R. (Eds.). (2019). *Explainable AI: interpreting, explaining and visualizing deep learning* (Vol. 11700). Springer Nature.

Samie, F., Bauer, L., & Henkel, J. (2016). Edge computing for the Internet of Things: A case study. *IEEE International Conference on Computer Design (ICCD)*, 105–112. .DOI: 10.1109/ICCD.2016.7738596

Sandler, M., Howard, A., Zhu, M., Zhmoginov, A., & Chen, L. C. (2018). MobileNetV2: Inverted residuals and linear bottlenecks. In *Proceedings of the IEEE Conference on Computer Vision and Pattern Recognition* (pp. 4510–4520). https://doi.org/DOI: 10.1109/CVPR.2018.00474

Santos, A., Cazzamatta, R., & Napolitano, C. J. (2025). Holding platforms accountable in the fight against misinformation: A cross-national analysis of state-established content moderation regulations. *The International Communication Gazette, 87*(8), 729–750. DOI: 10.1177/17480485251348550

Sarhaddi, F., Nguyen, N. T., Zuniga, A., Hui, P., Tarkoma, S., Flores, H., & Nurmi, P. (2025). Llms and iot: A comprehensive survey on large language models and the internet of things. *Authorea Preprints*.

Satyanarayanan, M. (2017). The emergence of edge computing. *Computer, 50*(1), 30–39.

Savin, A., & Nielsen, M. F. (2025). The data-driven home: Towards a more coherent regulatory framework for smart homes in the European Union. *Information & Communications Technology Law*, •••, 1–21. DOI: 10.1080/13600834.2025.2572918

Schissler, M. (2025). Beyond hate speech and misinformation: Facebook and the rohingya genocide in myanmar. *Journal of Genocide Research*, *27*(3), 445–470. DOI: 10.1080/14623528.2024.2375122

Schneble, C. O., Elger, B. S., & Shaw, D. (2018). The Cambridge Analytica affair and Internet-mediated research. *EMBO Reports*, *19*(8), e46579. DOI: 10.15252/embr.201846579

Sculley, D., Holt, G., Golovin, D., Davydov, E., Phillips, T., Ebner, D., & Dennison, D. (2015). Hidden technical debt in machine learning systems. *Advances in Neural Information Processing Systems*, •••, 28.

Shafagh, H., Burkhalter, L., Hithnawi, A., & Duquennoy, S. (2017). Towards blockchain-based auditable storage and sharing of IoT data. In *Proceedings of the 2017 Cloud Computing Security Workshop* (pp. 45–50). https://doi.org/DOI: 10.1145/3140649.3140656

Shaffique, M. R. (2024). Cyber Resilience Act 2022: A silver bullet for cybersecurity of IoT devices or a shot in the dark? *Computer Law & Security Review*, *54*, 106009. DOI: 10.1016/j.clsr.2024.106009

Shang, J., Ma, T., Xiao, C., & Sun, J. (2019). Pre-training of graph augmented transformers for medication recommendation. *arXiv preprint arXiv:1906.00346.*

Sharif, S., Zeadally, S., & Ejaz, W. (2024). Resource optimization in UAV-assisted IoT networks: The role of generative AI. *IEEE Internet of Things Magazine.*

Sharon, Y., Berend, D., Liu, Y., Shabtai, A., & Elovici, Y. (2022). Tantra: Timing-based adversarial network traffic reshaping attack. *IEEE Transactions on Information Forensics and Security*, *17*, 3225–3237.

Shetty, D. K., Vijaya Arjunan, R., Cenitta, D., Makkithaya, K., Hegde, N. V., & Bhatta, B, S. R., Salu, S., Aishwarya, T. R., Bhat, P., & Pullela, P. K. (2025). Analyzing AI regulation through literature and current trends. *Journal of Open Innovation*, *11*(1), 100508. DOI: 10.1016/j.joitmc.2025.100508

Shi, Y., Yang, K., Jiang, T., Zhang, J., & Letaief, K. B. (2020). Efficient Edge AI: Communication Communication-Efficient Edge AI: Algorithms and Systems. arXiv preprint arXiv:2002.09668. arXiv.

Shickel, B., Tighe, P. J., Bihorac, A., & Rashidi, P. (2017). Deep EHR: A survey of recent advances in deep learning techniques for electronic health record (EHR) analysis. *IEEE Journal of Biomedical and Health Informatics*, *22*(5), 1589–1604. PMID: 29989977

Shi, W., Cao, J., Zhang, Q., Li, Y., & Xu, L. (2016). Edge computing: Vision and challenges. *IEEE Internet of Things Journal*, *3*(5), 637–646. DOI: 10.1109/JIOT.2016.2579198

Shi, W., & Dustdar, S. (2016). The promise of edge computing. *Computer*, *49*(5), 78–81.

Shi, Y., Yang, K., Jiang, T., Zhang, J., & Letaief, K. B. (2020). Communication-efficient edge AI: Algorithms and systems [Preprint]. arXiv. https://arxiv.org/abs/2002.09668

Shlezinger, N., & Bajic, I. V. (2022). Collaborative Inference of IoT devices empowered with AI. arXiv preprint ArXiv:2207.11664. arXiv.

Shokri, R., Stronati, M., Song, C., & Shmatikov, V. (2017, May). Membership inference attacks against machine learning models. In *2017 IEEE symposium on security and privacy (SP)* (pp. 3-18). IEEE.

Siam, S. I., Ahn, H., Liu, L., Alam, S., Shen, H., Cao, Z., & Zhang, M. (2025). Artificial intelligence of things: A survey. *ACM Transactions on Sensor Networks*, *21*(1), 1–75.

Sicari, S., Rizzardi, A., Grieco, L. A., & Coen-Porisini, A. (2015). Security, privacy and trust in Internet of Things: The road ahead. *Computer Networks*, *76*, 146–164.

Silva, B. N., Khan, M., & Jung, C. (2018). Urban planning and smart city decision management empowered by real-time data processing using big data analytics. *Sensors (Basel)*, *18*(9), 2994. DOI: 10.3390/s18092994 PMID: 30205499

Simchon, A., Edwards, M., & Lewandowsky, S. (2024). The persuasive effects of political microtargeting in the age of generative artificial intelligence. *PNAS Nexus*, *3*(2), pgae035. Advance online publication. DOI: 10.1093/pnasnexus/pgae035

Sondeck, L. P., & Laurent, M. (2025). Practical and ready-to-use methodology to assess the re-identification risk in anonymized datasets. *Scientific Reports*, *15*, 23223. Advance online publication. DOI: 10.1038/s41598-025-04907-3

Sonicki, Z. (2024). Large multi-modal models – the present or future of artificial intelligence in medicine? *Croatian Medical Journal*, *65*(1), 1–2. DOI: 10.3325/cmj.2024.65.1

Sonkar, A. (2025). The Digital Personal Data Protection Act, 2023: Analysing Its Implications, Challenges, and Future Prospects. *International Cybersecurity Law Review*, •••, 1–23.

Srivastava, S. S., Ali, S. I., Srivastava, A. K., & Goswami, C. (2024). Improving 5G network performance with MIMO technology using beamforming algorithm. *ICTACT Journal on Communication Technology*, *15*(2), 3173–3178.

Srivastava, S. T. C., Sharmiladevi, D., Sugumar, D., Ali, S. I., Jones Mary, T. A., & Kumar, S. (2023). *Using a smart wearable device for monitoring social distance in smart cities*. In *2023 International Conference on Research Methodologies in Knowledge Management, Artificial Intelligence and Telecommunication Engineering (RMKMATE)* (pp. 1–5). IEEE. https://doi.org/DOI: 10.1109/RMKMATE59243.2023.10369118

Stevens, J., Ghapanchi, A. H., Purarjomandlangrudi, A., & Bruce, S. (2025). Patient experiences of remote patient monitoring: Implications for health literacy and therapeutic relationships. *Technologies*, *13*(10), 464. DOI: 10.3390/technologies13100464

Stokes, L. (2025). Ana position statement: The ethical use of artificial intelligence in nursing practice. *OJIN: The Online Journal of Issues in Nursing*, *30*(2). Advance online publication. DOI: 10.3912/OJIN.Vol30No02PoSCol03

Strubell, E., Ganesh, A., & McCallum, A. (2019). Energy and policy considerations for deep learning in NLP. In *Proceedings of the 57th Annual Meeting of the Association for Computational Linguistics* (pp. 3645–3650). DOI: 10.18653/v1/P19-1355

Sujatha, L., Hemasundari, M., Pode, S., Shrivastava, V., Shah, S. S., & Datta, P. (2024). IoT-driven smart cities: Leveraging big data and AI for sustainable urban development. *Journal of Informatics Education and Research*, *4*(3).

Sun, P., Shen, S., Wan, Y., Wu, Z., Fang, Z., & Gao, X. Z. (2024). A survey of iot privacy security: Architecture, technology, challenges, and trends. *IEEE Internet of Things Journal*, *11*(21), 34567–34591.

Sun, Y., Zhou, S., Xu, J., & Zhang, R. (2021). Energy-efficient federated learning over wireless communication networks. *IEEE Transactions on Wireless Communications*, *20*(3), 1935–1949. DOI: 10.1109/TWC.2020.3031787

Suthar, B., & Ali, S. I. (2025). *A survey on hand gesture sign language recognition with Arduino Leonardo*. In *2025 International Conference on Computational, Communication and Information Technology (ICCCIT)* (pp. 111–115). IEEE. https://doi.org/DOI: 10.1109/ICCCIT62592.2025.10927994

Sutton, R. S., & Barto, A. G. (2018). *Reinforcement learning: An introduction* (2nd ed.). MIT Press.

Taha, K. (2025). Big Data Analytics in IoT, Social Media, NLP, and Information Security: Trends, Challenges, and Applications. *Journal of Big Data*, *12*, 150.

Thompson, J. A., Hersch, D., Kasozi, R. N., Miner, M. H., & Adam, P. (2024). Disparities in offering enrollment in remote patient monitoring for covid-19. *Telemedicine Journal and e-Health*, *30*(3), 715–721. DOI: 10.1089/tmj.2023.0150

Ullah, A., Anwar, S. M., & Li, J.. (2024). Smart cities: The role of Internet of Things and machine learning in realizing a data-centric smart environment. *Complex & Intelligent Systems.*

UNESCO. (2021). Recommendation on the Ethics of Artificial Intelligence. https://unesdoc.unesco.org/ark:/48223/pf0000380455

Usman, Y., Ihejirika, C. J., Offor, S. N., Akl, R., & Chataut, R. (2025). Green cybersecurity: Leveraging ai, ml, and llms to optimize energy, threat detection, and sustainability frameworks. *IEEE Access : Practical Innovations, Open Solutions*, *13*, 159345–159379. DOI: 10.1109/ACCESS.2025.3602451

van de Poel, I. (2025). *Responsible AI, ethics, and the AI lifecycle: How to consider the human influence? AI and Ethics*. Springer., DOI: 10.1007/s43681-025-00666-z

Van der Pol, E., & Oliehoek, F. A. (2016). Coordinated deep reinforcement learners for traffic light control. *Proceedings of the NIPS Workshop.*

Van Zoonen, L. (2016). Privacy concerns in smart cities. *Government Information Quarterly*, *33*(3), 472–480.

Varshney, D., Zafar, A., Behera, N. K., & Ekbal, A. (2023). Knowledge grounded medical dialogue generation using augmented graphs. *Scientific Reports*, *13*(1), 3310. PMID: 36849466

Viswanathan, H. (2025, October 31). YNHHS reaches preliminary $18 million settlement over data breach. Yale Daily News. https://yaledailynews.com/blog/2025/10/31/ynhhs-reaches-preliminary-18-million-settlement-over-data-breach/

Wang, S., Tuor, T., Salonidis, T., Leung, K. K., Makaya, C., He, T., & Chan, K. (2019). Adaptive federated learning in resource constrained edge computing systems. IEEE Journal on Selected Areas in Communications, 37(6), 1205–1221. DOI: 10.1109/JSAC.2019.2904348

Wang, Q., Mao, Z., Wang, B., & Guo, L. (2017). Knowledge graph embedding: A survey of approaches and applications. *IEEE Transactions on Knowledge and Data Engineering*, *29*(12), 2724–2743.

Wang, X., Han, Y., Wang, C., Zhao, Q., Chen, X., & Chen, M. (2020). In-edge AI: Intelligentizing mobile edge computing, caching, and communication by federated learning. *IEEE Network*, *33*(5), 156–165. DOI: 10.1109/MNET.2019.1800286

Wang, X., Li, H., Kumar, A., & Chen, Z. (2025). Edge intelligence: Fundamentals, recent advances, and challenges. *IEEE Internet of Things Journal*. Advance online publication.

Wang, Z., Shi, Y., & Letaief, K. B. (2025). *Edge large AI models: Collaborative deployment and IoT applications* (Preprint). arXiv. https://arxiv.org/abs/2505.03139

Wu, Z., Pan, S., Chen, F., Long, G., Zhang, C., & Yu, P. S. (2021). A comprehensive survey on graph neural networks. *IEEE Transactions on Neural Networks and Learning Systems*, *32*(1), 4–24. DOI: 10.1109/TNNLS.2020.2978386 PMID: 32217482

Xing, H., Zhu, G., Liu, D., Li, Y., Liu, D., Zeng, Y., & Zhang, R. (2023). Task-oriented integrated sensing, computation, and communication design for wireless edge AI [Preprint]. arXiv. https://arxiv.org/abs/2306.06603

Xu, D., Li, T., Li, Y., Su, X., Tarkoma, S., Jiang, T., . . . Hui, P. (2021). Edge intelligence: Architectures, challenges, and applications. *arXiv preprint arXiv:2003.12172.*

Yang, Q., Liu, Y., Chen, T., & Tong, Y. (2019). Federated machine learning: Concept and applications. ACM Transactions on Intelligent Systems and Technology, 10(2), 1–19. .DOI: 10.1145/3298981

Yang, Z., Gao, W., Luo, C., Wang, L., Tang, F., Wen, X., & Zhan, J. (2022). Quality at the tail of machine learning inference. *arXiv preprint arXiv:2212.13925.*

Yang, C., Huang, Q., Li, Z., Liu, K., & Hu, F. (2017). Big Data and cloud computing: Innovation opportunities and challenges. *International Journal of Digital Earth*, *10*(1), 13–53.

Yang, M., Nazir, S., Xu, Q., & Ali, S. (2020). Deep Learning Algorithms and Multicriteria Decision-Making Used in Big Data: A Systematic Literature Review. *Complexity*, *2020*(1), 2836064.

Yazdinejad, A., Dehghantanha, A., Karimipour, H., Srivastava, G., & Parizi, R. M. (2024). A robust privacy-preserving federated learning model against model poisoning attacks. *IEEE Transactions on Information Forensics and Security*, *19*, 6693–6708.

Yothi, V., Sreelatha, T., Thiyagu, T. M., & Sowndharya, R. (2024). A data management system for smart cities leveraging artificial intelligence modeling techniques to enhance privacy and security. *Journal of Internet Services and Information Security*, *14*(1), 126–140.

Yu, M. & Sun, S. (2020). Policy-based reinforcement learning for time series anomaly detection. *Engineering Applications of Artificial Intelligence, 95*. 103919. 10.1016/j.engappai.2020.103919.

Zaharia, P. (2012). Introduction of the New Public Management in the Romanian and Swiss Local Public Administration. *Economic Insights - Trends and Challenges, 64*(4).

Zamani, A. (2022). Artificial Intelligence - The New. *Machine Learning*.

Zamani, A. S., Hashim, A. H. A., Shatat, A. S. A., Akhtar, M. M., Rizwanullah, M., & Mohamed, S. S. I. (2024). Implementation of machine learning techniques with big data and IoT to create effective prediction models for health informatics. *Biomedical Signal Processing and Control, 94*, 106247.

Zeng, L., Chen, X., Zhou, Z., Yang, L., & Zhang, J. (2020). CoEdge: Cooperative DNN inference with adaptive workload partitioning. *arXiv preprint arXiv:2012.03257*.

Zhai, K., Liang, Y., Cho, C., & Li, C. (2022). Task-oriented sensing, computation and communication integration for multi-device edge AI [Preprint]. arXiv. https://arxiv.org/abs/2207.00969

Zhang, C., Lin, J., & Wang, Y. (2021). Towards efficient deep learning inference in edge computing: A review. *IEEE Communications Surveys and Tutorials, 23*(3), 2107–2135.

Zhang, C., Xie, Y., Bai, H., Yu, B., Li, W., & Gao, Y. (2021). A survey on federated learning. *Knowledge-Based Systems, 216*, 106775. DOI: 10.1016/j.knosys.2021.106775 PMID: 34909232

Zhang, J., & Tao, D. (2020). Empowering things with intelligence: A survey of the progress, challenges, and opportunities in artificial intelligence of things. *IEEE Internet of Things Journal, 8*(10), 7789–7817.

Zhang, Y., Gong, Y., Shi, M., & Yang, X. (2026). Privacy risk of transportation location-Based data: Re-identification and de-anonymization. *Transportation Research Part C, Emerging Technologies, 183*, 105495.

Zhang, Y., Zhang, J., Yue, S., Lu, W., Ren, J., & Shen, X. (2024). Mobile generative ai: Opportunities and challenges. *IEEE Wireless Communications, 31*(4), 58–64.

Zhan, L., Dang, X., Xie, Z., Zeng, C., Wu, W., Zhang, X., Zhang, L., & Cai, X. (2025). Evaluating GPT-4o in infectious disease diagnostics and management: A comparative study with residents and specialists on accuracy, completeness, and clinical support potential. *Digital Health, 11*. Advance online publication. DOI: 10.1177/20552076251355797

Zhao, I. Y., Ma, Y. X., Yu, M. W. C., Liu, J., Dong, W. N., Pang, Q., Lu, X. Q., Molassiotis, A., Holroyd, E., & Wong, C. W. W. (2021). Ethics, integrity, and retributions of digital detection surveillance systems for infectious diseases: Systematic literature review. *Journal of Medical Internet Research, 23*(10), e32328. DOI: 10.2196/32328

Zhenning, L., Hao, Y., Guohui, Z., Shangjia, D., & Xu, C.-Z. (2021). Network-wide traffic signal control optimization using a multi-agent deep reinforcement learning. *Transportation Research Part C, Emerging Technologies, 125*, 103059. DOI: 10.1016/j.trc.2021.103059

Zhou, Z., Chen, X., Li, E., Zeng, L., Luo, K., & Zhang, J. (2019). Edge intelligence: Paving the last mile of artificial intelligence with edge computing. *Proceedings of the IEEE, 107*(8), 1738–1762. DOI: 10.1109/JPROC.2019.2918951

Zhu, G., Lyu, F., Jiao, J., Liu, Z., Chen, Y., Xu, J., & Zhang, R. (2023). Pushing AI to the wireless network edge: An overview on integrated sensing, communication, and computation toward 6G. *Science China. Information Sciences*. Advance online publication. DOI: 10.1007/s11432-022-3652-2

Zitnik, M., Agrawal, M., & Leskovec, J. (2018). Modeling polypharmacy side effects with graph convolutional networks. *Bioinformatics (Oxford, England), 34*(13), i457–i466. PMID: 29949996

About the Contributors

Abu Sarwar Zamani is currently working as an Asst. Professor at Prince Sattam bin Abdulaziz University, Alkharj, Kingdom of Saudi Arabia and as an Adjunct Senior Fellow in Kulliyyah of Engineering at International Islamic University Malaysia, Gombak, Malaysia. Previously he worked as a Senior Lecturer in Shaqra University and King Saud University, Kingdom of Saudi Arabia. He received his Ph.D. in Computer Science from Pacific Academy of Higher Education and Research University, India and Master in Computer Science from Hamdard University, New Delhi, India in 2007. His research interests are, AI, ML, IoT, Health Informatics, Big Data, Cloud Computing and Data Mining. He has more than 15 years of experience in teaching, research, and industries. He has published 100+ research papers in many reputed journals in high indexed outlets. He has around three international patents from Australia and India. He has completed numerous research projects that were financed by Saudi Arabia's Ministry of Education's Deanship of Scientific Research. He is currently working for numerous reputable journals, such as Springer, Elsevier, and MDPI, as an Academic Editor, Associate Editor, and Guest Editor.

Aisha Hassan Abdalla Hashim received her Ph.D in Computer Engineering (2007), M.Sc. in Computer Science (1996) and B.Sc. in Electronics Engineering (1990). She won the Best Graduating Ph.D Student Award during the IIUM Convocation ceremony in 2007. She joined IIUM in 1997 and is currently a Professor at the Department of Electrical and Computer Engineering. Professor Aisha has taught several courses related to Communication and Computer Engineering and is actively involved in curriculum development and programme accreditation. She has been a member of the Department Board of Studies for several years. She received the Best Teacher Award during IIUM Quality Day in 2007. Prof. Aisha has been appointed as external examiner/visiting professor/adjunct professor at different universities. Professor Aisha who is actively involved in research and postgraduate programmes, has published more than 200 journal/conference papers, and supervised/

co-supervised more than 40 Ph.D/Master's students. She received the Promising Researcher Award in 2009 during IIUM Quality Day. She has also received many medals/awards in different national/international research exhibitions. One of her research exhibitions won the Promising Commercial Value Award (Second Runner Up) in IRIIE 2014. As a researcher, she has secured research grants from IIUM, Ministry of Higher Education (MOHE) and Ministry of Science, Technology and Innovation (MOSTI). She has actively contributed as a reviewer /technical committee member in many journals/conferences. Professor Aisha has established several teaching/ research networks between IIUM and overseas universities. She has been appointed as IIUMÂ Internationalisation Ambassador to Sudan (October 2014) and has participated in initiating several MoUs as well as encouraging the PhD Student Mobility programme between IIUM and Sudanese Universities. Professor Aisha also participates in community services. She was appointed as a Board of Studies member at the International Islamic School, Malaysia. She also served as Parent/ Teacher Committee member at the school for more than 10 years.

Mobin Akhtar is Assistant professor of Computer Science at Riyadh Elm University (REU) Saudi Arabia with over 10 years of experience in Teaching. Before joining REU in Sep. 2018, he served Shaqra University as a Lecturer of Computer Science from August. 2009 to Sep. 2016, Md. Mobin Akhtar received his Master degree, M.Sc.Tech (IMCA), from JAMIA MILLIA ISLAMIA, NEW DELHI in 2008, and PHD degree in Computer Science from pacific university Udaipur, Rajasthan in JAN. 2019. His research interests span over the areas of Online Information System Development, Big Data, Internet of thing(IOT), IOMT and Cloud Computing. His current interests are in Artificial intelligence, and Big data. Besides teaching, he enjoys giving tech talks, reading biographies, reading world history and reading about new technology articles on the internet. His teaching abilities include innovative skills and extensive use of technology in teaching.

Hazra Imran is an Associate Professor of Khoury College of Computer Sciences, Northeastern University, Vancouver Canada. She has instructed over fifty courses in computer science at University of British Columbia (Canada), Langara College (Canada), Douglas College (Canada) and Hamdard University (India), with a class size ranges from 35 to 160. As an Assistant Professor of Computer Science at Hamdard University, she has supervised several graduate and under graduate students. She completed her Postdoctoral fellowship at Athabasca University in Canada, funded by MITACS under the guidance of Prof. Sabine Graf and Prof. Kinshuk at Athabasca University. She received PhD from School of Computer and Systems Sciences Jawaharlal Nehru University (JNU), New Delhi, India in 2012.

***

Ing. Otmane Azeroual is a world-renowned senior researcher, lecturer, and thought leader in digital transformation, artificial intelligence, and advanced data-driven research infrastructures. His groundbreaking interdisciplinary work at the nexus of computer science, higher education research, innovation management, and industry has set new standards in how data and AI reshape science and society. His research on the design, deployment, and critical evaluation of Current Research Information Systems (CRIS) — combined with cutting-edge AI-powered analytics — is internationally acclaimed and among the most cited in the field. Dr. Azeroual's pioneering contributions drive the evolution of intelligent data ecosystems that empower Open Science, elevate transparency, and revolutionize strategic decision-making in science policy worldwide. Holding a Ph.D. in Engineering Informatics and a robust foundation in business information systems and software engineering, he has authored numerous high-impact publications in top-tier journals and has been a sought-after keynote and plenary speaker at prestigious global conferences. His expertise is recognized by editorial boards and scientific committees internationally, where he shapes the future agenda of research data science. Bridging academia and private industry, Dr. Azeroual uniquely fuses rigorous theoretical insight with practical innovation. His leadership in both sectors fuels transformative digital strategies and sustainable technological solutions. As an inspiring educator, he equips emerging researchers and professionals with cutting-edge knowledge in AI, data science, research analytics, and project management — preparing them to excel in complex, dynamic environments. Passionate about harnessing AI for evidence-based governance, Dr. Azeroual actively collaborates across disciplines to build resilient, transparent, and data-driven research infrastructures that set global benchmarks. His visionary work not only advances scientific understanding but also catalyzes paradigm shifts that benefit institutions, governments, and society at large.

Daniel Raj K. is a postgraduate scholar in Computer Science Engineering at Dr. G.U. Pope College of Engineering, pursuing a Master of Engineering degree. He holds a Bachelor's degree in Information Technology from Kings Engineering College with a CGPA of 8.1. His research focuses on machine learning, deep learning, and intelligent systems. He has authored and reviewed multiple research papers published in reputed journals, including IEEE, IGI Global, and Scopus-indexed publications. He aims to pursue a Ph.D. and contribute to impactful research and quality education in the field of computer science.

Irfan Ahmad Khan is an Assistant Professor of Computer Science at Rai University with 17 years of academic and administrative experience, including 15 years at King Saud University, Riyadh, Saudi Arabia. His research interests include software quality and testing, AI-assisted quality frameworks in higher education. He is currently pursuing post-doctoral research from Lincoln University, Malaysia.

Shikha Khullar is an Associate Professor in the Department of Computer Science and Engineering at Poornima University, Jaipur. Her research interests include Artificial Intelligence, Internet of Things (IoT), Cloud Computing, and Smart City Technologies. She has contributed to several international book chapters and research publications and holds design patents. Dr. Khullar is passionate about leveraging emerging technologies for sustainable and intelligent systems.

Ausaf Malik is appointed as Professor at UILS, Chandigarh University, Mohali . He has over 15 years of experience in teaching and administration in various universities from India. He holds a doctorate from the prestigious institution and central university, Jamia Millia Islamia, New Delhi and a post graduate degree in law (LL.M) from Aligarh Muslim University, Aligarh. He has published over 16 research papers in National and International Journals, authored one book and has been an editor for two books. He has been a part of various International/National Seminars, Conferences, Moot Court Competitions and an invitee as a guest/chair for the respective competitions by eminent universities/colleges in India.

Nandhakumar R was born in Tamil Nadu, India on 10th March 2007. He is pursuing a B.E. degree in Computer Science and Engineering and is currently studying at Chennai Institute of Technology, India. He is a passionate research student with strong experience and enthusiasm for innovation, technology, and creative problem-solving. Driven by curiosity and a vision for advancement, he is dedicated to impactful and meaningful work that bridges design, technology, and real-world solutions, demonstrating a deep understanding of practical problem-solving. He has published six book chapters and 2 utility patents. This combination of research, innovation, and creative passion positions him as a versatile and forward-thinking professional, committed to shaping the future through technology and design.

S. Pavithra is an Associate Professor and Head of the Department in the Department of Computer Science and Engineering at Chennai Institute of Technology, Chennai, with a strong academic and research background. She has published over 55 research papers in Scopus-indexed journals and 3 papers in SCI-indexed journals, reflecting her active contribution to scientific research. Her innovative work has led to the granting of 40 utility patents and 1 design patent, showcasing her expertise in applied research and technology development. Additionally, she has contributed a book chapter, further extending her impact in the academic community. Her work exemplifies a blend of scholarly excellence and practical innovation.

Index

Symbols

A

B

C

D

E

F

G

H

I

K

M

N

P

R

S

www.ingramcontent.com/pod-product-compliance
Lightning Source LLC
LaVergne TN
LVHW060004031026
849161LV00025B/1367
9798337370460